Bridges to the Ancestors

David D. Harnish

Bridges to the Ancestors

Music, Myth, and Cultural Politics
at an Indonesian Festival

University of Hawai'i Press
Honolulu

Printed in the United States of America

11   10   09   08   07   06   6   5   4   3   2   1

LIBRARY OF CONGRESS CATALOGING-IN-PUBLICATION DATA

Harnish, David D., 1954–

Bridges to the ancestors : music, myth, and cultural politics
at an Indonesian festival / David D. Harnish.

p. cm.

Includes bibliographical references and index.

ISBN-13: 978-0-8248-2914-8 (hardcover : alk. paper)
ISBN-10: 0-8248-2914-X (hardcover : alk. paper)

1. Sasak (Indonesian people)—Indonesia—Lombok—Rites and ceremonies.
2. Sasak (Indonesian people)—Indonesia—Lombok—Religion.
3. Mythology, Balinese—Indonesia—Lombok. 4. Songs, Balinese—Indonesia—
Lombok. 5. Fasts and feasts—Indonesia—Lombok. 6. Political culture—Indonesia—
Lombok. 7. Muslims—Indonesia—Lombok. 8. Hindus—Indonesia—Lombok.
9. Lombok (Indonesia)—Social life and customs. 10. Lombok (Indonesia)—
Religious life and customs. I. Title.

DS632.S38H37 2006
394.265'09598'6—dc22
2005008742

Book design and composition by Diane Gleba Hall
Printed by The Maple-Vail Book Manufacturing Group

For my parents, Donald Prugh and Barbara Dick Harnish,
for I Wayan Kartawirya and Mangku Sanusi,
and for Maxine, Malini, Colin, and Gaby

Contents

Acknowledgments

A GREAT MANY people have assisted either in my research projects in Lombok and Bali or in preparing this text. While it is impossible to name everyone deserving of recognition, I must mention a number of people. I hope those individuals I have overlooked will forgive me.

I want to thank the officials and committees of the Fulbright-Hayes grant offices. I received two grants to conduct research in Lombok and Bali and the fieldwork would have been impossible without them. I also extend my appreciation to the Indonesian government research institute, LIPI, and to the regional government centers that helped me in Indonesia.

I cannot thank enough my Indonesian sponsors of different research trips: Dr. I Madé Bandem, Hj. Dra Sri Yaningsih, and H. Lalu Wiramaja. Pak Bandem and his wife, Swasthi Bandem, helped me establish contacts in Lombok. Bu Yaningsih and her staff at the Arts Section of the Regional Department of Education and Culture in Lombok were extremely helpful to my research. I deeply thank several members of this staff who became close informants and friends, particularly Max Arifin, Ida Wayan Pasha, and I Nengah Kayun, as well as an associate of the Education and Culture Department, R. Soesantyo. I want to thank other members within the Culture and Education Department, particularly Martinom, Lalu Gedé Suparman, and H. Lalu Wacana.

I am very grateful to my mentors at the University of Hawai'i and at the University of California at Los Angeles: respectively, Ricardo Trimillos and Sue

Carole DeVale. Both helped guide my creative energies in beneficial directions. I want also to thank Hardja Susilo, who first suggested that I conduct research in Lombok, and Timothy Rice, a key member of my dissertation committee. Others to whom I extend my appreciation include Lisa Ho, Larry Polansky, and Michelle Chin, who assisted in documenting various festivals. In addition, I thank Adam Zygmunt for technical assistance and Jennifer Furr, Wanda Bryant, and Jeffrey Ohlmann for other graphic help.

I appreciate the assistance and cooperation of the leaders and villagers of Lingsar, and I want to thank Sasak officials at the Lingsar temple, in particular the late priest Mangku Sanusi, his nephew Suparman Taufiq, and his brother and current priest, Asmin. I also thank the Balinese temple organization, the Yayasan Krama Pura Lingsar, especially the former head, Anak Agung Gedé Biarsah, the current head, I Wayan Kereped, and the common priest at Lingsar, I Jero Mangku Negara. I appreciate the consultations with the manager of the *batek baris* group, Saparia, and the musical director, Amaq Jasira, as well as with the shawm players, Amaq Sari and Amaq Salih, and I want to extend my gratitude to all of the Balinese and Sasak gamelan groups that performed at Lingsar over the research period. I thank Ida Padanda Ketut Rai for his audience with me, and greatly appreciate the consultations with I Gusti Bagus Ngurah, Ida Bagus Putu Basma, Padanda Istri Manuaba, I Gusti Jelantik Sunu, I Nengah Lagas, I Gedé Gumbreg, I Déwa Gedé Raka, Dr. I Wayan Dibia, Dr. I Nyoman Wenten, Thohil, Arbainjulianda, Farjaruddin, and Rahil.

I extend my deep gratitude to I Wayan Kartawirya, his wife, Ni Madé Darmi, and his family for their home hospitality during my stay with them during several periods of the 1980s. Kartawirya and his uncle, Mangku Kadek Saka, were two main Balinese teachers. I also thank again Lalu Wiramaja and his wife, Nur Wiramaja, for taking me in during Ramadan and informing and assisting me at every turn. Finally, I wish to thank my wife, Maxine Barry, and my children, Malini, Colin, and Gaby, for sacrificing their time, energy, and patience to allow me to finish this work.

CHAPTER ONE

Encounters, Constructions, Reflections

DURING A BREAK in the 1988 festival at Lingsar, the Sasak priest Sanusi and I sat on a pavilion in the temple, where he carefully responded to my questions on the schedule of rites and their meanings. Suddenly, the Balinese leader and grandson of the last Lombok Balinese king, Anak Agung Gedé Biarsah (Agung Biarsah), stormed in with an entourage of advisors and demanded to know if rumors were true that Balinese were precluded from carrying the main food offerings in festival processions. Tellingly, he spoke in Indonesian, rather than the regional Sasak language, which made his words formal and distant. He stated that many local Balinese were complaining about this rumor; they had always had access to the offerings, and the prospect of not touching or carrying the offerings (a locus of power) during processions was upsetting. Sanusi, overwhelmed and outnumbered, replied in polite Indonesian that "of course" Balinese could carry the offerings in turn with Sasak participants, "just like always," and that the rumors were untrue. Agung Biarsah, with his advisors in tow and mission accomplished, quickly departed.

There was more at stake in this interaction than simply access to the offerings—though that was also a serious issue for Balinese participants. Sanusi and Agung Biarsah were struggling over the ritual position that articulates which party is at the "center" of the festival and which is the "outsider." Agung Biarsah, as the heart of past political power, wanted to reclaim Lombok Balinese access to these offerings while at the same time continuing to dominate in other festival events, ultimately restating Balinese hegemony as center; Sanusi was trying to

1

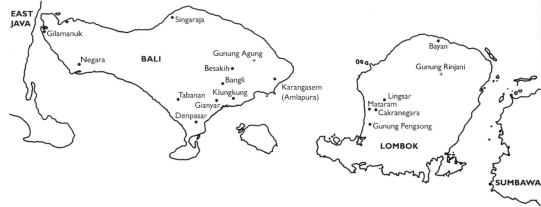

reconfigure the Sasak as center hosts and the Balinese as peripheral others, sym-bolized by exclusive Sasak access to power via the offerings. Though Agung Biarsah reclaimed the visible center on this occasion, the efforts of Sanusi, who died in 1993, and those of other Sasak have resulted in an enhanced acknowledgment of the Sasak contribution. Most Sasak, in fact, hold that they are the originators and hosts of the festival and that the Balinese are simply honored guests. I have never met a Balinese who agrees with this assessment.

This book is a broad ethnographic study of the Lingsar festival that addresses its players, performing arts, rites, histories, changes, and relationships with socio-cultural and political trends on the island of Lombok and nationally in Indonesia. The festival is a site of cultural struggle and a nexus of religious, political, artis-tic, and agrarian interests. It is a significant image- and identity-molding event, and many forces try to control the forms it takes, their meanings, and interpretations to further their own interests. Many decades ago the festival was considered the most important religious event in Lombok; now, while it preserves this function for many participants, the event has also become a contested institution for construct-ing ethnicity and asserting sociopolitical identity in postcolonial, modernist, and newly democratic Indonesia.

Any major festival provides an opportunity for a culture to define itself, as social worlds, sacred beliefs and objects, meaningful rites, and performing arts are revealed to refresh that culture. The participants are bonded as a unit, further grounded in their history and ideology, and in general come to know themselves better as a result of their encounter and experience. Festivals are ideal contexts for the negotiation of history, ethnicity, and identity; they also may reflect a people's response to contemporary circumstances, may erect boundaries of "us vs. them" to stimulate intraethnic experience, and may result not from some abstract impulse to celebrate culture but through the agency and decision-making of their partici-pants. The festival at Lingsar has one major feature that distinguishes it from most others worldwide: it is created by two ethnic groups and must accommodate the histories, experiences, and memories of both the local Hindu Balinese and the Muslim Sasak.

Lombok is a relatively neglected island neighboring Bali. Dominated by Java in medieval times, it was then colonized by Bali for over 150 years and the Dutch for the next fifty, so the indigenous population, the Sasak, have had little opportunity to develop an independent cultural identity. Their history with the migrant Balinese, the largest minority on the island, has often been tense. Memories of ethnic colonization run deep, and religion has been a major dividing factor. Among Sasak and other ethnic Muslim minorities in Lombok, the phrase *"yang penting Islam"* (what's important is Islam) has unifying, linking power; despite their centuries on the island, the Lombok Balinese, being Hindu, are excluded from this pact. The festival has historically been the forum to mediate religious and social tension and nurture Hindu-Muslim solidarity. Today, however, this union is less potent as religion, reform movements, modernization, and politics have instead promoted greater separation.

The festival, called Pujawali (worship return), is held annually at the temple in the village of Lingsar in the district of West Lombok (Lombok Barat). Participants and officials agree that it has primarily functioned to promote agricultural and human prosperity and to *menyatu* (unite) or *mempersatukan* (make one) Balinese and Sasak. The festival has also been a forum to revisit and reorder the past, and it helps to legitimize traditional Balinese and Sasak cultures in modern Lombok. The constant maneuvering and positioning in the festival indicate just how important the festival is to both groups as they struggle to express their ethnicity while negotiating the other camp, local religious leaders, and the regional government.

Music and dance are central to the festival for ritual purposes—playing at the right spot, initiating a rite, enacting a transformation—all provide an opportunity for participants to interpret the event and its history, and to construct and define ethnicity. Both camps present an array of diverse arts; a few of these exist only to serve the festival. Officials have said that the festival would not take place without its music, because music defines so many stages and completes or references worlds necessary for festival rites. Music is the public icon, the vehicle to move events forward, and the force for constructing place and ethnicity. As the soundscape for the festival, music allows its activities to happen.

IN THE WORLD OF FESTIVAL

Festival is a special context for the construction of ethnicity and socioreligious behavior and experience. As Cornell contends (2000:42), ethnicity can be a collective narrative that captures central understandings of a group. At Lingsar, Balinese and Sasak use an abundance of music and dance to construct and articulate their ethnicity—their collections of narratives—and orientations to the world at large, and these performing arts—themselves embodied narratives of past ideation—are refocused and finessed to respond to contemporary issues. Dance (at least at Lingsar) is the more clearly narrative medium, and its public ritual performances recast myth and redefine disputed identities (see Mendoza 2000).

Religious festivals are highly charged environments; expressive elements like music and dance that represent or unify a congregation attain a special status in such settings. Several participants of both camps at Lingsar have confirmed that music and other ritual arts and objects achieve a "heightened reality" or "symbolic life" during the festival. Music performance is also a key element in creating a magnified aesthetic state of liveliness known as *ramé*, a sociocultural goal for both groups. In the festival context, *ramé* refers to the bustling moments of music and dance, collective ritual activities, spiritual union, and to other climaxes within the event.

Participation requires physical, mental, and spiritual action, and participants learn how to interpret festival meanings through their accumulation of experience. Each festival provides a deepened foreknowledge for the next and fosters more mature ritual behavior and participant expectations. As one participant stated, *"Orang tua kami tak kasihtahu arti arti sajien atau pujawalinya. Kami harus mendapatnya sendiri"* (Our parents never told us about the meanings of offerings or of the festival. We had to discover these for ourselves). The festival experience becomes its own narrative of ethnic rediscovery, and the role of individual and group agency in the construction of meaning is clear.

In this sense each festival becomes a negotiation and renegotiation with a variety of entities and issues from the personal and intimate to the public and national. Each individual, party, and community experiences this negotiation process during each festival as all participants must consider what the festival represents, their personal and collective place within it, and how this relates to being a contemporary Indonesian citizen on the island of Lombok. The result is a redefinition of a myriad of identities that pertain to social, religious, and political orientation.

Major rituals and their performing arts are "shared institutions" that offer ways for participants to organize themselves, practice their culture, and assert their values (Spickard and Burroughs 2000). The festival and its music are thus forces to mould and generate culture. Stokes (1994:5) asserts that music constructs and mobilizes ethnicity and identity as it articulates the cultural self and distinguishes that self from the other. Performance at Lingsar erects and maintains boundaries of social identity, and establishes Sasak and Balinese ethnicities in positions of opposition. However, a paradox exists. While performance on a social level realizes respective cultural selves in opposition to one another, on a spiritual level it forges a unity between the groups—a unity that both groups sense and recognize as essential for festival success. Music performances are multidimensional and affect both groups.

TEMPLE AND FESTIVAL

The temple in the village of Lingsar (spouting water) was built above the most abundant water springs on the island. Temple organizations regulate irrigation water for much of the fertile rice-growing western plain of Lombok; this water also irrigates some fields in Central Lombok and long ago was directed as far away as

East Lombok.[1] The structure is often considered the "mother temple" for the local Balinese, and it is also a shrine to worship culture heroes for many Sasak; for both, it is the place to pray for rain and abundance, success in business and agriculture, and cures and boons.

The festival and its mythologies interweave historic events and ancestor spirits with the divine; this process allows various participant interpretations of the temple, the festival, and the performing arts. Though the organizations representing Balinese and Sasak interests would prefer uniform interpretations, the Pujawali itself, with its diverse rites and participants, does not support homogeneous themes or meanings but rather encourages divergent experiences and understandings.

The festival's success was a mandate for legitimation of past Balinese colonization (1740–1894), and today it remains one of the largest-scale events in Lombok. Perhaps 20,000 are directly involved in the festival, and well over 100,000 farmers and other individuals depend upon the temple and its festival to coordinate irrigation and increase the producing capacity of the earth. These people, to at least some extent, believe in the powers centralized at the temple and in the efficacy of the festival rites. The stature of the temple has attracted the attention of the regional government, which has been helping direct the festival and claiming some credit for its success as a symbolic mandate for their governance of the island.

Participants come to the festival not only for its efficacy but also for its spiritual, social, and musical experience. The festival dramatically unifies a large and unique congregation, and music and dance escort the participant through a special history. Ethnic tension, however, lies beneath the surface of cooperative behavior, and the festival is an event in which a struggle is played out over which group—Balinese or Sasak—owns the past, dominates the present, and best accesses the divine. There is constant contestation over the temple's history and meaning, and this contesting reveals the parties' agendas and respective positions.

The festival serves many purposes:

1. To provide a forum for communicating with the divine, however construed,
2. To help secure agricultural and human fertility, rainfall, boons, and cures,
3. To help regulate irrigation for the rice fields and agricultural organizations,
4. To furnish a forum in which to appropriately erect history, remember ancestors, and construct socioreligious ethnicity, and,
5. To allow the manipulation of that history and ethnicity to meet current needs, needs that continually adjust to various pressures by outside forces and new generations of participants.

Perhaps most importantly, the festival harmonizes relations between the Sasak and the local Balinese. In the past it was considered crucial that Balinese overlords and landowners commune and celebrate with farmers, who were mostly Sasak.

Today, participants claim that the unity created between the groups is essential in coordinating them, organizing irrigation needs, and maintaining peace. A Balinese leader, Wayan Kereped, stated that without the festival union Balinese and Sasak in Lombok might become "like the Palestinians and Israelis." Music and dance are primary catalysts in effecting transformations and reunifying these peoples.

THE PLAYERS

Lombok is due east of Bali and joins its neighbor island Sumbawa to form the Indonesian province of Nusa Tenggara Barat, one of the most strongly Islamic of Indonesia's provinces. Lombok and the Sasak people have been subject to extensive Hindu Javanese and later Islamic Javanese influence; Sumatra/Malay, Makassarese, and Sumbawanese Islamic influence; Balinese colonization and influence; Dutch colonization; Japanese occupation; and now the modern Indonesian government. The Sasak voice has rarely been dominant. Sasak culture today shares some elements with Sumbawa on one side and with Bali on the other, but it has a special relationship with Java because of past influences and the existence of differing Islamic practices: one older, syncretic, and associated with traditional social custom, and one newer, modern and divorced from traditional cultural patterns. The tensions between traditional and reformist Islam, ancestral spirits and Allah, myths and liturgies, and arts and religion are clear on both islands. The Balinese also enjoy a special relationship with Java. Many claim descent from Java (via Bali) and assert that they preserve a spiritual mandate to dominate political and religious life through ancestral links to the legendary Hindu Javanese empire, Majapahit.

The value of the temple can be viewed through the pasts and presents of festival participants. The Sasak, culturally related to the Javanese, Balinese, and Sumbawanese (in West Sumbawa), constitute over 90 percent of Lombok's population of 2.6 million. They are a society of Muslims, most of whom are "orthodox" (that is, they are party to the revitalization and reformation of Islam in Indonesia which has a Sunni basis) and Mecca-oriented. Some Sasak, however, practice a local, syncretic Islamic faith that combines indigenous beliefs with Islamic, Hindu, and Buddhist influences. It is this latter group of "traditional" Muslims who constitute nearly all of the Sasak participants at the festival. Today, they may number as few as 40,000 throughout Lombok, and most are gradually accepting a more orthodox Islamic worldview. The other Sasak who attend the festival are either moderates who retain some belief in the power of the land and ancestors, reformist Muslims who are primarily curious about the event, or government officials who seek to establish a presence there.

The Hindu Balinese, most of whom originate in the East Bali district of Karangasem, became the colonizers of neighboring Lombok and controlled the entire island from 1740 until 1894, when they were defeated by Dutch forces. Nearly all surviving Balinese chose to remain in Lombok, which they considered their home, rather than return to Bali. Today they number about 114,000. Both groups of festival participants—Balinese and traditional Muslim Sasak—are religious and political minorities, and both have experienced oppression. Since the festival now helps to legitimize their cultures—through its elaborate fanfare, government recognition, participant numbers, and acknowledged function—both camps have a large interest in the festival's success, and the event has become a prominent cornerstone of their religious and cultural self-identities. Chapter Two discusses these groups, their religious orientations, and their systems of music and ritual.

The Balinese and Sasak face different problems in Lombok. The former, the past colonizers, are now a religious minority in need of preserving their history and culture in response to the growing reconciliation of Sasak and Islamic culture. They are acting forcefully to maintain their presence at the festival, which the government considers primarily Sasak. The Sasak, who were prevented from experiencing a golden cultural age due to colonization and external influences, have gradually learned to temper religious values in order to preserve what is left of their past.

Sasak identity is not well defined. In the attempt to establish a culture based on Islamic principles initiated by late nineteenth-century religious leaders and nobility, the Sasak have swept aside traces of their earlier culture until very little remains of what can be designated "traditional culture." The Lingsar festival is one phenomenon that remains, and it offers a direct link to legendary Sasak heroes, culture, and identity. Religious leaders and the government have been working to Islamify or secularize enough festival rites to rationalize and even encourage Sasak participation as a means to preserve *khas* Sasak (original Sasak culture) in the face of the religious, political, social, and technological changes that are sweeping over Lombok. To some extent, these forces want to control the past and manipulate the notion of *khas* Sasak to assert a more forceful Sasak image. Music and dance are active and powerful icons that can be interpreted to formulate cultural identity and reconfigure the past, and local leaders have given considerable attention in framing the image of *khas* Sasak. Most agree that anything appearing to be of Balinese origin cannot, by definition, be *khas* Sasak. Thus any traditions that seem to share elements with Balinese arts are scrutinized and often discouraged or even banned.

MYTHS AND THE INNER POSITION

The Balinese and Sasak relate two different myths regarding the discovery and significance of the temple; these myths frame the interpretation of the festival and much of its music, and they reflect contemporary ethnicity and interethnic relations. The past is subject to debate and is the cause of frequent tension. At one time or another, each group has tried to impose its myth upon the other in an attempt to demonstrate that it is they who truly direct and are the center of the festival, that their rites are truly efficacious, and that it is they who advance the fertility of Lombok. At the same time they paint the other group as peripheral to the festival's success.

The struggle for the center position, highlighted in the first paragraph, has become a permanent feature. The issue of who has access to the offerings arose again during the 1990s (particularly in the 1994 and 1995 festivals), similar issues were apparent in 2001, and such tensions and postures will continue indefinitely due to the religious, political, and economic significance of the temple and its festival. Chapter Three interprets these problems within the respective myths of Lingsar and identifies the political positions of the Balinese and Sasak camps and the role of the government. Chapter Four details the events, activities, stages, and performing arts of the festival.

At Lingsar, myth (public/popular belief of its founding) and liturgy (scheduled rites of specialists) are two different spheres that rarely overlap. Hefner (1985:16) affirms that among the Tengger of East Java, what resides in public myth is often quite different from the liturgies of priests at the same event, and this could prove true at any contested religious event. During the Lingsar festival the human figures presented in the Lingsar myths—Datu Wali Milir for the Sasak and Anak Agung Ngurah Karangasem for the Balinese—are not invoked by the priests of either camp. The deities immediately associated with these figures are similarly ignored. Yet many participants interpret the festival through the myths and their political units. The distinctions between myth and liturgy in Lombok were probably caused by the questions posed by modernizing Indonesia and revitalized Islam, as both Balinese and traditional Sasak appear to have made an effort to "reshape" their "folk heritage so as to make it capable of meeting the challenge" of the current surrounding society (ibid.). This reshaping of heritage apparently stimulated an evolution of the Lingsar myths that I believe has accelerated over recent decades. The divergence of myth and liturgy has also affected the interpretation of the festival music. Some performances are held to support a mythic-political complex of meanings, others have a more liturgical function and connect directly to the priests and their rites, and a few combine elements that reach into both domains. Since the myths are subject to change, so too are the interpretations of the performing arts.

Balinese and Sasak participants realize that they are both linked to Lingsar, that beneath their argumentative exteriors they actually share many understandings, and that they must work together for the mutual success of the festival, and this has always served to unify them. The shared rites, in particular, create a sense of Turner's "communitas" (see especially 1969), where separate social roles and ethnic identity dissolve in the establishment of a unified spiritual order (a process discussed in Chapter Six). The religious goal of the festival is to guarantee through ritual processes sufficient rainfall and irrigation water for the rice fields. Water and its spiritual force are major symbols. The festival therefore has a universal appeal to the inhabitants of Lombok, Hindu Balinese and Muslim Sasak alike. The farmers of both groups have a considerable stake in the success of the festival, and they care very little about debates over history.

THE FIELDWORK ENCOUNTER

I first came to Lombok in 1983 to research music of the Balinese minority, following the findings of a single source available on local music (Seebass et al. 1976), and I attended the Lingsar festival as part of that project. I was astonished at the diversity of ritual and musical activity at the festival, and at the participation of the Sasak—a fact never mentioned by my local Balinese hosts. The Balinese and Sasak held mostly separate rites in separate spaces within the temple, but came together for other rites. Since there had been some sectarian violence between Balinese and Sasak, the unified actions and apparent solidarity in the joint rites were striking. The intermingling of the participants and their different forms of music was a unique experience; it seemed clear that this event was specific to Lingsar and could not happen elsewhere. At that time I was concentrating on the local Balinese music at the festival, and so other dimensions of meaning lay hidden within the folklore of the temple, the unique scheme of the festival, and the experiences of the participants. I returned to visit the temple in 1985, 1989, and 1995, and to again witness and research the festival in 1987, 1988, and 2001, and thus have since immersed myself in other aspects of the festival and have come to notice changes over the years.

Over the past two decades, a series of new developments have emerged as a result of pressure from interest groups (including the provincial and district governments), a new generation of more educated (or modern) participants, a changing political climate, and the fact that many officials and leaders have died and been replaced (see Chapter Seven). Some "traditions" considered requirements in 1983 no longer exist. In 2001 festival officials and participants acknowledged small changes over the years but insisted that the festival and its diverse meanings and functions were *tetap sama* (still the same). I soon realized that the notion of perpetuity—that everything within the festival must be validated or rationalized by historic practice—is the lynchpin of the event. Admitting to truly new developments, without historic precedence, would make those elements inauthentic; instead, apparent new developments are identified as *perbaikan* (improvements, here implying improvements on already existing models).

In the 1980s I took a structuralist approach to attempt to make sense of the festival's myriad activities, but in 2001 this proved inadequate to explain new developments. This volume thus combines an interpretive structuralism with new ethnography to contextualize and explicate meanings of performing arts and rites and to trace sociocultural changes and their resulting impact upon the arts. The festival, like other major events worldwide, is a barometer of change for the participants and their society and a malleable node of identity construction and negotiation. Such cultural texts are never fixed; they must be reinvented. Each festival is a new take on past practice, and the many histories, voices, and experiences that bring such life to the event can never be fully contained; these move and change in often unpredictable ways.

ISSUES AND CHANGES

My earlier work on Lingsar tended to focus on the importance of music in inter-action with context to generate meaning and on "structural homologies" linking music and cosmological forms. While these both have a place in the current study (see the musical analyses in Chapter Five), they are restricted to specific perfor-mative and religious dimensions and are not used to explain change.

A turning point in the modern realization of the festival was the death in 1993 of the Sasak priest Sanusi. The position was assumed by his brother, Asmin, who was neither well versed in the rites nor felt obligated to some traditions; thus began a series of changes. Their nephew Suparman Taufiq, a well-respected authority, stated that Asmin had never even attended the festival before he became priest and did not have the background to understand the various rites and crucial role of music. I believe that the changes initiated after 1993—new interpretations and the additions and omissions of specific music—led to increasingly more changes in subsequent years.

I met with Sanusi tens of times. He taught me a lot about the festival, particu-larly what it meant to the Sasak and to Lombok. He also spoke at length about the importance of the performing arts. He knew the names of all the rites and stages of the festival and could expound upon these for guests. His friendly, out-going manner and total grasp of the event was an asset to all participants at Lingsar. He worked well with the Balinese and with the government, and had in fact worked in government offices before assuming the position of priest in the 1960s. In contrast, his younger brother Asmin (Min) received little formal educa-tion and had no history with the festival until 1993. Suparman (Parman) told me that Min is "blind" (*buta*) toward the inner workings of the festival, and that he has "difficulty interacting with others" (*sulit berinteraksi*) and thus cannot explain what he does know. While most Sasak (and Balinese) respect Min, they realize that his knowledge is limited and that he is serving a role rather than leading the fes-tival. This issue arises in several chapters because many changes originate with the transition from Sanusi to Min.

Though the Balinese position has remained more consistent, a number of new developments have emerged over the past ten years, including the loss of an impor-tant gamelan, the addition of a new sacred temple dance, and a reconfiguration in the authority of the temple complex. New priorities are in place that did not exist in the 1980s. Both Balinese and Sasak are negotiating pressures from the gov-ernment, Islamic leaders, and Hindu organizations and making adjustments where necessary (see Chapters Three and Seven). Interpretations of the festival have consequently become more fluid, less coherent, and more prone to change.

STUDY OBJECTIVES AND REFLEXIVITY

This study aims to demonstrate the interrelationships of music and festival at Lingsar, explore how symbolic practices (performing arts, rites) shape socially active history, discuss issues of change and modernization in the festival, advance notions of individual agency, define Balinese and Sasak and their cultures in Lombok, and to present fairly the case for each group. The festival's value is today multifaceted, its meanings are diffuse, and it represents ethnic groups and social classes equally. Though I have been careful not to privilege any individual, ritual position, class, or ethnic group, the more well-known Balinese cultural model is sometimes presented first in a section in order to contrast with the lesser-known Sasak examples. Points of contrast are also made between Balinese culture in Bali and in Lombok to illuminate the unique nature of the latter in relation to Lingsar.

While I've devoted many years of research and thought to the festival, this is rarely a reflexive study; my experience is added only when necessary to illustrate change or contrast. One of my primary goals—a responsibility in fact—is to place the Lingsar event in the world of festivals. Thus several chapters describe the festival's properties (for example, their arts or rites) and processes. Much of the time I cite what Rice (1994:11) calls "generalized authors," in this case "the Balinese" and "the Sasak." These authors are often held to feel particular things, to bear certain attitudes, and to hold specific beliefs. While these authors consist of diverse voices and are not monolithic, the information ascribed to them has been established through extensive interviews with leaders and participants of each camp. I feel that it is necessary to discover and frame positions of similarity and contrast for respective Balinese and Sasak participants. However, participants within each camp often disagree, and divergent opinions are occasionally featured to demonstrate internal conflict.

I frequently use the word "tradition," also critiqued by Rice (ibid., 12–13), to describe those forms of music and behavior that represent the past and are in general highly valued. "Tradition" legitimizes the present for most participants and is a construct that defines a temporal continuum of moral order. Its antonym, "contemporary," refers to the current period, which, though modern, independent, and more "Islamic," is stripped of the values associated with ancestors and the past. For most people in Lombok today, the contemporary is preferable; however, for most participants at Lingsar, "contemporary" is seen as shallow, without spiritual basis, and lacking authenticity.

Throughout the text, I use the word "teacher" rather than "informant." I use it to refer to a large number of Balinese and Sasak, a few of whom are the late Mangku Sanusi, Mangku Asmin, the late Mangku Kadek Saka, I Wayan Kereped, Anak Agung Gedé Biarsah, Suparman Taufiq, Saparia, the late I Wayan Kartawirya, Mangku Negara, Lalu Gedé Suparman, Lalu Wiramaja, and the late Ida Padanda Ketut Rai. This book has grown out of discussions and interviews with these and many more individuals, from pertinent literature, and from my own observations over the years. I hope that I have given them all sufficient voice.

There was often confusion as to my role in the festival; I believe it was difficult for Sasak and Balinese to determine my identity. Participants, musicians, and ritual officials were used to seeing me at Lingsar, however, and I have become a very small part of the festival lore.[2] My research sponsorship often came from the regional Education and Culture Department. A few department officials had also researched the festival, and in the late 1980s they occasionally accompanied me to the site. These officials, to whom I am indebted, felt they were performing official business and therefore held as much authority as festival officiates, an attitude quite counter to my research approach. I was often viewed as an official or alternately as a foreign scholar and granted appropriate respect and distance. However, I usually wore *pakaian adat* (ceremonial clothing), which distinguished me from government officials, and many participants eventually grew comfortable discussing intimate aspects of their knowledge and experience. The Balinese and Sasak camps were consistently accommodating to me, and, perhaps wanting to court a more favorable opinion, invited me to eat in their respective compounds several times each day of the festival. Though my stomach was often quite full, the frequent experience of feasting together helped develop a closeness that I hope is reflected in this work.

One problem I constantly confronted was that the festival is a temporary event. The ten thousand or more participants at any festival scatter after five or fewer days, leaving very little time for meeting even a handful of them or the scores of musicians, let alone taking it all in and reflecting on it. While I was accessible to everyone and open to all viewpoints, I was also extremely busy documenting the event (by audiotape, minidisk, videotape, still photos, observation, occasional participation, fieldnotes) and interviewing teachers (and eating whenever invited). Most activities, often held simultaneously in different spaces, happen only once, making thorough coverage a very challenging proposition.[3]

In most years I held extensive conversations with participants and officials before and following the festival, but these discussions were, in a way, decontextualized; teachers' words were so much richer while the event was happening, when we were all witnessing and experiencing the festival together. In fact, I discovered that descriptions teachers gave about a festival beforehand often contradicted with what they said afterward, and what they said on both occasions frequently disagreed with my experiences at the same event. We all seemed to have selective memories, though perhaps this is not surprising. So much happens at each festival that our experiences reflect both our own subjective worlds and our positions in the ritual frame.

DIMENSIONS OF CHANGE

Since 1983 I have changed, the field of ethnomusicology has changed, and many aspects of the festival have changed; sadly, many people—festival teachers such as Sanusi, Mangku Saka, I Wayan Kartawirya, and Ida Padanda Ketut Rai—have died. Though some of these people still influence the festival (and my thoughts about it), the event has taken new directions.

In 1983 I was a Master of Arts in Ethnomusicology student from the University of Hawai'i conducting research on the music culture of the Balinese minority. In the late 1980s I was a doctoral student from UCLA looking specifically at the festival. As a professor I returned to the temple in the 1990s and again researched the festival in 2001. Some ideas that seemed intriguing in the 1980s did not interest me later, which shows either an evolution in my thinking or a change in my priorities. Ethnomusicology, of course, has shifted dramatically over those decades as well, moving from a positivist and objectivist perspective—where the researcher unquestioningly takes copious notes, extensively documents music for later analysis in the lab, maps data for geocultural regions, and in general aspires to act like a scientist in the field—to the researcher's becoming a more reflexive and interacting player—where s/he admittedly affects the environment, becomes part of the proceedings, scrutinizes biases, and prioritizes local voices. Changes in the discipline and in the researcher are natural developments that affect field method and interpretation.

In the 1980s I was strongly attracted to the notion of structural homologies between music and other ritual or belief systems operating at Lingsar or in cultures generally. Sugarman (1997:24) explains that the premise of this type of analysis is that "a community makes the music it does because something in that music's structure or style is logically consistent with central patterns of thinking and of behaving within the culture." The concept that gamelan music was homologous with cosmological structure reached its fruition during the 1980s after provocative works by Becker (1979, 1981), Becker and Becker (1981), DeVale (1977), and others. Becker and Becker developed the idea to suggest that "iconic" constructs in music reflected the "natural order" of existence. My attraction to these ideas stemmed from my interest in religion; the theories supported my bias toward music in ritual contexts as necessarily expressing religious or spiritual sentiments. It "made sense" that underlying structures of music and religious cosmology would be shared and that gamelan music could represent cosmological order. I actively looked for such connections in my work at Lingsar and privileged that information in early reports and in my dissertation (1991a).

I now feel that this argument limits a music's impact. While homologies are often confirmed by participants, priests, and musicians at Lingsar, simply stating that music structure is homologous with religious cosmology says little about a music's relationship to its immediate environment. Stokes (1994:4–5), in a similar critique, suggests that music does not simply reflect underlying cultural patterns and social structures as a static symbolic order but rather creates a unique sociocultural context for things to "happen." I have become more interested in how music shapes social behavior and experience and allows for a variety of behaviors to flourish.

Parallel to the changing face of the discipline, the researcher, and the festival over the last two decades were changes in the regional and national governments (from autocratic to chaotic and democratic). During these same years (1980s–1990s) the tourist industries in both Lombok and Bali experienced tremendous growth. Though it did not directly impact the festival, the 1997 recession and currency devaluation halted tourism expansion and government projects, and destabilized the government of dictatorial President Soeharto, who had been in power since 1966, inspiring massive protests that resulted in his resignation in 1998. This ushered in the hopeful era of *reformasi* (reformation), of democracy, of a freer press, and of freedom for splinter groups that had previously been restrained, including Islamic parties and organizations. These splinter groups began to burgeon and soon affected sociopolitical and cultural situations throughout the country.

As a result of newfound freedom for religious and political organizations, perceived police corruption, a declining economy and resources, and political infighting (and perhaps stimulated by disgruntled former powerbrokers), sectarian violence emerged in several areas and spilled over onto other islands. In January 2000 violence erupted in Lombok against Christian churches and businesses (mostly owned by Chinese-Indonesians, a frequent target of violence in Indonesia), apparently in reaction to ongoing Christian-Muslim violence in the Maluku islands. The young protagonists were affiliated with Islamic brotherhoods organized to control crime and deal with lawbreakers; these had formed because locals felt the police had become untrustworthy. Nearly every church and targeted business was destroyed; interestingly, the only churches saved were those located in Balinese communities that local Hindu Balinese decided to defend. Apart from one incident, the Balinese were not assaulted or threatened; nevertheless they armed themselves with knives, daggers, and clubs and kept watch over their communities throughout 2000. Many Sasak citizens were shocked at the violence and wanted to help or protect the victims, but they feared the gangs. A Sasak teacher and friend, Lalu Wiramaja, said as he looked absently toward the ground, "I didn't know that these things could happen here, but as I drove around the city (Mataram, the regional capital) I saw that it was."

This violence shattered the tourist industry, and many hotels, shops, and restaurants soon went out of business. Combined with the recession, this was a crippling blow to most everyone on the island. Many Sasak, including those responsible for the violence, became ashamed of such violent actions and pledged that it would never happen again. Though many Christians have returned and a freer political environment prevails, there remains an air of tension and fear.

According to Balinese and Sasak teachers, most of this tension has been absent at the festival; this is likely because participants were never involved with, nor sympathized with, reformist Islamic groups. One recent change, however, is the development of local security forces, *lang lang* (or *pecalang*) to watch over the proceedings. Several other minor changes are clear, including the manner in which the festival is locally publicized and reported, the policies and relationships with various government offices, the more visible authority of Muslim and Hindu reformist organizations, and the increasing attempts by outside forces to control and define the event. More changes are likely. Since 2001, regional autonomy has been granted, and Sasak have now largely replaced Javanese in district and provincial government posts. Most of these new officials are *haji* (local spelling for men who have completed the pilgrimage to Mecca) or Islamic leaders, and they have some authority over cultural events like the festival.

The bombings in Bali on October 12, 2002, that killed 202 people directly impacted tourism and spotlighted the growth of radical Islam and political disorder in Indonesia. Hotel occupancy rates in Bali and Lombok dropped from 70–90 percent to 10 percent; the numbers rose slightly in early 2003 but then the U.S.-Iraq war in March 2003, followed by fear of the SARS virus, caused another steep decline. Though tourist numbers have since risen, the local economy has not recovered, and continuing travel advisories from some major Western countries restrict a rebound. The devastating tsunami that struck Sumatra on December 26, 2004, may also stall the recovery of tourism.

When discussing Islam, one point to make clear is that Islamic organizations in Lombok, while "fundamentalist," have no relationships with national, Southeast Asian, or international militant groups. The major organizations have developed locally to promote the further Islamification of the province and to help unify and govern religious practice. Nevertheless, many formal and informal groups thrive and impact local culture. In the aftermath of the bombings and the local, national, and international tension caused by the U.S.-led war with Iraq, sources indicate that many Sasak are undergoing a self-reflection that will likely influence local politics.

The festival, however, does not depend on tourism, is not impacted directly by world events, and has an oblique, though growing, relationship with reformist Islam and modernism; it has existed in some form for over three hundred years and has adapted to great turmoil before. It seems likely that it will again accommodate any developments and continue prospering. The festival may, in fact, operate as a stabilizing mechanism in mediating local and external conflicts and rebalancing the worlds of Lombok.

CHAPTER TWO

Festivals and Cultures
of Lombok

THOUGH RARELY a subject of study in ethnomusicology, "festival" as concept and action has been extensively explored by anthropologists and folklorists. To my mind, the available literature divides into two camps: one defines festival as cultural representation revealing deeply held ethos and belief (following the lead of Victor Turner), and the other views it as public display mediating cultural or subaltern expressions or identities that may be ethnic, sexual, political, or any combination of these. This division arises not only from different methodologies but also from distinctive types of festivals. The former festivals tend to be "older," nurtured over decades or even centuries, rural, and may be religious in tone; the latter tend to be "newer" or in position to accommodate sociocultural change and often intended to reflect popular culture or contemporary life. Before 2001, I placed the Lingsar festival exclusively into the former; I see it now reflected in the latter as well. I suspect that an interaction between poles of concepts like "sacred" and "secular" occurs in most other festivals, as religious festivals "have evident secular implications, and secular ones almost invariably resort to metaphysics to gain solemnity and sanction for their events or for their sponsors" (Falassi 1987:3). This chapter addresses the notion of festival as it pertains to Lingsar, discusses festivals in Bali and Lombok, and situates the Lingsar festival as an event that bridges the two islands and helps to define both.

Festivals, particularly those more religious in orientation, are major ritual events and cultural performances that articulate concepts of identity and value.

They may involve a single family, clan, congregation, community, or an entire nation, and will embody a number of individual, interrelated rites or ritual performances (liturgies) within their structures. Festivals are closely related to the conception of celebration. When any social group celebrates a particular event or occasion, such as birth, harvest, or national independence, "it also celebrates itself" and creates "frames" for understanding symbolic objects and behaviors that express culture (Turner 1982:16). Such festivals are generally connected to specific phenomena or experience: the life cycle (birth, marriage, death), work (planting and harvesting), seasons of the year (solstice), religious beliefs (Muhammad's birthday), upward shifts in social status (potlatch), or shared community celebrations (Thanksgiving). Most kinds of festivals come to be associated with special types of attire, music, dance, food, drink, staging, physical and cultural environment, and sometimes masks and shrines—what Turner calls the "properties" of a festival (ibid.:12).

Festivals symbolically restate the arrangement of the natural or social world. These statements, which may be realized as rites within a festival, become memorable and repeatable. Festivals and other ritual events are part of the human impulse to intensify time and space within the community and to reveal mysteries while being engaged in revels (Abrahams 1987:177). Falassi (1987:2) presents an encompassing definition:

> . . . festival commonly means a periodically recurrent, social occasion in which, through a multiplicity of forms and a series of coordinated events, participate directly or indirectly and to various degrees, all members of a whole community, united by ethnic, linguistic, religious, historical bonds, and sharing a worldview. Both the social function and the symbolic meaning of the festival are closely related to a series of overt values that the community recognizes as essential to its ideology and worldview, to its social identity, its historical continuity, and to its physical survival, which is ultimately what festival celebrates.

While secular festivals reveal a culture's "mood of feeling, willing, and desiring, its mood of fantasizing" (Turner 1987:77), and tend to challenge the normal social order with antistructural behavior, religious festivals tend to reenact a mythic event, make a community "contemporary with the gods" (Eliade 1959:91), and help confirm a sense of primordial order. These festivals underscore the harmonies and continuities of a culture, "emphasizing the wholeness of the world's fabric," and the "deepest values of the group are simultaneously revealed and made mysterious" (Abrahams 1987:176–177). They may arise out of shared apprehensions in the face of somatic or social change, provide cultural definitions in response, and define the borders of transitions and transformations. These festivals sometimes rely on divine powers as served (or controlled) by ritual officers to activate the transformations. Although specialists such as priests assume leadership at religious festivals, collective action at some festivals achieves the highest level of personal meaning because behavior in unison conveys the message that the community exists and leads to broad communal experience.

Underpinning each festival activity are the social structure and history of the group(s) involved. Through its rules, patterns, and processes, festival "at once encapsulates the world of social relationships and the cosmos" as the community returns to the whole, a mythical time and place where coherence, connectedness, and efficacy characterize the social order (Drewel 1992:xv). Falassi (1987:3) indicates that if we consider that the primary function of festivals is

> . . . to renounce and then to announce culture, to renew periodically the lifestream of a community by creating new energy, and to give sanction to its institutions, the symbolic means to achieve it is to represent the primordial chaos before creation, or a historical disorder before the establishment of the culture, society, or regime where the festival happens to take place.

Many festivals are important vehicles to build, reinforce, or affirm ethnic identity, because they deconstruct then reconstruct culture in a fresh new light that binds the participants together and defines their core values. The culture is thus renewed and cultural identity is reestablished, as participants celebrate their past with restored vigor for the present. This is perhaps the most profound contribution of festival to a culture's physical and spiritual survival.

While festivals may be perpetuated from mythic times, their performance must accommodate the current time; festivals must accept and respond to the present to remain meaningful. Though a festival and its rites are repeatable, they are neither exactly reproduced nor experienced precisely the same way twice. They are subject to revision, and participants have the power to transform events as they negotiate the appropriateness of ritual canon (Drewel 1992:xiv, xviii). The participants, not their ancestors, are the major players in the event, and the festival must continue to serve their needs or it ceases to be significant and may be discontinued.

Within the special social and spiritual world of festival, participants modify their normal everyday behavior; they do not "act" normally. Many abstain from activities of everyday life and their actions and social roles may become distorted, inverted, stylized, or disguised (Falassi 1987:3). These individual and group actions and roles intensify and assume a symbolic character in accordance with the goals of the particular festival. Similarly, performing arts that may occur outside the festival take on special meanings when performed within the festival context.

The Lingsar Pujawali (Balinese: "to worship again") festival, held at Pura Lingsar (Lingsar temple), is, like other religious festivals, determined by a sacred calendar and carves out sacred time from profane time. A particular sequence of rites at the festival commences sacred time, subsequent rites bridge the present and past within this dimension of time, and another sequence of rites returns normal, historical time. As officials and participants engage in learned and rehearsed speaking and acting routines in the formal and ceremonial setting, this and other religious festivals gather their power to focus attention on the contrast between ordinary time and the extraordinary occasion.

The sacred always attracts the profane, and the Lingsar Pujawali conjoins seriousness with a sense of fun. The sacred also attracts politics, and various political forces vie to become associated with festivals. Some festivals, particularly those that serve minority interests or beliefs, face severe opposition from those in political power. However, the direct force of politics does not usually prevent celebration of major festivals, which can assume their own life and become impervious to direct outside interference (Cosentino 1986). Within a festival, diverse and competing interests are accommodated because the event is most often collectively organized for the common good and calls upon heterogeneity for unity (Drewel 1986).[1] These issues of cultural history, politics, and diverse interests will be further discussed in Chapter Three.

Balinese festivals are most frequently held at temples, and temples are the greatest realization of Hindu Balinese religious practice. The architecture and value of temples on Bali and Lombok are quite similar. As the Balinese assimilated in Lombok, however, a number of distinctions in temple festivals and religious behavior emerged that reflected their status as a minority. The discussion below indicates these distinctions in religious and musical culture, and how these inform Balinese orientation to the Lingsar temple. A subsequent exploration of Sasak religion and festivals provides background for their participation at Lingsar and the challenges faced by traditional Muslims in contemporary Lombok. The final discussion introduces the Lingsar temple and festival and briefly examines the various parties involved. Contrasts between the Balinese and Sasak religious orientations are highlighted throughout this chapter because they clarify respective positions within the frame of the Lingsar festival.

BALINESE TEMPLES AND RELIGION

Balinese temple festivals celebrate the anniversary of the temple's initial consecration and the meaning and myth of the particular temple. These festivals are true religious holidays, and participants organize into groups to carry out the work necessary for successful completion of a festival. Festivals are communal efforts, and they activate the collective work patterns and community cohesion typical of Balinese society. In Bali, women prepare the required communal offerings and their own family offerings, men slaughter animals and chop and cook the meat for the festival feast, and young people provide performances of dancing and music, usually within the context of boys' and girls' associations (Goris 1960:95). However, in Lombok these efforts are more specialized and less communal, and there is in general a lower level of community cohesion.

Balinese religion can be characterized as a syncretic form of Shaivite Hinduism, combining aspects of Buddhism along with indigenous beliefs in natural and ancestral deities. It prescribes a theological taxonomy of ritual sacrifices and indigenous rules pertaining to rite design and the number and type of offerings.

Customs can differ among the various districts and villages of Bali and Lombok. The Indonesian phrase *lain desa, lain adat* (different village, different custom), accurately pictures this situation where local religious traditions take priority over standard procedures or orthodox dogma. However, a greater uniformity of religious practice exists among the Balinese in Lombok than in Bali. Their minority status has encouraged a more centralized and defined core value system and religious identity.

The greatest institution of Balinese religion is the temple, and festivals held at temples are the most meaningful demonstrations of religious practice. Festivals determined annually (or seasonally) relate to a culture's need to create a special time in which to celebrate itself and engage in public, formal ritual. The Balinese have an intense need for this experience, particularly in Bali where temple festivals occur somewhere nearly every day and individuals are obligated to participate in five to ten or more yearly. The dates of temple festivals are determined by their initial consecration, which is normally established on a day of special power, such as the full moon. Festivals are, in a sense, birthdays of temples, part of the life cycle of the temple itself that began in mythic time, returns to that time during each festival, and will repeat and evolve indefinitely. Participants attend festivals because they are bound together to the same mythic time. Depending upon the individual (and the particular temple), participants pray to their past, to ancestral deities, to the high deities, and to God who unites them all. They also come to experience the power of mass devotion, to merge into a oneness of purpose, and to socialize with other participants with whom they share a particular history. The temporal power of the festival connects the present to the past, and participants reexperience their origins and history as a way of securing a safe and prosperous present and future.

The calendars used to determine festival dates are either the *uku*, a Javanese-Balinese calendar of thirty seven-day weeks equaling 210 days, or the Indian-derived *saka*, a solar-lunar calendar of 354–356 days.[2] In general, village and home temples (by far the most numerous) follow the *uku* year, while temples involved with the rice cycle or removed from the historic Hindu Javanese influence (i.e., those in remote areas in Bali and sprinkled throughout Lombok) follow the *saka* year. The length and processes of these various festivals can be quite distinct, yet their goals are the same. Every Balinese participates at a variety of temples that conjoin him/her to specific groups of villagers and descendants, and together these temples express his/her identity.

Temple festivals are one of five types of ritual prescribed by the theological Hindu Balinese taxonomy known as Panca Yadnya (five sacrifices), and these include Déwa Yadnya (sacrificial offerings for deities, i.e., temple festivals), Manusa Yadnya (sacrificial offerings for humans, i.e., life-cycle rituals), Pitra Yadnya (sacrificial offerings for ancestors, especially death ceremonies), Buta Yadnya (sacrificial offerings for malevolent spirits), and Resi Yadnya (sacrificial offerings made both to priests and by them).

In Balinese thought, a temple "is a place where concentrated divine living energy may come into our material world, a point of vital contact between the powers that give life and the human beings that worship those powers" (H. Geertz 1988:1).[3] There are numerous types of temples: the *kayangan tiga* (three temples), consisting of *pura puseh* (temple of origins), *pura desa* or *balé agung* (central village meeting temple), and *pura dalam* (temple of the dead); the *sad kayangan* (six temples), major temples thought to connect the land at six points;[4] the *pura jagat* or *pusering jagat* ("world" and "navel-of-the-world" temples) that connect many villages together; the *pura penataran* (temples for nobles); the *pura pamaksan* and *panti* (temples binding specific groups of descendants); the *pura dadia* (clan temples); the *pura merajan* and *sanggah* (home temples); the *pura melanting* (temples for commerce); temples associated with their geographies, such as *pura segara* (sea temples) and *pura bukit* (mountain temples); a variety of rice and irrigation temples (*pura ulon siwi, pura bedugal, pura subak, pura ulon carik,* and *pura empelan*); and still other temples with specific local functions. In 1973 Hooykaas (11) conservatively estimated the number of temples on Bali to be 20,000. In 1985 records showed that beyond the thousands of Balinese home temples there were just 217 "public" temples (binding larger congregations) registered with the government; perhaps twenty more of these have since been erected.

Of the many types of temple listed above, only a few exist in Lombok. The *kayangan tiga* configuration of three temples common in many villages does not exist. Nor are there true *pura puseh* or *pura desa*, and there are only five *pura dalam* throughout the entire island. The temples most central in the lives of the Lombok Balinese are the *pura pamaksan*, the temple of the immediate ward or hamlet within villages that bind specific groups of neighboring descendants. Other temples that group specific descendants (such as *pura dadia*) are absent in Lombok;[5] there is only one sea temple (*pura segara*) and no true rice temples. Some public temples, similar in many respects to *pura jagat* (world temples), unite large groups of Balinese together and relate to their common history.[6] Pura Lingsar, more than any other, binds the Balinese together as one ethnic community, and it has also assumed the function of a rice temple for agricultural organizations.

Festivals, called *odalan* (of which there are several types), *piodalan, usaba, aci,* or *pujawali*, are celebrated at all Balinese temples in Bali and Lombok.[7] H. Geertz (1988:2) provides an excellent overview of temples.

> Every temple is owned, made, and used by a particular group of people, whose ancestors gave of themselves to it, and whose descendants will too. It is the place where they make contact with the divine, for their own particular benefit and that of the immediate locality of the temple. Its ceremonies are directed, above all, at gaining and preserving the well-being of that group. The temple is not only a record of their life together, it is their life.

The space of the temple is sacred, and it is not humans but rather the gods who choose the ground for a temple (Goris 1960:103), which is always positioned along the proper directional axis (*kaja-kelod*). Most (excepting death temples) are located in the north (or towards mountains), northeast, or east of a given community and usually face southward or away from the mountains. This reflects the spiritual dichotomy inherent in the axis; the direction toward mountains has greater power and purity. The temple itself comes to represent a centralizing force of spiritual power. H. Geertz (1988:7) further explains:

> A temple and its altars is the intersection point of all the multiple worlds of the universe: the Great World of the cosmos, and all the Little Worlds of the village community, of the fields and streams and wooded areas around it, and of each human being in that realm.

The walls, gates, and yards of a temple mark off areas of increasing purity. The progression from normal space into the first courtyard of a temple through the great gateway (*candi bentar*) symbolizes crossing the boundary from profane to hallowed ground. From the first courtyard into a temple's middle courtyard symbolizes greater sacredness, and from the middle courtyard into the inner courtyard and its altar complex symbolizes the transition into the most pure, sacred space, that is inhabited by the gods during a festival. This temple construction, adhered to at Lingsar, thus maps a cosmological scheme that acknowledges three components or zones throughout the manifest world, known as Triangga (Budihardjo 1986:39).[8] The inner courtyard is the most sacred space, the highest ground physically, and positioned on the directional axis towards the mountains, while the middle courtyard is slightly less sacred, and the third is the least sacred space, the lowest temple ground, and furthest from the mountains.[9] In this way the temple is a living organism that reflects the lower-, middle-, and upper-world construct of the cosmos and within the human body, and the gates and altar structures come to represent the world. The temple is thus a representation of the universe, of "ourselves," and is itself an offering (H. Geertz 1988:7–8).

At temple festivals, participants honor the deified ancestors who founded the particular temple and, by doing so, honor the myth that the ritual enacts and the origin of the village involved. In Balinese thought, the divine constitutes the whole universe and all of its particles. Therefore to honor the deities is also to honor the divine substance within oneself and within all beings, living and inert (ibid.:6–7). The divine temporarily assumes the form of the deities invoked at festivals, and these deities enter the *palinggih* ("seat," the altars) or *pasimpangan* ("place to stop" for divine guests, sometimes glossed as "substitute") built and decorated specifically for them in the temples, which become their home during their visits on Earth. At some festivals, deities also enter and possess one or more participants and make their complaints and demands (if any) known through the possessed.

Through prescribed offerings, inducements, and prayers, participants ask the deities for blessings, safety, and health for themselves, their families, and/or their communities. The very act of participation is considered a request for blessings.

In Bali until the mid-twentieth century, most attendants (particularly men) participated in festivals simply by being present; they were not expected to join in the communal prayer generally known as Mabakti (Belo 1953:51). In contrast, the Balinese in Lombok, stirred by their minority status, participated at a greater level, and today nearly everyone on Bali and Lombok participates and prays collectively with fellow villagers.[10] Over the last twenty years many people have begun to pray at temples at various times of the year, and religious activity on both islands has dramatically increased. This turn towards religion is discussed further in Chapter Seven.

The plethora of offerings and additional decorations at a festival, such as woven palm-leaf plaits (*lamak*) and bamboo poles (*penyor*), all carry symbolic significance that becomes activated in the force of context and creates a solemnized atmosphere. As Turner (1982:16) asserts, all symbolic objects in celebrations "speak" and communicate ideas, relationships, and "truths" that are invisible or intangible. These virtual messages are greatly enhanced when they intermingle in the proper context. There is a layering of symbolism where individual messages and meanings are juxtaposed, coalescing into new heights of significance.

In addition to their religious nature, festivals are also major social occasions that bring together communities; they are unique social worlds. The temple becomes the theatrical center of a village that provides an opportunity for villagers to socialize and for young people to flirt. This social behavior is more restrained in Lombok because of the potential of ethnic tension and violence that might be caused by noise and activity disturbing nearby Sasak communities.

Processions are inevitably included and frequently proceed toward rivers or the sea to ritually bathe god-houses or figurines (if included), or to gather water used for other segments of the festival. In some festivals, processions depart for other sacred spots or temples, usually to invoke divine essence and/or neighboring deities. In either case, processions move through preestablished places, manipulating the space that exists in the environs. Marin (1987:223) calls the procession route a "spatial discourse" that articulates, according to rules and norms, the chosen path. Dibia (1985:64) describes Balinese processions as "a spectacular, powerful movement from a religious and theatrical standpoint," a "huge, glorious moving theatre," whereby the procession route becomes the stage. Music is always included in processions and is marching and militaristic in character, coloring the mission of the procession and marking its commencement and conclusion. Again, ritual activity is more restrained in Lombok. Processions are shorter, less frequent, and less rambunctious.

Music sanctifies the solemn moments of the festival, yet also enlivens the social atmosphere. According to both treatises and participants, the performing arts are sacrificial offerings and function to complete crucial parts of the festival. Music, for example, helps to invoke and entice the deities to come down from their abode on or above the mountains. It then entertains and keeps them in their temple altars for the festival's duration. Sacred temple dances before the deities present the most spiritually pure art of the village and constitute a special, required stage of many festivals. These dance and music offerings inform what is sacred to the culture members, constructing "a central cluster of ideas, images, feelings, and rhythmic interactions which constitute a kind of symbolic template or master pattern for the communications of a culture's most cherished beliefs, ideas, values, and sentiments" (Turner and Turner 1982:204).

Music, dance, and/or theater may be featured for other stages or rites of festivals. Here it is performed primarily for human attendants and functions to keep them present to share experiences and generate "communitas." Music serves at least three major purposes: 1) to invoke, address, and/or entertain deities, a critical function for festival success; 2) to provide the special soundscape or soundtrack of a festival, that changes to complement specific activities, stages, or rites; and 3) to educate or enculturate participants about their own socioreligious past and present.

An understanding of the spatial and temporal dimensions of a festival is crucial in understanding its meaning. The temple space is selected by the gods, positioned according to formulae, and built to represent the cosmos. The temple is the home on Earth of the deities and constitutes an offering to them. The festival is held on the same date as its consecration—an auspicious day generally selected to conjoin many special days in the calendar—which enhances the power of the moment. The festival also reactualizes the myth of the founding of the temple and village, as it honors the ancestral deities and invokes their presence into the festival. The past is thus conjoined to the present as the deities are made contemporary, and the notion of time transforms from profane to sacred.

Since 2001 it has become clear to me that the processes and interpretations of temple festivals are never static; Balinese religion is, and always has been, changing; it adapts to new times and environments. Ritual canon is frequently questioned and finessed into slightly new configurations; as a consequence, functions, including musical ones, remain the same though certain elements—for example, the pieces or even the type of gamelan—may change. While such dialectic processes have always been at work, the last few decades have seen far more challenges to the order. A number of debates have arisen in Bali that question the very basis of local Hinduism. Progressive scholars and Indian Hindu movements and organizations, such as those dedicated to the renowned guru Sai Baba and Haré Krishna International, have gained legitimate followings and currently hold influence with the main religious body, Parisadha Hindu Dharma, that seeks to organize and centralize religious practice. Several core issues directly impact upon temple festivals; one involves animal sacrifice. Such sacrifices are common in Balinese ritual but are disdained by reformists, and opposing groups often struggle to control major temple festivals. Festival gamelan performance has not yet been questioned by these reformists, many of who are musicians or artists themselves. Regular gatherings of the Indian-inspired groups, however, do not include gamelan music. Instead, congregants sing *bhajans* (North Indian–style devotional songs usually in Sanskrit) in a call-and-response format. A few of these organizations and individual reformers now reside in Lombok as well.

Lombok Balinese Religious Identity

Lombok Balinese maintain their Balinese identity through temple festivals, life-cycle rituals, ceremonial clothing, language, and food. Their culture and religion have had to adapt to the reality of minority status on an island outside of Bali. The native inhabitants, the Sasak, are Muslim, and the Balinese have become knowledgeable about both Islamic culture and the distinctions of their own religion and performing arts. As a minority, the Balinese constitute a prime example of tradition preservation and assimilation. Traditions considered necessary to maintain their integrity as a culture have been maintained strongly; those of lesser importance became flexible and have adapted to Lombok, sometimes assimilating Sasak elements (see Harnish 1990, 1992).

Although there has been ethnic friction, local Balinese generally blend well into Sasak society. They are often not easily distinguishable even for Lombok's own citizens. Several aspects of their ceremonial life, however, have changed as a result of life in Lombok. Sasak bureaucrats and friends are frequently invited to life-cycle ceremonies to foster good will, and this changes both the handling and content of food (pork must not be served) and the religious process, as speakers explain the ceremony and the rituals transform into entertainments. Further, Balinese restrain festival celebration to avoid ethnic friction and are particularly careful to refrain from activities during the early evening Muslim prayer of Magrìb. In general, Lombok Balinese are far more knowledgeable about Islam than their counterparts in Bali.

Everyone regards the Sasak as the original inhabitants and the Balinese as relative newcomers.[11] There are many early reports of Balinese settlements in West and Central Lombok, perhaps as early as the fifteenth century (see Hägerdal 2001 and Clegg 2004). Many of these eventually embraced Islam and automatically became Sasak; others maintained their religion and welcomed Balinese arriving a century or more later. In the late seventeenth century, Balinese troops battled and defeated Sasak kingdoms and Makassarese troops, but did not assume full political control of the island until shortly before 1740 (van der Kraan 1980:4–5). After their defeat by the Dutch in 1894, the Balinese became a religious minority under Dutch colonialism.[12] The Japanese supplanted the Dutch in 1942 and departed in 1945, whereupon Indonesia immediately claimed independence, though it was not fully realized until 1949 after Dutch efforts to recolonize Indonesia were finally repulsed. Once again the Balinese became a political minority. Today, the 114,000 or so Balinese are fluent in the Sasak and Balinese languages, as well as the national Indonesian language. Balinese and Sasak converse together in Sasak or, more frequently today, in Indonesian—particularly in urban settings and official institutions such as schools and government offices where Indonesian is the norm.

Most Balinese originate from the Karangasem district in East Bali and regard Lombok as their home, having lived there for many generations. They view Bali as a spiritual center and the source of ancestral deities and wisdom (Gerdin 1982:13). Many, however, have never been to Bali. When they arrived in Lombok, the Balinese found themselves on an island slightly smaller than Bali (4,700 km^2 and 5,591 km^2 respectively), and with a range of peaks and great volcanic mountain, Gunung Rinjani, slightly higher than Bali's Gunung Agung (3,726 m and 3,000 m respectively). In Bali, the great Gunung Agung was the focal point and center symbol of the world, the reference of direction of all good things, and the abode of Siwa (frequently referred to as Batara Gunung Agung) and the divine ancestors (Ramseyer 1986:95). The Balinese, like many island people, orient themselves in terms of a mountain-sea axis (*kaja-kelod*), with the mountains considered the high and pure space, *utama*, and the sea the low and impure space, *nista* (the middle human world is *madya*). Lombok Balinese oriented themselves to Lombok by establishing the great Gunung Rinjani as the focal center, the abode of the high god (Batara Gunung Rinjani) and the divine ancestors of Lombok, and Rinjani became recognized as a younger sibling of Agung. Mangku Ketut Narwadha, a priest at Lingsar, said directly in 2001 that Rinjani "holds" (*megang*) Lombok, just as Agung holds Bali and Mt. Seméru holds Java, and that the Balinese immediately acknowledged Rinjani's power. This reorientation and ontological flexibility helped Balinese culture and religion adapt to Lombok. This transplanted world-view is demonstrated by the addition of altars for Lombok deities, such as Batara Gunung Rinjani and Batara Gedé Lingsar (the deity of Lingsar), in every major temple on Lombok.

The meanings of temples and festivals are the same as in Bali. Festival fanfare, however, has been reduced to avoid ethnic confrontation, and historic developments permanently interrupted the role of the courts and temples as cultural institutions. The Dutch destroyed or dismantled every noble ruling house in 1894, immediately terminating the role and image of the courts. Several temples were similarly destroyed, and the Balinese—due to smaller numbers and the relatively late date of their permanent settlements (1700s–1800s)—never established the elaborate numbers of temples and temple complexes as in Bali.

The reality of mixed villages and the above changes in the traditional temple configuration prevented both some of the formations of community reciprocal work organizations (*banjar*) and the social cohesion of communities in Bali. The Balinese concept of *suka-duka* ("happy-sad"), where villagers will work through festive and sad times unified together as one body, does not apply to the more fragmented Lombok Balinese communities. Nevertheless, their society retains a sense of unity and common purpose; the minority status binds them together. In ceremonial life, all participants work cooperatively for the success of a temple festival, and ward members assist neighbors at life-cycle ceremonies with the understanding that the assistance will be reciprocated. Although historic events have reduced the visibility and vitality of Balinese culture, local Balinese have retained their identity by orienting themselves to Lombok, preserving their literary and much of their performing arts traditions, and maintaining their ceremonial life.

A central authority, Parisadha Hindu Dharma Indonesia (similar to that in Bali), was established in the late 1960s to help codify religious practice and unify and oversee the Hindu community in Lombok and the recent settlements of

Balinese in Sumbawa. The organization made little impact until the 1980s, when it issued a policy of ritual dress (also found in most of Bali): white and gold (for men; colors for women were not specified) at temple festivals, and black for cremations. I believe that the institution, which strives for homogeneity, will work to gradually eliminate the unique aspects of Balinese culture in Lombok, to codify religious practices at festivals and elsewhere, and to make behaviors more like those in Bali and more "Hindu." These trends are now clearly visible in Lombok.

As in Bali, Indian Hindu movements are finding participants. In 2001 I attended an evening of *bhajan* devotional singing dedicated to Sai Baba (and his previous incarnation), and was surprised at the number of congregants and the mastery over such a non-Balinese soundscape. Thus far, the Balinese involved with these movements continue to participate in temple festivals and the phenomenon may simply be symptomatic of the increased religiosity that seems to be occurring throughout Indonesia. To this date, no great struggles have yet emerged between reformers and traditionalists in Lombok. However, the Parisadha Hindu Dharma and Indian movements, as well as other forces within the Balinese community, may someday impact on the processes, instruments, musics, and interpretations of major temple festivals like the one at Lingsar.

Music, the State, and Religious Ritual

The Balinese performing arts that developed before the twentieth century are rooted in religion and function as a form of worship (see Harnish 1998a). In Bali, music and art were so ingrained into religion and daily life that no equivalents developed in the Balinese language except as components of ritual work (*karya*). At one time, it is believed, a majority of people were directly involved in artistic production, though this has become somewhat impractical in today's modern Bali (Harnish 2002). In Lombok, daily life rarely includes music or art, and today only a minority of Balinese have ever been involved in artistic production beyond the creation of offerings.

Balinese culture was firmly established in Lombok in the nineteenth century, although constant fighting between the seven Balinese ruling houses and frequent Sasak revolts prevented a flowering of Balinese arts. Nevertheless, there were several transplanted types of performing arts including the courtly *gambuh* theater, the *Semar pegulingan* court orchestra, and other court music and dance forms.[13] Kings and princes in Java, Bali, and Lombok all cultivated arts and sought gamelan orchestras as part of their legitimacy; for these nobles, power was "that intangible, mysterious, and divine energy which animates the universe" (Anderson 1972:7) and was concentrated in court regalia such as gamelan that could be accumulated to enhance their personal power. The rulers of Lombok, particularly the last king, Anak Agung (A. A.) Ngurah Karangasem, were among the wealthiest in Indonesia and had sufficient resources to sponsor courtly arts and to acquire as many gamelans as they wished. A. A. Ngurah Karangasem successfully completed the transplantation of Balinese culture to Lombok, and the Lombok

Balinese became spiritually and politically independent from Bali by the mid-nineteenth century.

Following the Dutch victory in 1894, the courtly forms promptly vanished and the notions of noble power were abandoned as the Balinese retained only those forms that were considered crucial for ritual purposes. These arts were also endangered because the centers of Balinese culture—the courts and temples—had either been obliterated by Dutch cannons or were in disarray. Before the turn of the twentieth century, however, a local representative from North Bali appointed by the Dutch, I Gusti Putu Geria—affectionately called "Gusti Patih" (noble minister)—helped restore Balinese music and dance in Lombok and contributed new musical instruments and his dance expertise. Like most migrants, the Balinese preserved those arts considered most important for cultural continuity—in their case, arts associated with religion—occasionally assimilating elements of the majority culture; they discarded or simply forgot about less vital forms, including—since the noble model had disintegrated—the courtly arts, and forged new traditions incorporating their new environment (see Harnish 1992).

TRADITIONAL SASAK RELIGION AND FESTIVALS

Up until the sixteenth century the religious practices on Bali and Lombok were probably very similar. Both Balinese and Sasak belief systems included animism and ancestor worship with traces of Hinduism and Buddhism, though Bali embraced a stronger Hindu element probably because it was physically closer to Hindu Java and more subject to Javanese influence. In the early sixteenth century the Hindu Javanese kingdom of Majapahit fell to Islamic forces and many of the artists and nobility migrated to Bali, where they introduced a deeper level of Hinduism; meanwhile in north Lombok, Muslim Javanese evangelists introduced a Sufi form of Islam. In the mid-to-late sixteenth century, a more "orthodox" Islam was introduced in the east by Muslims from Makassar and Sumbawa. From this time forward, the Balinese became more Hindu and the Sasak became more Muslim, and before another hundred years had passed, the first "official" Balinese expedition departed for Lombok. But while the Balinese incorporated their earlier belief system into a more monotheistic form of Hinduism, the Sasak lost most of their early beliefs in the drive to establish a purer form of reformist Islam.[14]

Due to their shared history, Bali and Lombok were grouped together politically by the national government in Java in the mid-twentieth century, despite the fact that their cultures practiced separate faiths. It was not until December 17, 1958, that the government established Bali as its own province and joined Lombok with Islamic Sumbawa into a separate province, Nusa Tenggara Barat (NTB). Table 2.1 provides a graphic synopsis of the history of Lombok.

Traditional Sasak festivals call into the present and reactualize the deeds and power of the ancestors. In Sasak belief, ancestors, particularly the first cultivators, bond and mediate between the descendants and the natural powers within the landscape, and eventually attain divine status (Pepplinkhuizen 1991:38). The Sasak have

TABLE 2.1. Historic Synopsis of Lombok

Before 13th century	Feudal kingdoms; Hindu/Buddhist/animist; limited Javanese influence
13th–14th centuries	Hindu kingdoms; Selaparang kingdom; clear Javanese influence
14th century	Hindu Javanese Majapahit empire defeats Sasak kingdoms
16th century	Sufi-type Islam introduced in north; Sunni-based Islam later in east
16th–17th centuries	Islamic kingdoms rise; Pejanggik and powerful Selaparang; first Balinese settlements established in west; Makassar influence in East and Central Lombok
17th century	Balinese control West Lombok
1678	Balinese defeat Selaparang and other Sasak kingdoms; divide Lombok between themselves and local figure, Banjar Getas
1738–1740	Balinese begin colonization of all Lombok
1740–1894	Balinese colonize Lombok, meeting occasional resistance
1894	Dutch defeat Balinese, begin colonization of Lombok
1942	Japanese supplant Dutch, begin occupation
1945	Japanese retreat; Indonesian independence claimed; Dutch attempt to regain control
1949	True independence achieved; national government appoints Javanese to govern Bali and Lombok
1958	Lombok joined with Sumbawa into province of NTB; continued Javanese governors
1998	First governor from NTB

never had the matrix of holy places that Bali has had, and only certain festivals have precise dates determined by a calendrical system, excepting, of course, Islamic rites such as Maulud (or Maulid, Muhammad's birthday) and the feast of Lebaran (Idul Fitri, usually spelled Eid el-Fitr outside of Indonesia), which is held at the end of the fasting month, Ramadan. From the Sasak ancestor cult developed a complex of death ceremonies perhaps more numerous and more complicated than those of Bali.[15] Unlike ancestors in Bali, Sasak ancestors are continually considered village members, and rites at gravesites probably constitute the foremost ritual activities of the traditional Sasak. The traditional worldview "indicates no definite boundary between living and dead villagers, or between the past and the future, which are considered aspects of the present" (Krulfield 1974:88), and ancestors share in village food production in the form of ritual offerings made to them. Rural Javanese hold similar rites in which family spirits are offered clothing, food, and drink (Hefner 1985:70); Sasak and traditional rural Javanese bury rather than cremate their dead and seem to share many beliefs and rituals toward the dead and ancestral deities.

Information on traditional death ceremonies, agricultural rites, and big feasts is limited partially because these events have grown extremely rare in contemporary Lombok (see, however, Polak 1978 and Ecklund 1977). There still exist traditions of feasting around ritual dates, but these traditions are not as codified as the Javanese Slametan and do not usually fall on dates in Islamic history as they do in Java (see C. Geertz 1960:78 and Hefner 1985:105). In the transition from a more syncretic to a more orthodox Islam, the *adat* (customary law) that held traditional festivities together in Lombok has grown weaker and weaker. Religious leaders have tried to eliminate traditional festivals and replace them with strictly Islamic ones, and they have achieved a high degree of success. Ironically, while many orthodox leaders have striven to remove *adat* and substitute it with modern Sasak/Indonesian fundamentalism, the new order has simply shifted the orientation of the traditional worldview. Instead of viewing the old Sasak courts and nobles as models of purity and spiritual power, for example, many now view Mecca and religious leaders in this light. But although many of the cultural changes have been superficial, traditional festivals and performing arts have been severely impacted. In order to be preserved within the general Sasak populace, festivals and arts must be Islamic in orientation and meaningful to the emerging Sasak/Indonesian cultural identity.

There are two main socioreligious groups within Sasak society: the smaller Waktu Telu or Wetu Telu ("three times" or "three stages"), and the much larger Waktu Lima ("five times"). The Waktu Telu are nominal or traditional Muslims, and the Waktu Lima are, for the most part, reformed orthodox Sunni Muslims.[16] The origin of these terms seems related to religious practice: the Waktu Lima ideally accept the five tenets of Islam and pray five times a day, while the Waktu Telu generally follow three different kinds of rituals (life-cycle, Islamic, and agricultural; see below), honor a trinity (usually conceived as God, the ancestors, and parents), and follow, in rituals, sacred sets of three.[17] Many state that Waktu Telu pray three times, rather than five times, a day, but this is not generally true as the majority do not pray at such regular intervals. Most within this group accept only the first of the five tenets of Islam (belief in Allah with Muhammad as His Prophet). Their beliefs represent a legacy of the original Sufi Javanese expedition to North Lombok, while those of the Waktu Lima have antecedents in the more orthodox Islam introduced in the east.

Four contemporary reasons account for the further development of the Waktu Lima in Lombok:

1. The influence of large numbers of non-Sasak peoples (Sumbawanese, Makassarese, Bugis, Arabs, Javanese, etc.) who are orthodox Muslims,
2. The pilgrimage to Mecca, where many Sasak receive religious training and are honored upon their return,
3. A surging twentieth-century pan-Indonesian-Islamic movement that unifies and inspires reformist Islam and the Waktu Lima, and,
4. The building of Islamic schools and boarding schools (*madrasah, pesantren*) and the fostering of religious education at these schools for many thousands of children in Lombok.

The founding of the local Islamic organization Nahdhutul Watan (NW) by TGH Zainuddin Abdul Majid in 1936, and its formal incorporation as an educational and social entity in 1953 had a tremendous impact upon Lombok's religious and political developments over the second half of the twentieth century. Abdul Majid himself took a government position in the 1950s and led the charge of *tuan gurus* (religious leaders) into the government. Particularly since the 1970s, many NW leaders and other *tuan gurus* have been members of the Indonesian parliament or have held important provincial government positions. Today, being a *tuan guru* or a *haji* is almost a requirement for most offices.

McVey (1995:318) states that the removal of Waktu Telu leaders from positions of authority in the early Dutch years greatly impoverished Waktu Telu villages and led to the first widespread desertion from the older faith. The Dutch wanted to further isolate the Waktu Telu and Waktu Lima to prevent any unity between them and thus decrease resistance to Dutch rule. Though they had to confront occasional Waktu Lima revolts, the Dutch had more trouble dealing with Waktu Telu. They feared their millennial complex and so worked to undermine their communities (Ecklund 1979:250–251). Leemann (1989a:40), for example, states that the close relationship between the Dutch government and Waktu Lima was considered necessary to govern effectively and resulted in a policy of eliminating village communal law over land in 1935. Since land—the spiritual and material basis of Waktu Telu communities—could suddenly be bought and sold, the policy worked to dissolve those communities and to further Waktu Lima enterprises and conversions. The post-Independence Javanese/Indonesian government has maintained and expanded policies favoring Waktu Lima. The government has viewed "proper" religion as progressive and a sign of civilization and acceptance of official authority (McVey 1995:323); from this perspective, the Waktu Telu were "backward," outside the mainstream, and uncivilized. Unlike the Balinese colonialists, both the Dutch and Indonesian governments have found much more in common with the Waktu Lima.

The Waktu Lima and the Waktu Telu mirror different worldviews that encompass different work patterns, village structures, clothing, ritual practices, and attitudes towards music and the performing arts. The Waktu Lima, for the most part, seek to follow Islamic law as outlined in Lombok to the fullest extent. Many are members of reformist religious organizations, such as the local NW or the national Muhammadiyah, that led the twentieth-century drive for purist reform in the observance of Islam in Lombok. Waktu Lima are both village and urban dwellers and work as traders, in small businesses, and in the government. Most follow common practices: they pray five times a day, pray at the mosque on Fridays, aspire to the Hajj, fast during daylight hours of Ramadan, and give the charitable *zakat*. Many, however, also maintain Sasak customs and attitudes and are "moderates." Like those with a stronger Islamic orientation, few of these people call themselves "Waktu Lima"; most simply call themselves "Muslims."

Most modernist Muslims insist that their practice of Islam is "pure" while that of the Waktu Telu is "false." In fact, the official attitude toward the Waktu Telu belief is that it is not a religion at all. Many officials have pointed out that the Waktu Telu neither have a comprehensive holy book (*kitab suci*) nor follow a codified series of rites, two requirements for the word "religion" (*agama*) as it is understood in Indonesia. Therefore, Waktu Telu merely embrace a set of "beliefs" (*kepercayaan*). Further, the full title of their practices is "Islam Waktu Telu." Since these practices are clearly not Islamic as outlined in the *Al Qur'an* and *hadith* literature, then they cannot be called "Islam" or "religion" at all.

Waktu Telu realize that their beliefs differ from those that are thoroughly Islamic, but many believe that their practice was originally mapped out by a culture hero, Pangeran Sangupati, who devised a version of Islam in proper accordance with the beliefs and customs of the Sasak.[18] Their contention, as explained by several teachers, is that as long as they continue their traditions, they will meet with safety and agricultural success; if they discontinue their *adat* and betray their ancestors, they will suffer sickness and famine. For those Waktu Telu who claim this myth, it helps affirm their cultural legitimacy. They have needed a response to the continuing pressure to change their customs and beliefs—pressure exerted by modern Muslim leaders who have questioned their cultural integrity. The Waktu Telu do not view themselves as "false" Muslims. As a consequence, I use the words "traditionalist," "nominal," or "syncretist" since they also acknowledge limits in their relation to general Islamic dogma. To modernist Muslims, the Waktu Telu are not "Muslim" at all since they follow neither the five pillars nor the behavioral requirements of Islam.

Although the poles between traditional/syncretic and orthodox/reformed appear hard and fixed, my research often indicates softer boundaries, and I have met a number of Sasak who constitute a third group: Muslims who continue certain *adat* practices or are sympathetic toward *adat*. Leemann (1989a:33) describes these moderates as "included in the process of Islamization" who identify themselves as Muslims but retain a "pre-Islamic body of thought."

Mark Woodward's work (1989) on Javanese Islam explores the beliefs of urban and rural dwellers in the Yogyakarta area. He articulates two main divisions of practice (normative Islam and Islam Jawa) and occasionally a third (reformist Islam). "Normative Islam" refers to the "set of prescribed behaviors that Allah, through the agency of Muhammad, has delineated for the Muslim community" and is linked to a royal cult (where rulership is equated with sainthood); "Islam Jawa" combines indigenous beliefs with Sufi mysticism and royal cult; and "reformist Islam" follows normative Islam (without the royal cult) and practitioners are often members of reformist organizations that subject all aspects of life to scripture.

These divisions help illuminate the situation in Lombok. "Waktu Lima" include those who follow either reformist or normative Islam (the latter more moderate and retaining some traditional cultural customs), and "Waktu Telu" include those similar to practitioners of Islam Jawa. The Waktu Telu, however, are diverse and their beliefs are difficult to define. Some are close in practice to normative Islam, others can hardly be called "Muslim" at all, and few are involved with Sufi mysticism, which is often apparently part of "orthodox" practices at some mosques, but all are tied to ancestral lands and *adat* customs. In contrast, many orthodox Muslims call their own practices *agama hilang adat* (here meaning religion without *adat*). These divisions present a continuum from reformist Islam through normative Islam to Waktu Telu, and individuals or whole villages may appear anywhere along that continuum. As a whole, the village of Lingsar follows normative Islam, with some on reformist and Waktu Telu poles. Although few call themselves Waktu Telu today because of the attached stigma, most Sasak participants at the Lingsar festival maintain *adat* customs; some are truly Waktu Telu and follow few Islamic practices, others are closer to normative Islam.

The few remaining Waktu Telu strongholds have been in the north, the mountains, and in rural West Lombok, while the Waktu Lima are found everywhere else, particularly in urban centers where they constitute nearly 100 percent of the Sasak population. Waktu Telu villages are somewhat isolated, while Waktu Lima villages dominate the main trade routes of the market economy. The Waktu Telu *adat* discourages a money economy and the selling of most agricultural products, including rice. Since the Waktu Lima have discarded *adat* and accept only Islamic law for moral and behavioral guidance, they have been relatively mobile and adept in money matters and have monopolized trade and finance in Lombok. Some have moved into or near Waktu Telu villages to act as market middlemen, bringing with them orthodox Islam and religious leaders who scrutinize Waktu Telu religious practice. As the Waktu Telu village opens up and moves into a money economy, its *adat* weakens and is gradually replaced by a Sasak version of Islamic law.[19]

In the 1980s local officials always described the village of Lingsar as strongly Islamic and thus somewhat at odds with its temple culture. As the story went, the last king, A. A. Ngurah Karangasem, had himself begun the local Islamic transformation by financing the Hajj pilgrimages of many individuals to Mecca as a reward for their hard work on the temple. These individuals returned to develop orthodox Islam in the village, and the temple soon became a strange anomaly in a sea of reformist Islam. In 2001, however, I learned that as recently as forty years ago Lingsar was still largely a Waktu Telu village.

In the early post-Independence years a political struggle ensued between the nationalist party (Partai Nasional Indonesia [PNI]) and the communist party

(Partai Komunis Indonesia [PKI]) throughout Indonesia. In Lombok the main arguments revolved around land reform, and the PKI proposed a complete re-allocation favoring farmers. Since these ideas favored *adat* and the land, many Waktu Telu were attracted. Lalu Wiramaja told me that the PKI enlisted Waktu Telu leaders, who in turn had their communities (mostly farmers) attend events and vote for the PKI party. The remaining Sasak nobility, who still wielded some influence among nonorthodox Sasak, were associated with the PNI, while reformist Muslims were members of Muslim parties such as Masyumi or Nahdatul Ulama.

In 1965 a supposed communist coup attempt in Jakarta—now thought to have been an internal military squabble or even an anti-leftist conspiracy—in which several military officials were killed sparked an anti-communist melee throughout the country. Many members of the PKI were slaughtered outright by the military and citizen vigilante squads, a few were offered the choice of suicide, and some were imprisoned and rehabilitated. Perhaps nearly one million died nationally (see Kahin 2003). Many of those killed in Lombok were Waktu Telu farmers and religious officials (*kiyai* and *pamangku*) who had been attracted to the ideas of land reform (see Zakaria 2001:37). Muller (1991:54) claims that many were slaughtered simply because some local reformists felt their beliefs were "unacceptable."

The entire affair worked to further destabilize and delegitimize the Waktu Telu, many of whom quickly began following *tuan gurus* and proclaimed themselves Waktu Lima for their own protection (Leemann 1989a:46). The government soon strongly encouraged the Waktu Telu to send their children to Islamic schools so that they could truly learn about the religion, and thus avoid misunderstandings in the future. The village of Lingsar, as well as nearby Narmada (a family center for the Sasak Lingsar priest), were hit hard by the slaughter and the following reform movement. Wiramaja states that the priest and his family "were all clearly Waktu Telu up to that point." Lingsar quickly assumed a more Islamic profile. Not coincidentally, major new problems concerning Sasak participation at the temple suddenly emerged. The temple and its festival were clearly not Islamic; thus it could be considered off limits for all Sasak.

Since it was assumed that communists could not follow religion and because the government wanted a direct hand in regulating religious activities, all Indonesians were ordered by the national government to register in 1967 as believers of one of four faiths (Cederroth 1981:77): Islam, Christianity (Protestantism or Catholicism), Buddhism, or Hinduism.[20] The Waktu Telu were thus compelled to choose Islam. As a result Waktu Telu religious practices, already in steep decline, were examined by religious officials with government authority and generally found to be impure and heretic. Through political pressure and even violent acts,[21] most remaining Waktu Telu eventually pledged allegiance to orthodox principles and discontinued syncretist practices. Among the 2.5 million Sasak today, it is very rare to find anyone who calls him/herself a Waktu Telu, and, in fact, "Waktu Telu" and "Waktu Lima" are terms that were officially abolished in 1968 and are less frequently used today. It is felt, incorrectly, that Waktu Telu and their culture no longer exist.

The above events strongly curtailed the frequency of traditional Sasak festivals, which may have been nearly as numerous and spectacular as Balinese events at one time. Reformist practice absorbed aspects of some traditional syncretist feasts and presented them within a new framework, such as in the Periapan communal meal on Maulid (though this feast has been in decline since the 1970s). Other traditional festivals, however, conflict directly with modernist observances and were never incorporated. These festivals have decreased dramatically, particularly after the 1960s. The remaining Waktu Telu in several areas are often afraid to hold major festivals because to do so would encourage socioreligious and economic persecution.

Nevertheless, a few Waktu Telu festivals still exist in rather remote villages; some others are continued by a small group of Sasak syncretic Buddhists, the Boda (sometimes called Sasak Aga [original Sasak]), who have maintained ritual practices once shared with the Waktu Telu (see Harnish 1994 and Leemann 1989a). Cederroth (1981:177) states that Waktu Telu religious rituals can be divided into three groups: 1) those of the life cycle, including birth, hair-cutting, circumcision, tooth-filing, marriage, and death (Polak 1978:126–178 describes some of these); 2) those called Syarat (Islamic law) more directly associated with Islam, such as Maulud, Lebaran, and local observances; and 3) calendrical rites connected to agricultural practices and fertility (the Lingsar Pujawali is one of these; Polak 1978:188–236 explores similar practices).[22] The latter rites and festivals bring specific groups or whole villages to participate and feast together to help secure prosperity and safety for the community. These festivals share elements with those in Bali and Java and are emphasized in the following discussion.

For the determination of traditional Sasak festivals, there does not appear to be a single traditional calendar system used throughout Lombok, but rather two systems with local variations. One is a solar-lunar calendar similar to the *saka* sometimes called *wariga*,[23] while the other, as indicated by Cederroth (1981:290–294), consists of eight years with intersecting months, weeks, and days, similar to the Javanese *windu* eight-year cycle. This *windu* calendar combines with a variation of the Muslim calendar to determine dates of acknowledged Islamic holidays and local Islamic observations. Polak (1978:279–333) suggests that the Waktu Telu originally borrowed calendrical systems from Java but did not account for time adjustments that eventually separated them; time deviations for Islamic rites often lead to conflict between Waktu Telu and Waktu Lima.

The remaining festivals associated with Waktu Telu known to the writer include the Pujawali at Lingsar; the Ngayu–ayu (beautiful, good things) held in Sembalun Bumbung, Lenek, and in some Boda villages;[24] and other festivals and communal feasts known generally as *gawé* (ritual feast) or *alip* (feast) and held in several villages, such as Suren and its environs, Sapit, Annyar, and Bayan.[25] Few of these festivals are associated with Islam; most concern fertility or an ancestral cult and celebrate ancestors' acts and deaths. While some festivals are held at or around sacred gravesites, known generally as *makam*, others are held at shrines in holy places known as *pedéwaq* (place of deities), *kemaliq* or *pepaliq* (sacred place with taboos), or *pepujan* (place of worship). Frequently an ancestor is believed to have mysteriously vanished at a particular spot, which might be a *makam* or *kemaliq*, and ceremonies and celebrations will be held around that spot (Polak 1978:340). This is the rationale at Lingsar for many Sasak. The shrine is believed to be the abode of deities, with a concentration of divine power, and the divine, as in Bali, is believed to both affect and exist within everything. The deities worshipped during such festivals are ancestors or spirits inhabiting particular sites thought to control prosperity and fertility at that site or throughout a region.

The term *kemaliq* can denote any sacred place protected by numerous taboos in Waktu Telu villages, including mosques and ancestor graves (Cederroth 1981:61), and the word is used for both the second courtyard and its altar at Lingsar. It commonly refers only to the courtyard of a shrine, and the term *pedéwaq* often defines the shrine itself. These are holy sites protected by taboos. Some shrines are located on high ground, probably to map a high–low dichotomy of spiritual power. They are also frequently positioned near water springs. Unlike the empty altars of Balinese temples, most Sasak shrines contain many erect stones or a single stone, thought to be supernaturally powerful or somehow directly connected to the deified ancestor and fertility. These stones often commemorate the ancestor and his supernatural power, and may be interpreted as phallus (*lingga*) symbols representing that power. During some ritual events the powers of the local landscape are invited to take up their "seat" in the altar stones to become divine protectors of the community (Pepplinkhuizen 1991:36). One or more stones are also usually found in Waktu Telu mosques.

Like Lombok Balinese, Waktu Telu acknowledge Gunung Rinjani as the symbolic center of their world conception, and Batara Rinjani (sometimes Batara Indra) is conceived as the original Sasak ancestor.[26] Deified ancestors can be traced to the same or a similarly powerful line, and some traditional Sasak noble classes (*perwangsa*) claim direct lineage to Batara Rinjani. Several Sasak mentioned that Rinjani is so important that the original interpretation of the Islamic pilgrimage meant climbing Gunung Rinjani rather than departing for Mecca. Traditional Sasak, like Balinese and many rural Javanese, believe in the power inherent in directions, that *daya*, or towards the mountain, is a more pure and sacred direction than *lauq*, or towards the sea. This sense of directionality likely informs the positioning of holy shrines, as in Bali; at Lingsar the *kemaliq* altar clearly has a directional basis, and some traditional villages, such as Bayan, are constructed with a similar orientation to help concentrate spiritual power.[27] As traditionalists begin to reform, the sacred direction towards the mountains and Gunung Rinjani shifts and becomes the direction towards Mecca.

The festivals held at these shrines, often to invoke rainfall or give thanks to deities, reenact the myth of the founding of the area and include many types of offerings, animal sacrifices, and one or more processions. The work is collective and the events are major social and religious occasions. Several religious officials contact and invoke deities and represent the villagers, but the primary goal is village participation as a form of worship and an experience of community. As in Bali, a number of performing arts are integral to the festival and constitute offerings: some are more sacred, more directed at deities, and serve to invoke deities; others are presented primarily to entertain the human attendants.

Sasak accommodated the Balinese colonialists in differing ways: Waktu Lima in East and Central Lombok struggled and frequently revolted, particularly when Balinese kings took Sasak daughters as concubines, and when they subjected Sasak to compulsory labor and military service, while Waktu Telu in the west, who shared some beliefs with Balinese, established fairly harmonious relations. Many Waktu Telu even fought with the Balinese against Waktu Lima during the latter's revolts in the nineteenth century. Balinese influence is still felt in West Lombok, and many Sasak understand the Balinese language, though they are not fluent speakers. The Sasak, however, have reclaimed their island and want to make visible their culture and religion. Mosques have been built in such plenitude around Lombok in recent years that other Indonesians often call Lombok *pulau seribu mesjid* (island of a thousand mosques). This phrase is inadequate as there are probably now more than two thousand mosques.

Throughout history, the Sasak, who were colonized and strongly influenced by Javanese, Makassarese, Balinese, Dutch, and Japanese, have rarely had political control of their island. While many of the previous generation have interpreted the political power of the national government as a new form of Javanese colonialism, Sasak have recently been appointed to most of the important positions within the regional government and now play a major political role. In a move lauded locally, the national government in 1998 appointed the first NTB-born and non-Javanese governor, H. Harun Al Rasyid (from Bima regency on Sumbawa), and currently there is a Sasak governor.

The government has taken steps to aid and develop Sasak cultural identity and has allowed Sasak religious leaders to foster religious identity, particularly after the 1997 recession, the ensuing fall of President Soeharto, and the relaxing of authoritarian rule. Many Islamic groups, built around *tuan gurus* or around mosques, then organized small-scale security forces to protect villages. Some *tuan gurus* were responsible for directing these forces to attack Christians in January 2000 in retaliation for the deaths of Muslims in sectarian violence in the Maluku islands (see Chapter One). This event was publicized worldwide and devastated the island's tourist trade, which had been rapidly expanding since the 1980s. Lingsar had always been on the tourist itinerary, and the industry had started to have an impact on some of the Lingsar performing arts (see Chapter Seven). The Ministry of Tourism (Kantor Parawisata) maintains influence at Lingsar, particularly among the Sasak who have most benefited from this contact.

Both the government and religious leaders have paid close attention to the Lingsar festival. While many religious leaders banned Sasak participation at the festival on the grounds that it is a "heathen" (non-Islamic) ritual, the government decided to help develop the festival as a tourist attraction and to bolster local cultural identity. To avoid religious problems, the government encourages Sasak attendance not as a practice of religion (*agama*), for which it clearly does not qualify, but as a continuation of cultural tradition (*budaya*), devoid of religious associations. This has allowed some remaining Waktu Telu (and those who retain a "pre-Islamic body of thought") to participate in the festival, but many do so for religious reasons.

Music, Ritual, and Religious Forces

Reflecting the political and religious problems of Lombok, the traditional music of the Waktu Telu has waned as the ritual contexts for performance have declined. Like the Balinese, most Waktu Telu performing arts were steeped in religion and used in worship, but the Islamic reform movement and associated religious organizations have fought against Waktu Telu ritual practices, adversely affecting the traditional arts. Many music forms have been lost, though musicians often created new forms which were acceptable and retained elements of earlier music (see Harnish 1998b).

Sasak ruling houses, which, as a Sasak friend called them, were simply "glorified huts," had limited political power, collected limited revenues, and though widespread controlled only limited areas. There were few traditions that expressed a Sasak court model of power. This is not surprising given the extensive colonizations of the island. However, the notion of kingship was vital to local belief, and religious concepts formed the basis for social structure and political organization. Nobility expressed authority and fulfilled responsibilities by sponsoring major rituals, and they often owned a number of gamelans that were used in such events as big feasts and communal ancestral grave cleanings. Ritual life maintained status. In the twentieth century the nobility's political power was eclipsed by religious organizations and *tuan gurus*, and many sponsored traditions have vanished; a few have fallen into the hands of villagers.

As with many Javanese and Balinese, struck bronze, the primary aesthetic in most gamelans, carries a special significance for the traditional Sasak. Bronze musical instruments, in fact, are often considered to embody power through which can flow the voice and wisdom of the ancestors (Harnish 1991a:181). For this reason, and because of the association with Waktu Telu ritual, some Islamic leaders have banned traditional bronze instruments in their areas of influence as a way to preclude the experience of and exposure to preformist Islamic culture. By the 1970s, music had become a sign of religious orientation: those who engaged traditional gamelans that used bronze instruments were Waktu Telu (or had similar sympathies); those who engaged ensembles without bronze instruments (what we might call "reformist gamelans") were Waktu Lima. These two types of ensembles embody some distinctive musical elements that will be discussed in Chapter Five. Interestingly, with government support, by 2001 many types of gamelans, particularly the *gendang beleq* (big drum) with its bronze instruments, had made a recovery and hundreds of performing groups had formed. While this change does indicate a mental switch and a relaxing of prohibitions, the renewed use of gamelan music is confined to entertainment, social activity, and identity-building, and does not play an integral purpose (i.e. marking a stage, completing a rite as at Lingsar) within a ceremony. Thus, most contemporary gamelan use has been de-ritualized, which might have ensured its survival in the transition to modernized and Islamified Lombok.

THE LINGSAR FESTIVAL

The village of Lingsar is located about twenty kilometers east from Cakranegara and Mataram, the centers of the ruling Balinese kingdoms. Mataram is also the seat of the provincial government. For many centuries, the temple *was* Lingsar, the principal reason for the existence of the village. The temple was the center, both physically and symbolically; virtually all villagers were farmers connected to it. The twentieth century brought many changes to this construct. The village expanded in all directions, and, though farming was still primary, businesses and schools opened, people began to move in and out, and villagers became increasingly more Islamic and opposed to the culture surrounding the temple. The festival today, however, still provides income and status to the village. Vendors and private transporters reap benefits from participants, the village earns some revenue through tourism, and the social networks and irrigation brokering reestablished at each festival secure Lingsar's access to water and the general economy.

Balinese and Sasak myths confirm that the temple is a "sacred site" where a deity from the divine world has intervened with mortals in our world to enact a miracle (see Eliade 1963 and Chapter Three). The temple has been a pilgrimage site for Balinese and Sasak over centuries; though some come at other times of the year, the vast majority comes for the festival. Like other sacred sites, music performances are meant to reproduce the temple's complex cultural mix and history and to represent the passage from this world to the other (Bohlman 1996:338). To participate in the ritual is to participate in myth. The music and festival mobilize participants, narrate the past within the framework of the present, and provide experiences for the construction and maintenance of personalized and group identities.

Performance Profile

The Lingsar Pujawali reenacts the legendary founding of the Lingsar water springs and joins in festivity and worship the migrant Balinese and Waktu Telu and some other Sasak. The festival also regulates the irrigation of much of West Lombok and serves to invoke rainfall, to realize a forum for direct contact with the divine, and to thank the deities for the past harvest. The Balinese and Sasak conduct respective rites, prepare respective offerings in respective courtyards, present respective performing arts, and even honor respective myths, but they participate and work for the success of the festival together. While the event is clearly part of religion (*agama*) for the Balinese, it has been embraced since the latter part of the twentieth century as an expression of *budaya* (culture) and *adat* (customary law) for the Sasak. Since the festival was clearly not Islamic, the change among the Sasak from religion to *budaya* and *adat* was necessary for their continued participation. It was also necessary for the Balinese; they could not hold the festival, as it has always existed, without the Sasak.

The Pura Lingsar complex, located in the western plain of Lombok, contains many sacred water springs and receives runoff from rivers that begin at Lake Segara Anak within the crater of Mt. Rinjani. During the last Balinese kingdom (1839–1894), the court annexed the festival and turned it into a state ceremony, asserting that the ruling house had the power to guarantee an abundant water supply and fertility in Lombok through holding a grand festival (Gerdin 1982:72, 216). The concept of king and ruling house became synonymous with water and prosperity, and the prime legitimation of power was the king's provision of water for his subjects, which occurred primarily through the Lingsar festival. This and other state ceremonies allowed the court to coordinate cultivation activities and control the irrigation system. Following the festival, for example, the farmers throughout the western plain would transplant rice seedlings into the fields, and later they would harvest together. Unlike the situation in Bali, where the irrigation organizations (*subak*) were independent from noble control, the organizations in Lombok, often mixtures of Balinese and Sasak farmers, were subordinate to the ruling houses.

Following the Dutch conquest of the Balinese and the ensuing Dutch colonization (1894–1942), the *subak* and other participants expected the Dutch, as successors to Balinese kings, to legitimize their rule by guaranteeing irrigation water and fertility in the same manner: by sponsoring major ceremonies like the Lingsar Pujawali. The Dutch contributed to the festival and repaired the temple (partially destroyed by Waktu Lima following the Balinese defeat), but did little to support grand festivals. With the help of nobles and the revenue derived from harvests of the temple lands, the festival managed to continue the same traditions without the courtly fanfare. This may have altered the meaning of the festival. Instead of the courts and rulers displaying their power and securing the water for the masses by way of the festival, it perhaps was only the high deities of Lombok and Bali who could bestow these favors.

The meaning of the festival has further dislodged from royal control since Indonesian Independence. Though the festival is sponsored primarily by the two rice harvests of the temple lands and by contributions from descendants of noble houses, the provincial government has been playing a larger role since the 1980s and the Krama Pura temple organization has access to other funding. Many grants for repairs and outright contributions have been offered to the Krama Pura; in fact, the government paid for the construction of a parking area in 1989 and for additional temple gates and a proscenium performance stage in 1993. I Wayan Kereped, the head (*ketua*) of the Krama Pura, mentioned in 2001 that he has not sought any government funding over the previous few years, though the Tourist

Office (Kantor Parawisata) now funds additional performing groups and local guides. While at one time the city and military police patrolling the festival were seen as contemporary versions of royal guards at the festival during Balinese colonization, these days the Lingsar village *lang lang* security force, Geresak ("friendly"), is also involved, demonstrating the cooperation between government and local agencies in furthering the interests of the participants and the island.

Since the introduction of shorter-maturation strains of rice in the 1970s–1980s, the festival no longer coordinates the rice cycle, and farmers may let their fields lie fallow at differing times, plant vegetables during short seasons, and even seek alternative sources of water. The festival, however, still helps control the irrigation of much of the western plain, and some farmers try to follow the earlier tradition of transplanting seedlings after the festival. The government efforts to assist in agriculture and festival coordination demonstrate that the government has the well-being of the farmers in mind and that it can help contribute to the general prosperity of Lombok. The various branches of the government have legitimized the festival, and their efforts may constitute a mandate for governing Lombok to local farmers.

From the Balinese perspective, the festival is determined by the *saka* year and occurs on the sixth full moon; from the Sasak perspective, it occurs on the seventh full moon of the *wariga* calendar. The Pura Lingsar complex actually consists of two temple structures: Pura Ulon (head temple) and Pura Lingsar or Pura Lingsar Barat (West Lingsar temple) (see Chapter Four). Both temples contain single exclusive Balinese courtyards called *gadoh* (work, source) and single shared courtyards called *kemaliq* (sacred place of many taboos). The altar complexes within the *gadoh* unify the high deities of Lombok and Bali and honor the Balinese Lingsar myth, while the *kemaliq* altars consist of many erect stones (like Sasak *pedéwaq*, *kemaliq*, and *makam* shrines) and the courtyards contain ponds fed by sacred water springs. The *kemaliq* of both temples, overseen by Sasak officials, are associated with irrigation water, and many Balinese consider them rice and irrigation temples.

Since the 1980s Sasak officials have contested the idea that the *kemaliq* of Pura Lingsar is part of the *pura*, a word that refers to a Balinese temple. Suparman Taufiq (Parman), the nephew of the current Sasak *pamangku* and in line to become the next one, reiterated his opposition to folding the *kemaliq* into the *pura* in 2001, despite the wall that surrounds and links both courtyards and creates one structure. According to the Sasak founding myth, the *kemaliq* existed before the coming of the Balinese to Lombok, and the nineteenth-century Balinese raja (A. A. Ngurah Karangasem) united the *gadoh* with the *kemaliq*. Consequently, to Parman and many others the *kemaliq* was originally in its own space and thus is still separate from the *pura*. Needless to say, the Balinese Krama Pura disagrees and has not been pleased with the emergence of this story and the *kemaliq*'s developing independence from the *gadoh*. The official marker and street signs, both designed by the government, are split on the issue. The street signs say simply "Pura Lingsar," but the marker on the temple says "Pura Lingsar dan Kemaliq" (Pura Lingsar and

Kemaliq). The latter is what Parman is suggesting. Through this semantic switch, the courtyards and temple itself are reconfigured, the *kemaliq* is no longer administrated by the *gadoh* or by the Balinese temple organization, and the Sasak myth is asserted as fact (see Chapter Three).

Pura Lingsar is the mother temple of Lombok for most Balinese. It is often likened to Pura Besakih in Bali, which unifies all as one island people. Lingsar is the place of worship for the Supreme Being, for the ancestral deities of Bali and Lombok, and for the high deities who "own" Lombok and Bali. Pura Lingsar is categorized as one of the great state temples, now collectively called *pura jagat* (world temples) or *pura umum* (public temples). When Balinese intellectuals conceive of six temples connecting six points (*sad kayangan*) as in Bali, Lingsar is generally the central temple. For the Waktu Telu, or more accurately the Waktu-Telu-like Sasak, the *kemaliq* has become a protected traditional shrine, the place of worship of high ancestral deities who control fertility, and the memorial to honor a particular culture hero, sometimes named Datu Wali Milir (see Chapter Three). The Sasak rites undertaken at Lingsar by officials and participants constitute some of the last remnants of early Sasak ritual tradition in the western plains of Lombok.

The festival is growing in popularity. Lombok Balinese and Sasak farmers and members of *subak* are obligated to attend. Most Balinese families and wards (*banjar* or *karang*), even those disassociated with rice cultivation, send at least one representative who takes offerings on the group's behalf, and frequently entire families and whole *banjar* attend. The festival is getting attention on Bali as well, and many interested Balinese from Bali now regularly attend the festival. There are several reasons for Balinese attendance: to pray for fertility and rainwater, to make vows in return for health, pregnancy, etc. to divine powers, to maintain relations with ancestors, to pray to God, to show solidarity with family and community, or simply to witness the spectacle.

The Balinese have probably always outnumbered the Sasak as participants in the festival, but their numbers have far exceeded the Sasak over the last few decades. Sasak attendance dipped from the 1960s to the early 1980s due to the fallout from the supposed attempted coup, religious registration, and pressure from Muslim leaders, but their participation began rising in the mid 1980s and continued to rise throughout most of the 1990s. Since the government has acknowledged the festival, contributed to its function, and therefore sanctioned it, Sasak from many parts of Lombok who still retain elements of Waktu Telu beliefs now feel encouraged to participate. Many orthodox Muslims attend now as well, though mostly to participate in the event known as Perang Topat (War of the Rice Squares).

The *topat* or *ketopat* (also *tupat* or *ketupat*; Balinese: *tipat* or *ketipat*) are cooked and hardened squares of rice fastened with palm leaves. The *topat* are offerings prepared by farmers (additional ones are made by local committees), and the Perang Topat involves two groups of people (largely men and boys)—one on each level of the temple's shared outer courtyard—who hurl the hundreds of *topat* at one another for fifteen to thirty minutes. The Perang Topat is wild and sometimes gets out of hand, and this is one event that joins fun with serious worship at the festival. It creates chaos from the serious order of the other festival rites and can be interpreted as antistructural behavior, as commoners throw *topat* at nobility, young throw them at old, Sasak at Balinese and vice versa, and even Sasak at Sasak and Balinese at Balinese.[28] Perang Topat is what Falassi (1987:5) would call a rite of competition without winners, a rite that works as a cathartic moment among more serious rites.

For most participants the event provides great secular enjoyment. But for the farmers the event generates the sacred qualities of the *topat* as offerings. The *topat* must be thrown in order to be transformed into received and blessed offerings. Following the Perang Topat, the farmers collect the *topat* and place them in their rice fields and irrigation channels (or within trees), and the *topat* are thought to guarantee fertility. When the farmers have scooped up the *topat* for their fields, then the "war" is over because none remain to throw. Since "rice war" rites occur at a few of the other remaining festivals in Lombok and do not seem to have to have an antecedent in Bali, the Perang Topat appears to be a Sasak contribution to the festival (though many Balinese disagree).[29]

The Pujawali activates the meaning and myths of the temple. It celebrates the temple, the ancestors, the high deities, and the transcendental divine. As the mother temple for many Lombok Balinese and now for some remaining Waktu Telu (since other shrines in the area are destroyed or obsolete), the temple is the forum to contact the controlling forces of their universe and pray for fertility, safety, prosperity, and virtually any other request. The Sasak Boda, local Chinese, and other residents of Lombok often attend the festival or visit and pray at the temple at other times. To visit and present offerings at the temple is to believe in the supernatural forces within nature and the spirit and ancestral worlds of Lombok.

There are many meanings of the temple and its festival for the people of Lombok, and to claim discovery and development of the area is to celebrate past ethnic glory and power. The Sasak and Balinese myths directly conflict and have contemporary political meanings. Most Sasak feel that Lingsar is an inheritance from their ancestors, since the island is often referred to as Gumi Sasak (Sasak world) and the high deities of Rinjani and Lingsar are considered Sasak ancestors. Most migrant Balinese, on the other hand, believe that they received a mandate to rule Lombok from these deities for a period of seven generations because the Sasak ruling houses were corrupt and impure and the power to rule was therefore shifted to their shoulders as righteous bearers of the Javanese Majapahit tradition. The Sasak and Balinese myths support their respective positions and indicate the importance of Lingsar in their worldviews. From this perspective, whoever owns Lingsar, its temple, and its festival, holds the spiritual power to control the destiny, fertility, and prosperity of Lombok.

CHAPTER THREE

Myths, Actors, and Politics

THE VILLAGE and temple of Lingsar are located in the heart of the western plain of Lombok, due south of a mountain informally called Gunung Nudaya (Northern Mountain), which lies on the westward side of the northern chain of mountains whose culmination is Gunung Rinjani. There are two major water springs at Lingsar, and irrigation dikes are built to use this water and rainwater to irrigate the rice fields throughout much of West Lombok and parts of Central Lombok. Each of these water springs is connected to one of the temples that comprise the Lingsar temple complex: the spring on the east side lies within Pura Ulon ("head temple") and that on the west side lies within Pura Lingsar. The temples are a bit over a hundred meters apart, and festivals are celebrated at them simultaneously. Additional water springs have created a small lake, and the Lingsar temple land, which consists of fifteen hectares (hectare = 2.47 acres), includes a garden and yields substantial biannual rice harvests.

Balinese and many Sasak agree that Pura Ulon is older than Pura Lingsar. Pura Lingsar is almost an exact replica of Pura Ulon; other near-duplicates are found in various parts of Lombok, generally at water springs. Most teachers state that either the last king of Lombok, A. A. Ngurah Karangasem (r. 1839–1894) or one of his sons built Pura Lingsar as a larger duplicate to expand and glorify the state ritual that the festival had become and to better unify the Sasak and Balinese participants and ethnic groups in general. One other reason is clear: Karangasem descended from a different lineage of nobles than that celebrated at Pura Ulon, and he wanted to create a new and distinct temple that nevertheless embodied all the main altar structures of Pura Ulon. Both temples have second courtyards called *kemaliq* (sacred place of supernatural sanctions) that include shrines of sacred rocks and ponds built over the two sacred water springs.[1] These water springs are a primary focus of folklore, and their discovery or creation is a central issue in the local Balinese and Sasak battle over history and temple designation.

The myths of Lingsar reveal how the past is incorporated into contemporary cultural identity; they also help inform the interpretation of the performing arts. The arts cannot be properly understood without exploring the respective myths; in fact I submit that to participate in a rite or a performing art is to participate in myth. These myths embody codes and imageries that are activated and referenced by the performing arts, called into the present, and manifested within the festival. Participants appear to interpret the arts using the same modes of conceptualization as they use to interpret history.

MYTH AND HISTORY COMPLEX

Eliade (1963:5–6) defines myth as a sacred story that narrates a sacred history relating to events that took place in primordial time, how, "through the deeds of supernatural beings, a reality came into existence." By knowing the myth, one knows the origin of things and can control and manipulate inherent elements. This knowledge can be experienced by ceremonially recounting the myth or by performing the ritual for which it is the justification. One "lives" the myth, which becomes "a charter for ritual performance" and a religious experience in mythological time (Leach 1972:239). The figures in myth become contemporary in ritual as one is transported into that time. Myth "expresses, enhances, and codifies belief," reveals moral wisdom, and provides a statement of reality "by which the present life, fates and activities of mankind are determined" (Eliade 1963:20). Contents and meanings of myths change over time when necessary, or, as Campbell (1988:135) suggests, myths and culture heroes evolve as culture evolves.

Levi-Strauss (1963:209) explains that the "operational value" of a myth "is timeless" and "explains the present and the past as well as the future." He states that if "there is a meaning to be found in mythology, it cannot reside in the isolated elements which enter into the composition of a myth, but only in the way those elements are combined." Thus the constituent units of a myth can be isolated and their relationships to other units can be examined to determine the structure of the myth—what makes it tick, what gives it meaning. Because he felt that any myth consists of all its versions, Levi-Strauss refuted those who search only for the "true" or "earlier" myth, considering all versions of a myth equally valid. He (ibid.:216–218) asserts that many scholars "have selected preferred versions" of a myth for study instead of analyzing all of them. This reduces the dimensional aspect of a myth and biases the results to support one or another version that is then reported as the only "true" version.

Herzfeld (1985:191) challenges the distinctions made between history and myth; this is, how scholars consider history factual and myth fictional. He states that history is just another mythology that can be "symbolically unpacked." History and myth are equally meaningful, and all variations of both are valid within their own context; in a hermeneutic sense there is no one myth or one history in any culture truer than any other existing myth or history.

In his analysis of the exegesis of national myths by institutional folklorists in Greece, Herzfeld demonstrates how ideological frameworks shape the results of scholarship. These myths are interpreted to mold the cultures of the geographical periphery of Greece into exponents of the cultural center to help foster a sense of national consciousness among Greeks. He explains that these folklore studies at the institutional level have been necessary to forge a national consciousness and identity out of a chaotic history (1982:144). As will be discussed later, the provincial government on Lombok has taken similar steps with similar goals in mind and uses Lingsar to define history and interpret regional cultural identity.

Appadurai (1981:202) explains that opposing factions in societies generate different myths that support political interests and that myth "debates" are culturally organized and structured to assert a political position. Within the competitive process involved in generating myths, values are defined, images are contrived, and interpretations are imposed by one group onto another. In the case of the Sasak and Lombok Balinese, the debate rages not over elements within which they acknowledge a common past, but rather within pasts in which major events are claimed exclusively. The inherent debatability of these events has direct political implications, and the past becomes a "conscious element of contemporary interactions" (ibid.:216). These contemporary interactions, mixed with new situations and evolving ethnic identities, inform the interpretations of the past and provide the political framework within which the debates are organized.

SOURCES AND STORIES

There are two basic mythic accounts of the origin, development, and meaning of the festival, one Balinese and one Sasak. The myths are concerned with who discovered the natural springs, who built and paid for the original shrine, who expanded on it, and who thus has present claim to the temple land and control of the irrigation dikes. Not surprisingly, the Balinese account favors the Balinese, while the Sasak account favors the Sasak. Though variations of the basic myths exist within both camps, respective key elements are uniform. Below I analyze these myths and their structures to examine key and transformational elements that lead to a meaningful interpretation of the festival experience. I also explore the role and position of the local government, the formal constraints on the myths, the opposing factions and their interests, and the political ramifications of the myths and their relationships with contemporary identity (see Harnish 1997:83–86).

It appears that the active debate over history began in recent years, perhaps only after the mid-1960s slaughter. During the time of Balinese colonization and their absolute control over the fertile rice-growing Lingsar area, it is highly unlikely that public differences on local history were tolerated, and perhaps they were unneeded. Throughout the twentieth century a reformist Islamic movement, fueled initially in reaction to Balinese colonization, progressively enveloped the socioreligious consciousness of the Sasak. The movement instigated a reevaluation of Sasak identity and instilled ethnic pride. This new orientation has no doubt helped breed the forceful emergence of Sasak folklore at Lingsar.

In response to modernization, national identity, and the scrutiny of religious leaders, the Sasak have outwardly become more Islamic. Local leaders have investigated Sasak socioreligious behavior to define actions that are "Islamic," "animist," or "Hindu Balinese," and also to promote their own version of Islamic practice (for example, Nahdhutul Watan or national Muhammadiyah). Religious leaders, striving to eliminate all non-Islamic practices among the nominal Muslim Sasak, forbade Sasak participation at the Lingsar festival in the late 1960s due to its "pagan" and Balinese elements. Sasak participation immediately decreased but did not disappear. The resulting arguments over Sasak Islamification and the delegitimation of the Waktu Telu helped fuel the war over Lingsar's history. The attention given to Lingsar by the government in the 1980s inspired an increased Sasak presence at the festival, although Sasak numbers have since stagnated and active participants have decreased.

Much of the controversy concerns which courtyard is more important during the festival and who controls the ritual. The two main courtyards within both temples are the *gadoh* and the *kemaliq*, terms that also apply to the main altar in each courtyard. The *gadoh* is exclusive to the Balinese and the *kemaliq* is shared. The officiating priest in the *kemaliq* is Sasak, and he is responsible for directing rituals and making specified offerings for the *kemaliq*. Most Sasak admit that Pura Ulon is older than Pura Lingsar, but insist that the *kemaliq* in the Pura Lingsar was already present when the Pura Ulon was built, that Pura Lingsar was constructed around the *kemaliq*, and that the *kemaliq* in Pura Ulon was only recently built and does not precede the one in Pura Lingsar. They also assert that the rituals in the *kemaliq* are the primary services of the festival. They accept the Balinese neither as leaders nor as joint partners but only as respected guests. Some Balinese, in response, state that the term *kemaliq* does not necessarily denote anything specifically Sasak, that it was built by Balinese, and that services there were relegated to the Sasak in order to give them a way to participate.

The Balinese Myth

I will present the full historical account of one Balinese, I Gusti Bagus Ngurah, because it interpolates all temple structures and the Balinese and Sasak kingdoms of the time. The versions of most other Balinese interviewed closely parallel Ngurah's in structure and content, and major events are similarly interpreted. As Gerdin (1982:26) experienced during her research among Balinese in Lombok, I also found that teachers were highly opinionated, that nobles of one former court could not let the version of a rival court stand unchallenged, and that they would stress their own ancestors' roles in the discovery of Lingsar and the rule of Lombok.

Following Ngurah's account, I provide one variation: a text written by I Goesti Bagoes Djlantik Blambangan, a Balinese district head in the 1930s during the Dutch administration.[2] The written text from the colonial period is included to permit analysis of how certain social and political realities have changed and how these changes may have had an impact on the structure and content of the myth. The written charter was only recently discovered and is not known by most Balinese.[3] I also briefly explore a recent Lombok Balinese booklet, written in response to Sasak publications, on the history and rituals at the festival.

First Balinese Version

This first Balinese version is my paraphrased translation from two interviews with Ngurah at his residence, the Puri Kelodan palace in Karangasem, East Bali, in 1988. He is regarded as an "objective" expert on history and is well read in *lontar* palm-leaf manuscripts. Further, his version incorporates inchoate elements of other Balinese accounts. He is also, however, a major player in the debate over history because it was his direct ancestor who became the first Balinese king of Lombok. In fact, the story begins with his ancestors and his palace residence, Puri Kelodan, a place still shrouded in mythic time.

> There was a kingdom ruled by three siblings in Karangasem who lived in Puri Kelodan [south palace]. Their sister, Ni Gusti Ayu Karang Winten, had borne a child in the Gunung Rata [a high pavilion within a palace] at Puri Kelodan, and this child's father was Batara Gunung Agung [the deity of Mt. Agung]. When the child was six months old, he ordered people to carry him up to Mt. Bagus [a foothill of Mt. Agung] and then to build a temple there. The child, Batara Alit Sakti, was carried up and then vanished [*moksa*: divine unification, with representative spiritual energy remaining at the place of transcendence]. Then a large temple called Pura Bukit [hill temple] was erected there in his honor.
>
> Later, a messenger carrying a letter from Datu Pejanggik [king/chief of Pejanggik kingdom in Central Lombok] came to Bali to search for a kingdom ruled by three siblings to ask for help to defeat a powerful enemy. This messenger searched all over Bali and finally found the Karangasem kingdom. He delivered the letter to I Gusti Ketut Karangasem, who consulted his siblings and decided that they could not refuse such a request. Karangasem then went to Pura Bukit to ask for blessings from Batara Alit Sakti [now in spirit form] and was told to take a regiment of two hundred men halfway between Bali and Lombok and then head for a small mountain on Lombok. The expedition was led by I Gusti Ketut Karangasem, Ida Ketut Subali, and Dané Mang Poleng. As they were leaving in fishing boats, leaves from trees around Pura Bukit fell and turned into butterflies and helped guide the boats to the small mountain in Lombok.

Upon arriving in Lombok, the expedition encountered a group of elders wearing white clothes and selling golden bananas, *ketopat* [rice squares], snacks, and chickens with white faces and feathers. The troops stopped to eat and rest, then Ida Ketut Subali and I Gusti Ketut Karangasem went to the top of the small mountain to meditate, seeking inspiration. They heard a voice [of Batara Pengsong] telling them to head northeast where they would encounter a voice and a revelation, and that they should rest whenever tired and hungry. As they descended from the mountain, which was to be named Pangsung [later named Pengsong] to honor their meeting with the mountain deity, they noticed that the group of elders had disappeared. They realized these elders were spirits and later would include the types of food they had received from the elders as offerings at the Pura Lingsar festival, a tradition still continued today.

They traveled northeast and rested and ate at an area now called Punikan. The area was completely covered with thick forest and was difficult to travel through. They had carried fruit from Bali and threw the seeds around the area, which eventually led to a large fruit harvest in the area still famous today. They needed a sign and asked for inspiration, then suddenly heard the sound of spouting water. They headed in the direction of the water and came upon the water spring of what is now Pura Ulon. This area they called Aiq Mual, overflowing water, and later, Lingsar, spouting water [Ngurah refers to the entire area]. I Gusti Ketut Karangasem prayed to Batara Alit Sakti and to the deity of the water spring, whose name is Batara Gedé Lingsar, and there appeared a regiment of two hundred men dressed in yellow sarongs and headpieces. This army consisted of spirits, but appeared as real men. When the two armies together approached the Pejanggik kingdom, opposing troops were confused and fearful and the armies won, continuing on to other kingdoms. Finally, they arrived at the last opposing kingdom, Selaparang. There they defeated Selaparang and took a sacred *bendé* [a small gong] with some Sasak back to Karangasem. Still today, descendants of these Sasak carry this gong during the temple festival at Pura Bukit that honors Batara Alit Sakti.

After consulting with his siblings, I Gusti Ketut Karangasem returned to Lombok. An agreement with Banjar Getas [the enemy of the Pejanggik kingdom with whom the Balinese sided] divided the island into east and west; Banjar Getas would rule the east and I Gusti Ketut Karangasem would rule the west as an extension of the Karangasem kingdom. It took many years to begin clearing and farming, establishing irrigation, and settling the area around Lingsar, because it was covered in thick forest. But eventually an area was cleared out and a temple [Pura Ulon] was built dedicated to the expedition and the royal family. One of the leaders of the expedition, Ida Ketut Subali, returned to Karangasem and became a *padanda* [high priest] and then returned to Lombok to help arrange the temple and to act as priest.

Pura Lingsar on the west side was built much later, after I Gusti Ketut Karangasem's lineage was defeated by a separate Karangasem lineage that had established a palace in Mataram. Whereas Pura Ulon is considered a family temple for the immediate family members of I Gusti Ketut Karangasem and of the others in the expedition, Pura Lingsar was intended as a public temple that would bring the general Balinese and Sasak populations together. It would also function as a rice temple for the *subak* [irrigation organizations]. The *gadoh* courtyards in both temples "define" a swirling place where man and God meet, recalling the time when I Gusti Ketut Karangasem met Batara Alit Sakti at Pura Bukit. The inner courtyard at Pura Bukit is also named *gadoh* in memory of that event. *Kemaliq* simply means to become sacred, and it is a Balinese, not a Sasak word. The formation of rocks within the *kemaliq* altar is for worship of Batara Wisnu [the Hindu god associated with water].

This account, couched in Balinese imagery, explains Lingsar's history in five stages: 1) the Batara Alit Sakti and pre-Lombok time, 2) the time of receiving the letter from Datu Pejanggik, 3) the mission and success in Lombok, 4) the victorious return to Karangasem, 5) and the rise to kingship and return to Lombok of the main figure, I Gusti Ketut Karangasem. In the pre-Lombok time the main characters—I Gusti Ketut Karangasem, Batara Alit Sakti, and Ni Gusti Ayu Karang Winten—are introduced and the divine relationship between the ruling nobles and the high deity of Bali, Batara Gunung Agung (the father of Batara Alit Sakti and the highest deity in Bali), is featured. Batara Alit Sakti and the construction of Pura Bukit are the products of the pact between Batara Gunung Agung and the nobles. This pact will lead to the divine intervention and assistance needed in the mission to Lombok. The main units of the account resemble those of a three-part *wayang kulit* shadow-play story. They begin with a peaceful palace scene which descends into confusion and chaos; next comes withdrawal and the seeking wisdom or power, followed by battling with the enemy; and finally comes acknowledgment of the righteous hero and the return to order and a peaceful palace. Table 3.1 depicts graphically the five units or stages of the Balinese account.

TABLE 3.1. Balinese Account

UNIT	SITUATION, EVENTS
Pre-Lombok time	peaceful, enter relations with deities
Letter from Datu Pejanggik	confusion, consultation and blessings and divine assistance
Mission to Lombok	trials, meditation and divine gift, victory
Return to Bali	triumphant return, successful rite of passage
Return to Lombok	return asking new status, new dynasty, Lingsar built

The pre-Lombok period is characterized by a kingdom ruled by siblings who have entered relations with the highest deity in Bali, Batara Gunung Agung. Their sister is impregnated (immaculately) by Batara Gunung Agung and she gives birth to Batara Alit Sakti, a child who spiritually vanishes at Mt. Bukit and requests that a temple be made for him. This temple establishes a forum that claims Batara Gunung Agung as the ultimate source (through his son) to directly access divine advice. Receiving the letter from Datu Pejanggik throws the world of I Gusti Ketut Karangasem into turbulence. He and his siblings feel that they cannot refuse assistance, yet feel confused and do not know how to prepare for battle. Karangasem consults Batara Alit Sakti at Pura Bukit and receives the divine information (almost a mandate) necessary to begin the mission. This stage deliberately states that I Gusti Ketut Karangasem was invited to come to Lombok, and this invitation becomes the political rationale for the expedition to Lombok. The Balinese therefore claim no intention of conquering or colonizing Lombok.[4]

The mission to Lombok is the main part of the story and describes the trials of Ketut Karangasem, Ida Ketut Subali, and the army. This unit continues the theme of divine assistance, highlighting how butterflies help guide the army, how a group of spirits provides food, how Batara Pengsong (the deity of the small mountain) gives direction, and how Batara Gedé Lingsar creates the water spring to call them and later provides a spirit army. The account is almost fatalistic, as if the deities had willed the Balinese to conquer and control Lombok, even though the Balinese only wanted to provide assistance to a fellow king. The Balinese are pictured as fulfilling a righteous duty supported by divine sources. Many Lombok Balinese nobles I consulted assert that their ancestors were the true heirs to the Majapahit tradition, referring to the legendary Majapahit kingdom of East Java. These nobles, who trace their genealogy there, believe that the divine energy and spiritual power of Majapahit had concentrated within their ancestors' kingdoms and that this concentrated power, which brings with it order and prosperity by its mere presence, provided a divine mandate to rule (see Gerdin 1982:75).

The concept of discovery is primary in the account. The Balinese, after traversing the Lombok strait in fishing boats, eventually encounter the water spring, which spouts forth to signal them to come to Lingsar. They find the water spring through both their own and divine efforts. I Gusti Ketut Karangasem meditates and prays at the top of Mt. Pengsong and, through the power of his spirituality, he is granted a revelation first to head toward Lingsar and then to encounter Batara Gedé Lingsar. Lingsar is his primary point of destination and discovery. His meditation and Majapahit pedigree lead to the divine gift of two hundred soldiers who are visible but spirits. This assures his victory in war, and, as a symbol of the total victory over the opposing kingdoms, he takes back with him to Karangasem a sacred gong and those who are in charge of it. This gong represents spiritual booty and enhances the power of the Karangasem court.

The fourth stage of the myth, the return to Karangasem, has I Gusti Ketut Karangasem returning home with his enhanced status as a victorious, righteous leader with the dharma of a ruler. After consultations with his siblings, he returns as king to rule over West Lombok for Karangasem, the final stage of the story. He is accompanied by Ida Ketut Subali, another culture hero credited with spiritual powers, who returns to Lombok after study as *padanda* to preside over the temples, festivals, and court ceremonies (most *padanda* in Lombok claim lineage to Ida Ketut Subali). Thus one culture hero returns as king, the other as high priest (attached to and legitimizing the kingship). Their passage through the tests of the expedition to Lombok are akin to elaborate rites of passage to the highest status positions available in Balinese society. The discovery of Lingsar is equivalent to the discovery of themselves and to the destiny of Lombok. Through Lingsar comes the creation of the royal court of Lombok-Karangasem, the fulfillment of history, the extended righteousness of Majapahit, and the realization of divine power.

A number of interlinked images are important in the Balinese conceptions of kings. For any ruler to be effective, he should worship before and have a special relationship to the closest highest mountain and its deities (Stuart-Fox 1991:23). The story features I Gusti Ketut Karangasem in consultation with Batara Alit Sakti at Pura Bukit in Bali and meditating on Mt. Pengsong in Lombok. At Mt. Bukit, Batara Alit Sakti directs him toward Lombok; at Mt. Pengsong, Karangasem proves his worth and purity through his meditation, and the deity directs him toward Lingsar. He is also related through blood to Batara Alit Sakti, and has an indirect relationship with Batara Gunung Agung, the highest deity of the mountain. Water is another prime image in the account, as it beckons Karangasem to Lingsar and provides the spirit army. Water equals prosperity and symbolizes Lingsar. These stories neatly interweave water, mountain, and divine kingship.

I Gusti Bagus Ngurah's account explains the relationship of Pura Ulon and Pura Lingsar in terms of function: Pura Ulon is essentially a family temple and Pura Lingsar a public temple that also serves as a rice temple. Pura Ulon was built by his direct ancestors and, during colonial times only family members and high-caste Balinese were allowed to pray in the *gadoh*, while commoner Balinese and participating Sasak were relegated to the *kemaliq* (nobles and other high-caste members also had full access to the *kemaliq*). In this way the family kept the divine power connection established in the *gadoh* exclusively among themselves and excluded commoners, nonrelatives, and Sasak alike. This connection is realized through the *gadoh*'s altar complex, which unifies the high deities of Bali and Lombok—Batara Gunung Agung and Batara Gunung Rinjani—into one powerful unit and contains a central altar dedicated to Batara Alit Sakti and his mortal mother, Ni Gusti Ayu Karang Winten, who is also a direct ancestor of the Lombok-Karangasem nobles (see Chapter Four). The expedition to Lombok is thus honored, and the deities who extended safety and success to the expedition are worshiped. The altar complex fully illustrates the divine pact between deities and the Karangasem nobles.

When Ngurah's lineage is defeated by the Mataram kingdom ruled by another line of relatives, Pura Lingsar is built to generalize the meaning of the area, its history and festival. The festival became a state ritual during the rule of the Mataram kingdom (1839–1894) and an elaborate ceremony for securing rain and fertility;

Lombok Balinese and Sasak were unified through collective effort. The Mataram court installed the vast irrigation system still extant today and positioned themselves as the "owners" of the water supply throughout West Lombok. The festival constituted a political demonstration of spiritually concentrated power, secured water and fertility, and the rulers became associated with prosperity. Thus the meaning of the festival changed from a central noble family honoring their ancestors to a public, living demonstration of the divine pact.

Although Pura Lingsar is supposed to be a replica of Pura Ulon, there is one important difference. The central altar in the *gadoh* is dedicated to Batara Alit Sakti and Batara Gedé Lingsar, and, unlike the altar in Pura Ulon, omits the mother of Batara Alit Sakti, who really does not hold much meaning for the general Lombok Balinese.[5] In this way Batara Gedé Lingsar, whose altar had been in the *kemaliq* of the Pura Ulon, was annexed by the *gadoh* in Pura Lingsar apparently to further centralize divine power into one courtyard. (The *kemaliq* altar remains a second spot dedicated to Batara Gedé Lingsar for participating Balinese.) The source of the power of sacred water for all Balinese is Batara Wisnu, the preserver within the Hindu Trinity, who is particularly manifest in the *kemaliq*. The festival is deeply profound because of the representation of the most prominent deities: Batara Gunung Agung and Batara Alit Sakti of Bali, Batara Gunung Rinjani and Batara Gedé Lingsar of Lombok, and the Indic Batara Wisnu.

Second Balinese Version

One written text provides a slightly different view of several parts of the story. *Riwajatnja Poera-poera dan Pedéwa'-pedéwa' di West-Lombok* (The history of Balinese and Sasak temples in West Lombok) was written by I Goesti Bagoes Djlantik Blambangan in the 1930s. Blambangan was the *punggawa* (head of a subdistrict) of Cakranegara Utara (an area historically connected to Lingsar) under the Dutch colonial administration, and he was probably required to submit this report on the socioreligious practices of Balinese and Sasak (both are included, but most of the report is lost) as part of his duties. This text was sent to me in 1989 by noted Bali scholar David Stuart-Fox, from the archives office in Buleleng, Bali. Since no one I interviewed in Lombok had any knowledge about such a document, I conclude that this record, written primarily in Indonesian, was probably delivered to Dutch officials in Buleleng without any copies having been offered to Balinese or Sasak community leaders. Perhaps this was the general procedure for such reports, or perhaps the information was deliberately withheld.

The Blambangan account, paraphrased in my translation below, states that I Gusti Ketut Karangasem rules the Karangasem region individually, not in collaboration with siblings. Karangasem sets off for Lombok "three hundred years ago" and the story continues:

> When Karangasem climbs up to Pura Bukit to meditate, Batara Bukit [not Batara Alit Sakti] asks him if he wants to expand his domain. Batara Bukit adds that if he wants to, he can defeat the people of Lombok but must first

go to Gunung Pengsong and ask for a divine gift [to insure victory in war] from the deity there. Later, Karangasem receives a letter from Lombok from Datu Selaparang [not Datu Pejanggik] asking for assistance in subduing Banjar Getas.

Karangasem heads for Pengsong with a platoon [no other figures are mentioned] and meditates there. Batara Pengsong tells him that he will receive the "gift" of military victory but that he must humbly ask for permission and the gift from Batara Gunung Rinjani and Batara Gedé Lingsar at Lingsar, because these are the deities who especially rule Lombok.

Banjar Getas knows of Karangasem's arrival in Lombok and meets him after Karangasem descends from Pengsong. He humbly introduces himself to Karangasem and explains that his friend's son-in-law was sent away by Datu Selaparang, who then took the man's wife and tried to rape her. When she refused, Datu Selaparang killed her husband. Getas came to his friend's aid while Datu Pejanggik came to defend Datu Selaparang. Since then they have tried to kill Getas and have debased him and his followers. He says he is not afraid of Datu Selaparang and Pejanggik, even though his followers number only forty, but that he is no match for Karangasem. If Karangasem kills him, he will not receive any reward of land from Selaparang or Pejanggik, who will continue to hold onto Lombok. But if he instead defeats these unfair rulers, as he should because he—as a great king—must defend what is fair, he will then be ennobled. Getas then surrenders himself to Karangasem, explaining that if Karangasem allows him to live, he will loyally follow into battle against Selaparang and Pejanggik.

Karangasem decides to protect Getas and battle Selaparang and Pejanggik, but first must go to Lingsar. Because Karangasem does not know where it is, Getas accompanies him to the Ancar River that leads to the water spring of Lingsar, and then Getas leaves to prepare for battle. At Lingsar, Karangasem discovers the water spring and stones that we still find today. But no one is around or lives there because the area is covered in thick forest. Here Karangasem meditates and humbly asks Batara Gunung Rinjani and Batara Gedé Lingsar for the gift of victory in war against Selaparang and Pejanggik. Batara Gedé Lingsar answers, "I have consented to your request. Take and govern Lombok as your kingdom. I give you the gift of victory in warfare and you cannot lose to the kings of this island. It is proper that these kings be defeated, since they are not fair and noble. I give you permission to rule Lombok to the limit of only seven generations, and you must come, exalt, and worship me."

The story continues with Karangasem defeating Pejanggik, Selaparang, and other kingdoms, then dividing the island between himself and Banjar Getas. The account states that Sasak were later brought to Lingsar from Central and East Lombok to work on irrigation with Balinese experts, and that Karangasem appointed a Sasak *pamangku* (priest) to guard the stones at Lingsar. Blambangan concludes by stating that this is how Balinese and Waktu Telu began worshipping Batara Gedé Lingsar, Batara Gunung Rinjani, and Batara Pengsong in Lombok. He explains that Pura Lingsar was built "about sixty years ago," meaning around 1870, though he never clearly states that Pura Ulon is the older temple.

This account is framed within a different set of political implications. Although Karangasem is drawn to Lombok because of the letter he receives from Datu Selaparang, he also wishes to extend his political domain there. He is even encouraged to go and granted assurance of victory by Batara Bukit (Batara Alit Sakti). The journey is clearly not as unselfish as the one in Ngurah's version. Today this story could cause ethnic friction, as it could be argued that the Balinese came primarily to colonize Lombok. At the time Blambangan wrote this account, the Dutch were fully in control of Lombok and the Balinese had little cause to worry about Sasak reaction. In contemporary Lombok, however, the minority Balinese would probably never suggest that Karangasem wanted to conquer Lombok. In fact, Ngurah repeated several times that the Balinese had no such intention.

It could also be interpreted that the Balinese were granted rule because the kings in Lombok were unfair and morally corrupt and therefore had lost the license to rule. This license was, in turn, granted to a great noble king, I Gusti Ketut Karangasem, by Batara Gedé Lingsar and other deities. This perspective concurs with that of many Balinese nobles that power and the mandate to rule had flowed to them from the Majapahit tradition. Along similar lines, many Balinese feel that Javanese incursions into Bali over the centuries had the same sense of righteousness: to purge selfish, unethical rulers and restore purity, harmony, and balance. Divine will and intervention into the rule of Lombok are stronger in this account than in Ngurah's version.

The discovery of Lingsar is unclear in Blambangan's version. Although the account states that Karangasem found the stones in the water spring and that no one lived in the area, it also states that Getas tells Karangasem to follow the Ancar River and that he will find the Lingsar water spring, implying that Getas (and therefore others) already knows of the water spring. This conflicts with Ngurah's (and most other Balinese) version that Karangasem is led to Lingsar by the sound of spouting water created by Batara Gedé Lingsar. The discovery aspect of the myth is deemphasized in Blambangan's account, while the divine will aspect is increased. The distinction may suggest that the water spring and its discovery have become more important over time. This is likely for both ideological and practical reasons. According to Blambangan, only two *subak* (Lingsar and Gagelang) benefited from the water springs in the 1930s. Today, however, over twenty *subak* need the water, and the springs (and residing deity) are viewed as the primary source of fertility and prosperity in Lombok. Claiming the discovery of the original spring is necessary today to legitimize the myth.

Blambangan seems to indicate that the water spring and *kemaliq* stones are at the Pura Lingsar location, meaning that the original location of the spring (and perhaps the first temple) is not Pura Ulon. This conflicts directly with contemporary Balinese versions (and many Sasak versions) which state that the original spouting spring was at the Pura Ulon site. The account also asserts that a Sasak *pamangku* was appointed by Karangasem to "guard" the spring, which thus explains the genesis of Sasak priests and participation.

Although several aspects differ from Ngurah's account, the discovery unit and the later description of the festival are couched in Balinese terms, and the Sasak are given an important, yet secondary function at the festival. With the exception of Banjar Getas, no local figures are given positive images or credited with any positive action (Getas is not a respected figure among most Sasak). Thus Blambangan's version follows the same structure as Ngurah's.

Ngurah mentioned Banjar Getas only once during his rendition of Lingsar's history, although after questioning he did clarify Getas's role in Lombok's history. Blambangan, on the other hand, mentions Getas early and frequently, and most Balinese and Sasak include Banjar Getas as a major character. Many accounts state that Getas is a sculptor who makes revealing statues of the wives of the rulers, and these wives all become enamored of Getas. In retaliation, Datu Pejanggik rapes Getas's wife and tries to kill Getas, but Getas is magically powerful and difficult to kill. This is why Datu Pejanggik, defended by Datu Selaparang, writes the letter to Karangasem.

Blambangan's variation features a friend's daughter threatened with rape and her husband murdered. When Getas attempts to help his friend, he is targeted by Datu Pejanggik and Datu Selaparang, one of whom then writes a letter inviting Karangasem to come to Lombok. These or similar stories have been published as historic fact in several local and foreign publications (see, for example Clegg 2004; Harnish 1985).

Ngurah probably does not give much weight to Banjar Getas in his version because it does not relate to his reference point as a direct descendant of I Gusti Ketut Karangasem. Since Ngurah lives in Bali, he may not be interested in the general history of Lombok, in which Banjar Getas is a very important character. Similarly he does not concern his version with Pura Lingsar because it was built by a different lineage and its meaning is not specific to his experience.

Third Balinese Version

To counter what it felt was false information promoted by the government, the head Krama Pura office for the province published a booklet, *Pura Lingsar Selayang Pandang* (Overview of Pura Lingsar) in 1989. The booklet does not recount the discovery of the water spring or the founding of the temple but merely presents "facts" about Lingsar, most of which were intended to be used with tourists. The booklet, however, has neither been translated nor distributed to tourists, and few people have read it. The authors clearly intended to provide a counterpoint to the Sasak myth, and ultimately assert that all of the rituals at Lingsar have been prescribed by the Indic Vedas. It states frankly at the beginning that A. A. Ketut Karangasem built Pura Ulon in 1658 and that A. A. Ngurah erected Pura Lingsar in 1753. The Sasak are said to "follow the teachings" of the Waktu Telu in the *kemaliq* and to worship with the Balinese Hindus. The *kemaliq* is one structure with the *gadoh* "that cannot be separated" (*tak terpisahkan*), meaning that the *kemaliq* and *gadoh* are inextricably part of one structure (p. 4). The booklet legitimizes many of its points by quoting Vedic literature.

Kereped, the leader of the Krama Pura, seemed to be embarrassed about the booklet and was reluctant to lend it to me in 2001 (I had neither seen, nor been aware of it). I believe his reluctance was based on the polarizing elements in the text, particularly with regard to the absolute Balinese claim over Lingsar. He had been trying over the past years to smooth relations with the Sasak camp; this booklet, if promoted as *the* Balinese position, could cause further division. One major point that Kereped agrees with, however, is the contention that the *kemaliq* and *gadoh* share a history and are part of one structure. All Balinese insist on this unity because it provides a cornerstone to the myth and to the festival meaning promoted among their community.

The Sasak acknowledge the age of Pura Ulon, but state that the *kemaliq* of Pura Lingsar is older and was discovered by a Sasak culture hero; thus that it is inherently separate from the *gadoh* and *pura*. In all Sasak versions of history, the coming and impact of the Balinese are prominently situated. The reverse, however, is not true. The account of I Gusti Bagus Ngurah does not incorporate any Sasak element. His and local Balinese accounts emphasize the spiritual power of Balinese leaders and the divine intervention of the deities. The Balinese systematically deny a Sasak role in the discovery of Lingsar.

The Sasak Myth

As with the Balinese, there are several Sasak versions that conflict. However, unlike the Balinese, the Sasak have enjoyed the support of local government, particularly the Education and Culture and the Tourism offices. They have published two books that include a Sasak version of Lingsar's history and a video that features a dramatic reenactment of the myth. Local tourist information and the Lingsar guides articulate a Sasak perspective regarding the discovery of Lingsar and the history between Sasak and Balinese.

I will present one full Sasak account of the history of Lingsar, then add parts of three other versions to illustrate important points of distinction determined from the perspective of the reference. A new version, also analyzed, is currently emerging. Two traditional manuscripts, *Babad Selaparang* and some versions of the *Babad Lombok*, discuss Banjar Getas (who is pictured as a traitor) and his involvement with the Balinese (see Marrison 1992:87–89). However, these manuscripts do not mention Lingsar and since they disagree on most points, they are not discussed here.

The full version of the Sasak myth below is translated from the book, *Upacara Tradisional Dalam Kaitannya dengan Peristiwa Alam dan Kepercayaan di Nusa Tenggara Barat* (Traditional ceremonies and their connections with elements of nature and beliefs in [the region of] Nusa Tenggara Barat), written by a team led by H. Lalu Wacana and published in 1984 by the regional Education and Culture

Department. This book can be considered the "official" version of history since it has been formally published by a government agency. Wacana is Sasak, considered pro-Sasak, and a *haji*. The two consultants engaged for the book were the recently deceased Sasak priest at Lingsar and a descendant of a former priest who became an orthodox Muslim *haji*. There were no Balinese consultants. Interestingly, these same Sasak consultants also provide variations of this account presented later in the chapter.

First Sasak Version

In a fashion similar to that Michael Herzfeld presents regarding institutional folk-loric studies in Greece (1982), the authors of this government publication attempt to formulate a unified Sasak identity out of a chaotic and colonized past, and they are introduced as objective scholars producing the "true" history. Their account falls under the "Legende" (Legend) subheading of the "Perang topat" (War of the rice squares) heading within the "Deskripsi upacara tradisional" (Description of traditional ceremonies) chapter of the book. My translation paraphrases the account, to which the writers have added commentary and from which some deletions have been made due to length.

> The Madain kingdom was located in the present village of Bertais, and it governed the whole of West Lombok. The king's name was Aria Baris Jerneng and his younger brother was Datu Bayan, who controlled the northern and mountain areas. The southern area was prosperous and there were thousands of small water springs. The people of Madain were farmers who loyally followed their local customs and worked hard. The king had fair policies and loved his people. The people believed in the forces in nature, that the world was full of spirits who influenced the path of humankind and could cause safety, difficulty, sickness, accidents, and so forth. The people bowed before and worshipped these spirits, both those who create safety and those who create accidents. Because of this, their lives were full of ceremonies.
>
> The king had two sons, Datu Pasek and Raden Mas Sumilir. Sumilir was in charge of the area around Lingsar and this was a beautiful area. People would stop and rest on journeys in the beautiful forest there and see the many flowers. Sumilir wanted to complete the beauty of the area, so he stuck a pole in the ground to search for a spring. Up spouted water, fresh and plentiful. The water flowed downward fluidly; the word for this in the Sasak language is *langser*, hence the name, Lingsar. Sumilir vanished in the water spring during meditation and people became saddened and did not take care of their lives. Sickness and epidemics raged throughout the kingdom.
>
> Sumilir's nephew, Datu Piling, was sleeping in the forest after a hunting expedition and suddenly met Sumilir, who invited Piling to meditate at the water spring. Sumilir said that anyone who wanted to meet him could come to see him. Piling later told all people who wanted to come see Sumilir to

bring *ketopat* [rice squares]. After everyone came in the late afternoon when the flowers droop because the sun is going down, Sumilir vanished again [*moksa*—leaving behind his spiritual essence] in the water spring, and was given the title Datu Wali Milir [king/chief and saint of Islam]. All the people present threw the *ketopat* and flowers and fruit into the spring, and this is how the Perang Topat began.

Peng, the son of Datu Piling [who was Sumilir's nephew], had three sons, the third of whom was to become the third priest of Lingsar [after Datu Piling and Peng]. The Balinese came to Lombok during this time, the sixteenth century, led by Gusti Ngurah Jelantik Karangasem. They were looking for a place to set up a temple. They landed at Gunung Pengsong and the deity of Pengsong told them that they should establish a temple halfway between Gunung Pengsong and Gunung Rinjani. Later the Balinese were to set up a temple on Pengsong as a sign of appreciation to the deity. Apparently the Balinese did not follow the directions exactly, and they went to Mt. Punikan, where they planted many different kinds of fruit from Bali. Gusti Ngurah heard the sound of spouting water and the Balinese went to Lingsar where they saw the *kemaliq*. Here is where they built a temple in a manner that unified Gunung Rinjani on Lombok and Gunung Agung on Bali. This mission was intended to unify the deities of Rinjani and Agung, and they constructed three shrines: one for the deity of Rinjani, one for that of Agung, and one for that of Bukit in East Bali. This unification also had as its goal the union of the Balinese and the Sasak. The consecration of the Balinese temple was performed to correspond with the full moon of the seventh month of the Sasak calendar. This was accompanied by a Pujawali festival, where the main activity was the Perang Topat.

The carrying out of the ritual and the work occurs in the *kemaliq*, while the temple is considered a great guest. The Balinese worship Batara Gedé Lingsar at the temple while the Sasak worship Datu Wali Milir. These two names carry the same understanding, that of Raden Mas Sumilir. Anak Agung Karangasem [who defeated I Gusti Bagus Ngurah's direct ancestors] built the newer temple complex at Lingsar in a lavish fashion. The rice fields of fifteen hectares are the possession of the [now deceased] Sasak priest Sanusi, through inheritance from his great-grandfather Wijaya.

The dynasty of Anak Agung Karangasem secured the unity of the Pujawali and Perang Topat. The Sasak priest continuously served as leader of the ritual. The goal of the festival for the Balinese is to pay respects to Batara Gedé Lingsar, while for the Sasak, it is to pay respects to Datu Wali Milir. For the Balinese, Pujawali means worship annually; for the Sasak, it means to worship Datu Wali Milir. The holder of the Pujawali is the Sasak priest, who is the inheritor from Datu Wali Milir. Though both Balinese and Sasak had the opportunity to illustrate their feelings of respect for the deity, gradually the Balinese activity began to color the festival. This can be seen historically by understanding that when Buling Putera [one of the

Sasak priests] became an orthodox Muslim, the village of Lingsar followed. Buling Putera was allowed to go to Mecca as a present from Anak Agung Karangasem after he had directed Sasak all over Lombok who came to work as a form of devotion on the new temple complex in the nineteenth century. Since then the villagers of Lingsar are only spectators at the Pujawali and Perang Topat. The villagers and many other Sasak feel that the festival has become too Balinese. Therefore, many of the Sasak no longer truly understand what the Perang Topat is about. The time of Perang Topat is supposed to remind us of an event in antiquity. This moment alone is pregnant with history and meaning.

This account can be broken down to five units. The first encompasses the pre-Lingsar period when life is idyllic and the Lingsar area is beautiful. Sumilir is a local noble who sticks a pole in the ground to find a water spring to complete and preserve the beauty of the area.

The second unit concerns the transformation of Sumilir into Datu Wali Milir, which involves his disappearing two times into the water spring. After the first disappearance, his presence is truly gone and great sadness and epidemics strike the land; during the second disappearance, he leaves behind his spiritual presence and the land and people become prosperous. The transformations can be seen as constituting a divine sacrifice, which includes an isolation period (between the two "disappearings") similar to myths of other sacred figures such as Jesus and the Buddha. When he vanishes a second time, he leaves his spiritual essence that will perpetuate abundance. The throwing of the *ketopat* and other items into the spring celebrates his sacrifice and initiates the Perang Topat, and Milir's sacrifice establishes a yearly ritual in his honor.

The third unit concerns the arrival of the Balinese, who are searching for a place to build a temple and land at Mt. Pengsong where they meet a deity who tells them to build a temple halfway between Mt. Pengsong and Mt. Rinjani. The Balinese, however, get lost and plant fruit before the group leader, Gusti Ngurah, hears the sound of spouting water and they find Lingsar. Here they build a temple near where they discover the *kemaliq*.

The fourth unit involves the intentional uniting of the deities of Mt. Rinjani and Mt. Agung on Bali by the Balinese, and by extension also the Sasak and the Balinese. This constitutes the common past among Sasak and local Balinese. The Sasak accommodate the Balinese and the Sasak priest is the leader of the ceremony. The Balinese have their own understanding of the festival, but the Sasak are in charge of it and do the important work.

The fifth unit acknowledges that reformist Muslim Sasak, such as those who live at Lingsar, no longer follow the ritual and implies that Sasak who do are not orthodox. The account ends with dire comments concerning the forgetting of the history and significance of the Perang Topat and Pujawali for the Sasak and how the ritual has taken on Balinese coloring. Table 3.2 presents graphically the main units of the Sasak account.

TABLE 3.2. Sasak Account

UNIT	SITUATION, EVENTS
Prehistory founding	idyllic setting; local noble sticks pole in ground
Sumilar-Milir transformation	mediates and vanishes in spring; sadness/epidemics, then prosperity
Balinese arrival	meet and directed by Pengsong, lost; hear springs
Deity-human unification	temple unity; Sasak ritual leadership
Islam and decline	orthodox movement; forgetting history; Balinese advances

The story begins, like Ngurah's version, along the lines of a *wayang* theme, with idyllic or peaceful palace imagery that is thrown into chaos. Then the Balinese seek a path to Lingsar. After the third unit, however, the two versions diverge. Instead of battle in the fourth unit, as in the Balinese myth, there is reconciliation and Sasak leadership (perhaps symbolizing a Sasak victory over the Balinese), and the fifth unit does not return to idyllic, peaceful palace imagery as in Ngurah's version, but instead expresses a forlorn sentiment.

The units of the myth are both religious and political. They are religious in the sense that Datu Wali Milir sacrifices himself for the prosperity of the Sasak. His withdrawal period into the spring leads to sadness and epidemics, but his triumphant return, his calling of the people together, and his supernatural transformation as he becomes the spirit of fertility and irrigation water, are performed out of his love for the people and the beauty of the land. The moment of *moksa* at the spring is the pivotal point as this establishes him as a permanent deity. His calling for people to visit him and bring *ketopat* initiates the Perang Topat, henceforth performed annually by ritual participants who remember his sacrifice. Some Sasak give him credit for establishing all ritual traditions at Lingsar, including the performing arts.

The last three units are more political and deal with accommodating the Balinese who renovated and rebuilt the *kemaliq*, constructed a temple adjoining it, and colonized the island, seizing the festival as a state ritual. As the history proceeds, it becomes clear that they have changed the festival to make it more Balinese. There is some resentment about this, although there is praise for their efforts to unify the deities of Lombok and Bali as well as the Sasak and Balinese people. The Indonesian terms used, *menyatu* (to become one) and *mempersatukan* (to make one), carry social and religious significance for both parties. It is clear in all Sasak versions that the Sasak greatly admire the efforts of Anak Agung Karangasem to unify the people. However, there are also forlorn statements concerning the loss of meaning and history for the Sasak, part of which is blamed on Balinese dominance in the festival. Two transformational keys in the myth are Milir's sacrifices—both his "loss," when his spirit is truly absent, and his *moksa*, when he becomes permanently attached to Lingsar—and the coming of the Balinese and the transformation of primarily a Sasak ritual into a Balinese one.

All Sasak versions I collected claim that the Sasak are the true holders of the ritual and Balinese are great guests. In interviews the late Sasak priest Sanusi and his nephew, Suparman Taufiq (Parman), stressed this and gave numerous examples of Balinese deference to them for ritual guidance or for special offerings that only Sasak can make. In all versions there is also the assertion that fifteen hectares of land belong to the Sasak priest as part of his inheritance from Datu Wali Milir. This land produces two or more crops (rice and vegetable) per year and is the source of irrigation water. The claim has direct political significance because the Lombok Balinese control all of the land in the immediate vicinity of the temple complex, and, in consultation with the government, *subak* organizations, and independent Sasak farmers, also regulate irrigation. While the financial and agricultural benefits of the fifteen hectares help finance the festival, the Sasak claim to this land may demonstrate that they feel marginalized and frustrated at a clearly unequal power relationship. The last three units of the story indicate the tension between Sasak and Balinese regarding the temple and irrigation control, and illustrates the corporate and status benefits of maintaining the yield.

In general, Sasak versions stress the primacy of the Sasak ritual: that a Sasak culture hero founded Lingsar and established the traditions, that the land and ritual were Sasak, and that it was the Sasak who accommodated the Balinese colonizers. The constituent units of the myth inform one another and enhance implied meanings, creating a religious and political story that represents contemporary Sasak ethnic-religious identity and constructs a collective past. The story recaptures that past, and provides the origins of the larger Sasak culture.

Second Sasak Version

Another publication, *Sejarah Timbulnya Bangunan Kemaliq Lingsar* (History of the building of the *kemaliq*) by Haji Ahmad Syarani in 1986, contains a version that differs on several significant counts from the *Upacara Tradisional* version, even though Syarani was also a main consultant in that publication. In this self-published booklet, there is no mention of Raden Mas Sumilir, and the hero is from Java. His name is Datuk Milir and he is responsible for bringing and spreading Islam in Lombok, an act that also deepens his own faith. He is made king by the people and frequently travels around the island, visiting villages and giving advice, and climbing mountains and viewing nature. Unlike the idyllic state described in the *Upacara Tradisional* version, the natural environment is dry, arid, and fallow, though still beautiful as "a creation of God." Datuk Milir is very moved and wants to help the land and people that he loves. He meditates on God and recites Islamic prayers in the forest, reflecting upon life, God, and Lombok. He puts a cane into the ground, and sleeps, sitting through the night. In the morning he peers at the mountains and recites prayers again. Then he grabs his cane and it shakes, and when he pulls it out of the ground, up gushes the water spring. He vanishes into the water spring only once but due to his *moksa*, prayers, and sacrifice, the land becomes fertile and prosperous. The account of the Balinese coming to

Lombok is also a bit different. Instead of the Pengsong deity giving direction, it is a ray of light that directs the newly arrived Balinese to Lingsar.

The main differences here are that the land is arid, not idyllic, and that Datu Wali Milir is Datuk Milir and is neither known as Raden Mas Sumilir nor is a local noble but is instead from Java. He brings Islam to Lombok, does not withdraw his presence from the environment (he performs *moksa*, leaving his presence permanently in the spring), and nominal and orthodox Islam are not distinguished. Muslims are said to attend to the festival as an expression of local Islam, and the hero is an Islamic saint and teacher who is honored at the festival. This account further emphasizes the importance of Milir. He saves the land from infertility with his sacrifice and prayers to God, establishes the traditions at Lingsar, and brings Islam to Lombok. This establishes him as evangelistic saint and further strengthens the Sasak claim to the festival and land. Contemporary religious identity may have flavored the story to make it meaningful to today's Sasak Muslims. This account makes the festival more Islamic.

In 2001 Parman told me that he was the one who actually wrote this account and that he simply put it under the name of his great-uncle, Haji Ahmad Syarani. If this is true, it is curious. The names are modified from other accounts which Parman has helped shape (see, for example, the third version below), and the less-educated writing style reflects an author lacking a grasp of modern Indonesian. If Parman did write the book, he employed a style that might represent a man like his great-uncle. I suspect that he may have worked with Syarani, whom Wacana lists as a consultant on the first version above, when Syarani was writing this version of the myth, or developed the text from Syarani's perspective.

Third Sasak Version

A third version comes from several interviews with the late priest Sanusi and his nephew Parman in the late 1980s. They state that Datu Wali Milir was sent by the Wali Sanga ("nine saints," legendary Javanese evangelists) in Java to bring Islam to Lombok. He is also sometimes called Raden Mas Sumilir, and thus this story incorporates elements of the two published versions. Parman asserts that the people of Lombok were not ready to follow the five tenets of Islam and therefore Milir introduced only three (appropriate for the Waktu Telu ["three times"]), thereby accommodating problems of religious interpretation and allowing for the later development of orthodox Islam among the Sasak. Both Sanusi and Parman say that the Sasak do not believe Datu Wali Milir ever died and that they meet and remember Milir during the ceremony. Milir *is* the water spring, and the festival is a forum to pay respects and remember him. His presence through *moksa* is the vital and sacralizing force within the water.

The political units of this version follow those of the published ones. Sanusi, however, added that Datu Wali Milir was led to Lingsar with the help of Batara Gunung Rinjani, the high deity of Mt. Rinjani considered the original Sasak ancestor by traditional Muslims. I interpret this statement to decrease the importance of Milir and his sacrifice and, to some extent, negate the Islamic founding of Lingsar. Sanusi reaffirmed a nominal Muslim belief concerning natural deities, thus refuting the more Islamic version of Syarani (or Parman).

In a later publication, *Sejarah Daerah Nusa Tenggara Barat* (The history of Nusa Tenggara Barat), Wacana, who led the team of writers for both this book and *Upacara Tradisional*, states that the founding figure of Lingsar was Datu Sela-parang, and he does not mention Datu Wali Milir (Proyek Penelitian 1988:138).[6] Although the name of the founding figure is different and unrelated—he is a king from the East Lombok Selaparang kingdom—Wacana reaffirms that when the Balinese arrived, there was already a *kemaliq* and a ceremonial tradition. This seems to be the crucial point of the Sasak versions: that they preceded the Bali-nese and continue the more important ritual traditions at Lingsar. The name of the founding figure is relatively unimportant.

The 2001 Version

After Sanusi died in 1993, I attempted to meet with Mangku Asmin (Min), his younger brother, who replaced Sanusi as *pamangku*. When I finally met Min in 1995, I found him difficult to speak with; he did not answer questions directly and did not want to, or was unable to, respond to some questions. In 2001 I seemed to have the same problem. Although polite, he dismissed me rather quickly and although he remained warm, he was also distant. Parman explained that Min is *buta* (blind), unknowledgeable and unable to answer questions, and that he knows only the *teknis* (technical) points of running the ceremonies but none of the his-tory or proper names of the rites. He added that Min had never attended the Pujawali before his older brother died and thus had to learn the ceremonies from scratch with Parman's help. The head of the temple organization, I Wayan Kereped, indicated that the Krama Pura had wanted Parman to assume the *pamangku* position after Sanusi died. Parman, however, declined; Parman also said that the males of the previous generation (including both Sanusi and Min) had the first claim to the position and Min apparently wanted to become *pamangku*. If Parman's analysis is correct, and I believe it is, then many of the changes at Lingsar can be attributed to Min's different orientation to and less experience with the Pujawali (see Chapters Five and Seven).

Parman states that when it comes to experience, he is *tertua* (the eldest); thus he feels freer to speak his mind. He moved out from Lingsar into another family area in nearby Narmada in the mid 1990s, yet remains the main authority when he returns to the temple. Working with the Ministry of Tourism, he has trained the guides that help tourists when they come to Lingsar, and he is the contact person for the local police and government offices during preparations for the festival. Parman is a government employee himself in the Ministry of Law, and he works closely with Kereped to negotiate festival schedules, changes, and rites. In 2001 he told me that now, under the era of democracy in Indonesia, he can finally tell the "real" (*yang benar*) history of Lingsar. He claimed that all stories beforehand were deliberately inaccurate because earlier years did not embrace "openness" (*yang terbuka*) and reform (*reformasi*). It is parts of this story, combined with the Sasak versions above, that guides tell tourists who visit the temple.

Parman says that the true hero who came to Lingsar was Haji Abdul Maliq, and that the "Maliq" in *kemaliq* came from his name. This man departed from Java with two siblings—a man, Haji Abdul Rauf, also known as Raden Mas Ketupati, and a woman, Déwi Rinjani Sakti. They landed in Bayan, a northern village, a center of Waktu Telu culture and one of the few remaining strongholds. They carried their bamboo boat from Bayan down to Lingsar. Abdul Maliq is credited with creating the water spring, performing *moksa* to preserve the spring, and introducing Islam. Thus, though again the name of the deity is changed, the basic units of the story are the same. The Sasak are at the site before the Balinese, the water spring is given a miraculous founding, and an Islamic evangelist sacrifices himself to perpetuate the spring.

What is different here is that three individuals arrive—they are Javanese from the powerful Démak kingdom (sixteenth century) from Java's north coast—they arrive in Bayan and move their boat across land to Lingsar, which links the founding of Waktu Telu belief directly with Lingsar, and these actions become the basis for the Batek dance (see Chapters Four and Five). In addition, Déwi Anjani Sakti, Haji Abdul Maliq's sister, becomes a major ancestral Sasak deity after her death and resides in the sacred lake, Danau Rinjani, on Gunung Rinjani.[7] The brother, Haji Abdul Rauf, is linked through his other name, Raden Mas Ketupati, to the Perang Topat, although Parman explains that the rite still celebrates Haji Abdul Maliq's sacrifice.

Upon hearing this tale from Parman, I wrote in my field notebook, "Was I in the presence of some new evolving myth, or was I in the presence of a great unfolding, previously secret truth?" The former seemed far more likely. This was a new narrative that linked Lingsar with the Waktu Telu center of Bayan and with Démak in Java, and it also explained the origin of the local deity Déwi Anjani. Parman went on to say that he and Mangku Sanusi had made up the name Datu Wali Milir and the earlier story (though other Sasak claim to have known the story and name independently). He also mentioned that the first Balinese Anak Agung took a wife from this lineage and well understood the history of Haji Abdul Maliq, a notion that would be strongly contested by Balinese teachers. Though the narrative implications differ, the transformational keys in the account correspond to other Sasak versions. The Islamic and Javanese connections are maintained, the sacrifice remains, the conversion to fertile land is preserved, and the early and independent *kemaliq* is established. The tale more strongly associates Lingsar with Waktu Telu, associates the founding with the introduction of Islam, explicates the origins of a major island deity, and provides the narrative of the Batek dance. This account gives the Lingsar festival an even higher profile.

I do not know if this story will become the dominant Sasak myth. The others are supported by books and a video; this one currently stands alone. In time, however, it could become the "official" Sasak account, particularly given Parman's influence among the Sasak at Lingsar and officials in the government, but for now only Parman, some of the related family at Lingsar, myself, and a few of the guides are aware of it. I am certain that other Sasak worshipping at Lingsar are unaware of the name Haji Abdul Maliq; in fact, many do not know the name Datu Wali Milir and either have no name for the deity or refer to it as Batara Lingsar.

In the discussions below, this newer version is not prioritized; the name Haji Abdul Maliq is unstated. Instead, Datu Wali Milir stands in for the Sasak hero. The name of this figure is not as important as what he represents, and the proposed characters (Milir, Maliq, Selaparang) all envelop Islam, fertility, and sacrifice. By their presence, all symbolize the Sasak discovery and implied ownership over the land and festival.

Kereped, the head of the Balinese Krama Pura organization, has learned that parts of the recent story, along with other Sasak versions, are what local guides are telling to tourists when they visit the temple. During my time in Lombok in 2001 he made it clear that he was going to take some action to change this situation. What most disturbs him is the contention that the *kemaliq* is separate from the *pura*. Fajaruddin, a guide who immediately assigned himself to me and followed me everywhere in the complex, stated that the most important part of the history is that the *kemaliq* is separate from the *pura*. He said that he gets mad when other guides describe the *pura* as one unit. Kereped, on the other hand, will accept the Sasak myth being presented to tourists only on condition that the *kemaliq* is stated as belonging to the *pura*. He said that to separate them, Lingsar and Lombok risk becoming "like Yugoslavia."

FURTHER INTERPRETATIONS

The moment of the discovery of Lingsar is a primary occurrence in all accounts. In *Upacara Tradisional*, Datu Wali Milir finally sacrifices himself in the water spring to complete the beauty of the area and ensure its fertility. In Syarani, Datuk Milir transforms both himself and the land with his sacrifice because of his love of the people and the land. He disappears and performs *moksa* in the spring that he had been praying to Allah to find, and the land changes from fallow to fertile. According to Sanusi and Parman (in the 1980s), Milir has not died and still lives in the water spring; he is the spirit of the spring and preserves it. Parman's 2001 version maintains the same idea with a new hero. In Balinese accounts (except Blambangan's), I Gusti Ketut Karangasem is led to Lingsar by the signal of spouting water initiated by Batara Gedé Lingsar. After a series of trials and occasions of divine assistance, he is provided with a spirit army to assure safety and victory in battle.

In all the accounts the discovery of the water spring is key. Without Milir and the water spring, the Sasak would suffer epidemics and the land would lie fallow; without Batara Gedé Lingsar and Batara Alit Sakti, the Balinese would not know where to go in Lombok, would lose their battle, and the unjust Sasak kings would continue to rule. The spouting of the water spring is the source of fertility and victory, of moral authority and divine power. For the Sasak, it is Datu Wali Milir and his *moksa* sacrifice that establishes the *kemaliq* as a monument to honor him. For the Balinese, it is the provision of a spirit platoon and the guarantee of safety in battle that establishes an altar for Batara Gedé Lingsar, one for Batara Alit Sakti as the main guide of the journey, and one each for the high deities Batara Gunung Rinjani and Batara Gunung Agung (who symbolically unify and ancestralize Bali and Lombok) within the *gadoh*. The primary figures worshiped at Lingsar are the saint, Datu Wali Milir, and the natural deity, Batara Gedé Lingsar, because they are directly associated with the water spring, moral authority, divine power, fertility, and irrigation.

Unlike Datu Wali Milir in the Sasak accounts, Batara Gedé Lingsar and the discovery of the spring have little to do with fertility in the Balinese accounts. This deity directs the Balinese to victory, helps overthrow unjust rule in Lombok, and is at first more associated with the return to moral order than fertility. The link of Batara Gedé Lingsar with fertility and water begins after Pura Ulon is built, then accentuated when Pura Lingsar is constructed. Eventually, he is understood to be the source of fertility and the spring, and the deity through which flows the power of Batara Wisnu (water). The *kemaliq* of Pura Lingsar, with these affilations intact, becomes the only Balinese rice temple in Lombok.[8]

The mortal figure in the Sasak accounts, Datu Wali Milir, transforms into a deity as he vanishes into the spring. The primary mortal figures in the Balinese accounts, I Gusti Ketut Karangasem and Ida Ketut Subali, become king and high priest respectively. All these figures go through rites of passage or of transformation, and their discovery of Lingsar is key in the history of Lombok.

One distinction in the myths concerns the individual efforts of Milir and Karangasem. Through Milir's individual effort, he discovers the spring, and his mission was to increase fertility, beautify the area, and introduce Islam. Karangasem's efforts in meditation and prayer help his path toward success in his military mission in Lombok, but he is given assistance by a number of natural deities who direct him. Karangasem is not later deified as is Milir. Milir's individual effort plays a greater role in the Lingsar discovery, since Karangasem receives substantial divine aid. The late Lombok Balinese priest, Mangku Saka, mentioned that this difference reflects the respective practices of Hinduism and Islam on Lombok in which there is a greater emphasis on collectivism in Hinduism and on individualism in Islam.

Mythical thought "builds up structures by fitting together events, or rather the remains of events," and myths "use a structure to produce what is itself an object consisting of a set of events" (Levi-Strauss 1966:22, 26). Local Balinese and Sasak agree that recent history—that is, since the building of the new temple complex in the nineteenth century—is part of a shared past. It is in the events preceding this period that conflicts emerge. To the Balinese, Lingsar was discovered by a Balinese noble; to the Sasak, it was a Sasak noble or Javanese noble evangelist. These and other claims are recast into the present and reenacted in ceremony as a demonstration that each group has ritual and political dominion. Though in direct opposition, the structures of the claims are essentially the same. Each account includes a prediscovery and discovery unit, a divine-providence unit (spiritual transformation or supernatural intervention), a direct or implied ethnic-relationship unit, a ritual leadership unit, and an attitude toward the present. The units together interpret events synchronically and diachronically; they mutually inform one another and lead to clear statements regarding political entity and ethnic identity. The units are consistently ordered and structured, and to a large extent it is the structure of the myths rather than their specific details that conveys the significance and meaning (Leach 1972:239). The sources also attempt to explain how ongoing traditions such as Perang Topat were initiated, thus linking current practices to precedents that confirm their interpretations.

Meaning is communicated through the identification of founders and ancestors, assertion of their religions and spiritual powers, and subordination of the other group. The friction inherent in the stories is a social and political reality, and the Balinese and the Sasak are opposing factions in a battle over history. The battle is not only over territory, it also concerns the mystical possession of the island and which religion is more spiritually powerful. The structure of the accounts is simple: it is a chronological narration in which one or more characters face problems that are resolved through human and divine action. The figures in all the versions are imbued with supernatural power, or receive power or guidance through supernatural means, which provides a divine rationale for the superior ethnic position asserted by each group.

The myths provide more than just rationales for the festival; they are celebrations of ethnicity. Cornell (2000) explores how ethnicity is a collective narrative that captures central understandings vital to a group. These "understandings" are rampant in all the Lingsar myth accounts. The Balinese explain their origins and missions in Lombok; the Sasak negotiate traditional and orthodox Islam and define their shared purpose at Lingsar. People spoke to me about history with great passion and seemed to relish their ethnicity in the process. Lingsar looms large in the lives of most festival participants; the ethnicities of Lombok Balinese and participating Sasak are largely enfolded within their myth narratives.

Constraints on the Interviews

I interviewed a wide variety of parties to collect the Lingsar myths. In 1987 I interviewed the Sasak priest Sanusi several times, and we discussed myths in the midst of other conversations. Parman was sometimes present and participating at these talks. In addition, I interviewed Parman alone and also conferred with Saparia (a leader of the Sasak organization) alone about the myths. Among local Balinese I conversed extensively with the late Wayan Kartawirya, a commoner directly connected to Lingsar who had a love of history and debate; with his late uncle and priest, Mangku Saka; and with A. A. Biarsah, a grandson of the last king, as well as his retinue of nobles and priests. In 1988 I spent two days interviewing Gusti Bagus Ngurah in Bali and then returned to Lombok for further interviews with each of the parties above, as well as with other Balinese and Sasak. In the 1990s some of these individuals again articulated to me their ideas on history. I also tried to discuss myth with Asmin (Min), but found he had little interest in the subject. In 2001 I approached several new individuals in both camps, and Parman was very eager to tell me the "authentic" myth.

Each interview had its constraints, and new contexts seemed to generate subtly different nuances in the stories teachers told. Sanusi, for instance, often spoke with me on a pavilion with several others listening, and in that situation he made emphatic points about Sasak leadership; privately he was more soft-spoken and less adamant about these same issues. Gdé Mandia, head of the Parisadha Hindu Dharma organization that oversees Hindu events in Lombok, essentially agreed with the Balinese myth while Wayan Kereped, of the Lingsar Krama Pura organization, was in the room. Later, however, he hinted that the Sasak might just possibly have been at the Lingsar site before the Balinese. This astounded me. No other Balinese had ever allowed for such a possibility. He was quick to add that, if so, they would have been thoroughly Waktu Telu Sasak. Though I often felt oversaturated with accounts, the numerous tellings provided a wide perspective on various viewpoints.

Rarely did Sasak and Balinese speak of the myth when they were together; that might have raised conflict. Whenever I was in "mixed" company, Balinese and Sasak were polite and indirect. On one occasion, however, Parman, Kartawirya, and I were discussing history and the conversation almost became heated. Parman acceded on some points they both felt were important (for example, the line of descent of the Sasak priest, the coming of the Balinese), but held his ground on other issues. After several minutes of intense discussion, however, they concluded that they were united and in agreement. Instead of arguing against each other, or about Balinese or Sasak positions, they instead declared that any problems experienced at the festival must originate with other parties who want to disturb the peace and unity. Kartawirya said excitedly, "*Mengapa mereka mau menggangu kita?*" ("Why do they want to disturb us?"—the "us" here including both Balinese and Sasak). Parman wholeheartedly agreed, "*Kita bisa mengurus semuanya sendiri*" ("We can take care of everything ourselves," meaning that no outsiders [including the government] were needed for anything). At this point the conversation concluded, and we all seemed to feel satisfied, united, and invigorated.

Current Conflicts and the Government

The regional government, in trying to raise the visibility of Sasak ethnicity, has interviewed the Sasak actors and published their versions. In addition, officials have been trying to alter the meaning of the festival from a "religious" to a "traditional" or "cultural" one in order to separate Sasak participation from any religious implications. In my conversations with Sasak and Javanese (the latter in government service), nearly all claim that the Waktu Telu faith is not a religion and that the temple is clearly not an Islamic institution; therefore Sasak participation at Lingsar cannot be, by definition, "religious." As a consequence, Sasak participating at the festival are continuing a tradition of ethnic identity expression or perpetuating a custom (*adat*); they are not fulfilling any religious obligations. The participation is often called "connected to tradition" (*terikat dengan tradisi*) or "cultural" (*terikat dengan budaya*). Concomitantly, however, most Sasak leaders state that the Balinese must come to the Sasak priest for ritual direction. The Balinese, on the other hand, state their own position emphatically and refuse to allow the Sasak past to be imposed upon them. Their versions of the myth (and hence the festival) glorify the colonial past when they held power over Lombok. For local Balinese the past was idyllic. Since then, they have been reduced to a minority with little political visibility.

Due to the tension among the Sasak with regard to attendance at and belief in the festival, the drive to publicize and promote Sasak culture as both "local" and "national," and its mandate to regulate sociocultural life, the regional government has assumed some power over the festival. In terms of publications and publicity, government institutions have sided with the Sasak. However, there are many conflicting interests. The Tourist Office wants to promote tourism at the festival, and Balinese performing arts and decor are colorful spectacles that attract tourists. The government is also still obligated to uphold the five Indonesian principles of Pancasila, which protect the minority Balinese in undertaking events crucial to their religion.[9] At the present time, therefore, the Balinese must be free to conduct their rituals, and the government may be obligated to assist them if requested.

In 1987 the regional government took overt steps to apply some control over the festival. Government leaders invited a Balinese group, composed mostly of artists from Bali, to perform in the evening. They limited other recreational arts to one evening and prohibited the Sasak social/fertility dance, Gandrung (see Chapters Six and Eight). These unprecedented actions were sharply criticized by the Krama Pura temple organization. The officials claimed that they were trying to keep the peace at the festival. Several times in the 1980s evening events had attracted belligerent crowds and there had been outbreaks of violence. By intervening as they did, the government was asserting that it was at least partially responsible for festival success and security. At earlier festivals, the military and local police personnel had been sent to help manage the crowds, but the government had never directly dictated festival events.

In 1988 the government had an even bigger role. Sanusi, the late Sasak priest, invited the regional governor, Wasito, to attend the festival and feast with dignitaries in Sanusi's compound at Lingsar. With the approval of the Krama Pura, the Sasak priest generally invites local figures such as district leaders, village headmen, and heads of district and local military and police. However, on this occasion, Sanusi invited the governor and failed, perhaps deliberately, to inform the Krama Pura. Members of Krama Pura, whose leader at the time was Agung Biarsah (the grandson of the last Lombok Balinese king), felt slighted when they realized they had not been informed. As a result they quickly developed a plan to greet Governor Wasito and give him a tour of the grounds. The Sasak organization envisioned a similar plan. After negotiations, it was decided that one Balinese and one Sasak leader should give short introductory speeches and then allow the governor to address the gathered participants and spectators at the festival. The groups, working together, decided to build a stage overlooking the site of the Perang Topat.

After touring the grounds and briefly interrupting activities on the main day of the festival, the governor and his entourage sat by the stage while the Balinese and Sasak representatives presented their speeches and introduced the governor. By the time the governor spoke, so much time had elapsed that the ritual proceedings had been seriously disrupted. Many events that are normally separate had to be performed simultaneously, and the Perang Topat began before all participants were prepared. The governor is now invited annually, and he or the lieutenant governor attends each festival, placing constant time pressure on the officials, rites, and performing arts.

The government widened the road into the temple complex and constructed a parking area in 1989; they paid for new temple gates and a proscenium stage in 1993. The Krama Pura agreed to these plans, but it is not clear whether Sanusi was consulted. Afterwards, however, he told me that it made the temple *lebih bagus* (better). Most Balinese voiced their pleasure with these *perbaikan* (improvements), though one man, Kayun, said that the temple had as a result lost some of its *khas* (original character).

The new structures follow Balinese form, and the parking space allows the village to charge a parking fee. In the late 1990s local guides were engaged to accompany tourists for additional donations. Government officials have identified the festival as a major tourist event. They want the government and temple closely linked and wish to receive credit for their assistance. These efforts suggest a desire to exert some control over the temple and festival.

The government has discovered a unique phenomenon of Lombok and wants to announce it to tourists, dignitaries, and locals alike. Lombok TV, the local television station, not only gave the festival substantial airtime in 2001, but in fact the coverage equaled that of Idul Fitri (the day of celebration after Ramadan) and Lebaran Topat (a local Islamic holiday).

The festival not only raises the stature of Lombok nationally and attracts tourists and revenue, it is also a context in which to mold regional identity and give definition to a melange of inchoate values—national, local, political, and religious. The government is proud (as are the Balinese and the Sasak) that the festival is the embodiment of the interethnic tolerance implied within the Pancasila principles. Sanusi often mentioned, sometimes in public interviews with Lombok Balinese officials, who nodded in agreement, that the government had not formulated the principles of Pancasila until the 1940s, while they, at Lingsar, had achieved them centuries earlier. Virtually every participant, guide, and official says the same thing today.

The insistence that fifteen hectares of land around the temple are actually a Sasak inheritance, as described in Sasak accounts, has received heated debate in some quarters. Balinese stress that they had never heard of such a story and that it, along with the figure of Datu Wali Milir, was made up as a device to appropriate the land. In the mid-1980s the government leader of West Lombok, Ratmaji, made it clear in a letter that he would tolerate neither friction at the festival nor changes in the festival process. Thus he would not consider the Sasak claim. His position asserted that the government both safeguards the festival and secures its success; he probably also knew that any disruption in festival meaning could lead to violence. Since their participation is a legitimate practice of religion, Balinese may always find support within the government—which tends to promote religiosity.

Regardless of which story is "true," the Sasak contention may indicate that there is unequal redistribution of the yield from this land or perhaps an unfavorable regulation of irrigation. The Krama Pura organization has controlled the lands and springs since national Independence, and farmers and villagers are largely dependent upon its benevolence. In contemporary Lombok the fact that a small religious minority has such authority over agriculture and irrigation water may seem troubling to a modern citizenry.

In 1988, in a move to demonstrate his independence from the Krama Pura, Sanusi refused to accept from Agung Biarsah the traditional donation (*pelaba*), a system of gifts to Sasak priests at Lingsar that has probably been in place for centuries. This refusal is now permanent. As further proof of his independence, Sanusi repainted the *kemaliq* according to his own taste, which several Balinese felt was wanting. They were appalled, but took no action. Sanusi had successfully severed the *kemaliq* from the direct control of the Krama Pura.

By 2001 Sasak officials had publicly separated the *kemaliq* from the *gadoh*, or, as Parman states, from the *pura*. The *kemaliq* is open year round for tourists to visit. They are requested to wear a *dodot* (a scarf-like material) around their waist and to provide a small donation for the rental. With Tourist Office cooperation and a donation and guide system, the Sasak position over the *kemaliq* has grown stronger since Sanusi's death. For certain ceremonies, however, the Balinese take over the whole space. From the Balinese perspective, the *kemaliq* is the second courtyard of the *pura* and it is a shared space. Kereped says that he has no problem with the actions (i.e., tourist development) of Sasak officials, but maintains that the *kemaliq* is part of the *pura* and that his organization, the Krama Pura, has ultimate authority over it. The verbal clash over the land seems to have died down, perhaps because with the guide and tourist system, and with the frequent use of the *kemaliq* for other ceremonies throughout the year, the Sasak position has become financially stronger. However, the fact that a new history may be emerging indicates continuing discord.

Political Positions of the Players

The Sasak have seen their numbers shrink or become less informed and the Balinese presence increase, and players like Parman and Sanusi have worked to rationalize and empower Sasak participation. The forceful expression of myth is a result of these developments. Many Sasak with traditional sympathies have experienced pressure to act, worship, and dress like orthodox Muslims; they have, as a consequence, struggled to find a response and a redefined cultural identity. The local Balinese, on the other hand, feel threatened by the reformist Islamic movement, the increasing role of the Sasak, the power of the *tuan gurus* and *hajis* in local government, and their isolation as a minority. They are reacting aggressively to ensure their religion's expression, integrity, and continuity at the festival and in Lombok generally. All these feelings impact the emotions and the interpretations of the past and result in dogmatic, conflicting mythologies.

During conversations, some teachers were not overly concerned about the names of founding figures or the precise order of their deeds. What seemed important was their ethnic group and social level, their group's pact with divine forces, the insignificance and yet also the achievement of "oneness" with the other group, and the imagery of spouting water and prosperity and its ownership.

Sasak versions include the coming of the Balinese—and do not necessarily deny their divine aid—but declare that the *kemaliq*, which honors the hero's sacrifice, was established beforehand. A kingdom was nearby and the land was either idyllic, as in *Upacara Tradisional*, or arid and fallow, as in Syarani, or that the enterprise was intended to spread Islam, as in Parman's 2001 account. The island, the deity, and the festival are Sasak. The ritual tradition has been handed down from generation to generation to Sanusi and now to the current priest, Min, who directs and controls the festival as did his ancestors.[10]

The Balinese mention only Datu Pejanggik and Datu Selaparang as Sasak characters in the myth (Banjar Getas is sometimes an expelled Javanese noble) and claim that no one lived at Lingsar, which was covered in thick forest. The deities willed that the Balinese should govern Lombok and defeat the unjust Sasak kings, who had lost the mandate to rule. The Balinese were "pure," with a concentration of moral power transferred from the Majapahit empire. Batara Gedé Lingsar confirmed this fact by supplying the spirit army to I Gusti Ketut Karangasem. Apart from the letter that supplied a rationale for invading, the Balinese do not acknowledge a Sasak role in Lingsar's discovery. They claim Lingsar exclusively to themselves, and assert that the Sasak created the figure of Datu Wali Milir as a way to claim the temple grounds and yields. The Balinese systematically deny the cornerstones of the Sasak myth.

The regional government has made it clear that it does not want any disturbance in the festival tradition, and that it safeguards the event as the modern rulers of Lombok. Under the rubric of Pancasila, the government is obligated to protect the festival as an integral part of the local Hindu faith. Sasak complaints are ignored because, as Muslims, their participation cannot be religious and because a redistribution of the temple lands would undoubtedly lead to violence.

Following the anti-communist slaughter and resulting contraction of Waktu Telu in the late 1960s, Sanusi was ordered by a military commander to refrain from officiating at the festival. The festival was deemed "pagan" and "Balinese," and Sanusi, who had registered as a Muslim, could therefore not participate. The Lombok Balinese came to his aid and insisted that the festival could not be carried out without him, and the order was rescinded. Since the mid-1980s Sanusi and now

Min have needed protection from neither the government nor local religious leaders, and they have distanced themselves from the Balinese.[11] Both the figure of Sasak priest and the festival itself have received government acknowledgment, and Sasak participation has increased over the years. Participants do not appear to be intimidated, and some travel from other parts of Lombok. In 2001 most of the Sasak participants were older and less educated; younger people, though they may have watched, rarely participated actively.

Understanding of the festival has changed over the years for all parties and will change again in the future. External forces—government, religious leaders, national developments—have impacted recent interpretations. The government stance is to view the festival both as a part of Balinese Hinduism and as a "traditional ceremony" of the Sasak detached from religion. Along with Sasak officials, the government has encouraged Sasak participation to strengthen ethnic identity and develop the festival as a tourist attraction.

In declaring and demonstrating his—and by extension, "Sasak"—independence from the Krama Pura, Sanusi's motive may have been more religious than political. Pepplinkhuizen (1991:37) states that among traditional cultures east of Bali, the highest deity is double-gendered and reconciles binary powers. Polak (1978:339–340) confirms that Waktu Telu construct male and female attributes within the divine and that gender binarism is conflated as other dualities. I believe that Sanusi, an active Waktu Telu most of his life, worked to reconfigure his relationship with the Balinese to fit this structure, with Sasak representing the female, earth, inside, cool (fertile and hospitable), rock, and elder, while Balinese was male, heaven, outside, hot, tree, and younger. Balinese are disconnected from the original Sasak ancestors and politically dominant, therefore male (controlling), heaven (covering earth), hot (excitable, inhospitable), and tree (covering rock); originating from Bali, they are outside and younger. The complementary duality of Balinese and Sasak merges into the representation of the high deity, the unification of binary powers and the "three" (two into one) of the Waktu Telu. Sanusi, in fact, stated that Balinese and Sasak are like the main two offerings (male and female *kebon odeq*, see Chapter Four), like king and queen, and felt his side equal if not superior to the Balinese (see Harnish 2001). His independence may have brought the realization of separation and reconciliation into sharper focus.

The current priest, Min, positions the Balinese similarly. He asserts that the Sasak (and *kemaliq*) are spiritually independent and "hardly need" (*tak begitu perlu*) the Balinese at the festival. Apart from these few statements, he says little. He is a much quieter man and rarely deals with the Balinese. Parman is the main conduit to the Balinese and with the outside world in general, and his opinions were largely shaped by Sanusi, who officiated for thirty years. Parman contended vehemently several times, "We do not follow the Balinese, the Balinese follow us" (*Kita tak ikut mereka, mereka ikut kita*), which situates Sasak as the masters of the festival. I do not believe he would ever say this to Kereped, with whom he shares a warm relationship; he reserves most of his political points for me and for other Sasak and tourist guides.

Despite the festival goal of unity, the Sasak-Balinese relationship has rarely been harmonious. This is not unusual in the world of festivals. Competing interests in many cultures conjoin together in festivals for the common good, then return to hostile relationships afterwards. The decision by Agung Biarsah in 1987 to assume leadership of the Krama Pura was looked upon as a good sign by both groups. Lombok Balinese had needed a high-profile leader and Biarsah, as the grandson of the last king, certainly filled that position.[12] Sasak respected Biarsah because his grandfather took a Sasak noble as one of his wives (Biarsah's grandmother), built Pura Lingsar, sent some hardworking Sasak to Mecca, and worked to unify Sasak and Balinese. However, Biarsah was not an effective leader and resigned from this position in 1989 (his role was always "temporary," he told me). A lesser noble assumed the position, succeeded by a temporary commoner over following years. Relations further deteriorated.

Since assuming the leadership position in 1993, Kereped has healed some rifts between the camps. As a competent and respected commoner, his stature completes the transition from feudal to modern in the Krama Pura profile. He has not requested government help, and perhaps has isolated the Krama Pura from government support—which is now linked to the *kemaliq*. He does, however, confer with organizations such as Parisadha Hindu Dharma and the Buddhist and Hindu subsection of the Ministry of Religion. Under his watch, several new elements in music and dance have been introduced into the festival. His efforts on behalf of all parties have been appreciated and his relations with Sasak officials and the people of Lingsar (he is a resident) remain warm. However, the tension over history and ownership perseveres.

The 1988 festival saw its share of inauspicious violence. A statue at the entrance of the *gadoh* was knocked over before the festival, and a small explosive rocket was fired into Sanusi's compound the same evening. One of the people responsible was the grandson of the Sasak *pamangku* of the Pura Ulon *kemaliq*. The priest, Lebar (Bar), reacted by suddenly dying without a descendant to take his place. Most people were saddened but felt it appropriate: Bar was so embarrassed his grandson could behave so irreverently that he simply died, which evidenced his feelings of intense guilt. A quiet Waktu Telu man whose life stretched far back into the Dutch period, Bar was never part of the battle over history, and in his last years he curtailed rituals at the Pura Ulon *kemaliq*.[13] His death symbolized the end of the earlier era and perhaps allowed Sanusi and other Sasak to relegate Pura Ulon to irrelevancy. No *pamangku* has taken Bar's place; instead there have been women called *petunggu* (waiters) who help people when they come to the Pura Ulon *kemaliq*. Some still come to worship or request water for illnesses, though it is unclear how many of these are Sasak.

Meanwhile, the numbers at the festival keep growing. The guide Fajaruddin estimated the total on the main day alone in 2001 at 20,000. Violence occasionally erupts, often initiated by drunken celebrants, but with around a hundred military police, a hundred members of the *lang lang* security force, and the same number of Krama Pura members present, troublemakers are intimidated and incidents are quickly stopped. Despite its reformist orientation, the village of Lingsar has embraced the festival as its heritage. In the 1980s few outside of the *pamangku*'s immediate community seemed involved; today most villagers seem somehow connected, either via a village organization (such as the *lang lang*), in a performing group, or as a vendor. As the festival has grown, so have some of its problems, but the Lingsar organizations, along with the government, have discovered many solutions. No violence was reported over recent years.

Assessment

The past is perceived in the context of the present. Balinese and Sasak teachers present histories, organized around current political and religious problems and reflecting their particular identities. Each source expresses perspectives in response to these problems from his/her own reference point. For example, Syarani (or ghostwriter Parman), a *haji*, foregrounds the Islamic nature of the Lingsar discovery: Milir was an evangelist, the discovery was accompanied by prayers to Allah, and the festival is an expression of local Islam. Sanusi, the traditional *pamangku* (representing the "pre-Islamic element" in Waktu Telu communities, charged with contacting "spirits and ancestors" [Leemann 1989a:27]), describes how Batara Rinjani, the high deity and original ancestor, helped lead Milir to Lingsar. Balinese nobles emphasize the role of a noble, I Gusti Ketut Karangasem, while Balinese priests give equal credit to Ida Ketut Subali, who would become the first Balinese priest in Lombok.

All actors are aware of the other group's myth, and some seem to tailor their version specifically in reaction. I Jero Mangku Negara, the common-caste Balinese priest at Lingsar, stated emphatically in 1988 that the Sasak not only had no role in the discovery of Lingsar, they also had no religion, and that Ida Ketut Subali's elder brother who built the *kemaliq*, gave the Sasak their (Waktu Telu) religion. This sharply critical account reflects both an intolerance of opposing accounts and the bitter experience of living as a religious minority. Individual stories mirror individual experience and disposition, and combine to articulate general ethnic perspectives for each group.

Many Sasak are not proud of their history; this is perhaps why reformist Islam as an alternative cultural marker has proven so successful. They have almost always been a colonized people, and feel that they have little to offer to the Indonesian mosaic of cultures. Too often associated with Bali, they strive to separate themselves from the Balinese. The notion of *khas Sasak* (original Sasak) must reject anything that smacks of being Balinese. Leaders emphasize differences in religion, food, life-cycle rituals (particularly circumcisions),[14] and clothing as being distinct from Balinese culture. The Lingsar myth, asserting self-direction and independence from the Balinese, is a proud foothold in the past, and the festival offers a path through history to reclaim their island and identity.

Lombok Balinese have their own myth and claims over the area that are partially demonstrated by the physical temple and altar structures that symbolize their authority. For many, the story is a way to situate and reexperience the glory of their culture, and also, perhaps, to transform their reality of being a religious minority separated from their ancestral island. They own and will fight for their illustrious past; several indicated that they might be willing to die to defend the Balinese position. The versions range from ignoring Sasak contributions to Balinese culture heroes giving the Sasak a religion. The former expresses a colonial attitude toward the Sasak as second-class people, while the latter exudes the bitterness of a religious minority with few political rights. Blambangan's account from the 1930s asserts that the Balinese controlled the festival and its history, but admits Sasak presence and contributions. Comparing Blambangan with current accounts indicates how much more contested history has become.

Wallis (1979:20) recounts how an archetypal Indonesian myth controlled the way the Javanese interpreted local historical events, and how plot conventions from the stories about Panji (a legendary noble Javanese lover and hero) could be used to legitimize the claims of kings and dynasties. Battle victories, marriages to those of competing realms, and comparisons of heroic deeds linking local figures with those of the Panji stories were themes contrived to assume control over an area. This mapping of events and characters to myth is in effect at Lingsar. Balinese have invoked the will of deities to legitimize control, adding that they entered Lombok to rectify the rule of unjust kings and to expand the righteous power of the Javanese Majapahit empire.[15] The Sasak have countered with a figure invoking the powerful Wali Sanga evangelists of Java, transplanting a new and pure religion into Lombok and introducing a sacrifice element that mystically creates and regenerates fertility and prosperity. The Panji story itself is referenced within Sasak performing arts and stakes a claim for the Lingsar lands (see Chapter Five).

Quite apart from these accounts is the practical reality of farmers needing sufficient irrigation water to achieve ample rice yields. Farmers have shown scant interest in the political elements; most care little about debates over history and would not benefit with any changes. The farmers I have spoken with seem to live in the present, and the festival offers an opportunity to pray to whatever deity controls fertility, rainfall, and irrigation water. Farmers' attendance and participation is largely traditional and obligatory; many are afraid not to attend. This is true even for some strongly Muslim farmers, who would rather face irate religious leaders than miss the festival and suffer possible hardships.

Today, a great many different kinds of people—farmers, nobles, merchants, students, bureaucrats, tourists, Sasak Muslims, Balinese Hindus, Sasak Buddhists, Christians, Chinese—attend the festival. Some are spectators, some are active participants. All of them constitute the realization of the festival in contemporary Lombok. The festival therefore contains multiple meanings and, like its past, is subject to multiple interpretations and experiences.

The altar, with dressed stones, in the shared *kemaliq* courtyard in Pura Lingsar, 2001.

Suparman Taufiq (Parman) (r.), the main force for the Sasak, and I Wayan Kereped, the head of the Balinese temple organization, on the opening day, 2001.

Cross-dressed Batek/Telek dancers (a scout, two warriors, and king [in back]) during the first procession, 1988. (Photo by Lisa Ho.)

The gamelan *gong kuna* club from Pagutan performs outside the Balinese *gadoh* courtyard on the first festival day, 2001.

Sasak musician Amaq Sari plays the *preret* shawm for a Balinese
cleansing ceremony in the *kemaliq* courtyard, 2001.

The gamelan *gong gilak* club from Pagutan in the first procession, 2001.

A Topeng Keras (strong male) dancer performs during Topeng Sidha Karya outside the Balinese *gadoh* courtyard on the main festival day, 1988. The temple gate is in the background. (Photo by Lisa Ho.)

The modern but sacred Rejang Déwa dance performed by the club Sanggar Tari Suci in the Balinese *gadoh* courtyard on the main festival day, 2001.

The singing club Sekar Alit performs *kidung* praise poetry in the shared *kemaliq* courtyard on the main day, 2001.

The gamelan *tambur* musicians ready to lead the first festival procession out into profane space, 2001.

Amaq Jasira (in dark glasses) leads the Sasak Baris dancers in the first procession, 1988.
(Photo by Lisa Ho.)

Dancers perform the Canang Sari offering dance in the Balinese *gadoh* courtyard on the main day, moving from outside the temple into the courtyard, 2001.

The Gandrung social/fertility dance with gamelan *gong* Sasak in the Sasak compound, 1988.

The head-carried *momot* (toward the front, under parasol) containing divine liquid and the *kebon odeq* are circumambulated within the shared *kemaliq* courtyard, 2001.

The onset of Perang Topat (War of the Rice Squares) outside the *kemaliq* courtyard, 2001. Hundreds of people on the lower (shown) and upper courtyards wait to grab and hurl the *topat* rice squares at their opponents.

Sasak women prepare the main festival offerings, the male and female *kebon odeq*, 2001.

The gamelan *baris* club, in a Sasak procession, enters the shared *kemaliq* courtyard on the first festival day, 2001.

Cross-dressed Batek/Telek dancers (a scout and two warriors) on the road following the first procession, 2001.

The Sasak gamelan *gendang beleq* club from Montor village performs in the *kemaliq* courtyard, 2001. The boys and young men perform a set choreography.

The Sasak priest Mangku Asmin (Min) opens the *kebon odeq* offerings and the *momot* bottle (foreground) as the last rite of the festival, 2001.

CHAPTER FOUR

Temple Units, Performing Arts,
and Festival Rites

THE TWO TEMPLES of Lingsar are Pura Ulon, also called Pura Aiq Mual, and Pura Lingsar, also called Pura Lingsar Barat. For this discussion of physical arrangements, I will put aside the assertion that the *kemaliq* is separate from the *gadoh* and say that within both temples there are *gadoh* and *kemaliq* courtyards. The Pura Lingsar *kemaliq* is larger and much more active than that in Pura Ulon.

TEMPLE STRUCTURES AND ALTARS

The *kemaliq* in both temples are built on lower ground and seventeen steps rise upward to connect the *gadoh* and *kemaliq* courtyards. The temples are separated by a little over a hundred meters of rice fields, with Pura Ulon situated to the east of Pura Lingsar (see Figure 4.1).

In front of Pura Lingsar to the immediate west is a large unnamed outer courtyard with higher (outside the *gadoh*) and lower (outside the *kemaliq*) sections. Further west are the living quarters of the Balinese *pamangku*, currently I Jero Mangku Negara, and the Sasak *pamangku*, Asmin or Min (the position formerly held by Sanusi).[1] Both *pamangku* receive these compounds as well as traditional compensation, *tanah pecatu* (rice-growing land), from the Krama Pura temple organization for their services. The Sasak compound is especially important in the sequence of events during the festival.

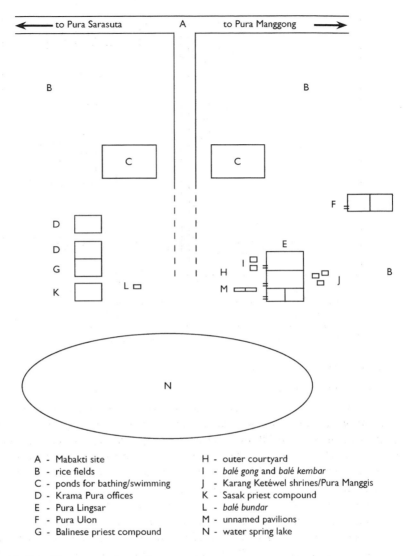

←— to Pura Sarasuta   A   to Pura Manggong —→

A - Mabakti site
B - rice fields
C - ponds for bathing/swimming
D - Krama Pura offices
E - Pura Lingsar
F - Pura Ulon
G - Balinese priest compound
H - outer courtyard
I - *balé gong* and *balé kembar*
J - Karang Ketéwel shrines/Pura Manggis
K - Sasak priest compound
L - *balé bundar*
M - unnamed pavilions
N - water spring lake

FIGURE 4.1. Pura Lingsar complex and environs

The *gadoh* and *kemaliq* of Pura Lingsar are supposed to be identical with those of the Pura Ulon. However, there are several differences in the altars, called *palinggih* (seat) or *pasimpangan* (place to stop), of the *gadoh* and the various *balé* (open pavilions) of the *kemaliq* (compare Figures 4.2 and 4.3). The central altar of the Pura Ulon *gadoh* is dedicated to Batara Alit Sakti and his human mother, Ni Gusti Ayu Karang Winten (Figure 4.2 C and D), while that in the Pura Lingsar *gadoh* represents Batara Alit Sakti and Batara Gedé Lingsar (Figure 4.3 B and C). In both *gadoh*, the altar east of this central shrine is dedicated to Batara Rinjani (Figure

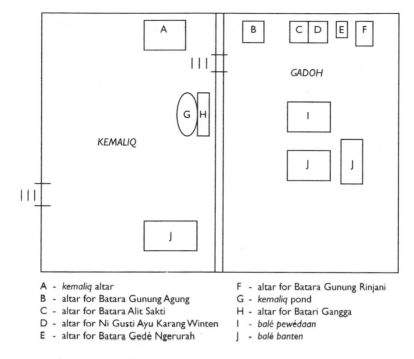

A - *kemaliq* altar
B - altar for Batara Gunung Agung
C - altar for Batara Alit Sakti
D - altar for Ni Gusti Ayu Karang Winten
E - altar for Batara Gedé Ngerurah

F - altar for Batara Gunung Rinjani
G - *kemaliq* pond
H - altar for Batari Gangga
I - *balé pewédaan*
J - *balé banten*

FIGURE 4.2. Main units Pura Ulon

4.2 F and Figure 4.3 E), while that on the west represents Batara Agung in the form of a *padmasana* (lotus throne) altar, also called *sanggar agung* (great altar) (Figure 4.2 B and Figure 4.3 A).[2] Both *gadoh* (and perhaps all Balinese temples) include a small *palinggih* for Batara Gedé Ngerurah, a deity who guards and protects the inner space of the temple (Figure 4.2 E and Figure 4.3 D) and is often considered a "translator" of the deities in other Balinese temples.

In the Pura Ulon *kemaliq*, the water spring pond (Figure 4.2 G) is separate from the main altar and dedicated to Batara Gedé Lingsar, while the pond and altar in Pura Lingsar (Figure 4.3 H and I) are side-by-side as one unit and dedicated to Batara Gedé Lingsar for the Balinese and to Datu Wali Milir (or other hero) for most Sasak.[3] This latter altar consists of approximately forty erect stones that are washed and dressed in yellow and white cloth. Stone altars are common at shrines and gravesites among nominal Muslim and Boda of Lombok, and may constitute remnants of a megalithic culture. Sanusi claimed that these stones were brought by representatives of villages who worked on *kemaliq* construction long ago, and that the stones maintain descendants' rights to participate at festivals. Others stated that the stones are objects of concentrated power associated with fertility and ancestral worship. Stones often link descendants with the deified ancestors who first cultivated the land, and these ancestors form a link between descendants and the deities that control the natural powers of the landscape. Similarly, van Baal

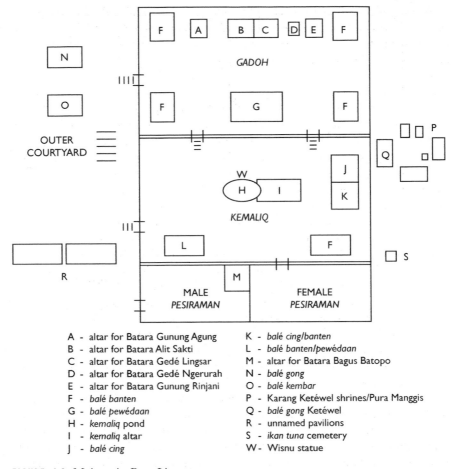

A - altar for Batara Gunung Agung
B - altar for Batara Alit Sakti
C - altar for Batara Gedé Lingsar
D - altar for Batara Gedé Ngerurah
E - altar for Batara Gunung Rinjani
F - *balé banten*
G - *balé pewédaan*
H - *kemaliq* pond
I - *kemaliq* altar
J - *balé cing*

K - *balé cing/banten*
L - *balé banten/pewédaan*
M - altar for Batara Bagus Batopo
N - *balé gong*
O - *balé kembar*
P - Karang Ketéwel shrines/Pura Manggis
Q - *balé gong* Ketéwel
R - unnamed pavilions
S - *ikan tuna* cemetery
W - Wisnu statue

FIGURE 4.3. Main units Pura Lingsar

(1976:24) states that stones in holy places in Bayan (a Waktu Telu stronghold) are associated with the deified ancestor; they emanate purity, prevent malevolent spirits from entering, and encourage general prosperity.

Behind the pond in the Pura Lingsar *kemaliq* is a prominent statue of Batara Wisnu (the member of the Hindu Trinity associated with water) riding the bird-man deity Garuda (Figure 4.3 W), while a small shrine behind the pond in the Pura Ulon *kemaliq* is dedicated to Batari Gangga (goddess of the rivers; sometimes a male figure, Batara Gangga) (Figure 4.2 H).[4] For the Balinese, the statue Hinduizes the *kemaliq* and clarifies that they worship Batara Wisnu through the manifestation of Batara Gedé Lingsar at the pond. The statue, some Balinese say, demonstrates that they worship an acknowledged Hindu god in the *kemaliq* and not simply a local deity or Sasak ancestor. The statue was reportedly placed there in the early twentieth century; before then, perhaps such a statement was unnecessary.

Many pavilions in both *gadoh* and *kemaliq* are called *balé banten*, referring to a space in which to store offerings (Figure 4.2 J and Figure 4.3 F). There are so many offerings at festivals that extra makeshift *balé banten* must be erected. The *padanda* priests in the *gadoh* courtyards officiate from the *balé pewédaan* (a pavilion for Vedic recitation) (Figure 4.2 I and Figure 4.3 G); directly in front of them are makeshift structures filled with offerings to be blessed and presented to deities. One other *padanda* officiates from a pavilion in the Pura Lingsar *kemaliq*; however, it is located on the side rather than the center of that space (Figure 4.3 L) and is called a *balé banten* rather than a *balé pewédaan*. One unique pavilion in the *kemaliq*, *balé cing* (Figure 4.3 J), is named after a wealthy Chinese merchant who financed its construction in fulfillment of a personal vow.

A last distinction between the two temples is the third courtyard in Pura Lingsar, which is used for bathing and called the *pesiraman* (a term referring to bathing). A wall within the *pesiraman* separates the men's and women's sections which contain four and five water spouts respectively (equaling the ritual number nine). Within the men's area lies a shrine for an obscure deity, Batara Bagus Batopo (Figure 4.3 M), who is also represented at Pura Bukit in East Bali—the temple that honors Batara Alit Sakti in the Balinese myth. This special shrine was supposedly added in the early twentieth century as a contribution from the village of Pagutan. Shortly thereafter, another addition, a series of shrines called Pura Manggis, were built behind the east wall of Pura Lingsar (Figure 4.3 P and Q) by members of the Karang Ketéwel ward in Cakranegara Timur.

Several pavilions are located in the outer courtyard. Those in front of the *kemaliq* have no particular names (Figure 4.1 M and Figure 4.3 R), but the two in front of the *gadoh* are called the *balé gong* (gamelan pavilion) and *balé kembar* ("paired" pavilion, referring to its relationship with the *balé gong*; it is also sometimes also called *balé gong*) (Figure 4.1 I and Figure 4.3 N and O). Further west lies the *balé bundar* ("round," even though it is a rectangular pavilion) (Figure 4.1 L)[5] and the living quarters of the two *pamangku* (Figure 4.1 G and K). Yayasan Krama Pura Lingsar offices are just north of these quarters (Figure 4.1 D) along with two small buildings used for temporary housing during festivals. To the south is a small lake created by the runoff from the springs (Figure 4.1 N), with adjacent women's (northeast side) and men's (west side) bathing spots. Further north are two small ponds, with old statues in them, that long ago were used for bathing (Figure 4.1 C).

Living in the springs and *kemaliq* ponds are fresh water eels (Sasak: *ikan tuna*; Balinese: *ikan julit* or *bejulit*) that swim throughout the area and can grow to two meters and more in length. The eels are considered sacred as protectors and preservers or manifestations of the deity. No one is permitted to catch or disturb them in the ponds. Visitors and participants, however, are allowed to feed the eels boiled eggs,[6] and they can be caught outside the temple. A few meters south of the Karang Ketéwel shrines is a small, marked cemetery for the eels that die in the pond (Figure 4.3 S). There is no such cemetery outside Pura Ulon, but officials state that eels rarely enter there; thus there are more and larger fish in the Pura Ulon pond.

Many changes have occurred at the temple site. For decades, vehicles could easily drive up to the outer courtyard. In 1989, however, a gate was built to prevent cars from entering, and then a lot was constructed to park vehicles for a token charge. Since the late 1990s guides await guests just inside the outer wall of the temple, and a few Sasak provide *dodot* scarves and access to the *kemaliq*. The monies raised are supposed to go to *kemaliq* upkeep, though it is clear that at least part of the collected revenue goes to the employees.

With government funds, the Krama Pura completed a stage (*wantilan* or *balé kesenian*) in 1993 near the ponds (Figure 4.1 C) on the east side of the road into the temple, as well as three new Balinese-style temple gates (*candi bentar*): a large gate over the road by the two ponds, a smaller gate over the same road between the outer courtyard of the *gadoh* on the east and the Krama Pura offices on the west, and a third one of similar size over the entrance to the *gadoh*. More changes will likely take place in the coming years because all forces at work—the government, the Sasak organization, and Krama Pura—are busy trying to further their own interests.

MUSIC AND DANCE

Sasak and Balinese participants present a variety of performing arts that together constitute a unique mosaic of sound and motion. One cannot encounter these combined varieties of music elsewhere in Lombok, and the unity of ethnicities and arts is certainly as great as anywhere in Indonesia. This chapter provides brief introductions to the arts and defines the arrangement of events at the festival as they appeared in the 1980s and in 2001. More detailed information is presented in Chapter Five.

One performance considered mandatory at the festival is the Batek Baris dance ("step line"; sometimes called Baris, although it is unrelated to the famous Balinese dance). Almost everyone agrees that the festival cannot take place without the performance, which features eight soldiers carrying rifles and performing drill moves led by a commandant brandishing a sword and barking orders in Sasak and Dutch. This martial dance is generally believed to be a Sasak contribution,[7] and it is associated with another dance at the festival, called Batek or Telek (this Telek has no relationship to the dance in Bali; see Chapter Five). Until the 1980s these arts were context-specific and never performed outside of this festival (except for certain rare, associated festivals).[8] Now, however, the Lingsar club frequently performs for tourists and for national holidays in which local arts are paraded. The group in the 1990s even performed at the well-known Hotel Mutiara and at the Taman Mini stage in the Indonesian capital of Jakarta.

The gamelan *tambur* accompanies the Baris dance. It consists only of a large, double-headed *tambur* drum and a medium-sized gong (sometimes called *boqboq*) and is performed in processions. A few musicians have referred to it in English as "drum band." This gamelan is enfolded into another, the gamelan *baris* ("line" gamelan), that accompanies the Batek/Telek dance, a dance combining the Baris dancers with three to five young women cross-dressed as heroes. The gamelan *baris* adds a bowed lute, bamboo flute, two additional drums, two individually struck kettle-gongs, and a small set of cymbals to the gamelan *tambur*'s drum and gong. Sanusi, Min, and Balinese officials state that this ensemble, particularly the game-, lan *tambur*, is "owned" by the temple generally and by the *kemaliq* specifically. Many of the instruments are kept in a "purified" pavilion in the Sasak compound.

Other forms of Sasak music at Lingsar have included gamelan *gong* Sasak, *preret* performance, and *gendang beleq*. The *gong* Sasak is a twentieth-century ensemble derived from the traditional gamelan *oncer* and processional gamelan *tawa-tawa*, and modeled upon the modern Balinese gamelan *gong kebyar* (see below), which consists of hanging gongs, a gong chime, several small and large metallophones, a lead metallophone, two drums, and a set of cymbals. The *gong* Sasak performs instrumentals and accompanies the Sasak social and fertility dance called Gandrung (love). One particular club from Montor village accompanies the Gandrung dance so often that it is called both gamelan *gandrung* and *gong* Montor. The ensemble is also broken down to form a processional gamelan *baleganjur*, styled after the Lombok Balinese ensemble of the same name. It consists of gongs, drums, and cymbals. Often known as *beleganjur* in Bali, the ensemble in Lombok, shared by local Balinese and a few Sasak groups, features a smaller instrumentarium and energetically accompanies processions.

The *preret* or *pereret* is a wooden double-reed instrument used to perform instrumental versions of sacred poetry. The free-meter pieces accompany the production and processions of the main Sasak offerings. Most years have featured two players; some years three have come although they did not play together. Performance has been either solo or in duet with one instrumentalist following the melody of the other. The *preret* players have frequently participated in processions. One or more Balinese *preret* players might join in processions, but this is not required of Balinese participants; they do so only as part of a personal vow (*kaul*) or devoted action (*niat*). For a number of reasons discussed further in Chapter Five, the *preret* players have only rarely come to Lingsar since the death of Sanusi in 1993. In 2001 one player was invited by the Krama Pura to perform for the Balinese purification ceremony within the *kemaliq*, and two Balinese players performed separately in some processions.

Gendang beleq is a gamelan consisting of two (occasionally four) large (*beleq*) drums, a timekeeper, many handheld cymbals, and two or three gongs. To my knowledge no *gendang beleq* had ever played at Lingsar before 1997. Parman, however, said that "long ago" (*dulu*) a related ensemble had performed, thus providing an antecedent for the current practice. No other Sasak or Balinese teachers agreed. Since the festival, particularly from the Sasak perspective, must preserve a consistent link to the past (when practices were designated by a culture hero), this claim provides a rationale for what would otherwise be a new (and less authentic) development. Since about 1990 the "development" and spread of *gendang beleq* throughout Lombok has been part of a government project to "de-traditionalize" (see Heelas 1996) and essentially reinvent and popularize select arts to mold and modernize local identity (see Chapter Seven). In 2001 four clubs (*sekaha* [*seka*], *sanggar*) performed at the Pujawali in processions, within the *kemaliq*, and on their own outside of the temple complex.

Several Balinese performing arts are "necessary" to complete the Lingsar festival experience for the Balinese participants. First of all, the Lingsar Pujawali, a major festival at a major temple, features the gamelan *gong kuna*, the primary Balinese ceremonial gamelan in Lombok. The gamelan—several hanging and horizontally mounted gongs, eight resting-bar metallophones, two large suspended-bar metallophones, two gong-chimes, two drums, and two to six sets of cymbals—opens the festival and performs throughout most days. The ceremonial repertoire, *lelambatan* (slow pieces), permits other activities and provides the festival soundscape. Until recently two separate *gong kuna* clubs performed at the festival. One of the gamelans was "returned" (*dikembalikan*) to Bali, because an ancestral village there made an official request for it.[9] Now only one group performs at Lingsar.

Gamelan *gong kuna* clubs include the instruments to form gamelan *gong gilak*, processional ensembles—similar though distinct from gamelan *baleganjur*—that consist of gongs, drums, cymbals, and two sets of pairs of kettle-gongs. *Gong gilak* perform martial, upbeat music in all processions including Balinese. With the substitution of some metallophones and a different repertoire, the *gong kuna* clubs also transform into modern gamelan *gong kebyar* to accompany dances and theater performances and play purely for recreation during free time particularly on the final festival day. The *gong kebyar* style, featuring rapid and virtuosic passages, came to Lombok from Bali in the 1930s and was soon presented at festivals like Lingsar's.

Since 1996 a new form of music—sung *kidung* poetry praising deities in the high Balinese and Javanese languages and featuring women and sometimes a male leader—has been part of the proceedings. Many state that *kidung* adds an important spiritual dimension. One or more clubs perform in either or both the *kemaliq* and *gadoh* on the main day. The forces behind this addition—the Krama Pura and

TABLE 4.1. Balinese and Sasak Performing Arts

DATE	BALINESE ARTS	SASAK ARTS
Since 1990	*kidung* singing	gamelan *gendang beleq*
	Rejang Déwa dance	
Since 1930	gamelan *gong kebyar*	gamelan *gong* Sasak
"Traditional"	gamelan *gong kuna*	gamelan *tambur*
	gamelan *gong gilak*	gamelan *baris*
	Canang Sari dance	*preret*
	Topeng Sidha Karya dance	Batek Baris dance
		Batek/Telek dance
		Gandrung dance

the modernist Parisadha Hindu Dharma organization—apparently wanted to present an acknowledged Hindu music form from Bali; I postulate that it is related to an increased religiosity found in Lombok and throughout Indonesia. The amplified, chanted music floats above the other sonic phenomena.

For many decades, if not centuries, the primary Balinese dance performed at temple festivals in Lombok has been Ngolahang Canang Sari (hereafter Canang Sari), a sacred male temple dance in which the *canang sari* (essence of betel nut) offerings are "danced." The dance, associated with Lingsar *dari dulu* (here meaning "since the beginning"), is performed in the *gadoh* on the main day and has gone through a transition over the past decade. Another dance with an established history at Lingsar is the masked Topeng Sidha Karya ("masked successful work," which refers to the carrying out of a festival), a dance drama meant to coincide with the services of the high priests. Two or three performers portray stock characters who abstractly depict the chronicles of Lingsar. In some years, for any number of reasons, this dance has not been held.

About 1997 a newly choreographed dance from Bali, Rejang Déwa (temple dance for the gods), that combined a variety of movements from sacred dances, was introduced into Lombok. It features eight female dancers in yellow dresses and unique headdresses. Like Canang Sari, this dance is performed on the main day of festival in the *gadoh*; some Balinese teachers state that it is now the main ritual dance. On occasion, more secular type Balinese dances are performed during the evening on the new stage outside of the temple. (Prior to 1993 these were held beside the *balé gong*.) Though not integral to the festival liturgy, they serve the important social function of providing a shared art, for both Balinese and Sasak are audience members.

Table 4.1 shows all of the Balinese and Sasak performing arts mentioned above, and in some cases their approximate dates of introduction into the festival. Not indicated here are the program deletions or lesser roles assigned to several "traditional" arts over recent years, such as Sasak *preret* music, the Balinese Topeng Sidha Karya dance drama, and the Sasak Gandrung dance. Tables 4.2–4.4 will later connect these arts to their contexts.

FESTIVAL EVENTS

There are five acknowledged days of the festival and several weeks of preparation. The Krama Pura is ultimately responsible for the preparations and successful completion of the festival. This organization, consisting entirely of Balinese, coordinates the events and finances the festival with the two harvests from the temple land. The Krama Pura technically oversees all activities and regularly confers with Sasak leaders to facilitate well-organized festivals.

Within recent decades the informal Sasak organization surrounding the Sasak *pamangku* has assumed responsibility for the Pura Lingsar *kemaliq* and undertaken separate preparations. The Balinese and Sasak organizations have moved further apart in recent years and the Sasak group has acquired authority over many *kemaliq* events. When Sanusi first declined the traditional money offered by the Krama Pura for *kemaliq* preparations in 1988, the *kemaliq* was symbolically severed from Krama Pura control. Since then it has become financially independent through donations for regular ritual services and new government and private contributions. The *kemaliq* is now available for tourists to enter for a voluntary donation. Many Balinese feel that Sanusi appropriated the *kemaliq* and all of the activities held there, but his perspective was that *kemaliq* activities are essentially Sasak and should therefore be maintained by Sasak. Min told me that he has no intention of renewing traditional relations with the Krama Pura, that he works with that organization only when undertaking the festival, and that he does so on an equal basis.

The activities and liturgy at the festival provide the framework for the festival events and experiences. The rites described below are almost the same every year, but small changes occur. For instance, some events shared by Balinese and Sasak were separated in a few festivals of the 1990s due to overcrowding; similarly, two Balinese worship services, rather than the one outlined below, have occasionally been necessary in the *gadoh* due to the number of congregants. The terms provided here that define Sasak rites all come from Sanusi. From our interaction, it is clear that Min is unfamiliar with some of this terminology. It is possible that Sasak rites are undergoing redefinition and that some of the terms used here will soon pass out of living memory.

Preparations

About one week before the festival, Balinese men from various communities, particularly farmers from *subak* organizations, participate in the cooperative work called *gotong royong* and clear away weeds and other growth from the main paths the processions will take and from the sides and interior of the temple. Separately, Sasak farmers clear the area in front of the *kemaliq*. Other Sasak, under directions from and often including the *pamangku*, sometimes paint or make repairs within the *kemaliq*. I frequently found Sanusi or Min weeding or painting during these preparations.

In following days, materials for offerings and decorations are gathered. Before each festival the Krama Pura swells from eight permanent members to over a hundred. The extra people are in charge of various tasks, and they and their families finalize the required offerings and decorations. Most of the decorations are completed in the *gadoh*, which buzzes with activity. Members arrange material and offerings for specific altars in the *gadoh* and *kemaliq* and those for particular processions. Experienced, elderly women usually oversee the offerings (some men share expertise, but offerings are primarily women's domain). An appointed member is responsible for engaging gamelan *gong kuna* performers and other artists.

From the early 1980s until 2000, three Balinese gamelan groups consistently performed. The first was the gamelan *gong kuna* from Karang Ketéwel, Cakranegara. This club performed on a *balé gong* within the Pura Manggis shrines (built by their ancestors) behind the east wall of Pura Lingsar. The second was a gamelan *gong gilak* assembled from that *gong kuna*. And the third was another *gong gilak* from Karang Bayan in Narmada; these musicians representing Pura Ulon performed in processions. Both the Karang Ketéwel and Karang Bayan groups had historic obligations to the temple. In 2000, however, the Karang Ketéwel gamelan *gong kuna* was "returned" to Karang Ketéwel in Bali and the *gong gilak* from Karang Bayan was replaced by a smaller gamelan *baleganjur*, reportedly due to deterioration of the *gong gilak*'s kettle-gongs.

The most "functionally" important Balinese music is provided by the *gong kuna* club on the main *balé gong* outside the *gadoh* of Pura Lingsar. This group is rarely the same in consecutive years; a club either offers its services or is selected from among many in Lombok. Pura Lingsar, unlike village temples, does not obligate one group or one village for this task. As the public mother temple, performance opportunities are open to any *gong kuna* clubs who seek to contribute their talents and represent their communities at Lingsar.[10] This honored voluntary service is called *ngayah*, and the Krama Pura tries to rotate this annual task among active groups.

The informal Sasak organization contacts the necessary dancers and musicians before the festival. Normally all performers from previous years will participate; occasionally one or more dancers decides not to perform, and the organization then seeks, not always successfully, to find replacements. The gamelan *tambur/baris* and *preret* musicians used to participate regularly; performing was an honor that passed through male descent, and most held their places until death. The performers at the festival in 1995 were nearly the same as in 1983 (my first encounter with the festival). By 2001, however, the *preret* players were rarely invited to perform, and four deceased gamelan *baris* leaders had been replaced by related musicians. Today, such responsibilities are not so prescribed, particularly as some descendants have opted not to participate—often because of a personal change of religious orientation—and therefore performers must be drawn from a larger pool of volunteers. The *gong* Sasak club, with some new members all from Montor village, continues its participation; since the club performs nonritual pieces, "religion" has not been a major issue. The *gendang beleq* players are boys and young men. There is no pattern of membership; males may choose to join clubs for shorter or longer periods. Different clubs are invited each year.

Among the Sasak, gender plays perhaps a bigger role in determining tasks. Postmenopausal women are in charge of preparing materials and offerings and cleaning the instruments used in the rituals (Proyek Inventarisasi 1984:107–108). Unlike the Balinese, it is an absolute requirement that only elderly Sasak women assume these tasks presumably because they no longer menstruate (a taboo around the temple), are beyond the passionate stage of life, and are therefore more "pure." Men are responsible for building a temporary extended roof over the *kemaliq* altar courtyard and for dressing the forty-odd stones in the *kemaliq* altar with yellow or white material. These colors are ritually pure and have male/female associations (see Ramseyer 1991:60); white is also a Waktu Telu color. The men decorate the altar in a prescribed manner: some material is hung from the back wall and other material draped from the poles and thatched roof in preparations known collectively as *abah-abah* (the Balinese also use this term). Like the ingredients in offerings and the material used for Balinese altars, the Sasak items (particular leaves, Chinese coins, fruit) carry symbolic meanings and the hung material embodies color symbolism. The *abah-abah* generally takes place one day before the opening day of the ceremony. By this time both Sasak and Balinese have made arrangements for feasts and have acquired suitable water buffalo for sacrifice. Both have prepared the numerous parasols, flags, and bamboo poles that are used in the processions and as additional decor.

The Sasak *pamangku* conducts personal preparations. Sanusi hung many individual pieces of material called *bebaliq* or *kemaliq* from a support beam within the pavilion of Sasak offerings in his compound. Most of this material was associated with a ritual of the same name that is supposed to be carried out for babies who as youths and adults will enter the *kemaliq* or *gadoh*.[11] The *bebaliq/kemaliq* were ancient heirlooms; some were remnants of rituals conducted for important Sasak and Balinese ancestors. Several larger pieces displayed were associated only with the *kemaliq*. This phenomenon of material "consecrated" to the *kemaliq* indicates the shrine's age and the status of the *pamangku* (Bolland & Polak 1971:168–169).[12] The *pamangku* thus demonstrates his clout by hanging these materials during the festival. In 2001 Min seemed to continue this tradition, though only a few pieces of material were displayed.

Nine rounds of cockfights are generally held on the day prior to the opening day of the festival: three each in front of the Pura Ulon, the Pura Lingsar *gadoh*, and the Pura Lingsar *kemaliq*. These bloodletting rituals—necessary to placate malevolent spirits—are limited to prevent excessive gambling.[13] Sanusi, again going his own direction, preferred to cut the head of a small chick before the *kemaliq* in 1988 instead of holding cockfights there. Although this angered some Balinese, he felt that cockfights are part of Balinese tradition and should not be followed by Sasak. Min has normally allowed cockfights, but the Balinese have been conducting this rite themselves.

The Opening Day

The opening day—sometime between early November and late December—falls one day before the full moon of the sixth month of the Balinese *saka* calendar and of the seventh month of the Sasak *wariga* calendar.[14] The primary festival day is the full moon day, but the day before, called Pengadagang (birth, creation) or Pemendak (meeting) by the Balinese and Penaek Gawé (beginning of festive work) by the Sasak, initiates the festival and is full of activity.

In the early morning the invited gamelan *gong kuna* begins to play on the *balé gong*, one of two pavilions in the Pura Lingsar's outer courtyard, signaling the official opening of the festival. (The gamelan *gong kuna* group from Karang Ketéwel used to begin later in the morning in the Pura Manggis shrine area.) Around midday the gamelan *baris* sets up on the *balé kembar* and performs intermittently with the *gong kuna*, though pieces frequently overlap. These gamelan clubs present offerings called *peras gong* ("legitimatize *gong*," consisting of cooked and uncooked rice, chicken, fruit, Chinese coins, and sweets) before starting to play. The gongs accept these offerings on behalf of their respective ensembles. The gamelan *baris* also receives *daksina* (south) offerings (rice, eggs, white thread, coconuts, and nuts), and all of the instruments are ritually purified with the water from the *kemaliq*. Throughout the day, food stalls are erected in parts of the complex and more and more people arrive, most of them carrying individual offerings of various shapes and sizes.

Since the late 1990s one or more *gendang beleq* ensembles have performed at various times of the day, usually in the afternoon when crowds were present. Since they include a detailed choreography, these groups require an audience; performance is more presentational than any other form at Lingsar. Each club works hard on coordination, movement, and precision to impress onlookers. Many of the clubs that have performed at Lingsar over the past few years have secured grants from the government tourist office; several have received training from government experts in dance and music. (Two clubs are housed in Lingsar itself, but normally only one of these performs per year.) *Gendang beleq* is a purely male form, and most clubs consist of preteens and teenagers. The government and community seem to have agreed that this musical activity is beneficial for youth, and a plethora of clubs have formed throughout the island since the mid 1990s.

When they were invited to perform (yearly prior to 1993), the *preret* players would start at midmorning in the Sasak compound just west of the temple complex. One or two players would begin performing the piece "Turun Daun," which opened the festival for Sasak participants. (One player was sufficient, and one was usually late.) Immediately following, elderly Sasak women began making the *kebon odeq* (little garden) and *pesaji* (food offering) offerings. Until 1993 "Turun Daun" was considered a requirement to precede the preparation of these offerings; it was also played when the offerings were completed several hours later. (In 2001 the women began to make the offerings after a brief prayer.) The players would perform other pieces in between or after these periods but played "Turun Daun" before and following the creation of the offerings. Observing this process was so fascinating that on one occasion I took notes that appeared in modified form in an article (2001):

> The *preret* (wooden oboe) player, Amaq Sari, takes his seat within the pavilion, next to the altar where the postmenopausal women are preparing the materials needed for the offerings. The priest, Sanusi, nods in his direction and Sari begins "Turun Daun," the piece that invites deities to descend. The music is shrill, penetrating, inescapable. The women then gather the materials—fruits, Chinese coins, flowers, seeds—and slowly create the *kebon odeq*, the two offerings which, according to Sanusi, unify dualities "like king and queen, male and female, and Balinese and Sasak." Sari continues

"Turun Daun" indefinitely. Some years, he (or "they," when his partner shows up) stops the piece to perform another but he performs only that piece today. He must continue playing until the women are done; similarly, they cannot begin until after he does. *Preret* performance enframes this event. Finally the women are done; the offerings meet the specific prescriptions for their preparation. The completed *kebon odeq* will be carried in the front of almost all processions, people will request and compete to carry them, and, in between processions they will be "seated" in the main Sasak shrine beside the sacred water spring-fed pool. Amaq Sari stops playing, folds his *preret* into some cloth, nods to Sanusi for permission to leave, and goes into the outer courtyard to chew betel nut. For the moment, his job is done. But the next procession is soon to start, and he will then walk beside the *kebon odeq* to various sacred places within the environs of Lingsar. . . .

This tradition, which endured for perhaps centuries, seems to have ceased (see Chapters Five and Seven), though perhaps someday it will be revived.

The two *kebon odeq* offerings, one male (*lanang*) and one female (*isteri*), are the most important Sasak offerings, and they are made within a special small pavilion called *balé penyimpenan* (pavilion for storage of sacred objects) within a small courtyard in the *pamangku*'s compound.[15] The term *kebon odeq* refers to a little garden that signifies greatness and sublimity, and the offerings themselves symbolize prosperity and cosmological properties. The coupling of male and female representations is required in rice cultivation ceremonies among Waktu Telu to promote fertility and prosperity and to symbolize other dualities (body/soul, life/death) that require each other (see Polak 1978:188–235). The two *kebon odeq* embody this principle; many Balinese offerings also join male and female attributes (see below). Sanusi conflated *lanang* and *isteri* as king and queen and as Balinese and Sasak.

The offerings contain three (*telu*) spatial areas: bottom, middle, and top. The bottom consists primarily of seeds, leaves, Chinese coins, and thread placed on a tray; the middle consists of a cut-open coconut wrapped in prescribed leaves with eighteen bamboo spears and items such as betel leaves and yellow bananas; and the top consists of ripe fruit (including gender-specific pineapple for the *lanang* and papaya for the *isteri*) fixed on the spears with many flowers rising far atop of the coconut. Sanusi stated that the tripartite *kebon odeq* structure symbolizes the base, middle, and upper parts of the cosmos. Proyek Inventarisasi (1984:71) declares that the offerings are symbolic of the great world mountain and universe.

The *pesaji* are covered food offerings on wooden trays consisting of steamed rice and side dishes, such as cooked meat on spears (*saté*) and peanuts. *Pesaji* (and other smaller offerings) are considered subordinate to the *kebon odeq*. They are made in a lower-level pavilion within the same courtyard as the *kebon odeq*; before 1993 these offerings had to be produced in increments of nine. On the first day there were usually nine or eighteen produced, but on the following day there were often twenty-seven or thirty-six or more. Nine is prominent in the making of all Sasak offerings: in theory there must be nine types of materials in the *pesaji*, nine or increments of nine of certain lesser offerings, and nine materials and nine bamboo spears within both *kebon odeq*. Teachers report that this numerological significance is related to ritual formulas that utilize the number, the sum of the four directions and their subdivisions and center, the number of the legendary Javanese Islamic evangelists known as the Wali Sanga, and even the number of outdoor bathing spots. Since 1993, however, the prescription for *pesaji* in increments of nine has been relaxed; I also found that the women producing the offerings are now reluctant to discuss the process.

After the *kebon odeq* are constructed, the Sasak *pamangku* and the women begin preparing the *momot*, an empty bottle sealed and covered with prescribed types of leaves and thread. The empty bottle will be carried in processions and placed within the *kemaliq*, to be opened only after the final procession of the final day. When finally opened by the *pamangku* before many witnesses, there is almost always some mysterious liquid within the bottle, considered *tirta* (holy water) and bestowed by the deity. Sanusi and others state that the amount of water in the bottle is directly representative of the amount of rainfall for the coming year, and hence the degree of prosperity. The water thus symbolizes the relative success of the festival. Great anticipation wells among participants before the *momot*'s unveiling. In 2001 the bottle was empty or had so little in it that Min was clearly disappointed. Nevertheless, people fought over the leaves and materials that had covered the bottle (these are considered blessed), and most said that the sparse or absent liquid would not necessarily translate into a drought or a poor harvest. And indeed, though not a good year, there was no drought and harvest was sufficient.

During the opening day some of the prescribed Balinese offerings are still in process in the *gadoh*. Elderly women and their assistants finish at least seventeen types of offerings, and prescribed numbers of these offerings are placed in covered altars within the *gadoh* and *kemaliq* courtyards. Balinese offerings are generically called *banten*, and more specifically *banten suci* or *banten luhur* for the *déwa-déwi* upperworld deities and *banten sor* for the *buta kala* underworld spirits. The *buta kala* are associated with propitiatory ceremonies that include offerings of blood or animal sacrifices called *(ma)caru* or *(pi)segeh* and are held by the gate into the *gadoh* and before the main prayers within the *gadoh*.

Teachers and scholars (e.g., Ramseyer 1986) say that the essence of the *banten suci* offerings symbolizes the universe or macrocosms and microcosms through representations of the tripartite cosmos and/or complementary opposites, which, through their duality, achieve balance and harmony. The late Mangku Saka, for instance, mentioned that an egg and a coconut represent the female and Earth property in the *suci* (lit. "pure": a specific type within *banten suci*) offering, while banana and bamboo represents the male property in the *daksina*. These offerings are always placed together in covered altars, symbolizing the unity of binary energies and creation and fertility. Many offerings also provide items the deities need to attend the festival, such as special food, betel nut for chewing, water for bathing or ritual purification, flowers for adornment, clothing material, combs, mirrors, and so forth.

The activities in the Pura Ulon resemble those in the west temple, but on a smaller scale. Neither *kebon odeq* offerings nor the *momot* tradition have been prepared in the *kemaliq* for many years, and the decor there is held to a minimum. Balinese offerings are fewer in number and follow a slightly different set of requirements. Until the late 1990s the Krama Pura had little to do with Pura Ulon; those responsible for the temple for centuries were the direct descendants of the troops who had first come to Lombok. These participants, from Karang Bayan in Narmada, were under the longtime leadership of I Gusti Jelantik Sunu and were entirely responsible for the Pura Ulon festival and all of its expenses. Since the late 1990s the costs have been borne by the Krama Pura and this organization now selects the officiating *pamangku* and *padanda*. In terms of leadership, performing arts, and priests, the Pura Ulon has lost its independence and been folded into the greater Pura Lingsar entity.

For many years no performing arts were presented in the Pura Ulon, but then in 2001 a modern gamelan *gong kebyar* club performed within the *gadoh*. According to Gusti Sunu, decades ago a gamelan *gong kuna* from Karang Bayan performed regularly, but the instruments fell into disrepair. Remaining club members then brought only the gamelan *gong gilak* instruments to play in processions; by 2000, however, the kettle-gongs of this ensemble had deteriorated, so musicians brought just the gamelan *baleganjur* instruments (gongs, drums, and cymbals). Some reports claim that *preret* used to be played in Pura Ulon, but whether the performers were Sasak or Balinese and whether performance functioned as at Pura Lingsar are unknown. The last Sasak *pamangku* for the Pura Ulon *kemaliq*, Bar, died in 1988, and it is possible that no one will ever assume his position; therefore, Sasak observations of rites at the *kemaliq* are very minimal. The Sasak "waitress" (*petunggu*) at the *kemaliq*, currently Inaq Muarduning (Muar, daughter of Bar), neither conducts official rites nor uses music in any way. It is likely that both the *kemaliq* and the *gadoh* have always been less active than those of Pura Lingsar.

Following late-morning bloodletting rituals (*pisegeh*) of chicks, which again cleanse the area of negative forces in the *gadoh* spaces of Pura Ulon and Pura Lingsar, a small group from Pura Ulon walks out of the temple complex between 1:00 and 2:00 p.m. to the main road, then heads westward to Pura Sarasuta alongside the Sarasuta River. They carry ritual instruments and two bottles; one will later be dressed in white cloth and the other in red cloth representing Batara Gunung Agung and Batara Alit Sakti, respectively. While an appointed member continues further west and obtains water from a spring at Saraswili for the bottle representing Batara Alit Sakti, the remaining group places some water from a spring at Pura Sarasuta in the bottle representing Batara Gunung Agung. Balinese teachers uniformly report that these actions symbolize the arrival on Lombok from Bali of Batara Gunung Agung and Batara Alit Sakti. Then the whole group proceeds back toward Lingsar. This procession and the one described below are called Mendak Tirta (meet holy water); the sacred and symbolic nature of water is emphasized.

Around 3:00 p.m. a large procession moves from Pura Lingsar eastward to Pura Manggong in Kumbung led by the Batek Baris and gamelan *baris* with *gong gilak* groups participating.[16] Immediately following the Batek Baris dancers is a group from Pura Ulon, led by the current officiating *pamangku*, Mangku Ketut Narwadha (for many years Mangku Wayan Gedog), which must always be the first group due to the "elder" status of Pura Ulon. Then comes the group from the Pura Lingsar *gadoh*, led by *pamangku* Negara; last comes the group from Pura Manggis (located behind the eastern wall of Pura Lingsar), the "youngest" of the temple structures. At Pura Manggong, the collective receives water and places it into two bottles— one covered with black and one with yellow material, representing Batara Gunung Rinjani and Batara Gedé Lingsar, respectively.[17] These vessels and those above are then named for the deities they represent.

This large group returns to Lingsar and stops at the crossroads where the dirt road leading south to the temple meets the paved road that runs east-west. Here they meet the group that has just returned from Pura Sarasuta, and they erect and decorate a makeshift altar positioned on the north side of the road, facing south- ward as in a temple, and within it place the four clothed bottles of water with other ritual objects. While most of the gamelans continue playing, two or three Balinese *pamangku* conduct a service unifying the forces of Bali—Batara Gunung Agung and Batara Alit Sakti—with the forces of Lombok—Batara Gunung Rinjani and Batara Gedé Lingsar. The waters, the deities and their powers, and the islands are symbolically married. Mangku Saka used the Indonesian words *pemaduan* (blend- ing) and *perkawinan* (marriage) to refer to this ceremony.

The traffic on this road is interrupted throughout the day and comes to a halt during the services at the crossroads. Most of the Balinese who are present par- ticipate in prayer, called Mabakti (to do devotion) or Muspa (flower), and sit on both roads facing the altar containing the vessels/deities while the gamelans (*gong gilak*s, gamelan *tambur*) generally continue playing. In 2001, all stopped playing except for a Balinese *preret* player who played for his own spiritual reasons. The gamelan *tambur* players left to prepare for another performance (see below) and the *gong gilak* musicians participated in the prayers. The few Sasak present do not participate in worship. It is significant that Sasak participate in neither the proces- sion to Sarasuta (where water is collected representing Bali) nor the prayers unify- ing Lombok and Bali, yet some do participate in the procession to Kumbung and receive and accompany the Lombok deities.[18] People state that the Sasak contri- bution is "traditional" and carried over from an earlier time when they believed in Batara Gunung Rinjani. Some Sasak assert that they help, accompany, and even protect the Balinese mission; this is likely due to the military association of Batek Baris and gamelan *tambur*.

Following the prayers, the procession forms again and enters the temple, though in 2001 the Batek Baris dancers performed on the road to the temple, in- advertently restraining some people from returning. While Balinese officials place the vessels/deities in their appropriate altars in the courtyards, a group of mostly Sasak enters the Sasak *pamangku*'s compound; everyone else disperses and prepares for the next event. A short time later, an assembly forms at the *pamangku*'s com- pound and the *kebon odeq*, with the *momot* and *pesaji*, are escorted to the front of the *kemaliq* in a procession called Mendak Kebon Odeq. All Sasak performing arts groups accompany the procession, which occurs around 4:00 to 5:00 p.m. Following this is Ngilahang Kaoq in Sasak or Mailahang Kebo in Balinese (both meaning "encircle with water buffalo"), a procession in which a buffalo is walked around the exterior of the Pura Lingsar complex three times. Approximately two thousand congregants are led by the Batek Baris dancers with gamelan *baris* and Telek dancers, one group of participants carrying ritual instruments and decor representing Pura Ulon, one group representing the Pura Lingsar *gadoh*, one group representing the Pura Lingsar *kemaliq*, and one or two buffaloes (two in 2001) and the men who drive the buffalo and prevent it from running off. The processional gamelans, including one or more *gendang beleq*, participate; before 1993, *preret* players did too. A number of Balinese *pamangku* officiate while the Sasak *pamangku* directs.

After the third circumambulation, the Sasak *pamangku* directs a line to enter the *kemaliq*. (Many Balinese and Sasak do not follow.) Upon a cue, the entering participants proceed around the *kemaliq* altar and pond three times, led once again by the Batek Baris, the gamelan *baris*, the Telek dancers, and, since the late 1990s, several *gendang beleq*. This procession is called both Ngilahang Kebon Odeq (encircle with *kebon odeq*) and Ngilahang Pesaji (encircle with *pesaji*). The Sasak gamelan *baleganjur* joins the procession (adding to the cacophony of gamelan *baris* and several rambunctious *gendang beleq*), and the *kebon odeq, pesaji, momot*, and the Balinese *kemaliq* offerings are all carried around in prescribed order. (Before 1993, the piercing *preret*s also performed.) Then the procession stops in front of the shrine and the main offerings are placed on a space called *sesangkok*, while others are positioned on other pavilions in the *kemaliq*. The Telek dancers usually perform in front of the altar, and sometimes the audience is requested to sit down. The dance is held near dusk, and is often rather solemn and quiet. While other clubs stop playing, the gamelan *baris* accompanies the dance.

The Sasak *pamangku* then leads an Upacara Geria (ceremony to cause many things to come) ritual, sometimes called Ngaturang Pesaji (offer up *pesaji*), which takes place in front of the altar and dedicates the offerings to the deity.[19] One or more gamelans (and formerly the *preret* players) perform as the *pamangku* silently mouths prayers and mantra formulas with incense and burning coconut smoke rising in front of him. Although I am uncertain of Min's practice (he does not feel comfortable discussing the topic), participants described Sanusi's language on this occasion as a mixture of Arabic and Old Sasak. Sanusi himself, however, told me it was all Sasak and that other participants were free to pray in any language. When asked about whether he invoked the name Datu Wali Milir during his worship, Sanusi answered quietly that the name of the residing deity is actually not Datu Wali Milir and that he was not allowed to verbalize the name, although he would silently mouth this name during part of his service.[20] During Upacara Geria, the participants, a mixture of Sasak and Balinese, pray with their hands above their head and flowers between the middle fingers, similar to the general practice with Balinese prayers. When the *pamangku* is finished, assistants provide and sprinkle participants with holy water from the pond, and then everyone leaves.

While this is going on, the Balinese hold a smaller procession within the *gadoh* called Purwédaksina (east-south), where participants circle the area in front of pavilions and altars clockwise three times, with accompaniment by the associated *gong gilak* groups. Afterwards, ceremonies and prayers are conducted in the *gadoh* of both Pura Lingsar and Pura Ulon, not by common *pamangku* priests but by *padanda* high priests. These priests recite Wéda (Vedic) texts during the ritual stage known as Mawéda (to do Wéda). A large number of congregates (particularly at Pura Lingsar) then follow in the collective Mabakti prayers. For similar prayers the next day, the number of congregates will double, triple, or even quadruple.

Padanda must all come from the *brahmana* caste, unlike *pamangku*, who are normally commoners. To attain the status of *padanda* requires many years of rigorous training in learning ritual formulas, the uses of ritual instruments, processes of self- and water purifications, spiritual techniques such as yoga, and so forth. *Padanda* are held to be spiritually pure. Unlike *pamangku*, *padanda* are rarely connected to specific temples. At Lingsar, however, two *padanda* were strongly associated with Lingsar: the late Ida Padanda Ketut Rai for the Pura Lingsar *gadoh*, and Padanda Istri Manuaba for the Pura Ulon. Rai was considered supernaturally powerful by everyone I spoke with (and hence, beneficial to the festival). He was in direct lineage from the first *padanda* of Lingsar and Lombok (Ida Ketut Subali) according to legend. The services of the *padanda* are now requested of available and appropriate candidates. Manuaba, a *padanda istri* ("wife" *padanda*, meaning her husband, now deceased, was a priest), resides in Karang Bayan and was obligated through lineage to Pura Ulon; she retired in the late 1990s and the replacement for her position is now selected from among other *padanda*. Interestingly, the Krama Pura continues to invite other *padanda istri* for Pura Ulon. The prayers within the *gadoh* and *kemaliq* conclude the activities of the first day, but there may be more secular music and dance performances in the evening. Though initially planned, no evening performances were actually held in 2001.

The Main Day

The full moon and main festival day is called Rainan Karya (day of work) among the Balinese, Perang Topat (war of the rice squares) or simply Pujawali (worship return) among the Sasak, and Hari Puncak (culmination day) in Indonesian. In the early morning two buffalo are slaughtered, one each in the Balinese and Sasak compounds. Both rituals are conducted by Muslim officials known as *kiyai*, and the head and right front leg of the Sasak buffalo are hung in a tree within the *kemaliq*, while the head of the Balinese buffalo will be carried in procession.[21]

This morning also begins with gamelan *gong kuna* in the *balé gong*, shortly followed by gamelan *baris* in the adjacent *balé kembar*; in previous years the Karang Ketéwel *gong kuna* and *preret* players also performed in their respective places (the *preret* accompanied the making of new *pesaji* offerings). In the early afternoon the gamelan *gong* Sasak club sets up on the *balé bundar* and begins to play, and one or more *gendang beleq* performs intermittently outside the temple complex or near the Sasak compound.

Around midday farmers begin bringing *topat* (cooked and hardened rice squares fastened with palm leaves), and these are collected in the *kemaliq*. Supposedly, *topat* also must be made in increments of nine—nine, eighteen, twenty-seven, and so forth—but I was unable to confirm whether many farmers follow this prescription. The farmers should be members of the Lingsar *subak* or others utilizing water from Lingsar, but many Sasak and Balinese farmers from other areas of Lombok bring their own *topat*, and temple officials often make many more. The Sasak *pamangku* and his assistants purify the *topat* with water from the *kemaliq* pond throughout the day and place the purified *topat* in front of the altar.

In the early afternoon the new *pesaji* are carried in a procession called Mendak Pesaji (meet offerings) to the *kemaliq*, accompanied by the Batek Baris dancers, gamelan *baris*, *gendang beleq* ensembles, and usually the Sasak gamelan *baleganjur*; *preret* players used to be included. Around midafternoon, feasts are held in the Sasak and Balinese compounds. The Sasak *pamangku* and the associated organization invite many local government and military officials as well as important community members to their feast. Krama Pura members hold a feast known as Mengibung (eat in abundance), which involves groups of eight men who each sit around and solemnly partake of mountain-shaped mounds of rice.[22] Both groups consume meat from the slaughtered buffaloes.

Balinese begin coming to Lingsar in droves in the early afternoon, carrying new offerings. Many go to Pura Ulon to pray before bringing offerings to the Pura Lingsar *gadoh*.[23] Though only one Balinese *pamangku* officially works and lives at Lingsar, many more assist during busy moments, and Krama Pura members help coordinate events. The congregants store their offerings within the altars until filled, and then within the side *balé banten* pavilions. The *pamangku* are in charge of acknowledging and arranging the individual offerings in the altars. More and more people congregate within the *gadoh* and *kemaliq* and outside the temple, and the participants' energy and sense of expectation reaches a higher level as they prepare for the main activities to begin.

By this time the Balinese *padanda* have begun Mawéda. They also offer the *banten* offerings to deities in a rite called Mabanten. A second Hindu *padanda* of the Buda (Buddhist) sect has joined the first (a Siwa or Shaivite) on his right (according to prescription, the *padanda* Buda must be on the right of the *padanda* Siwa) on the *gadoh*'s *balé pawedaan*; a third (of either sect, though usually Siwa) performs on a *balé banten* in the *kemaliq*, and a fourth officiates in Pura Ulon. The gamelan *gong kuna* in the *balé gong* makes a few instrument substitutions and is transformed into a modern gamelan *gong kebyar* to better perform theater repertoire and accompany the masked Topeng Sidha Karya dance, held next to the *balé gong*. Once featured annually, *topeng* (masked dance theatre) is now sometimes excluded due to time constraints.

As officials with loudspeakers direct the flow and timing of events in both courtyards, people in the *gadoh* sit before the altars and prepare to pray. After *topeng* is finished in the outer courtyard, Rejang Déwa dancers—eight women dressed in yellow and white—enter the *gadoh* and dance in the center. The music from the *balé gong* outside the *gadoh* is amplified by microphones and piped into the courtyard. This choreography is set; unlike Canang Sari, there is no improvisation. No Balinese officials I spoke with, including Krama Pura leader Kereped, could remember the year that the dance was first invited to Lingsar, but it appears to have been either 1997 or 1998. This new sacred dance now shares top billing with Canang Sari.

Next, Canang Sari begins just outside the *gadoh*'s entrance. Until the 1990s this dance featured five males who "danced" the special *canang sari* offerings into the *gadoh* and handed them over to *pamangku*, who arranged them in the proper altars. In 2001 over twenty dancers, including women and children along with men, danced in a long line to the center of the *gadoh*. In addition, the quality of offerings had changed; a *pamangku*, who was clearly disappointed, confirmed my observation that the offerings were smaller and less ornate than in earlier years.

When completed, all performing arts stop and the *padanda* begin chanting the mantra "Trisandya," a ritual praise text in Middle Javanese associated with temple festivals; most congregants follow along. After this, they begin the Mabakti prayers (sometimes called Panca Sembah due to the five times of raising hands, palms and fingers together), led by one of the *padanda*, who keeps a constant rhythm with his *genta* handbell. Then congregants receive holy water from assistants and drink and purify themselves in a process known as Nunas Tirta (request holy water).

Meanwhile a procession, again called Ngilahang Pesaji, begins in the *kemaliq*. It circles the altar three times and includes Batek Baris and Telek dancers, gamelan *baris*, several *gendang beleq*, Sasak gamelan *baleganjur* (and formerly *preret* players), ritual objects of all sorts, and *pesaji* and Balinese offerings. The Batek/Telek dancers may again perform in front of the stone altar.

The Sasak *pamangku* then leads a *geria* ceremony called Ngaturang Pesaji, which takes place under the makeshift covering in front of the altar. (In the 1980s, the performing arts sometimes fell silent, perhaps out of courtesy for the Balinese who were praying in the *kemaliq*. In 2001 all gamelans, including three *gendang beleq*, continued playing; the volume was astonishing.) After this, the *topat* are taken out onto the western wall of the *kemaliq*, and participants gather in the outer, shared courtyard to participate in the Perang Topat. Over the past few years it has been customary for the governor to throw the first *topat*, though some "naughty" youth often obtain and throw one or more *topat* before the governor has his chance. This event was well covered by the media in 2001. As assistants or *lang lang* members begin throwing the *topat* into the outer courtyard, the participants, squared off on the lower and higher levels of the outer courtyard, start pelting each other with them.[24]

The Perang Topat lasts from fifteen to thirty minutes (depending on how long farmers take to scoop up the *topat*). The event ends when there are no more available *topat*, after which most participants go home. Farmers place the *topat* in their rice fields or on trees. The *topat*, now considered blessed offerings, are believed to guarantee agricultural fertility. Many farmers do not transplant new seedlings into the fields until after completion of the Perang Topat (and the placing of *topat* in the fields) in accordance with a past rule, a fact that demonstrates the continuing festival function of systematizing and coordinating the rice cycle.[25] For many participants the Perang Topat is the culmination of the festival. Most government dignitaries, orthodox Muslims, visitors from Bali, and tourists now leave and do not return for later events.

There are sometimes evening performances of Balinese theater or modern Balinese dances.[26] These performances are accompanied by a modern gamelan *gong kebyar* and performed on the new *balé kesenian* stage outside the temple complex. (Prior to 1993 they were held near the *balé gong.*) Performances feature private groups or clubs from institutions on Lombok or sometimes on Bali. The audiences are mixed Balinese and Sasak. One or both of the following two nights may include performances as well. The Krama Pura, in consultation with police and local security, decides whether these performances should go forward based on their perception of public safety and the numbers of police available to prevent disruptions or violence. No groups performed in 2001; in 2004, a group from Bali performed.

The Sasak Gandrung social dance may be held on any one of these evenings or in between events during the days. This dance, accompanied by the gamelan *gong* Sasak, takes place by the *balé bundar*, *balé kembar*, or within the Sasak compound. It features a solo female (the Gandrung) who sings and dances then selects a series of dance partners from the audience. Gandrung has a history at Lingsar, and, though missing a spot in the official liturgy, it has traditional functions as entertainment and as a fertility dance (see Chapter Five). Although the dance was planned for 2001, the dancer was apparently not invited. When Sanusi was *pamangku*, it was required.

The Final Days

The two days following the main day are called Bengang in Balinese and Lalang in Sasak (empty), and there are no collective activities at the temple. Individual Sasak and Balinese (as well as local Chinese and Buddhist Sasak) who have made personal vows at the *kemaliq* generally pay their respects (financially and spiritually) during these days. In the *gadoh*, Balinese continue to bring offerings and pray to complete vows, to avoid the mass of people on the other days, or simply because they cannot attend during the other days (several festivals are held concurrently). Pura Ulon is quiet during these days, though groups from Karang Bayan continue to sleep in the temple (as others do in a less-organized fashion in the *kemaliq* and *gadoh* of Pura Lingsar) and occasionally individuals or groups come to worship.

The final day (the third past the full moon) is called Penglemek (fertile soil, referring to the state of the rice fields after the festival) in Balinese and Beteteh (discard, describing the later state of the *kebon odeq*) in Sasak. The gamelans, such as the gamelan *gong kuna* on the *balé gong*, are again playing from the morning onwards. More *pesaji* offerings (formerly with *preret* accompaniment) are made in the Sasak compound, and in the early afternoon a Mendak Pesaji procession again occurs from the compound to the *kemaliq*. The Batek Baris dancers, gamelan *baris*, Batek/Telek dancers, gamelan *baleganjur*, *gendang beleq* ensembles (and formerly *preret* players) all join in the procession. Following the procession, the Sasak *pamangku* leads a *geria* ceremony generally called Ngaturang Pesaji or more specifically Nunas Pamit (request to leave, interpreted by Sanusi and Parman as representing the *pesaji* departing from the *kebon odeq* and the separation of participants and deity). Following this, the *pesaji* are taken out of the *kemaliq* and returned to the compound.

Two *padanda*, one each in *kemaliq* and *gadoh* (and a third in Pura Ulon), begin their services in the midafternoon. Balinese congregants in both courtyards perform the Muspa prayer and generally the "Trisandya" mantra with the *padanda*, then follow with holy-water purification called Nunas Merta (*merta*: the elixir of life), referring to the water that was placed within the altars at the onset of the festival. On this final day, after the deities have resided in those same altars, the water, formally *tirta* and already holy, has become *merta* or *amerta* because it has touched the divine. Some of this water is mixed with other water and placed in bottles brought by individuals to the *gadoh*.

Next, processions within the *kemaliq* and *gadoh* (and within Pura Ulon) encircle the altars in those courtyards three times. The Balinese procession is again called Purwédaksina. For the Sasak, the procession is called both Ngilahang Kebon Odeq and Beteteh, and it marks the third occasion (the other two being the first and second days of the festival) of circumambulating the altar thrice during the festival, equaling a total of the ritually important nine times. Sanusi inferred and others explained that the first of three represents birth, the second, life, and the third, death; this three-part structure concurs with Waktu Telu practices elsewhere. The direction of the circumambulations is always clockwise. The two Balinese Purwédaksina processions (on the opening and final days) within the Pura Lingsar *gadoh* are also clockwise.[27]

Following these inner processions, the participants come out and form a major, shared procession, again headed by Batek Baris dancers and followed by the Pura Ulon group, the Pura Lingsar *gadoh* group, the *kemaliq* group, and the Pura Manggis group at the end. Ideally, all gamelans and *preret* players are included. This procession, called Penglemek or Melukar (to send back) for the Balinese and Beteteh for the Sasak, goes to Pura Sarasuta and a bridge at the Sarasuta River. The Balinese proceed to pray at Pura Sarasuta and throw some offerings in the river, while the Sasak stop at the river, and, after a prayer and sometimes a brief Batek/Telek performance (first performed in 1988), the Sasak *pamangku* and/or his assistants throw the *kebon odeq* into the river.

During Min's years, he then takes and opens the *momot* bottle, shares whatever water is there, leaves all the materials (which are quickly snatched by the faithful), and departs as the festival concludes. During Sanusi's years, however, the *momot* bottle was returned to the Sasak compound where to solo *preret* performance it was ceremoniously opened by the *pamangku* and the contents revealed to all. My eye-witness accounts and available photographs confirm that the bottle was 25 to 35 percent filled during the 1980s. In 2001 it was empty or nearly so. Sanusi would mix the powerful water in the bottle, considered manifested by the deity, with other water from the *kemaliq*. The participants still in attendance, mostly farmers and a majority of them Balinese, purified themselves with this water and/or put some of it in small containers and returned home.

Tables 4.2 through 4.4 outline chronologically the Sasak and Balinese events and performing arts for the three active days—the opening, main, and final days—of the festival. The tables consider only major events; the *preret* perfor-mance, currently suspended, is retained for analysis, as is the *gong kuna* for the Pura Manggis shrines; both could return someday. Similarly, the gamelan at Pura Ulon is considered a *gong gilak* rather than a *baleganjur*.

SIGNIFICANCE OF THE FESTIVAL RITES

The Lingsar Pujawali shares many characteristics with major festivals worldwide. Falassi (1987:4), for example, describes how framing rituals, which open and sacralize a festival, introduce a temporal interruption creating "time out of time," a special dimension that divides the festival internally as in movements within myth narra-tives. The gamelan *gong kuna* initiates this dimension and opens the festival for the Balinese, who then engage in preparing offerings; formerly, the *preret* opened the festival for the Sasak, who then engaged in making offerings. The loud music marks the transition from mundane to sacred time, and all performing arts divide the festival into meaningful fragments that help construct the ethnic narratives.

The next stage is reached when waters representing Batara Gunung Agung, Batara Alit Sakti, Batara Gunung Rinjani, and Batara Gedé Lingsar are married, and when Mendak Kebon Odeq and Mabakti greet the divine. The deities are then present, establishing a time continuum to the past; it is this continuum that gives the deities authority. This notion creates, sustains, and molds the myths; the myths, in turn, are the rationale of the festival. The festival reawakens the continuum.

The structural divisions embedded in the myths closely mirror the temporal dimension of the festival. Just as meaningful units occur before the discovery of Lingsar, the initial opening rites (preparation stage) begin before the coming of the deities. Reflecting heterogeneity and the dual ethnicities, the opening rites fram-ing the festival experience are held separately. Further transformations happen during the next stage when the deities arrive. Much of the following rediscovery stage—when the deities are present and abundance and righteousness are mani-fest—is shared. The closing rites—as the deities return to their respective abodes and boons (such as fertility) are granted—are partially shared.

Rites of purification are performed to placate or purge evil or negative forces from the festival site (Falassi 1987:4). At Lingsar, these take the form of cockfights

TABLE 4.2. Events and Performing Arts: Opening Day (Sasak: Penaek Gawé; Balinese: Pengadagang/Pemendak)

TIME	SASAK EVENT	SASAK PERFORMING ARTS	BALINESE EVENT	BALINESE PERFORMING ARTS
Morning				*gong kuna*
	kebon odeq, *pesaji* made[1]	*preret*	*banten* made	*gong kuna;* *gong kuna* (Manggis)
Midday		gamelan *baris*		*gong kuna;* *gong kuna* (Manggis)
Afternoon		*gendang beleq*	Mendak Tirta to Sarasuta	
	Mendak Tirta to Kumbung;	gamelan *tambur;* Batek Baris	Mendak Tirta to Kumbung;	*gong gilak;* *gong gilak* (Ulon); *gong gilak* (Manggis)
		gamelan *tambur*	Mabakti at crossroads	all three *gong gilak*[2]
	Mendak Kebon Odeq;	gamelan *baris;* Batek/Telek; *preret; gendang beleq;* *baleganjur*		
	Ngilahang Kaoq;	gamelan *baris;* Batek/Telek; *preret; gendang beleq;* *baleganjur*	Mallahang Kebo;	*gong gilak;* *gong gilak* (Manggis)
	Ngilahang Kebon Odeq Pesaji;	gamelan *baris;* Batek/Telek; *preret; gendang beleq;* *baleganjur*	Purwédaksina	*gong gilak*
	Ngaturang Pesaji;	gamelan *baris;* *baleganjur;* *preret; gendang beleq*	Mawéda; Mabakti	

1. In 2001 these offerings were made in the early afternoon. I was told this was due to Friday prayers.
2. As mentioned in the text, the Balinese musicians stopped playing in 2001 to participate in prayers while a Balinese man, Ketut Riana, played *preret*. The *tambur* musicians left to prepare to accompany the Batek Baris dance on the road leading into the temple.

and *banten sor, caru,* and *pisegeh* offerings, as well as ritual sacrifices of two water buffaloes. The rites are directed at negative forces to either placate or transform them for the duration of the event. Many participants, particularly among the Balinese, also conduct personal rites to purify their bodies and spirits and stave off negative internal energies. The *padanda*s must conduct a number of self-purification rituals before appearing at the festival, and then a series of others

TABLE 4.3. Events and Performing Arts: Main Day (Sasak: Perang Topat/Pujawali; Balinese: Rainan Karya)

| | SASAK | | BALINESE | |
TIME	EVENT	PERFORMING ARTS	EVENT	PERFORMING ARTS
Morning				gong kuna
	pesaji made	preret	banten made	gong kuna; gong kuna (Manggis)
Midday		gamelan baris; gong Sasak		gong kuna; gong kuna (Manggis)
Afternoon	Mendak Pesaji	gamelan baris; Batek/Telek; preret; gendang beleq; baleganjur		
	Ngilahang Pesaji;	gamelan baris; Batek/Telek; preret; gendang beleq; baleganjur	Mawéda	gong kebyar; topeng; Rejang Déwa; kidung; Canang Sari; gong kuna (Manggis)
	Ngaturang Pesaji;	Usually as above[1]	Mabakti	
	Perang Topat[2]		Perang Topat	

1. The musicians perform during Ngaturang Pesaji on both opening and final days; at times, they may abstain on the main day perhaps out of courtesy to the Balinese, who cease performing arts before Mabakti prayers (which may precede or coincide with Ngaturang Pesaji), when there is silence except for the *padandas'* *genta* bells. In 2001 the gamelans performed right through the rite.
2. A man strikes a wooden slit drum, *kulkul*, during the Perang Topat. The gong of the gamelan *baris* is often sounded throughout as well. The respective rhythms are unrelated.

before they invoke the deities. Participants state that performances of the gamelan *tambur* and gamelan *gong gilak* similarly help clear negative forces from the environment. Such purifications are a major element in the festival.

What Falassi (ibid.:4) calls "rites of conspicuous display"—which permit "the most important symbolic elements of the community to be seen, touched, adored, or worshipped"— abound at the festival. The display includes offerings, flags, parasols, lances and other weapons (such as the rifles of the Baris dancers), the *momot* bottle, water bottles for the deities, weavings and decorations, *bebaliq* cloth, the ritual instruments of the priests, and, of course, the musical instruments of all the ensembles, especially the gamelan *tambur*, which represents the sacred bounty of the temple. Seeing and hearing this gamelan played exposes one to that sacredness and realm of the ancestors. The above together demonstrate the power of the temple and its ability to safeguard prosperity.

TABLE 4.4. Events and Performing Arts: Final Day (Sasak: Beteteh; Balinese: Penglemek)

TIME	SASAK		BALINESE	
	EVENT	PERFORMING ARTS	EVENT	PERFORMING ARTS
Morning	*pesaji* made	*preret*		*gong kuna*
Midday	Mendak Pesaji	*gamelan baris*; Batek/Telek; *preret*; *gendang beleq*; *baleganjur*		
	Ngaturang Pesaji;	gamelan *baris*; Batek/Telek; *preret*; *gendang beleq*; *baleganjur*		
Afternoon			Mawéda	*gong kuna*;[1] *gong kuna* (Manggis)
			Mabakti	
	Ngilahang Kebon Odeq;	gamelan *baris*; Batek/Telek; *preret*; *gendang beleq*; *baleganjur*	Purwédaksina	*baleganjur*[2]
	Beteteh	gamelan *baris*; Batek/Telek; *preret*; *gendang beleq*; *baleganjur*	Penglemek	*baleganjur*; *gong gilak* (Manggis); *gong gilak* (Ulon)
	momot opening	*preret*	*momot opening*[3]	

1. This *gong kuna* group often assumes its *gong kebyar* form and plays *kebyar* repertoire.
2. There has been a tendency for the *gong kuna* group to assume the *baleganjur* form in these contexts, though the *gong gilak* form is equally appropriate.
3. Although not a Balinese event, more than half of those attending were Balinese in the 1980s. Since Min's time, the bottle has been opened at the river rather than at the Sasak compound, and *preret* players have not participated. I suspect that fewer Balinese now participate as well.

Falassi (ibid.) also mentions "rites of conspicuous consumption," generally feasts, as important moments in festivals. The Sasak host several feasts in their compound and invite important local officials and the governor. The feasts exhibit excessive abundance, as plentiful meals are rather solemnly eaten together. The Balinese engage in the Mengibung rite of consuming mountains of rice in groups of eight (eight around the center [rice] as in ritual formula), but never eating too much and always leaving some for the deities. These rites cannot be underestimated because "ritual food is also a means to communicate with gods and ancestors" (ibid.), and spiritually unifies those participating together.

The "ritual drama" is the rite that generally reenacts and brings to life the myth of a festival. I believe that the existence of two different ethnic groups with separate beliefs prevented the formation of a unified theatrical tradition at Lingsar. Instead, two dramas occur separately: the Topeng Sidha Karya masked dance for the Balinese, and the Batek Baris/Telek combined dance for the Sasak. Through masked characterizations, Topeng Sidha Karya calls the "powerful past of East Javanese courts into the present as a way of collecting together one major part of the Balinese conception of the cosmos into the festival" and weaves the temple and its environs into the grand scheme of the Balinese chronicles (Harnish 1989). The performances at Lingsar are specific to Lombok and meant to explicate the founding myth, though much of the message is abstract, and few participants can hear the narrative. Nevertheless, the main point of Balinese discovery—the moral authority of ancestral heroes—is clear. The Batek Baris/Telek dance, on the other hand, is considered a dramatization of the Sasak founding myth (regardless of the figures involved). The performance symbolizes the coming of the deity and hero, links this figure with Java, Islam, and several legends simultaneously, and stakes a claim for authority over the temple and festival (see Chapter Five). While Topeng Sidha Karya occurs only once, and sometimes not at all, the Batek/Telek dance is enacted several times.

Falassi (ibid.:4–5) mentions two other standard festival events: "rites of reversal," where social roles are reversed or inverted; and "rites of competition," often symbolic games that create a cathartic moment among the other rites. Both these ritual types appear to be squeezed into the Perang Topat at Lingsar. Although social roles are not reversed so that nobles are treated like commoners or vice versa, no social roles are acknowledged during the "war of the rice squares." Commoners throw *topat* at nobles and other commoners alike, while nobles do the same. Farmers throw at each other and at educated leaders, who throw at each other and back at them; tourists are also frequent targets. Gdé Mandia, the current head of the Balinese organization Parisadha Hindu Dharma, stated that getting hit by *topat* is like getting blessed.

It could be that at one time Balinese were on one side of the courtyard (outside the *gadoh*) while Sasak were on the other (outside the *kemaliq*); some tourist information states that this is the case. However, although there is a larger concentration of Balinese on the north side, there is a mixture of Balinese and Sasak on the south side. The Perang Topat realizes one goal of the festival: ethnic and social unity. It is this unity that constitutes antistructure, as ethnic friction and social division dissolve into ethnic harmony, unity of purpose, and fun. This unity is evident throughout much of the festival, but reaches its zenith during the Perang Topat.

For most participants and especially for the farmers, the festival provides an opportunity to directly sense the deities that control the rain and prosperity of the area, and to acquire boons. In addition to the blessed *topat*, holy water is available from the altars in the *gadoh* and *kemaliq* and from the *momot* bottle. The divinely manifest water can be used to sprinkle into irrigation dikes or around trees or other plants, with a promise of a fertile, prosperous harvest. Most people, however, drink and ritually cleanse themselves with this water; it is believed to prevent or cure disease. For some Sasak, the water is considered a magical gift from the ancestral hero. The *kemaliq*, like other remaining Waktu Telu shrines, is a monument dedicated to remembering legendary events and ancestors; it is also an institution to acquire favors and to obtain the ancestors' help and repay them for benefits received (see Polak 1978:340).[28]

I submit, however, that remembering the precise events and names of the ancestors is not as important as the act of participation. It is ritual action by the farmers (particularly preparing the *topat* and other offerings) that is their form of worship, and this action helps guarantee fertility and rainwater. Farmers and rural Sasak from remote areas of Lombok may have different understandings of the myth and the role of the temple and its festival, but they believe that the temple and their participation in the festival can affect transformations in the natural world and impact directly upon their lives.

Sasak participation probably began to decrease at Lingsar in the early twentieth century in response to the emergence of orthodox Islam, Dutch policies, and the resulting decline of the Waktu Telu. Later Indonesian policies and the actions of local Islamic organizations, religious leaders in regional government, the slaughter of 1965–1966, and religious registration have doubtless encouraged the downward spiral of Sasak involvement.

In the 1980s the government earmarked Lingsar as a tourist destination and the festival as a protected and encouraged event. Sasak from both nearby and remote areas have since either returned or come for the first time. Waktu Telu from nearby and northern areas come to Lingsar to worship centralized ancestral powers. These people, with similar takes on history, are easily recognized by their "traditional" clothing. Those from eastern, southern, and urban areas seem inspired to attend for differing reasons. Rahil, a late Waktu Telu leader from Lenek in East Lombok, told me that he felt Lingsar was a particularly powerful place. He was aware of the popular Sasak myth, though he had his own ideas about the temple's history. He believed that connecting with natural powers (i.e., the springs) and with the deities, and generating harmony with the local Balinese were the main goals of the festival.

When asked why they come, most respondents from outside West Lombok simply say that they have a garden or that their family has a history of participation or that they heard about Perang Topat. Their individual histories and positions in the ritual frame are diverse, and few come from families with generations of festival experience. Many Sasak from urban areas stand on the periphery and simply absorb the event. Some of these are modern Muslims, and, though they do not share in the beliefs inherent in the Sasak rites, they come to watch the spectacle and to participate in the Perang Topat, which can be viewed as an entertaining secular event. It seems that many Sasak generate their own meanings.

While most who are truly Waktu Telu participants are old or uneducated farmers, a number of young people also participate in the processions and the Perang Topat. I am uncertain where many of these people position themselves on the

Waktu Telu-Waktu Lima continuum. The Sasak are being encouraged to attend the event as a traditional secular event disconnected from religious beliefs. Though this has increased Sasak participation and many new participants are younger and disengaged from religious practices (e.g., prayers), others come to actively participate and embrace the belief structure. One man who came for the first time in 1988 mentioned that he wanted to make vows for the health of his family. From my observations these latter participants are moderates (normative Muslims) who maintain some traditional beliefs while also following the formal tenets of Islam. Several interpreted their experience at the festival in an Islamic light.

One such individual told me, *"Allah memberikan tempat ini untuk memuja"* (Allah gave us this place to worship). This statement articulates the feelings of many participants—that this traditional shrine was bestowed upon the Sasak as a way to worship God—and it confirms both traditional and Islamic perspectives on the meanings of the temple. Because the festival is now promoted and protected, moderates and nominal Muslims will not be harassed for participation; their participation is welcomed.[29] The recent efforts to reinterpret the founding myth and further Islamify aspects of the festival have made the event more acceptable to the general public. Several teachers, including Sanusi, have also mapped Islamic numerology onto temple structures to ease a transition to further Islamic interpretation (see Chapter Six). The current intraethnic Sasak tolerance toward the festival is unprecedented over the last hundred years, though most believe that participants attend out of a cultural obligation, not because of religious beliefs.

Most Balinese I've spoken with hold that Pura Lingsar is the most important temple in Lombok. Like the Sasak, the Balinese participants have various reasons for attending the festival, but all of these reasons appear somewhat connected to religious beliefs. Those who are farmers come because the festival is a *subak* event and the temple governs both when seedlings are transplanted into the rice fields and the flow of irrigation water. Farmers are also obligated to prepare *topat* and participate in the Perang Topat. Afterwards, they collect the blessed *topat* and perhaps some holy water to place into their fields. For agriculturists who do not receive irrigation water from Lingsar, it is still the temple to pray to the deities who are thought to "control" (*kuasai*) or "hold" (*pegang*) the rain and fertility of the island. For all Balinese related to the founders of the temple and the first mission from Bali, attendance is obligatory to remember their ancestors and the unification of Bali and Lombok. For urban and educated Balinese, the festival is an opportunity to pray to God and His manifestations.

Many other Balinese attend to regain a sense of identity. One teacher, Kartawirya, once said, *"Di mana bisa dapat déwa-déwi yang lebih kuat?"* (Where can you find more powerful deities?) The altar structure in the *gadoh* is unique to Lingsar: Batara Gunung Agung, the highest deity on Bali, and his son, Batara Alit Sakti, who directed the Balinese to Lombok, are revered next to Batara Gunung Rinjani, the highest deity on Lombok, and Batara Gedé Lingsar, the powerful natural deity who guided the Balinese to victory and is the source of fertility on the island, channeling the power of Batara Wisnu. The transplanted Balinese reestablish their community and remember who they are, where they come from, and how and why they live on Lombok. The past is honored and refocused into the present, and participants seem renewed and refreshed by the experience. Many participants also come from Bali, where the festival has grown popular in media reports. Some of these hail from East Bali and have a connection to families and traditions in Lombok, others are intellectuals who study religion and spirituality, several hope to collect holy water, and still others are simply curious.

Ritual Competency

"Siapa saja boleh bersembayang di sini" (Anyone can worship here), said Sanusi; Balinese officials concurred. All participants of whatever persuasion can pray at Lingsar, and ceremonies may be conducted for anyone. Participation does not require a specialized knowledge, because congregants participate at their own level via their social, economic, religious, and ethnic frame.

All participants are not equal, of course. The arrangement when sitting before altars, the interaction with officials, the level of participation and potential benefits, and the ceremonial clothing worn all signal the different status of individuals. Clothing is particularly indicative. The altars and the stones in the *kemaliq* altar are all clothed and anthropomorphized as elegant and noble participants, and the musics establish frameworks that ennoble higher castes. The wealthier and high-caste individuals have access to more refined clothing and greater ritual knowledge and benefits. Agung Biarsah wears his powerful heirloom kris (dagger) and sits before the main altar; no one sits in front of him, and the performance of the festival legitimizes his legacy. One Sasak, Haziz, wears the white cap that marks him as *haji*; he says that this shows who he is and where he has been, but it also demonstrates that he had the resources to go to Mecca and he is addressed respectfully by other participants. There is no conflict in his mind between orthodox Islam and his participation at Lingsar.[30] Despite the inequalities, the festival overall is representative; that is, the priests conduct rites and performers perform for the benefit of everyone, for increasing the capacity of the Earth, and for bringing rainwater to the irrigation channels and rice fields. In these, everyone shares.

There are three functional days of the festival: the opening, main, and final days, with two "empty" days before the final day. Some Balinese state that the duration of five days is important to align the life of the festival with the four cardinal directions and the center (the main day). The three functional days align the festival with the concept of birth, life, and death, which are associated with the opening, main, and final days, respectively. Ida Padanda Ketut Rai indicated that the rites of the *padanda* called *upiti* (birth), *setiti* (life), and *pralina* (death) equate the meaning of the day with the life of the festival. The three-ness that pervades the festival is also found in the three occasions for circumambulating the *kemaliq* altar structures (each occasion including three circumambulations); the three circumambulations of the *gadoh* altars; the three circumambulations of the temple complex; the three·spatial levels within offerings; and the Hindu Trinity of Brahma, Wisnu, and Siwa, whose functions are giving life, preserving life, and terminating life, which in turn relates back to *upiti*, *setiti*, and *pralina*. This three-ness, along with a complimentary duality and other cosmological elements, is believed to exist within the music, the musical instruments, and the very temple itself. These ideas are largely shared with active Waktu Telu, and they inform much of the music.

CHAPTER FIVE

Music: History, Cosmology, and Content

THE IDEA OF meaning in music assumes that a given music embodies semiotic messages or constructs or reinforces in sound organization concepts of social order, gender, religion, or identity recognized by culture members. These points are primarily reflective; that is, music may express a common sentiment or reflect or represent the given social order of its listeners and producers. Music is not, of course, limited to a reflective parameter of meaning, and no performance "can have exactly the same meaning for every listener or every performer" since ". . . the meanings of the gamelan or in dance performances are multiple, many-layered and constantly shifting" (Becker 1993:1). The "meanings" of the varieties of music at Lingsar that have been reported to me have indeed shifted or changed over time, just as the participants and officials, myths, liturgy, and my own interpretive lens have altered over time.[1]

Any discussion of musical meaning must also address the interpretive process of its discovery. I propose that content, context, and function synergize to create meaning in music, meaning that may derive both from acknowledged homologies (or other reflective or iconic properties) and from musically constructed frameworks for behaviors and experiences to happen. Those particular behaviors and experiences then become associated with a given music (content and contextualization) and provide foreknowledge for future interpretations and experiences with that and other musics. This foreknowledge generates expectations for the next encounter in a hermeneutic process that progressively develops mature ritual behavior and meaningful associations with particular musics and contextual simultaneities.

Context, a prime determinant of meaning, influences and shapes musical performance; a given composition will have different meanings in different contexts and may be performed differently as well (see Qureshi 1986, 1987). Content, of course, is fundamental in positing any ideas about meaning. Function is still another integral element in the meaning of music, particularly at religious events such as Lingsar where the acknowledged function of a given music announces much of its meaning and shapes the interpretation of its performance.

This chapter follows a modified structuralist approach to situate both Balinese and Sasak music at Lingsar. I interpret some of the salient religious and political meanings as articulated by participants and pertinent literature, explore tensions of structure and reception, and analyze the music content in relation to homology, social order, and personal orientation. While some music issues such as narrative apply equally to Balinese and Sasak forms, others such as cosmology for the Balinese or conflict and identity for the Sasak, are more specific to one or the other.

CONCEPTUAL FRAMEWORK OF GAMELAN MUSIC

Like other forms of music, gamelan music—whether Javanese, Balinese, or Sasak—reflects the culture and the people who produce it. Becker (1979:197) asserts:

> All music systems are infused with the concepts and systems of organization of the surrounding society, concepts which are also manifested in other systems of the society. The same concepts which control the organization of other kinds of experience within a culture control the organization of music and determine the selection of a limited pool of elements from the infinite possibilities of acoustic sound. Music systems are but one way in which the people of a given culture conceptualize and make sense of their world.

Music systems are thus related to other systems in any culture, and the formulations of other cultural experiences are related to those found within the organization of musical sound. While not always a crucial argument, in religious settings this interconnectedness between music and other systems helps formulate religious experience and behavior.

Gamelan music has often been observed as embodying social values and order in Javanese and Balinese cultures (see Keeler 1975), though more studies of extramusical significance have centered on cosmology. The music of cultures influenced by Hindu or Buddhist cosmological doctrine seem in general to exhibit a high degree of such symbolism. Gamelan music, as a presentation of the ordering of sound, is a "dynamic and ethereal phenomenon" and an "appropriate and natural cosmological symbol" (Simms 1993:68–69).

Music, Time, and Cosmology

> In Java, the fundamental governing principle in gamelan music is the cyclic
> recurrence of a melodic/temporal unit, which is a musical manifestation of
> the way in which the passage of time is also ordered. In Java, time is repre-
> sented as cyclical. (Becker 1979:198)

Javanese, Balinese, and Sasak gamelan music utilize cyclic or regenerative
phrase structures, and these cultures traditionally acknowledge the passage of time
as cyclic (linear time is, of course, also recognized and now prominent). The traditional calendars used by the Javanese, Balinese, and Sasak interweave and coincide
at structural points of determined significance, just as do the gamelan traditions.
Gamelan music, with its construction of time and musical parts of differing
lengths continuously cycling and coinciding at specific moments, has an "iconic"
relationship with these calendars. The points of coincidence of the several concurrent cycles in both calendars and music have special "power," where the energies
of special days or of musical parts synergize to create special moments in time.
Becker and Becker (1981:207) say:

> . . . the most prominent feature of iconic power in Javanese or Balinese
> music is coincidence—small coincidence and large coincidence—small
> coincidings and large coincidings of cycling sounds, all iconic with the cycles
> of calendars and cosmos and thus . . . completely "natural."

The "natural" passage of time in musical and cosmological conception is therefore conceived as a cyclic configuration within which are smaller and larger
cyclings coinciding at special points of emphases. Smaller cycles move within
larger cycles, and points of cycle coincidence mark important moments of time
in both gamelan music and calendar systems.

Time cycles are divided, then subdivided, then subdivided again, and can be
subdivided further with increasingly more specific purposes, and this telescoping
subdivision is represented in the instrumental parts and phrase structures of
gamelan music. This method of dividing and subdividing time and acknowledging points of coincidence is seen in an individual Balinese life cycle, where particular days are selected to mark and celebrate stages in life (birth, name-giving,
hair-clipping, tooth-filing, marriage, death) because of the auspicious coincidings
(and thus greater specificity) of time cycles on those days. Just as certain days coincide to mark important moments in a person's life cycle, tonal coincidings occur
within the cycle of the largest time frame in gamelan music and mark the moments
of emphases (Becker & Becker 1981:210). Gamelan music therefore draws "power"
and "beauty" by its statement of the reality of the passage of time as it occurs
within nature, life, and the cosmos.

DeVale and Dibia (1991) have suggested that Balinese gamelan music can be
mapped onto village social order and onto the central puppet (*kayonan*) used in

wayang kulit, two other ideas of music reflecting underlying values and referencing related symbology. In another work, DeVale (1977) asserts that gamelan music structure is a metaphor for cosmic structure, homologous with those of other art forms such as batik, the design and morphology of gamelan instruments, and the meditation gardens of Javanese nobility. Though some of the homology concepts advanced by DeVale and Becker are not supported by local voices, the ideas generally resonate with my observations and are confirmed by several teachers. Some Balinese musicians and scholars are attracted to these notions; in both Bali and Lombok some have concurred that strong links connect music, calendrical time, art and architectural structure, and cosmology. These ideas are more stretched in Sasak gamelan music because fewer instruments are creating internal coincidences. However, several Sasak, including elder musicians Rahil and Saparia, "see" a relationship between Sasak music, time, and cosmological structure. Reformist Sasak leaders clearly sense the connection between music, indigenous belief, and Hindu-Buddhist concepts. Several have attempted to ban the cyclic, referential gamelan music in an effort to prevent its potential influence and to encourage the formulation of an oppositional musical premise founded instead on Islamic principles.

Becker and Becker (1981:164) have referred to ritual gamelan music as an aural mandala, an aural structure of the cosmos or sonic cosmogram.[2] I (1991b) have called gamelan music an active ritual offering and sacred soundscape, and DeVale (1991:256) has defined it as a form of psychocosmogony, a spatiotemporal re-creation of the self and cosmos where the microcosm and macrocosm are re-created as one. Tenzer (1998:21) suggests that the periodic and regenerative structures of gamelan melodies are apt metaphors for the life, death, and reincarnation cycles associated with Hindu beliefs. Gamelan music, in this reflective mode, embodies concepts of the passage of time as well as a wide range of multidimensional aural symbols that express or reflect particular aspects of cosmology and reality. This homology paradigm also holds that similar underlying patterns are found within the structure of temples, villages, noble houses, religious offerings, and ritual formulas. While this paradigm has some bearing on music and its meaning at Lingsar, it should be flexible rather than fixed since cosmological ideas are also flexible and prone to reinterpretation.

BALINESE MUSIC: STRUCTURING COSMOLOGY

Among Balinese, much of this flexibility of the homology paradigm is embodied in the notion of *desa/kala/patra*, where the place, time, and circumstance determines the appropriate activity and its interpretation (see Chapter Seven).

Concepts Underlying Balinese Music

Two *lontar* manuscripts, the *Prakempa* and *Aji Gurnita*, provide a more indigenous perspective on homologies, and both define music as divinely constructed. The

Prakempa, apparently written sometime during the nineteenth century, states that Sang Hyang Tri Wisesa (God; the union of Brahma, Wisnu, Siwa) created the Earth through yoga and gave "voice," sound, color, written syllables, and directions to the dark, desert-like world (Bandem 1986:31). Colors, deities, voices, and musical tones were ascribed to directions, their subdivisions, and the center, and there then emerged and combined ten voices throughout the cosmos. Five of these became the scale *pélog* and five became the scale *slendro*.[3] The essence of these ten voices or tones, which created a union between the god Semara (represented by *pélog*) and the goddess Ratih (*slendro*), further merged into seven tones (from which both could derive) that unified the three worlds of the macrocosms (*akasa* [sky], *pertiwi* [earth], *apah* [water]), called *suara genta pinara pitu* (ibid.:34–35). Out of this seven-tone system emerged the gamelan *gambuh* (called *meladprana* in this *lontar*), from which other Balinese musical systems originate.

Bandem (ibid.:11) asserts that the gamelan (here spelled "gambelan," the original Balinese word) and music cannot be separated from the balance of Balinese life and that they harmonize humans with God, nature, and with all humankind. He lists ten philosophical "dimensions" that create harmony within humankind, and several of these dimensions unite cosmological and religious systems with musical systems. Music has a special relationship with religion and cosmology; it is developed upon structural elements shared with cosmology and has an efficacy to transform reality (time and space) and to create balance and harmony.

In the *Aji Gurnita*, Balinese gamelans are related to one of the gods of the four directions (Vickers 1985:146), and musical tones are connected with mystical syllables that give expression to the universe and allow humans to commune and achieve balance with the divine. Ramstedt (1993:78–80), elaborating on the idea, suggests that music and ritual express and support a balanced universal order (dharma), thereby preventing chaos (*adharma*). This order provides reference points for individual, social, and political action, and presents modes of behavior and attitude to which culture members aspire. The Balinese have granted music the role of embodying and sustaining these ontological foundations of their society (Tenzer 1998:16); it serves to help balance the cosmos and provide moral guidance.

Both *Prakempa* and *Aji Gurnita* describe the sensual aspect of music—how the male/female binarism as realized by the god Semara and goddess Ratih and their sexual union (two into one) as king and queen inform musical systems.[4] Semara is represented by white sperm, the five waters, and the five *pélog* tones, while Ratih is represented by red essence, the five fires, and the five *slendro* tones. Together these ten tones, which represent the four cardinal directions, their subdivisions, and the two centers (Siwa and Buddha; other times considered different names for the same center), turn existence and the cosmos (Bandem 1986:43). Music creates one out of the binary relationship of male and female (and through extension, other binarisms), and unifies the three divisions within the macrocosm and the microcosm and the cardinal points to invoke the spiritual center. Musical tones and their arrangement are joined with syllables (with which mantra ritual formulas are

TABLE 5.1. Relationship of Musical Tones with Other Phenomena

TONE	DIRECTION	GOD	COLOR
dang	east	Iswara	white
ding	south	Brahma	red
deng	west	Mahadéwa	yellow
dung	north	Wisnu	black
dong	center	Siwa	polycolor

chanted), gods, colors, directions, and love, and, through performance, music creates balance with the cosmos. The "voices" of many instruments are also conceived as having counterpoints in the neck and head (ibid.:71–75), representing internal psychic energies which are also balanced through performance.

The *Prakempa* declares that whoever fails to carry out required procedures or disrupts the balance inherent in music and the cosmos is punished by being sent to hell (*neraka*). Teachers have often mentioned that ritual music and musical instruments embody power, and that the instruments must be treated with respect and positioned correctly, and that the performance must proceed according to schedule and with as few mistakes as possible. Accordingly, there are a number of taboos and sanctions surrounding ritual gamelan in Bali (and Java and Lombok) that prevent the spiritual pollution or imbalance that invites chaos and danger (*adharma*), and is avoided at all cost. Music and gamelan constitute a supernatural and relatively secret (nonpublic) science, and require knowledge and training to perform properly. Many Balinese and Sasak teachers at Lingsar discussed this issue. The music is treated with respect, as its inherent power can turn negative if the instruments are not properly treated or if someone trespasses upon one of sanctions or taboos of performance. Parman, for example, mentioned that several women experienced miscarriages because they had approached the gamelan *baris* when they were impure (*sebel*), i.e., menstruating.

I believe that "knowledge" of music implies power similar to the notion of the knowledge that empowers the priestly caste as mediators of the gods. The following diagram, taken from the *Prakempa*, indicates the relationship of the five *pélog* musical tones in Balinese music (*dang, ding, deng, dung, dong*) with five cardinal directions, gods, and ceremonial colors.[5] The formulas of priests are, in fact, very similar in design, and priests must always assign sounds and deities to the cardinal directions for their rituals to achieve efficacy. Table 5.1 shows the relationship of the tones to various phenomena.

I do not mean by this discussion to exoticize the festival and its participants. The *Prakempa* and *Aji Gurnita* are court manuscripts primarily concerned with refined court gamelans and the esoteric interpretations of music. They appear to have been written by courtly scribes of the *brahmana* caste who sought to enhance the mysticism and beauty of courtly arts to ennoble the kings. There is very little practical musical information in these treatises, and they are not meant as manuals for musicians. In fact, they were probably never intended for musicians (not commoners at least), and many—perhaps most—musicians even today have never heard of these treatises. The texts, however, link music directly with cosmology and religion, and discuss function, efficacy, and context, and these concepts are useful for understanding the festival. Both manuscripts also mention the gamelan *gong* and gamelan *bebonangan*, which equate respectively with the gamelans *gong kuna* and gong *gilak* (and *baleganjur*) in Lombok.

According to both *lontar*s, the gamelan *gong*, created by the priests of the skies, is associated with the heavens. It symbolizes the sound of the collection of the priests and the nine gods (unifying the cosmos) in the heavens, and the great sound of the gamelan shakes the stratosphere and attracts them all together (Bandem 1986:89). This function is replicated at Balinese temple festivals where the gamelan *gong* calls together the deities of the cosmos and of the locale, who are attracted by its powerful sound. The music also draws the human participants and marks the development of the festival. The musical instruments represent cosmological, extramusical ideas; for example, the large gong symbolizes heaven and the unity of the Brahma, Wisnu, and Siwa spheres, while the smaller hanging gong represents the "collection of all that is pure" (ibid.:61). Discussions below address how these ideas are acknowledged in the Balinese music at Lingsar, but these are not the only loci of meaning for many participants also see the music as a framework prone to multiple interpretations in generating actions and transformations.

Gamelan *Gong Kuna*

The gamelan *gong kuna*, the main ceremonial ensemble of the Lombok Balinese, is a gamelan *gong*-type orchestra and a smaller counterpart to Bali's gamelan *gong gedé*. In Bali, few complete *gong gedé* survive; most were melted down and reforged as modern gamelan *gong kebyar*.[6] In Lombok there remain six complete *gong kuna* (a seventh was "returned" to Bali) and two or more incomplete ensembles; at least a few others were melted down or destroyed by the Japanese, Dutch, or Sasak.[7] Teachers state that these ensembles were associated with the Lombok courts during Balinese rule, just as the *gong gedé* were owned by courts in Bali. The gamelans were needed to perform at major temple festivals (such as Lingsar, which became a state ceremony), for life-cycle rituals of the nobility and for meetings between kings and princes of the seven noble houses in Lombok.

The Lombok Balinese *lontar Pegambuhan* shows that the courts supported other courtly performing arts such as *gambuh* theater, and teachers state that the courts held two or more *Semar pegulingan* court gamelans. However, nothing remains of these gamelans and their traditions in Lombok. When the Balinese courts were defeated in 1894, all courtly traditions vanished. The remaining gamelan *gong kuna* were probably passed on to the neighboring wards of the noble houses, just as the gamelan *gong gedé* and other court orchestras were passed from courts to villages in Bali following the final Dutch military victory in 1908.

Gong kuna instruments consist of two large hanging gongs called *gong ageng* (a "male," *lanang*, and a lower-pitched "female," *wadon*); one smaller hanging gong, *kempul* (normally *kempur* in Bali); a horizontally mounted kettle-gong called *kempli*; two *kendang* double-headed drums (*lanang* and *wadon*); usually eight resting-bar metallophones collectively called *gangsa jongkok*; two large *jegogan* suspended-bar metallophones; a single row gong chime of ten kettles called *trompong*; a single row gong chime of twelve kettles called *barangan* (or *trompong barangan*); from two to six sets of cymbals generically called *ceng-ceng*; and sometimes an additional hanging gong called *bendé* (Harnish 1992:38).[8]

Today, *gong gedé* and *gong kuna* are performed primarily at temple festivals, and at life-cycle rituals if the host family can afford the usual compensation of transportation and cigarettes, drinks, and snacks for the players. Both are tuned to the scale *selisir*, a hemitonic pentatonic tonality derived from the heptatonic *pélog* parent scale (often called *saih pitu*), although there is neither a concept of fixed pitch nor of absolute intervalic structure (see Tenzer 2000:27–33).

The *gong kuna* repertoire, like that of the *gong gedé*, consists of two types of compositions (*tabuh, gending*) usually called *gangsaran* (fast, "fluent" pieces) and *lelambatan* (slow pieces; also called *gending ageng* [great pieces]). *Gending gong* and *pegongan* also refer to the repertoire, particularly to *lelambatan* pieces. Very few *gangsaran* pieces are played in Lombok, and, in fact, the term *gangsaran* is not understood by many musicians. Performances often include only a single *gangsaran*, usually the *gending* "Macan Angelur" (Shouting tiger),[9] or "Longgor" (Burning tree). *Gangsaran* pieces are generally played at fast tempi and utilize a phrase structure of eight pulses per gong stroke; melodies, however, are not usually restricted to a single gong cycle and may extend over as many as four gong strokes (thirty-two beats) as in the case of "Macan Angelur." *Lelambatan* compositions, on the other hand, make up the primary repertoire. Pieces may include up to 128 core melody pulses per gong stroke, and the complete melody is both concluded and initiated with the gong. It is the *lelambatan* repertoire that most clearly embodies structures based on cosmological design. Mangku Saka, using terms such as *mikrokosm* (microcosm), *makrokosm* (macrocosm), and *alam semesta* (universe), stated that this repertoire expresses cosmic order and attempts to impose that order when performed in context.

Specific terms define the forms of *lelambatan* pieces. The term *tabuh* (to beat, strike, play music) is generally followed by a number denoting the number of *kempul* and (particularly) *kempli* strokes per gong stroke, or *gongan*.[10] For example, *tabuh empat* (four strokes) means that there are four *kempul* and *kempli* strokes per *gongan*, and also that there are sixty-four core melody or *pokok* (trunk) beats per *gongan*. There are 16 beats between *kempul* strokes, the *kempul* on beats 8, 24, 40, and 56,[11] and 16 beats between *kempli* strokes, the *kempli* on beats 16, 32, 48, and 64. The repertoire on both islands consists of pieces in the *tabuh empat, tabuh enam* (six strokes, 96 beats), and *tabuh kutus* (eight strokes, 128 beats) phrase structures. These terms convey to the musicians both the number of *kempul* and *kempli* strokes and the *pokok* tones per *gongan*.

Lelambatan in Lombok consist of *pengawit* ("what comes first," the mostly free meter introduction; also called *kawitan*), *pengawak* ("body," the main part of the piece), *penyibit* ("squeezed," a melody in higher register),[12] *peniba* or *pengiba* (from *kiwa*, meaning "left"; a short, fast section), and the *pengecet* ("additional," an allegretto), which leads to the final gong stroke and conclusion of the piece. Of these, the *pengawit*, *pengawak*, and *pengecet* constitute the basic form of *lelambatan* compositions; other parts are subsumed within one of these sections. Playing style and additional transitional sections distinguish Lombok versions from those of Bali.

Among the sections the *pengawak* is the most important. When names are given to the pieces—"Kabar Alus" (Good news), "Tuhu-tuhu Dara" (Sincere maiden), "Nangis Buleleng" (The cry of Buleleng), "Madu Kara" (Red honey), "Galang Kangin" (Light in the east)—they apply to the *pengawak*. In Lombok most clubs know the titles of relatively few pieces and tend to refer to compositions as *"tabuh* this" or *"tabuh* that." The *pengawak* is the largest part of any *gending*; its performance comprises well over 50 percent of a piece. Other metric sections are sometimes seen as contractions of the *pengawak*.

As part of the punctuation, the two *jegogan* bass metallophones stress the *pokok* melody, usually at a one-to-four ratio to the *pokok* realized by the *gangsa jongkok*. If we take a sixty-four-beat *tabuh empat* form (the most common), the *jegogan* are sounded on beats four, eight, twelve, sixteen, and so forth, a total of sixteen times at four-beat intervals; the *kempul* is struck on beats eight, twenty-four, forty, and fifty-six, and the *kempli* is sounded on beats sixteen, thirty-two, forty-eight, and sixty-four. The *jegogan* coincides with both *kempul* and *kempli*, and falls on an additional eight structural beats without other punctuation. Figure 5.1 provides a visual display of the punctuation of the *gong ageng*, *kempul*, and *kempli* within *tabuh empat*, and Figure 5.2 adds the *jegogan* and core melody. For these figures, G = gong, P = *kempul*, K = *kempli*, and J = *jegogan*.

From these figures we can see that the *kempli* strokes divide the *gongan* into four equal parts; one stroke coincides with the *gong*, further emphasizing the main point of coincidence in the cycle. The *kempul* strokes subdivide the four *kempli* divisions, resulting in eight equal points (four *kempli* and four *kempul*) in the *gongan*. The circular display demonstrates the similarity between a *gong* cycle and the cardinal directions and their subdivisions—the *kempli* indicating the cardinal points and the *kempul* their subdivisions.

The *jegogan* strokes add another layer of punctuation (see Figure 5.2) and equally subdivide the *kempul* and *kempli* cycles, indicating further points of coincidence on every *gong*, *kempli*, and *kempul* stroke, and dividing the *gong* cycle into sixteen equal parts. These large, five-keyed instruments are struck simultaneously by one player and tuned slightly apart to create a large beat or vibrato (*ombak*). While most other Balinese gamelans are known for the shimmering effect created by the *ombak*, in *gong kuna* only *jegogan* present this feature. The figure shows the relationship between *jegogan*, *gong*s, and core melody (*pokok*).

The eight five-keyed *gangsa jongkok* ("squatting bronze") play the *pokok* and are tuned at the same pitch; they come in three sizes and octaves. There are four

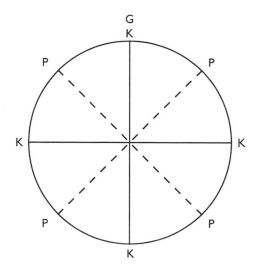

FIGURE 5.1. Basic punctuation primary gongs in *tabuh empat*

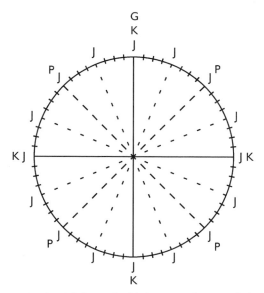

FIGURE 5.2. Basic punctuation *tabuh empat*, with *jegogan* and core melody

middle-octave and two high and two low metallophones. Four musicians each play a pair of instruments: either one low- and one middle-octave instrument, or one middle- and one high-octave instrument.

The solo *trompong* gong-chime performer plays the *pengawit* introduction alone, then ornaments the *pokok* played by the *gangsa jongkok* in the *pengawak* and other metric sections, frequently as an expanded reiteration. For all major points within a *gongan*, the *trompong* performs a tonal coincidence with the *pokok*, further emphasizing these points in the structure. The instrumentalist often coincides with the melody at other points as well, but can add embellishments between the melody beats as appropriate. *Trompong* performance adds another layer of melody and a subdivision to the phrase structure.

Table 5.2 indicates the flow from section to section of virtually any *lelambatan* composition among all *gong kuna* groups. (Numbers of some repetitions and tempi are, of course, prone to change.) It begins with the *pengawit* introduction and features statements of the *pengawak* (and *penyibit* alteration), then moves through several transitional sections (*pelainan, peniba, tabuh gangsar*), and eventually concludes with the *pengecet*. The *pengawak/penyibit* alternation is by far the largest portion of the piece and has the slowest tempo. The *pengecet* section condenses the punctuation and repeats a melody many times while accelerating. Three numbered sections constitute the basic form. The tempi of the various sections normally accelerate going in to a new section, and ritard after settling into the new or repeated section.[13]

DeVale and Dibia (1991:35), among other foreign and Balinese scholars, assert that the three basic compositional sections (*pengawit, pengawak, pengecet*) have anthropomorphic associations with the head, body, and leg/foot, respectively; a contention supported by the meaning of the terms themselves (see below). The form follows the tripartite structures of the macrocosm and microcosm, of musical instrument morphology (see DeVale 1977), as well as those of offerings, temples, pavilions, and other types of architectural design. Tenzer (1990) describes this

TABLE 5.2. *Lelambatan* Composition in *Tabuh Empat* Phrase Structure

SECTION		NUMBER OF GONGAN	BEATS PER GONGAN	TEMPO (GENERAL) POKOK = MM
1. *Pengawit*		none	none	none
2. *Pengawak*		1, 1/2	64	60
	Pelainan	1/2	32	73
	Penyibit	2	64	68
	Pengawak	1, 1/2	64	64
	Pelainan	1/2	32	77
	Penyibit	7/8	56	72
	Pelainan	1/8	8	73
	Tabuh Gangsar	2	32	73
	Pelainan	1	8	67
	Peniba	10	8	64
3. *Pengecet*		many 10s	8	110–123

TABLE 5.3. Density Ratio *Gong Kuna* Instruments to Gong Stroke in *Pengawak*

INSTRUMENT	DENSITY RATIO
ceng-ceng and *barangan*	512:1
trompong	128:1 or 256:1
gangsa jongkok (*pokok*)	64:1
jegogan	16:1
kempul and *kempli*	4:1
gong ageng	1:1

three-part music form as a metaphorical journey from the mountain through the middle world to the sea, thus moving from the most sacred to the most secular sphere and evoking the same cosmic structure that informs temple designs. The nonmetric *pengawit* section (head, mountain) may be interpreted as related to non-metric sacred chant, the most sacred of musical arts. The *pengawak* is the body, where the main part of the piece is realized. An increase in tempo marks the *penge-cet* (foot, sea), and the phrase structure contracts and takes on the punctuation of *gong gilak* pieces related to underworld spirits; the *pengecet* section also gradually accelerates over the numerous repeats. This completes the journey from the mountain to the sea or from the head to the foot (from most sacred to least sacred), and also from slowest to fastest, constituting both metaphor and homol-ogy in the form of a *gending*. Culture expert Ida Wayan Pasha confirmed that the performance of these pieces is like such a journey.

The drummers are the ensemble leaders responsible for establishing tempo and for signaling a composition's transitions and conclusions. The *kendang lanang* (male) player generally plays a pattern working with the main beat (*polos* = basic), and the *kendang wadon* (female) player plays a pattern working off of the main beat (*sangsih* = other), with the two together forming an interlocking figure. This con-cept of two gender-associated, interlocking parts is replicated on the twelve kettle *barangan* gong chime, which is played in continuous figuration by four men at an eight-to-one ratio with the *pokok* during most of the piece and four-to-one ratio during the *pengecet*. Two men play a *polos* part at two different octaves, while two others play the *sangsih* part at two different octaves.

The cymbal or *ceng-ceng* section normally includes a *ceng-ceng* or smaller *rincik*, a set which includes two upturned cymbals on a base that are struck with counter-parts held by the performer in each hand, along with a single, larger cymbal on a base struck with its counterpart. The *ceng-ceng* or *rincik* is played at the fastest den-sity referent (the fastest pulse) along with the *barangan*: eight-to-one with the *pokok* during the *pengawak*, and four-to-one during the *pengecet*. Occasionally, smaller cymbals are also included.

Table 5.3 presents the density ratios of the instruments of the *gong kuna* to the gong stroke in a *tabuh empat* structure. The table indicates the layers of activity for all the instruments, beginning with the most frequently played but least important, the *ceng-ceng*, and ending with the least frequently played but most important, the *gong ageng*. The table illustrates the cyclings and coincidences within the music.

The table also shows the 512:1 ratio between the *barangan*/*ceng-ceng* and *gong ageng* in *tabuh empat*. In *tabuh enam*, the ratio is 768:1 and in *tabuh kutus* 1,024:1, thus providing ever smaller cycles rotating within larger cycles. Figure 5.3 illustrates these cyclings within one-quarter of a *gongan* (one *kempli* cycle); these provide the framework for structural homologies.

The program of pieces at festivals usually begins with the *gangsaran* "Macan Angelur." Afterwards a second *gangsaran* may be played or, more likely, one or more *tabuh empat* pieces, then a *tabuh enam* piece, followed by a *tabuh kutus* piece. Since *tabuh empat* pieces outnumber all others, more of them are played. If the *sekaha gong* does not know many pieces, they will play their repertoire, take a break, and then repeat the pieces in the same order, beginning with smaller forms and progressing to larger ones.

The late venerable priest Ida Padanda Ketut Rai, who conducted services at Lingsar for decades, thought that the ritual formulas of the high priest and the invocation of the deities, called *upiti* (birth), *setiti* (life), and *pralina* (death), relate to the creation, sustenance, and termination of music. The life of a composition

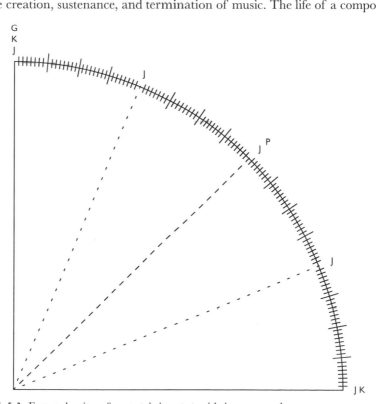

FIGURE 5.3. Fastest density referent, *tabuh empat*, with *barangan* and *ceng-ceng*

revolves around the gong, particularly the first and last strokes that create and terminate a piece. The Hindu Trinity mirrors this same tripartite formula—Brahma creates life, Wisnu sustains life, and Siwa destroys life. The *gong kuna*'s regenerative music can thus be seen to recreate this tripartite scheme, embodied in the three sections of a *lelambatan* piece. The music also works to unify male and female instruments and parts (*lanang/wadon* instruments; *polos/sangsih* figurations), and, through association, other binarisms (see Harnish 1997). This principle is reified within Balinese culture by the Semara/Ratih and *kaja/kelod* axes as well as by the term *rwa bhinnéda*, the dualism (and its resolution) that makes up the whole. While only the more philosophical Lombok Balinese discuss such connections, these individuals happen to be respected, elderly, intellectual artists such as Gedé Drawi, Wayan Wirya, and Ida Wayan Pasha.

I believe that it is through these structuring elements and cosmological homologies that the music can achieve its power and reflect an aural mandala representing the forces of dharma. Many participants hold that the music calls down deities and attest to the power of the gamelan to purify and balance individuals and the temple space. The focused contextualization of the music shapes experience because it reminds participants why they are present and can work as a vehicle for greater spiritual realization. As Kartawirya once said, the music "*sadari kami bahwa déwa-déwi datang*" (makes us aware that the deities have come).

Gamelan *Gong Gilak*

The processional *gong gilak* (excitement, fast gong) is also known in Bali, but the ensembles there are scarce and rarely differentiated from the gamelan *beleganjur* (war spirit) or gamelan *bebonangan* (kettle-gong) of Bali (see Bakan 1999). The Lombok *gong gilak* consists of the two *gong ageng*, *kempul*, and *kendang* instruments of the *gong kuna*, combined with a set of processional cymbals (*ceng-ceng kopyak*), a timekeeping kettle-gong called a *petuk*, and two small gong chimes of two kettle-gongs apiece called *réong*. This instrumentarium is virtually the same as that of the gamelan *beleganjur* of Bali; only the number and case of the kettle-gongs differ. Gamelan "*baleganjur*" (local spelling) also exist in Lombok and may substitute for *gong gilak*, but such groups do not include kettle-gongs.[14] The *Aji Gurnita* refers to an ensemble (*bebonangan*) with precisely the instrumentation and function of the *gong gilak* (see Vickers 1985:169).

In myth, the gamelan *baleganjur* was created for and is associated with spirits of the underworld (*buta kala*), in contrast with the gamelan *gong*, created for priests and gods. The functions and associations of these two ensembles form a zenith/nadir binarism not unlike others such as day/night, head/foot, and male/female. Participants have suggested two differing interpretations regarding the functions of the sonically powerful *baleganjur* music: the first, that they are meant to intimidate underworld spirits, and the second, that they invite the *buta kala* to the festival to be placated and transformed into helpful agents for successful completion of the festival. In either case any threat from underworld spirits or malevolent, *adharmic* forces is dissipated.

The *gong gilak* safeguards festival processions by proudly announcing the event with its martial quality and frightening off visible and invisible mischief-makers. Its performance creates a powerful and sacred aura that protects the procession as it moves from sacred, purified temple space into profane space. Mangku Gedog, who officiated at Pura Ulon for many years, stated that the music "*memperlingdungi kami di pawĕ*" (protects us in the procession) and expands the space of the temple into the environment. The *Aji Gurnita* asserts that the music is so powerful that when it is played, "the world feels like it is shaking to the sound of thunder"; and it functions to lead and magically protect soldiers in warfare, to glorify the weapons of state, and to accompany kings to meetings (Vickers 1985:165). The first two functions are realized by the gamelan protecting the procession and extending its purified space, while accompanying all the ritual implements and weapons (such as lances) of the temple. The third function was evident in Lombok long ago when such ensembles reportedly accompanied princes in processions to palaces. A few participants have stated that the music escorts deities in processions.

The repertoire, *gilakan*, refers to the strong, exciting nature of the pieces. McPhee (1966:94) considers *gilakan* the most condensed of the *gangsaran* forms. The players I have spoken with over the years seemed to concur; they conceived of the repertoire as short, powerful pieces derived from the gamelan *gong*. The pieces maintain values inherent in *lelambatan*, but are faster, livelier, and more repetitive. The phrase structure, identified by interlocking *réong* patterns, comprises eight beats per *gongan*; the form (*bentuk*) is identical with *pengecet* sections of *lelambatan* pieces. Balinese action pieces used in dance and theater employ similar forms, though the first *kempur* stroke on beat 3 (see below) is usually absent. *Gilak* music has aroused less cosmological speculation, but DeVale (personal communication) suggests that the quickly rotating and circulating pieces may constitute an intimidating cosmological statement—a notion echoed in different terms by local specialists such as Gedé Drawi and Ida Wayan Pasha. The *gong gilak* compositional phrase structure can be illustrated as follows, where G stands for *gong* and P for *kempul*:

	G	.	.	P	G	P	.	P	(G)
Beats:	8	1	2	3	4	5	6	7	(8)

The cymbals drop in and out of the cycles, entering in interlocking *polos-sangsih* figurations to intensify the music, but dropping out altogether in softer sections. The drums (both *lanang* and *wadon*) signal these changes to the musicians and indicate where the pieces should end. During a procession only one piece is generally played, and its tempo is roughly constant.

Eight-beat phrase structures are generally associated with strong or coarse natures, and with excitement and the inability to control one's emotions—qualities associated with underworld spirits or unrefined characters. The *lelambatan* and *gilakan* repertoires seem to symbolize their audiences and elements. The audience of *lelambatan* consists of deities and so the performance features large forms and multiple musical layers, while the audience of gilakan consists of underworld spirits and so the performance features small, rapid, and clearly delimited percussive cycles. The gamelans themselves form a functional, complementary duality.

Padanda and Genta

The *padanda* add another level of meaningful activity as they chant their Sanskrit liturgy and ring their *genta* bells. The liturgy, language, and figure of the *padanda* possess "a venerable, other-worldly quality through associations with a distant sacred past and with an esoteric scholarly tradition" (Wallis 1979:93). These priests introduce an Indian-derived aspect of the festival, a theological component that underlies the Hindu-Buddhist universe and constitutes a detached holiness in contrast to congregant communalism.[15] The *padanda* alter their voice quality, somewhat obscuring the words that they use to address the divine, in the same way that their rites are not clearly audible to the public (except when using microphones) since they are physically isolated (on the *balé pewédaan*) and spiritually isolated (entering into communion with the divine). By achieving a union of the body as microcosm with the universe as macrocosm and mapping all the mystic syllables in their proper position through ritual, the *padanda*'s soul is replaced by the Supreme Being and he/she can then prepare the holy water, the boon the participants are seeking (ibid.:104).

Today the voice of the *padanda* is amplified at festivals and clearly audible. They create a rhythmic drone with their voices, forming sacred words and creating a background of cosmically charged Indic value. The *genta* bell stands out as well, and its constant rhythmic ringing is a sanctifying ostinato that mixes within the gamelan music matrix. The late Ida Padanda Ketut Rai mentioned that the ringing of the *genta* awakens participants spiritually and prepares them to concentrate on God; Rai and other teachers made similar statements regarding the music in general. It is important to restate that the liturgy and the ringing of the *genta* are not directly related to the myths of Lingsar; their function is to introduce sacralizing Indic values necessary for major festivals. These exist in a dimension apart from the congregants' more popular practices, such as myth, but both are necessary to complete the efficacy and experience of acknowledged major festivals like Lingsar.

Dances

The two Balinese dances historically linked to Lingsar are Canang Sari and *topeng*. The accompaniment derives from dance pieces that are not associated with the ceremonial repertoires described above. "Tabuh Telu" (Three strokes, a *gangsaran*-like piece of sixteen beats) is a composition commonly used to accompany Canang Sari. Certain clubs prefer different pieces; since they do not rehearse and are rarely trained, those dancing care little about the selected piece. Topeng features a succession of characters who are introduced and accompanied by pieces associated with those characters that are entitled "Topeng (This Character)" or "Topeng (That Character)." Rejang Déwa, the new, modern-style dance introduced in 1997, is accompanied by a gamelan *gong kebyar* piece of the same name; the piece and movements borrow some ideas from ritual forms but are otherwise squarely in the late twentieth-century *kebyar* idiom.

Canang Sari features dancers in a row carrying the *canang sari* (essence of betel nut) offerings from outside the temple in to the *gadoh* and up to the priests, who take the offerings and place them within altars. The dance represents the path of congregants and symbolizes a journey from least sacred to sacred within the *gadoh* ("outside" to "inside"). The usually untrained dancers improvise their movements; though sometimes well-known individuals, most are simply congregants. Balinese sacred temple dances usually have little choreography and are humble requests from the people themselves. While formerly performed only by men, today women and children may participate as well, and the number of dancers has swelled from five to more than twenty. Their public, communal efforts reflect a different category of performance from *topeng*, and are a polar opposite from the isolated, ritualized *padanda* and the tightly choreographed, presentational Rejang Déwa.

Canang Sari, though distinct from male offering dances in Bali (generically called *baris pendet*), has been the most common sacred temple dance at Lombok Balinese temples; it is not unique to Lingsar. Before the mid 1990s the dance included clear fertility elements, as the men "danced" the offerings decorated with embroidered goddess symbols on the attached *lamak* plaits and in the shape of a *cili* (rice goddess). In those years women congregants sometimes stood and improvised with one or more of the men—who were often deliberately humorous. Laughter was acceptable, though it often made more conservative Balinese, who felt that the dance should be performed with as little individuality as possible, uncomfortable.[16] Until 2001 each time I witnessed the festival it rained so terribly hard that Canang Sari was shortened and the dancers practically ran from outside the *gadoh* to the altars, swiftly handed the offerings to priests, and raced for cover under the pavilions. In 2001 it did not rain at all, and the dancers performed for twenty minutes. With over twenty dancers entering the temple, they needed that much time to reach the priests, deliver their offerings, improvise a little, and then dance back into the crowd.

Formerly, the *canang sari* offerings had to be danced for their elements to become active (similar to how *topat* must be thrown to be transformed). The ingredients were associated with binary male and female powers (betel nut, flowers, fruit); attached were woven plaits of fertility symbols (each slightly different) in the *cili* shape, which gave the offerings a strong female element. The carefully constructed offerings were dedicated to the *gadoh* altars and their deities. Mangku Saka mentioned that after being danced, the offerings symbolically became what they represented. Like other Balinese and Sasak elements that were ritually combined, such as the waters after Mendak Tirta, there was a symbolic marriage of the offerings, the divine, and the male dancers. According to many (Saka, Sunu, Kartawirya), the men dancing with the offerings (which were representations of the feminine divine) helped generate fertility and its manifestation as rainwater. The hard rain at Lingsar was auspicious and demonstrated the auspicious results of ritual invocation and worship. Except for the dancers (who got drenched) and myself (who had to protect my equipment), everyone was happy with the rainfall during the dance. In the late 1990s, as the number of dancers increased, the quality of the offerings decreased and the value of the dance changed (see Chapter Seven).

Topeng is a masked theater of two or three male dancers who act out several characters: coarse noblemen, refined noblemen, clown sidekicks, supernaturally powerful characters, court ladies, and so forth. Most of these are stock characters and the clowns—the only speaking figures—are charged with creating a story outline that the actors improvise. Troupes at Lingsar seem to change from year to year, along with the length of the performance and the number of characters.

The *topeng* dance vocabulary acknowledges the Triangga (the three spheres of the manifest world) (Dibia, personal communication): refined characters move slowly with concentrated upper-body movements, while coarse characters emphasize strong, more active lower-body movements, forming a space-movement homology with cosmology. A similar structure (that is, slower/refined and faster/coarse) is seen both in the music forms discussed above, in design motifs on instrument cases (see below), in the elements used in offerings, and in the temple construction itself.

While Canang Sari is an offering dance associated with the congregants that formerly involved fertility symbolism, *topeng* is performed by skilled or even semi-professional artists. It "establishes a link with the ancestral world" (Slattum 1992:12) and demonstrates the victory of the mythical forces supporting the cosmic order (dharma) over those which do not (*adharma*), while combining elements to make that order exist here and now (Ramstedt 1993:84–85). The performance, and by extension the festival itself, thus come to represent that cosmic order, and it is in this light that Balinese culture heroes achieve their status. The performance reveals the political elements within the Balinese myth that assert Balinese hegemony—as a force for the cosmic order—over the festival and its proceedings. No one is sure how long *topeng* has been performed at Lingsar, and no one is sure how often it has been performed or when it will again be held. Mangku Negara once said, "*Saya senang topeng ada di sini karena topengnya artinya ini upacara Bali*" (I'm happy that *topeng* is performed here because it signifies that this is a Balinese ceremony). To Negara, *topeng* made the festival and its history distinctly Balinese and not Sasak.

The masks themselves are often considered "lightning rods" to collect a portion of cosmic energy (H. Geertz 1992:8) and to have often been empowered with the spirits of ancestors, performances, and festivals. Many old masks are sacred, and rituals are often held to "marry" a dancer to his masks. In a performance, masks manifest ancestors who then exist side-by-side with their descendants and enforce cosmic balance through successful battles with negative forces. The clown characters (*penasar* and *bondres*) retell these stories with contemporary reflection, interpolating the given performance context and informing audiences of the struggles and successes of the main characters.

The story performed at Lingsar is supposed to be the same each time, according to teachers such as Kereped and Komang Kantun. One dancer (Madri) called it *Babad Kerajaan Lombok* (The chronicle of the [Balinese] Lombok kingdoms); Gdé Mandia thought it might be *Babad Lingsar* (The chronicle of Lingsar). In either case Lingsar is a feature, but the story is so abstract, so short (due to time constraints), and so nearly inaudible to the audience (due to so many simultaneous events) that the only notion really communicated is the coming of the Balinese and righteousness to Lombok. Balinese ancestors are credited with bringing cosmic balance to Lombok and this transformation is recreated once again at the festival. Performance, regardless of the given story, makes this point by its presentation alone.

The final *topeng* character is Sidha Karya ("successful work," often translated as "able ceremony"), a wild-haired, leering, white-faced supernatural being who is not connected to the story. In Topeng Sidha Karya (the usual show at Lingsar), this character is necessary to guarantee the festival's success. He performs a blessing and throws holy water and a handful of Chinese coins and yellow rice (symbols of prosperity) to the audience while often grabbing children, then giving them money (Slattum 1992:26). Kereped stated that this was the most appropriate character for Lingsar and other festivals. Sidha Karya is a positive force to guarantee rainwater, health, and prosperity. He is also associated with the ancestors and nobility, two major forces credited with festival success.

Rejang Déwa was created around 1988 by Swasthi Widjaja Bandem at the college conservatory of arts (STSI, now ISI) in Bali.[17] The dance came to Lombok in the mid-1990s and was immediately accepted for performance as a sacred dance at a number of important temples (Pura Gunung Sari, Pura Méru, Pura Lingsar, etc.). Though the dance and its music quote ritual expression and the dance is thought to combine aspects of sacred dances of Bali, it requires set costumes (based on East Bali models), choreography, and music and is reminiscent of other Balinese music and dance of the late twentieth century. The Parisadha Hindu Dharma in Lombok, the religious organization that authorized its approval, apparently wanted another characteristically Balinese element in the festival, one that was modern and linked the Lombok Balinese with their brethren in Bali. The performance is now central to the Balinese part of the festival, performed before Canang Sari on the main day within the *gadoh*. The dance, featuring eight women carrying offerings and wearing yellow and bare-shouldered costumes, presents contemporary notions of the sacred and, in a sense, modernizes Balinese performing arts at Lingsar (see Chapter Seven).

SASAK MUSIC: CONFLICTS AND NARRATIVES

Sasak music shares some developments with Balinese music; both were influenced by Javanese settlements, migrations, and invasions. Large populations on both islands, particularly those of noble descent, claim lineage from Java. As in some other cultural spheres, the concept of Java legitimizes status.[18] Many Sasak nobles, however, have to admit that their Javanese ancestors came to Lombok via Bali. Still today, any Balinese who converts to Islam automatically becomes Sasak. This has made discerning what is Sasak from what is Balinese a fuzzy undertaking.

During the period of complete Balinese colonization (1739–1894), Balinese ideas inspired many Sasak musicians, and, on the surface, "traditional" Sasak music shares elements with Balinese music. This similarity has been part of the problem for modernizing Lombok. Some Sasak leaders, in promoting *khas* Sasak (original Sasak culture), have striven to remove what they perceive as "Balinese" elements in the arts from contemporary life, and thus have occasionally banned certain forms.[19] Most musicians, however, acknowledge two streams of influence into Sasak arts: one from Hindu Java and Bali and the other from the Islamic world including parts of the Near East, Sumatra/Malaysia, and Muslim Java (see Harnish 1998b). The music at Lingsar is related to the Java/Bali stream, but most of it has been spared criticism because of its connection to the festival, now held to be *khas* Sasak.

Concepts Underlying Sasak Music

Sasak music has not been well documented; no *lontar* indicate its nature and origins. Unlike Balinese music (see, for example, Kunst and Kunst-V.1925; McPhee 1966; Herbst 1997; and Tenzer 2000) and especially Javanese music (in such recent studies as Brinner 1995 and Sumarsam 1995), no formal theory speaks for Sasak music or performance practice and no indigenous literature links their musical systems with other systems. Sasak tunings, modes, ensembles, and vocal forms are not codified, and musicians rarely verbalize about the techniques, practices, and meanings of music. However, general patterns of instrumentation and music forms among Sasak ensembles, similar poetic forms used for vocal song throughout Lombok, and a body of research data together provide an outline for Sasak music.

Sasak gamelan music is based on cyclic phrase structures like Balinese and Javanese gamelan music. The conception of time is likewise cyclic, as indicated in the *wariga* and *windu* Sasak calendars, and coincidings of smaller cycles with larger cycles occur in both time and music as among the Balinese and Javanese, though fewer instruments provide inner punctuations and coincidings. The ensembles at Lingsar (*baris*, *gong* Sasak, *gendang beleq*) provide sound structures that help define Sasak culture. The late Waktu Telu leader Rahil was an outspoken musician who occasionally discussed extramusical meanings. He felt that gamelan music structure was related to the arrangement of a traditional Sasak village, with its mountain/sea directional axis and its set of open pavilions that subdivide the axis.[20] The frequency of binarisms, threes, and nines in ritual formulas and their placement within the music indicates a mapping phenomenon shared with Balinese music. It is clear today, however, that fewer Sasak would be inclined to interpret pre-Islamic gamelan music in a religious light; any music held to have structure related to cosmology would be discouraged due to the current dominating idiom of orthodox Islam. Sasak music and its meaning are thus more strongly contested than Balinese music, where concepts of music and religious cosmology are nurtured.

Ida Wayan Pasha is a Lombok Balinese with some Sasak blood who is respected for his mastery of many Balinese and Sasak forms. He is also a former Education and Culture official who has been searching to discover a Sasak music theory for several decades. His opinion, largely supported by musicians and my findings, is that Sasak "modes" (*pateat*) derive from an unnamed single heptatonic series. These modes include unnamed scales of four and five tones. He feels that although the scales are similar in some respects to *pélog* and *slendro*, as understood particularly in Bali, these terms should not be used when describing Sasak music.[21] Consequently, I use "*pélog*-like" and "*slendro*-like" below.

Among the Sasak, music is a sign of religious orientation and embodies elements related to beliefs and social networks (Harnish 1988:123); it is thus a site of cultural tension. The problem has become more apparent because of the often-public transition most Sasak have made from a nominally Islamic worldview to a reformist Islamic one, to greater polarization between Waktu Lima and Waktu Telu, and to the disavowal or the proscribing of "traditional" rites and associated musics. The ensembles affiliated with the Waktu Telu are primarily composed of bronze instruments—often associated with ancestor worship—and are sometimes banned in orthodox villages. These ensembles use *gongan* phrase structures, with smaller cycles rotating within larger ones, and feature a composite melody derived from the interlocking figurations of instruments like kettle-gongs. My earlier observations and work with teachers (1988, 1998b) suggested that these music elements relate both to a cohesive community order based on traditional patterns of kinship and reciprocal work patterns, and to a concept of balanced cyclic time and the world of the ancestors. This structural homology links music elements (such as composite melodies and cyclicity) with Waktu Telu sociocultural patterns and cosmology; it contrasts markedly with Sasak music of the second stream.

Ensembles associated with Waktu Lima/modernist Muslims omit composite melodies, gongs and bronze instruments, gong-type structures, and *pélog*-like and *slendro*-like tonalities. They instead feature stringed instruments (violins, plucked lutes) and more vocals (sometimes in Arabic), and normally produce a monophonic or heterophonic melodic texture. These musical elements relate both to the greater mobility, individualism, and modern orientation of orthodox Muslims, and to concepts of linear time, hierarchy, and monotheism. The music, along with connected beliefs and orientations, articulates a different vision of the individual and the social order.

Some religious leaders (particularly *tuan gurus* of the 1970s and 1980s) became aware of the distinctions between the two streams of music and of the link between music and religious and personal orientation; they have therefore sought to prohibit the music and performance contexts of the Waktu Telu. In seeking to ban certain styles, these leaders demonstrate a concern that such forms of music may adversely affect and influence people. They have sought to preclude the experience of traditional music as a way to dismantle traditional beliefs (Harnish 1988:133).

Reformist Islamic leaders in Lombok have disapproved of the Lingsar festival; some have even used the word *kafir* (pagan) for the event. The music, however, has sometimes been ignored, perhaps because of its support in certain government offices such as Tourism and Education and Culture. One style that has been openly criticized is *preret* music, which formerly accompanied many of the ritual activities at the festival. The few remaining Sasak *preret* players of the ceremonial repertoire in Lombok frequently encounter antagonism because their music and performance symbolize what religious leaders have striven to remove from Lombok. Amaq Salih told me that he cannot practice in his home because neighbors accuse him of being a non-Muslim and tell him to stop. The music honors deities and embodies the emotive melodies of poetry addressing the pre-orthodox divine; it has become an icon for belief in ancestors and invocation to deities.

The gamelan *tambur/baris*, on the other hand, has received approval from many modern Muslims, some of whom, like the remaining Waktu Telu, have told me that the ensemble is sacred and represents authentic Sasak culture. The music of this ensemble consists of monophonic or heterophonic melodies played on a flute and bowed lute, and the ensemble includes occasional vocalists singing related melodies, thus meeting requirements for modern Sasak music. The gamelan *tambur/baris* also, however, features several prominent bronze instruments such as a gong, includes a counterpart percussive melody produced by two interlocking kettle-gongs, and is a sacred heirloom with a nominal Muslim ritual function, which all qualify it as a Waktu Telu ensemble. These elements combine to create a unique ensemble that embodies aspects of both Waktu Telu and reformist worldviews.

Gamelan *Tambur/Baris*

The gamelan is shrouded in mystery and even its name is unclear. Many Balinese insist on calling it gamelan *tambur*, while most Sasak persist in calling it gamelan *baris*. Part of this confusion lies in the basic instrumentation of the gamelan *tambur*, which consists solely of the gong and *tambur* drum, and the instrumentation of the gamelan *baris*, which adds a *redeb* (a spiked, bowed lute, also called *rebab*), a *suling* (bamboo flute), a *kenat* (single kettle-gong, often called *kenot*), a *kajar* (counterpart kettle-gong with sunken boss), two *kendang* drums (*lanang* and *wadon*), and *rincik* (small, upturned cymbals on a base). When the other instruments are added, the function of the gong and *tambur* changes so drastically that the gamelan *tambur* becomes the gamelan *baris*. The *tambur* is often called *jidur* in this new context.

The gamelan, particularly the *tambur* and gong, is held as sacred. The gong is believed to have curative powers if heard at the right time of day; Parman mentioned one occasion when the sound of the gong cured cysts in the neck of a relative. The *tambur* and especially the gong are wrapped in *kain poleng*, a black-and-white cloth symbolizing the harmonizing of negative and positive energies (that is, the unification of binarism) into protective power (see Hauser-Schaublin 1991).[22] These two instruments, again particularly the gong (as with Balinese and Javanese gamelan), must receive offerings, and all instruments receive water from the spring in the *kemaliq* before use. This functions as a request for the use of the instruments and reconsecrates the gamelan with the *kemaliq*.

The main ritual music of the gamelan *tambur* is "Tak Tak Pong," a piece representing three *tambur* beats (the two *tak* represented in the onomatopoeic title) and one gong and *tambur* beat together. This form of four *tambur* strokes to one gong stroke, which is consistent throughout a performance, is indicated below where T indicates the *tambur* and G indicates the gong.

<pre>
T T T T T T T T T T T T T T T T etc.
   G   G   G   G   etc.
</pre>

Generally the ensemble accompanies processions; the beats, consistent in tempo, represent steps. A second piece, "Tamburan," features the gong struck over and over again with a fast drum roll on the *tambur*. "Tamburan" accompanies the Baris dancers who perform a quasi-military routine just outside the *kemaliq* and, since the mid 1990s, on the main road into the temple. This gamelan *tambur* and the few in Bali are sacred and associated with warfare and processions into warfare. Ida Wayan Pasha and other teachers compare the gamelan *tambur* with European military drum bands. It is believed that, like the gamelan *baleganjur* and gamelan *gong gilak*, there is a magical protective power in the instruments and music of this gamelan.

The gamelan *tambur* accompanies the steps of the Baris dancers, men who wear Dutch military outfits and carry obsolete or false rifles. The dancers are eight soldiers and a *komanden* (commandant) who carries a sword and shouts orders in a combination of Sasak and Dutch. Sanusi and Jasira (who played the *komandan* for decades) state that the total number of dancers (nine) is connected to the nine directions (four cardinal directions, their subdivisions, and center), the design of offerings, the making of *topat*, and the nine Wali Sanga. On occasion, a few teachers have told me, not all nine men have shown up, so the dance had to use only eight or seven. Although they sometimes behave in a humorous way, these dancers symbolically protect the festival and lead the processions with serious expressions. The *komanden* is particularly fierce and stays in role throughout most of the festival. In the 1980s I never approached Jasira unless he was taking a break (that is, had his sword down or hat or sunglasses removed) because his behavior was unpredictable.

The gamelan *baris* adds the other instruments and performs a completely different repertoire. No specific term defines this repertoire, which reportedly consists of up to thirty pieces but normally involves only four or five during the festival. These pieces are simply called *gending* (melodic or vocal composition) or *lagu* (song). The music bears a similarity with that of the gamelan *wayang* Sasak, the ensemble that accompanies the Sasak shadow play. Both ensembles consist of a *kenat,* a *kajar,* two *kendang,* a gong, and *rincik,* and they feature a *suling.* In both, there is a tendency for the *kenat, kajar, kendang,* and *rincik* to double the fastest density referent both when leading to a gong stroke and when accompanying fast dance steps. Part of the repertoire is also related: both ensembles use the *gendïng* "Janggel" (Walking) prominently in performance. Often connected to "Janggel" in gamelan *baris* performances is "Balekuwu" (a coastal area). Other pieces include "Nyanyi" (Sing), "Pantun" (a poetic form), "Pejarakan" (an East Javanese kingdom), "Telek" (a legendary couple), and "Jepon" (a flower). Song titles do not seem important and according to Saparia, the former head of the Sasak organization, and in my own experience, the musicians often confuse them. The lead *kendang* player may cut short any piece or signal transitions at any time.

"Janggel" (also called "Janggel Batek") continues the basic "Tak Tak Pong" structure with *tambur* and gong both played at a four-to-one ratio. The melody overlaid in this structure, performed by *redeb* and *suling* and occasionally a female vocalist, consists of 64 *gongan* beats or 256 *tambur* beats and three sections: "Aja Lali" (Do not forget), "Ukur Gulung" (Watch the headpiece) and "Umbak Gangsur" (Rising wave). Jasira interpreted the song structure as anthropomorphic and related to the three levels of *kebon odeq,* which makes it similar in this respect to the Balinese understanding of *lelambatan.* The *tambur* and gong divide the piece into a number of four-beat units and provide a constant background ostinato.

Another piece, "Pantun," represents a second poetic repertoire and consists of a long single melody performed in a phrase structure of thirty-six beats (indicated by the *tambur*) per single gong stroke. Other pieces with extended melodies within single *gongan* are "Telek," with eighty beats, and "Jepon," with sixty-four beats; these structures with differing or unusual lengths indicate consideration of the demands of the poetic line. There are thus two types of pieces: those which continue the *tambur*-to-gong ratio of four-to-one and add a melody over many gong strokes, and those which feature a long single melody of multiple phrases within a single *gongan* cycle. The lead musicians of the ensemble—the late Amaq Sarwi (*kendang*), the late Amaq Ratima (*kendang*), the late Amaq Raina (*suling*), and the still living Amaq Raidin (*redeb*)—have asserted that the repertoire, particularly of the latter style, is structured around poetry. However, they did not use terms to distinguish the differing types of pieces.

The two kettle-gongs, *kajar* and *kenat,* are played by single musicians who perform continuous interlocking parts. The *kajar* is struck with a small wooden hammer and the *kenat* with a wooden stick. Both instruments can produce several different sounds because the players can strike them on the boss, the side of the boss (except for the *kajar,* which has a sunken boss), or on the shoulder, and can dampen the sounds or leave them open. Similar to the instruments in gamelan *wayang* Sasak, the *kajar* part replicates the *kendang lanang* (male drum) and the *kenat,* the *kendang wadon* (female drum); players admit to sometimes improvising patterns that are immediately responded to by their partner. The *kajar* player may also interject a "bing" stroke in the middle of fast patterns. Occasionally, at slow tempi, the *kenat* sounds every other core pulse.

	1	2	3	4	5	6	7	8	9	10	11	12	13	14	15	16
Kenat					•			•								
Kajar			•			•		•	•							
Rincik			•		•		•		•			•				
Tambur	•				•				•			•				
Gong	•															

FIGURE 5.4. Punctuation in "Pejarakan"

The *rincik* is played by a single musician at the fastest density referent pulse (often supported by the *kajar* and *kenat*), but, unlike most Balinese cymbals, it is played irregularly in differing rhythmic figurations. The *tambur* keeps the main pulse like a *petuk*, although in a slow tempo the player often syncopates every other beat. The gong assumes its function as the phrase marker for the largest melodic units in pieces like "Telek" and both initiates and terminates the cycles like those of the *gong kuna*. Figure 5.4 indicates the basic parts for *tambur, kajar, kenat,* and *rincik* in a slow tempo of a Janggel-style piece, "Pejarakan." Using a TUBS-type notation, each box of Figure 5.4 represents a sixteenth pulse. These basic parts are subject to spontaneous variation.

The *kajar* and *kenat* often enter an interlocking pattern that intensifies during increased tempi within the performance. When coming to the end of the complete melody, all instruments frequently play at twice their normal density, then relax following the gong stroke. When a vocalist is singing or the group is in procession, the tempo remains relaxed and the percussive instruments play more intermittently. Then, as the singer drops out and the dancers begin performing, the music grows louder, intensifies, and except for the gong player, the instrumentalists double the density reference.

Amaq Raidin, along with other musicians, states that the *redeb* and *suling* have gender associations and are related to vocal music. When featured, a female vocalist sings texts derived from a type of poetry known as *lelakaq*—poems of love, nature, and parting. Like most Sasak poetry, the content and melodies of *lelakaq* are sad or melancholy. The melodies are said to be from "long ago" (*dulu*), but the song texts are not sacred. They use the *pantun* form, a rhyming couplet found throughout the archipelago. The text and language structures are fairly flexible; different words, including Indonesian words, may be inserted. On occasion, parts of a text can be changed. Teachers report that the words are secondary in importance to the melody. Musicians such as Martinom and Rahil, who come from other parts of Lombok, showed that they could identify the type of poetry solely by its melody; with five distinct dialects throughout Lombok preventing easy comprehension, melody and contour are the primary ways musicians recognize song and poetic style.

The melodies of the *redeb* and *suling* involve a variety of tuning systems: pentatonic *pélog*-like scales ("Jepon"), pentatonic *slendro*-like scales ("Janggel," "Pantun"), and tetratonic *slendro*-like scales ("Pejarakan"). Unlike the fixed pitches on metallophones, the *redeb* and *suling* can play any tonality. Because they are the only melodic instruments, the musicians playing them perform mellifluous lines rather than core melodies. Musicians (Amaq Raidin, Amaq Raina) say they "*membawa gending*" (carry the melody), and they play in close heterophony.

"Pejarakan" uses a tetratonic *slendro*-like scale without semitones. Two repeated melodic phrases of eight gong strokes each follow one another in a form of AA'BB'; these are repeated many times. The piece functions to request permission of the deity to depart from the festival. The melody of both instruments is continuous, with the *suling* blown in a circular breathing technique and the *redeb* bowed actively to provide constant sound. Figure 5.5 displays only one statement of the A phrase and one statement of the B phrase from the complete melody, along with *tambur* and gong structure.

The transcription uses staff notation to better show the descending glissandi (from c" to a#" on a gong beat in the seventh measure of the A melody, from c" to a#" in the fourth measure of B, and from a#" to g' in the seventh measure of B) that mark significant performance moments. Teachers state that glissandi on main beats, especially those that do not resolve to the main tone (g' in this piece) are what give the piece its color and make it melancholy. Lalu Gedé Suparman, a respected musician and scholar, asserts that glissandi present the "sudden shadow of the mountain," an enhancement of the melancholy. Similarly, the fact that the end of the A melody resolves on a#" and not g' (the primary tone) creates a sense of nonfulfillment and hence further melancholy. These melodic elements color

FIGURE 5.5. Melodies of "Pejarakan" (Lingsar, November 23, 1988)

much of Sasak music and are probably why most Sasak consider their music sad and melancholy. The pitches fluctuate and are approximately d#"-30, c" +32, a#'+22, and g' +30. My recording was made at Lingsar, November 23, 1988, the first day of the 1988 festival.

One stanza of text, sung hesitantly because the vocalist had forgotten many of the words, is below (submitted by Saparia) with my translation into English beside it. The form is *pantun*, with a structure of ending vowel sounds of é, a, é, a. The first two lines are called *sampiran*, a technique to create assonance without contributing to the intended meaning of the poetic content.

Beli raret aji selaé,	Buy dried beef twenty-five rupiah,
Tolang pauk bejerintang,	Mango seeds fall from the trees,
Kaji pamit epen gawé,	Excuse me, owner of the house,
Kadung jauk desa Lingsar.	Because Lingsar village is far.

Though the first two lines are not meant to contribute to the meaning of the couplet, occasionally, as here, there is a meaningful coincidence. For example, the second line, "Mango seeds fall from the trees," foregrounds an emotional element (i.e., seeds falling, symbolizing departure and separation) to the last two lines, which then politely ask permission to depart. "Departure" has been given several meanings: in the first, the song alludes to leaving home en route to Lingsar, specifically on leaving family; the second talks about departing from the deities and returning home; and the third requests that the *pesaji* offerings depart from the *kebon odeq* before the *kebon odeq* are carried in the final procession and thrown in the Sarasuta River. Parman gave me the first meaning. Sanusi and Saparia gave me the second two. Such poetic texts are often polysemous, allowing for further sad or melancholy interpretations and experiences of various dimensions of departure and separation. Like *preret* music (see below), the emotional intent of the poem is embedded in the melody and contour and can be understood without lyrics.

The gamelan *baris* accompanies the Batek or Telek part of the Batek Baris dance, and also frequently accompanies the Baris dancers with pieces like "Janggel" and "Pejarakan." The Batek/Telek dancers are usually four or five young women cross-dressed as noble and warrior figures. Most say that these figures derive from the Panji cycle of East Javanese stories as found in Balinese *gambuh* and *arja* theater. In its complete form (sometimes a few of the women do not attend), there are a king, a general, a scout, and two principal noble warriors called *batek*. Sasak teachers before 2001 stated that the figures represented Datu Wali Milir as king and the others his entourage, dramatizing his initial arrival at Lingsar. Parman said in 2001 that there are only three main dancers, who represent Haji Abdul Maliq, the culture hero in the new myth, and his two siblings. The Baris platoon are seen as the guardians of the king and his party.

The two *batek* noble warriors who head the other *batek* dancers (the king, the general, and the scout) are often called *telek*. These two are related to a local legend of a princess who falls in love with a commoner artist. Parman in the 1980s and others explained that when the king discovers their love, he demands that they circle the kingdom singing of their folly. This kingdom is believed to have existed near Lingsar, and the story forms the basis for a theater form called Amaq Darmi in the surrounding area. Balinese teachers state that Telek is the original Lingsar dance and that the other characters have been added.[23] The dance intermixes gender in two ways: in the cross-dressing of the women who portray heroic male characters, and in the balance created between these women and the male Baris dancers. Mangku Saka, the late Balinese priest who witnessed the dance tens of times, believed that this was a type of marriage (*perkawinan*) similar to that of the waters of Mendak Tirta (see Chapter Four).

The cross-dressed dancers, usually accompanied by a female vocalist, follow the Baris dancers in the processions. At given points, the procession stops and the dancers perform. Much of the time they simply walk. The female vocalist will occasionally sing; at other times she dances. The *redeb*, *suling*, and singer follow the same melody that emerges in close heterophony. The women also dance in front of the *kemaliq* altar as part of Ngaturang Pesaji, which Mangku Sanusi situated as a performance for the deity.

The sound of the *redeb* (male) and that of the *suling* (female) also unites binary forces and promotes fertility. Mangku Sanusi answered my question about why the instruments are played together by saying "*seperti laki dan wanita*" (like male and female). Teacher Ida Wayan Pasha confirmed that most ritual and artistic focus at Lingsar is on promoting fertility (*kesuburan*) through coupling duality.

The unity of *suling* and *redeb* is also connected to Balinese theater and the *malat* stories of Panji—the legendary crown prince and great lover from Kahuripan in Java. The instruments appear in the Balinese court gamelan *gambuh*, the costumes of the Batek/Telek dancers are based on characters from the *malat* stories (very similar to those in Balinese *arja* theater), and Sasak teachers such as Sanusi and Saparia often called the dancers "Panji." The Panji stories are associated with the refinement of sociocultural life in legendary Hindu Java (non-Indic, non-Balinese) and are usually concerned with battles, heroism, moral behavior, and romance. Although there is a Hindu association, the stories provide the rich indigenous Indonesian imagery that both Hindu and Islamic nobles have emulated, and they are acceptable to and enjoyed by most Sasak.

This dance, however, is also a reenactment of the Telek legend of two lovers, a princess and a commoner, who must circle a kingdom at Lingsar as a penance; the piece in the repertoire, "Telek," and the term *telek* to describe the two Batek dancers, reveal this association. The "voices" of the *redeb* and *suling*, associated with male and female energies and romance, are considered by some to be especially appropriate to accompany the Telek figures, their dance, and a tragic love affair.

The entire Batek dance is, in addition, a dramatization of the coming of the Sasak culture hero, usually conceived as Datu Wali Milir. The Batek/Telek characters represent the king and his entourage and the Baris dancers are his troops. This interpretation illustrates the politicized myth of Lingsar, where Datu Wali

Milir is sent to Lombok from Java to introduce Islam, and he controls the area before the coming of the Balinese.

The Baris dance, which protects processions with its martial qualities, is another agent of this multidimensional performance. The repertoire is stark and the costumes and weapons are drawn from the most powerful images in Lombok's history: Dutch military uniforms and rifles. Sanusi said that before they wore these outfits, the dancers carried kris (daggers) and wore black with long yellow *slendang* (scarves).

Through images, functions, contexts, and contents, the Batek/Telek and Baris dances and gamelan *tambur/baris* express a variety of meanings simultaneously; meanings which specify "Lingsar" and both traditional and contemporary Sasak culture. These arts bridge the wide gulf of the traditional, ancestral worlds and the modern, Islamic worlds among the Sasak, and they carry the acknowledgement of *khas* Sasak.

Preret

The *preret* and its ceremonial repertoire are associated with deities among both Sasak and Balinese.[24] The initial performance at Lingsar used to mark the beginning of the festival for the Sasak, and its concluding performance, when the *momot* bottle was opened, signified the end of the festival for everyone. Since 1993, when Min inherited the position of Sasak priest from his brother Sanusi, it is unlikely that the instrument has been used in this way. These days it seems that only the Balinese are interested in engaging either of the elderly *preret* players from Sanusi's years (see Chapters Four and Seven).

The Lombok Balinese often use the *preret* for other temple festivals, and one or more players commonly come to Lingsar to perform on their own during processions. Evidence indicates that the migrant Balinese borrowed the practice from Sasak (see Harnish 1990 and 1992). The main tradition at Lingsar, however, was always a Sasak activity, originating from similar performance practices at other pre-orthodox shrines. In the 1980s Balinese teachers said that it was important to have the sound of *preret* at Lingsar to add to and complete the sense of a festival, but that performance in the *kemaliq* was sufficient. They also recognized the *preret*'s crucial function in inviting the deities to descend into and remain in the altars throughout the festival's duration. All participants I spoke with confirmed that the *preret* created a powerful expression of faith and praise. In 2001 several people said that they hoped the Sasak *preret* tradition might someday return to the festival.

The primary *preret gending* in the ceremonial repertoire is "Turun Daun" (Slowly gently descend), and it was played to open the festival and mark the making of the *kebon odeq*, completion of *kebon odeq*, the making and completion of *pesaji*, and during ceremonies within the *kemaliq*. It served to contact the divine world before work on the *kebon odeq* could begin, much like puppeteers in *wayang* theater utter a few Sanskrit syllables before daring to manipulate their puppets. "Turun Daun" could also be played in procession, though other pieces, such as

"Pendaratan Alep" (Proceed slowly) and "Rerangsangan" (Stimulation), were more generally played. Three other pieces performed were "Jodak Digol" (Crow eggs, known by the Balinese as "Guak Maling Taloh" [Crow steals egg]) to accompany the removal of *pesaji* and other offerings from the *kemaliq*; "Pang Pang Pau" (Mango trees) to accompany the opening and dispensing of water from the *momot* bottle;[25] and "Asep Menyan" (Rising smoke) played during ceremonies in the *kemaliq* to accompany prayers and incense smoke as it rose up to deities.

The main instrumental piece and its poem, "Turun Daun," can stand for the repertoire. The poem is a type known as *badede* ("to make happy," especially rocking a baby to sleep) and specifically as *pendede*. *Pendede* refers specifically to a type of *badede* directed at ancestral and natural deities, and the poems praise or invoke these deities or exorcise malevolent spirits. *Badede* normally consist of couplet verse forms, though there are also duplet forms, of from two to twelve couplets in High Sasak language. Most of this indigenous poetry, developed among the Waktu Telu, has disappeared during the Islamification of the Sasak. Two *preret* players with decades of experience at Lingsar, Amaq Sari and Amaq Salih, have been pressured to stop playing, and the tradition may die out. Both Sari and Salih are over seventy (neither knows the year they were born), and there are no young Sasak players. Amaq Sari reported in 2001 that, though he is now rarely invited to Lingsar, he still plays at a few other rites in West Lombok. He was also happy that the Balinese invited him in 2001. The single piece he played was "Turun Daun."

In 1983 I heard this piece sung by a number of people in the *kemaliq*, but most did not know the text well and simply hummed along with one or two leaders. Few people, in fact, know the poem; the only musician I met who could sing more than a single stanza was I Wayan Kuta, a Balinese man who has long since died. The Balinese use this piece in just the same way as the tradition at Lingsar: to invite deities to descend into the temple. In both Sasak and Balinese traditions, the piece is played instrumentally and very rarely sung. Like gamelan *baris* pieces and even Balinese *kidung*, it is the melody that primarily defines the piece.

Wallis (1973:11–12) suggests that moods are attributed to both melody and verse form, that each form has its own particular melodic patterns, and that the meaning of the text and verse form is encoded into the melody. He states that listeners can recognize the verse form of a text from its melodic performance and that the melodies embody the feeling of the text and form. Teachers in Lombok have frequently demonstrated this ability to know the form, function, mood, and meaning of a piece simply from hearing its melodic performance, even though there are melodic and form variations from area to area. In both Bali and Lombok, melodic contour is the most important signifying factor for the identity of a piece. In solo singing or playing, expansion and contraction of melodic material is allowable as long as the integrity of the contour is maintained. *Badede* like "Turun Daun" are sacred ritual poems with recognizable verse forms, melodies, and melodic contours. Below are two stanzas of "Turun Daun" as sung by Kuta, transcribed by I Wayan Kartawirya, and translated by Kartawirya and me.

Turun daun si gedong sari,	Slowly, gently descend into a dwelling of beauty,
Mumbul katon swarga mulia,	A clear vision/voice of majestic heaven,
Langan desidé nurunang sari,	The divine path brings down revelation,
Sarin merta sari sedana.	Purity and sustenance.
Kukus katon si putih jati,	An appearance of white, sparkling clouds,
Margin desidé micayang,	That the divine path gives,
Kaji ngaturang pangebakti,	Followers pay homage,
Si ketek parek le desidé.	Before God.

"Turun Daun," like most other couplet *badede*, is structured with lines ending with vowel sounds: "i," "a," "i," and "a." The last line of the second stanza, however, does not conform properly and concludes with "é" rather than "a." In performance, Kuta compensated for this by embellishing the word *desidé* with an "a" syllable to complete the melody (see Harnish 1985:142–150; 1990:210). Unlike most other *badede*, that follow the *sampiran* structure, all four lines are meaningful. Each line explores various perspectives on the divine path of deities descending into temple altars. This is precisely why traditional Sasak and Balinese consider the piece so appropriate and essential at temple and shrine ceremonies.

Instrumental performance on *preret* may have been preferred over vocal versions due to the sonic power of the instrument, which far exceeds any possible vocal rendition. The melody, above all, conveys the sensation of homage, and the piercing *preret* sound directly affects the attendants. Mangku Sanusi and Ida Padanda Ketut Rai both stated that the *preret* reached into participants as it rose to the heavens and invited deities to the festival, acting like a bridge between the human and heavenly worlds. The first line of "Turun Daun," "Slowly, gently descend into a dwelling of beauty," directly implores the deities to descend into the altars, the "dwelling of beauty" in the *kemaliq* and temple.

Cyclic repetitions of melodic phrases of literary material such as priestly texts may aid in the realization of the unchanging relationships "which exist throughout the universe" (Wallis 1979:123). Several Balinese and Sasak have mentioned that they concentrated on the *preret* to refine their inner selves before prayer. The *preret* players used to perform during the prayers within the *kemaliq* for this reason: to help purify the attendants and the space and time of the prayers.

Sari and Salih used to play "Turun Daun" together if both were present, or solo if they were alone. A third *preret* player, Amaq Andar, sometimes attended to fill in when one of the other players needed a rest. Some of the Balinese players who have come to Lingsar over the years—Wayan Darta and Ketut Riana, for instance—have participated on their own in one or more processions playing "Turun Daun" by themselves. However, the unique version was the duo performance of Sari and Salih, and the festival was the only place such a phenomenon was known in Lombok. In the 1980s the players stated that their combined performance "strengthens the piece" (*lebih kuat*). (In the hope that they may play again at Lingsar, the following paragraphs are in present tense.)

While performing solo allows a player to improvise, Sari and Salih simplify their versions to play together. One player, usually Sari, leads the other. The second player heterophonically follows the same melodic contour one or two seconds behind the first. Performance includes many sustained tones, often covering many seconds each, therefore both musicians are often playing the same pitch. When it is time to approach another structural pitch, the first player performs his ornaments in the approach to that new pitch, then reaches and sustains it. The second player waits a moment while sustaining the previous pitch, then performs his own ornaments in approaching the succeeding pitch, then reaches and sustains it.

"Turun Daun," like most of the *preret* repertoire, uses a pentatonic *pélog*-like scale (see below) and consists of four melodic phrases. Each phrase constitutes one half of a line, two phrases equal one line, and the four phrases equal two lines of poetry. These four phrases, which constitute one melodic cycle, must be repeated once to complete a couplet stanza of poetry. The *preret* players, however, are rarely concerned with the connection of their performance to the poetry and make little effort to conclude at a coincidence with the end of a stanza.

One-half of the complete cycle (two melodic phrases, one line of poetry) from a *preret* performance at the Sasak priest's shrine during the 1987 festival is transcribed in Figure 5.6. The phrases are indicated in the melody as A and B (omitting C and D). The pitches—roughly g'-8, a^{b}'+18, c''-15, d''+14, and e^{b}''+30—are indicated from lower to higher as 1, 2, 3, 4, and 5 in a linear, graphic notational format. The spaces between pitches indicate relative intervals; for example, the largest interval—between pitches 2 and 3, nearly a major 3rd—is represented by greater space than the others. A timeline in seconds is provided beneath each graph. This was the fifth repeated cycle, and it was longer and more elaborate than earlier cycles in the performance. (The players experienced tuning problems in earlier cycles.) Salih follows Sari and in several instances both play their own ornamentation simultaneously. Note that the beginning of the A phrase is taken from the fifth cycle. Normally Sari would begin the piece solo, with Salih entering after a moment. Here, however, because this cycle begins from the end of the previous one, Salih is still playing the final tone of the previous cycle.

"Turun Daun" serves several purposes. The melodic contour and content index reverence and homage and invoke and represent the deity. The performance acts to suspend the normal passage of time through extended, elaborated cycles and a continuous stream of sound (Harnish 1992:49). It also sanctifies the making of *kebon odeq* and *pesaji*, helps purify the space of the *kemaliq* during the Ngaturang Pesaji prayers, contacts the deity world and acts as a bridge between worlds, and spiritually "reaches into" the participants with its sonic power.

Al Faruqi (1983:22) suggests that in sacred nonmetric music, such as Gregorian and Islamic chant, there is a tendency for upward-leading openings and downward-leading terminations. The A opening melodic phrase of "Turun

Daun," after momentarily sounding the main (beginning and final) tone, begins with an upward leap, and the D melodic phrase gradually descends, hinting at the end of the phrase, until finally reaching and sustaining the final tone. There is a tendency in sacred musics such as this to avoid metric sensibilities and fluctuations of intensity, to be, in a sense, otherworldly. Wallis (1979:108–110) states that Sanskrit mantra and ritual formulas work similarly, and that they often begin with the mystical word *ong* sung quickly on a low tone before leaping to the opening melodic phrase. This serves to signal that the music is "completely attuned to mind, body, and energies and to the corresponding cosmological counterparts" and symbolizes part of the cultural past deserving respect and awe. Performance of "Turun Daun" briefly sounds the lower and main tone (pitch 2, the "tonic") before beginning the actual first melodic phrase. This may work to frame the significance of the piece, give the music its otherworldly quality, and mark the transformation of time.

The sonic power of the *preret* cannot be overstressed. Because it is a single, transportable instrument, the players easily enter the shrine in both the Sasak compound and the *kemaliq* and sit beside the congregants. The piercing and continuous sound is inescapable, and the emotive melodies directly strike and affect the congregants, many of whom concentrate on the sound to purify their inner selves before prayer. Like the *padanda*'s ritual formulas that are chanted in an altered voice to contact the divine world, the *preret*'s "voice" is altered (nonhuman), extraordinary, and extra loud to contact the divine world. Unlike the Sanskrit mantra and formulas of the *padanda*, however, the *preret*'s invocations and sanctifications are mostly public and nonsecretive; they are as much this-worldly as otherworldly. The music acts as intermediary between the divine and human worlds, allowing humans access to the deities and the deities a bridge to descend into the temple and human world.

Until 2001 I thought that the *preret*'s music was among the most sacred at Lingsar and could not be absent. Due to sociocultural and political changes, however, its function is no longer considered necessary (see Chapter Seven).

Gamelan *Gong* Sasak

Although it does not play an integral role in the formal sequence of rites, the gamelan *gong* Sasak plays music similar in design to the *lelambatan* repertoire of the *gong kuna* and contributes its "voice" (a significant element in the development of *ramé*) to the realization of the festival. The ensemble performs in the *balé bundar*, which is set apart from the temple (see Figure 4.1), symbolizing its distance from the festival's central events. The *gong* Sasak is a modern ensemble somewhat modeled after the *gong kebyar*, and it ornaments and alters the traditional sound organization in accordance with its era of development; that is, the music features fast tempi and complex interlocking parts. However, it is also a Sasak gamelan, related to the *tawa-tawa* (the processional ensemble supplying the gongs) and *oncer* (the ensemble contributing the gong-chime and drumming style), and it reflects

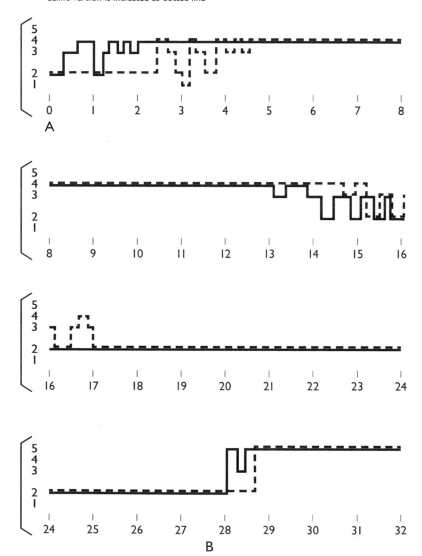

Key: Sari's version is indicated as solid line
Salih's version is indicated as dotted line

FIGURE 5.6. "Turun Daun" as performed by Amaq Sari and Amaq Salih (Lingsar, December 5, 1987)

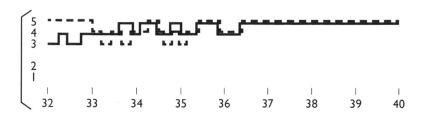

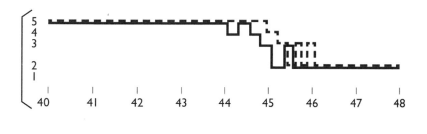

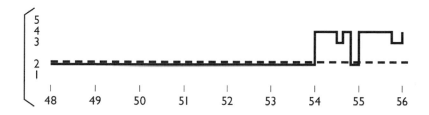

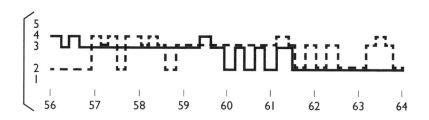

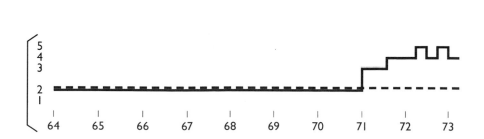

Sasak modernized tradition. The repertoire is a combination of original pieces for the *gong* Sasak, borrowed compositions from gamelans *tawa-tawa* and *oncer*, and borrowed pieces from *gong kebyar*.

The gamelan also accompanies the Gandrung dance usually within the Sasak compound, where its distance from the temple may enhance both its social and flirtatious nature and the fertility elements of the dance. The ensemble, headed by Amaq Wati, is from Montor village and has performed at Lingsar for over thirty years. The club is so strongly associated with Gandrung that it is often called game-lan *gandrung* and has taken the official title Sekaha Gandrung. The accompanying piece is also called "Gandrung." It consists of three sections in ternary form ("Gandrung," "Lampung Gunung" [Fall from the mountain], and "Gandrung"), and the players embellish the piece to fit the invited dancer. The gamelan's position and function in the ritual frame symbolize its character: its "voice" is modern Sasak—less acceptable as an offering and more associated with entertainment but linked to Gandrung. Like *preret*, however, the Gandrung dance seems to have fallen from favor; it is unclear when it was last performed and when it will again appear (see Chapter Seven).

The *gong* Sasak performers assemble the gamelan's cymbals, drums, and gongs to create a gamelan *baleganjur*, and they accompany nearly all of the Sasak processions. Like the Balinese *baleganjur*, the ensemble and performance is associated with underworld spirits and has a protective and martial function. It is played constantly in the processions and within the *kemaliq* and heightens the state of *ramé*. The repertoire is "Baleganjuran" or "Rangsangan," and there are eight or four *petuk* strokes (the timekeeping kettle-gong) per *gongan*. The performers of *gong* Sasak and *baleganjur* fulfill different functions throughout the festival.

Gendang Beleq

I had not seen a gamelan *gendang beleq* at the festival before 2001. The complicated rationales for its appearance at Lingsar are explicated in Chapter Seven. *Gendang beleq*, sometimes called gamelan *oncer* or regional names, was the traditional model for Sasak ensembles. The main instruments were the two large (*beleq*) drums, the *réong* kettles (normally two pairs, two kettles in two beakers like *gong gilak*), from four to eight *ceng-ceng* cymbals, a *petuk* timekeeper, a hanging gong, sometimes one or two small gongs (including the *oncer*), and sometimes one or more aerophones (usually *suling*). The tetratonic ensemble traditionally performed at a number of different occasions: life-cycle rites (especially marriages and circumcisions), ceremonies to invoke rainfall or aligned with the rice cycle, and national and regional holidays. The gamelan accompanied the *gendang beleq* dance as well as a traditional theater form called *kayaq* (see Harnish 1998b). Prior to the 1990s the *gendang beleq* dance featured the drummers, who dramatically confronted one another and played interlocking figurations on their drums, then moved off in different directions until it was time for another confrontation.

The dance currently in vogue throughout the island features not the drummers (who may, nevertheless, dance around a bit) but the *ceng-ceng* players. Sixteen or more players perform tight choreography, and, instead of mature men, the performers are boys and young men. Over the past few decades the gamelan had been waning along with Waktu Telu culture. The regional government wanted to preserve the ensemble, partially as an emblem of *khas* Sasak, though officials faced an influential clergy increasingly intolerant of traditional arts. After government officials witnessed Bali's successful development of *kreasi beleganjur* (new gamelan *beleganjur* pieces) for youth in 1986 (see Bakan 1999), a number of projects were undertaken to revive *gendang beleq* and young boys were targeted as performers. As religious leaders dropped their opposition, the government (with some in its ranks from clergy) helped pay for ensembles and teachers, and communities embraced the revival. This renaissance removed *gendang beleq* from many of its traditional contexts. As it went through a process of detraditionalization and secularization, the art was placed in the hands of officials and communities who revised the dances and increased the number of *ceng-ceng* players (sometimes the number of *réong* players as well). Today, when a *suling* is included, it must be well amplified to counter the greatly enhanced ensemble volume.

The ensembles were first introduced into the festival in 1997. In 2001 four gamelans were present. Two of these performed intermittently outside of the *kemaliq* in the open courtyard; three clubs performed within the *kemaliq* and one (Hujan Mas) was from Lingsar village. Though the *gendang beleq* addition may be renegotiated from year to year, it seems to have found a semipermanent place in the festival. The music and choreography, while reinvented, are based on traditional cyclic eight-beat patterns.

Dances

The Sasak Baris, Batek Baris, and Gandrung dances have been introduced and largely described. According to many participants, the Baris dance (the soldiers and commandant) conveys martial protective force and crystallizes into a political message by integrating the power of the Sasak deity. The Batek Baris dance expands the political imagery and dramatizes the arrival and triumph of the deity with his entourage through a combination of characterization, costume, terminology, and music. Until the late 1980s I always assumed that the Gandrung dance was a light or bawdy moment among more serious rites.

Aspects of Batek Baris and Gandrung dances, however, directly relate to the fertility invocation of the festival. The dances mix male and female together: the Batek Baris dance combines the nine male Baris dancers with the three to five female Batek dancers, and Gandrung features an alluring female enticing males to dance with her. These dances embody more fertility elements than their Balinese counterparts.

The Batek/Telek dance involves a symbolic marriage of gender as young women cross-dress as powerful male figures, perhaps representing the double-gendered aspect of the Sasak deity and serving as a balanced offering. The Indic-Javanese notion of *sekti* (*sakti*, *kesaktian*)—supernatural power initiated through union of male and female principles—helps explain fertility generation. *Sekti*, a term coined independently by a couple of teachers, is considered female energy and often the consort of a male deity, who, through sexual union, provides the male deity with his power. In the Batek/Telek dance women represent the *sekti* of the residing deity represented as king and noble entourage, realizing the androgynous power of the divine. The Baris dancers, the protectors of the sacred noble and double-gendered Batek dancers, are male counterparts to the female dancers. The *redeb* and *suling* constitute another gender coupling. Seemingly shrouded within the mystic of East Javanese courtly life, these instruments in concert connote ritual power and sexual fertility. The Batek/Telek performance in addition explicates the Sasak discovery myth, unites that myth with the local Telek legend, and links Sasak heritage with both East Javanese court tradition and Islam.

The Gandrung dance, enveloping male and female energy in direct and close interaction, is similar to *joged* and *gandrung* dances in Bali, to *gandrung* and *seblang* performances in East Java, to *tayuban* in Central Java, and to *ketuk tilu* in Sunda (West Java). The Balinese, Sasak, and East Javanese *gandrung* all formerly featured a male transvestite dancing with male partners; the dance has featured female dancers in Lombok and East Java for many decades. In East Java, Gandrung is a more secular offshoot of the sacred Seblang and is perhaps most like the Sasak Gandrung, which retains similarities with Javanese rice fertility dances. Today in Lombok, Gandrung is normally considered secular. In ritual contexts, however, it can achieve a different consideration and at Lingsar it has served both fertility and entertainment purposes.

The Gandrung dancer often performs in the central courtyard within the compound of the Sasak priest. In the 1980s and (presumably) earlier, she was taken by the priest into the small courtyard where the *kebon odeq* are made. The priest recited some words (spoken or silent, this was never clear) and lit some incense, then the two returned to the main central courtyard where some offerings were placed near the *gong* Sasak gongs. Sanusi and the dancer Padmawati said little on this subject, and Min did not respond at all.

The Gandrung, holding a fan, sits in the middle of the courtyard near the gamelan and the audience sits all around. At a signal the gamelan begins "Gandrung" and the dancer sings in indirect and abstract language about how she is a maiden looking for a mate, using the tonal material and tempo of the ensemble. After a while she stands and starts waving and turning her fan as she continues singing. Then she begins thrusting her hips side-to-side in an erotic fashion and starts to dance around the middle of the courtyard. After a few minutes, she moves towards the audience. When she spots someone she wishes to dance with, she throws her scarf (*slendang*) at him and then returns to her original position as the players conclude the piece with a gong stroke. The music begins anew and she again sings, eventually standing, and then dancing as her male partner (*nibing*) dances and approaches her. The couple perform a spontaneous duet which may be erotic, artistic, or humorous depending on the partner and the dancer's response. When done, he gives her some money (the equivalent of a few cents) and rejoins the crowd as the Gandrung returns to the gamelan and sits, readying herself to repeat the procedure again and again. The dancer looks for community leaders, other dancers, good-looking young men, and anyone sure to entertain the crowd (including foreign scholars). It rained during most performances I saw, an auspicious sign. Sutton (1993:140) indicates that it always seems to rain (a fertility association) during Seblang in Bakungan, East Java, even when performed during the dry season.

Unlike Seblang, the Gandrung dancer does not enter trance. Yet she, like the Seblang, is for the moment the embodiment of the local female deity, enticing male partners into sexual interaction and activating fertility by setting in motion the symbolic marriage of the divine with the community. The male/female union is necessary to achieve efficacy, and "sexual and agricultural fertility suggest one another metaphorically" (ibid.:139). The rainmaking associated with these fertility/social dances symbolically connotes "abundant rice, loving marriages, happiness, and many children" (Foley 1992:35). Since the 1980s, however, the role of Gandrung has decreased along with other music and activities related to Waktu Telu practices.

MUSICAL INSTRUMENTS

Musical instruments can illuminate cosmology, tensions, and sociomusical culture. At transformative rituals like Lingsar, the instruments themselves often have extramusical meanings beyond their "voices" and contextual values though intricately related to both. As DeVale (1991:256) asserts, "musical instruments are in themselves symbolic systems," or "symbolic subsystems of the larger aesthetic system defined by a culture for itself as a whole." These subsystems "not only reflect the larger system, but can help explain it."

All gamelans at the festival are greatly respected; they are given proper names and thought to embody a spirit presence, usually associated with the gong. Gamelans receive offerings (*peras gong* and *daksina*, and sometimes holy water from the pond) before they are played. This is usually done via the gongs, the conduit through which the gamelan's spirit flows or is awakened.

Instruments at Lingsar

DeVale and Dibia (1991) convincingly demonstrate that Balinese gamelan instruments are material culture constructed upon the same underlying concepts that inform pavilions, temples, home compounds, village arrangements, musical compositions, and offerings. Tripartite structures (for example, head/body/foot or *utama/madya/nista*) abound within the instruments and their cases. Three horizontal and vertical sections (3 x 3) on most instruments together create a structure of nine parts, representing the Nawa Sanga, the center-periphery cosmic map that governs the nine sections of Balinese homes, temples and their courtyards, ritual formulas, and even the way seedlings are planted in rice fields. Other divisions form complementary dualities (*lanang/wadon*). Some Balinese consider gamelan instruments as living organisms, just as they "view their towns, temples and houses as living organisms" (Budihardjo 1986:34).

Just as offerings have little meaning until activated by a ritual agent, the instruments are simply symbolic figures like any others until they receive offerings and incense and are played in context. Then inherent meanings spark to life and their power flows into the festival atmosphere. Several, particularly Mangku Saka, articulated this process of transformation from static to active symbol. Like music and structure, instruments merge tripartite and polar forces and can explain much of the religious meaning of the festival.

The *Prakempa* treatise mentions virtually every instrument in a gamelan and its value: the gong, for example, is as heaven and the unity of the Hindu Trinity, the *kempul* is the collection of all purity, the *trompong* is the lotus flower, and so forth (Bandem 1986:61, 69). The *lontar* also asserts that music is "attracting" and "sweet" and affects every part and organ of the body. The sensual power of the instruments cannot be overlooked; instruments create acoustical waves that physically strike participants. This is something that static architectural structures like offerings and temples cannot do. Through the sensations of sound, sight, and touch, the instruments spiritually affect and help transform participants.

DeVale and Dibia (1991:40–41) posit that Balinese gamelans reflect and are musical icons of village social structure, where drums are political leaders, gongs respected elders, higher metallophones youngsters, *ceng-ceng* children, and so forth. These ideas resonate with Turner's (1982:19) assessment that such ritual objects "are the product, center, and soul of a social group's self-manifestation."

No Sasak instruments are more important than the gong and drum of the gamelan *tambur*. For most participants these instruments are icons for Lingsar and the sacred property of the *kemaliq* originally possessed by deified ancestors. Their very presence represents what Falassi (1987:4) would call a rite of conspicuous display because these sacred secrets of the Sasak/Lingsar institution are publicly displayed and sounded for the benefit of everyone. The *tambur* embodies the secrets of the ancestors, and curative powers are attributed to the gong. Both are wrapped in the supernaturally protective *kain poleng* and these boldly guide processions into impure space.

The gamelan *baris*, combining Waktu Telu and modernist music elements, performs music that is *khas* Sasak, a vital concept in contemporary Lombok where "authentic" culture has largely become obsolete. The *suling* and *redeb* represent male and female, a crucial pairing in the accompaniment of intermixed gender dances. The gamelan *gong Sasak* and *baleganjur* add further bronze voices to the *ramé* atmosphere; from a traditionalist perspective, bronze is a vehicle through which ancestral wisdom flows to descendents. These instruments, so similar to their Balinese counterparts, represent similar values for many Sasak participants.

Though now rarely performed, the *preret* fulfilled a strongly religious function. Its voice was a bridge to the ancestral world, a medium to address the divine, and a frame for the *kebon odeq*. Interestingly, the instrument did not receive offerings, was not considered sacred, and had little extramusical value, though players often interpreted it anthropomorphically as head (reed, pirouette, staple), body (bore), and foot (attached bell) (Harnish 1988). Today, it seems that the *preret* is only heard at Lingsar when Balinese invite Sasak players or when Balinese players perform in processions.

Sanusi once said that Balinese and Sasak are like the two *kebon odeq* and king and queen. When the gamelan *baris* is playing on the *balé kembar* across from the *gong kuna* in the *balé gong*, an equality of purpose emerges that unifies the heterogeneity. This *menyatu* (becoming one) is the merging of two into one equaling three, the Waktu Telu ideal, and it is this experience that generates fertility and is ultimately the goal of the festival.

Musical instruments—given names, offerings, and holy water—are cultural objects that all participants encounter at Lingsar. As emblems they "explode with meanings, for they are invested with the accumulated energies and experiences of past practice" and the "history of the culture" (Abrahams 1982:161). Instruments are valued, tangible products of cosmological ideation with affective, transformative power. They speak about and express notions of the divine and provide narrative frameworks that define community values and the given performance. The instruments and their music do not simply remind participants of the past, their real efficacy is to re-present the energies they represent; to re-create what is being symbolized.

CHAPTER SIX

Explorations of Meaning

WHAT DRAWS PEOPLE to Lingsar? Balinese participants have a list of religious reasons; Sasak participation, though originally religious, is today problematic and in transition, combining religious beliefs (i.e., powers in nature and ancestors) with cultural obligation. Power, family, and social relations no doubt also play a part. While there is a "culture" among participants in which people share certain understandings, this culture is not singular or unified. It is diverse, consisting of contesting parties within both Sasak and Balinese camps. Ideology, personal experience, and history bring people to the event, but participants embrace differing interpretive schemes and come away from the festival with unique impressions and reflections. Distinct understandings, discourses, and experiential realms reside among the parties; though often without conscious reflection, individuals renegotiate those realms and situate their experiences accordingly. The myths, rather than simply rationalizations for conducting the festival, are expressions of and account for these differing schemes.

Music directs and generates these understandings and experiential realms, as it attracts, affects, and reflects the participants. With its power to mobilize the sentiments and actions of people, music can symbolize the conflicts that separate various parties, highlight divisions within each party, and ultimately transcend divisions to create a greater whole. Historical discourses shape activities within the performance arena; each story speaks to a dimension of the whole event and also reflects the whole event. This chapter discusses the underpinnings of these discourses, as well as those of music and dance as they work in context to shape the participants' experience. Overlapping dimensions—context, performance, personal experience, and semiotics—help explicate the meanings in the music.

CONTEXT, PERFORMANCE, AND EXPERIENCE

The study of music and context has become increasingly important over the past several decades as ethnomusicologists have sought to look beyond "the music itself" for new dimensions of meaning. Blacking (1995:45, orig. published 1969) was one of the first to explain that music can communicate its messages only if presented in the proper social context. Nketia (1990:79–80), promoting context-sensitive research, argues that since "a performance in many ways brings a renewal of shared knowledge and experience, the contextual approach enables one to observe how this experience unfolds both in the musical processes and in the interaction of those present." The Lingsar festival is a multifaceted setting for the interpretation of music as it is understood and experienced by the participants in which contextualization—music's integral relationships with time, space, persons, and actions—is central. This type of analysis resonates with Feld's communications approach (1994:78), where musical meaning is "interactive, residing in dialectic relations between form and content, stream and information, code and message, culture and behavior, production and reception, construction and interpretation."

During an inactive period at the 1988 festival, I asked the late Balinese *pamangku* Saka whether or not I might enter Balinese altars in the *gadoh* to examine the offerings. His response, translated below, was very telling:

> Of course you can go take a look. What are offerings anyway? Just a few items here and there. But who's brave enough to approach these offerings when the *padanda* is offering them up to God, or to stand up upon the altar when everyone is concentrating in prayer towards the altars and the gods are seated in the altars? These things are alive, you don't disturb them. This is like the flag. What is a flag? It is just a piece of material of white and red [the Indonesian flag]. But who's brave enough to climb the flagpole and rip up the flag when President Soeharto is saluting it on Independence Day with all of his generals together, and his armies are shooting in the air in salute while the entire country is silent in respect? Then these things are alive, you don't disturb them.

Saka's point was that symbols and their ingredients are meaningless until activated in the force of context—often through a party or agent (*padanda* or president). Similarly, the festival music may be important on its own but achieves an elevated power and acknowledgement during rites.

Based largely, though not entirely, on teachers' commentary and categories, my approach does not examine how context shapes performance or otherwise impacts upon it as some studies do (see Qureshi 1986 and 1987), nor how the audience in some sense co-creates the performance as in other studies (see Feld 1990). Instead, it examines how musical systems interlock with other sets of symbolism or symbolic acts. Temple festivals are multidimensional events; it is most rewarding to understand how the various dimensions intermingle and how, in a Geertzian sense, deep meaning is squeezed from this intermingling. Below I examine the relationships of music to other contextual elements, and explore how participants sense meanings of the festival through the musical performances, that is, how music informs the stages of the festival and defines their purpose.

Performance Aspects, Semiotics, and Identity

What I call the formal aspects of performance incorporates the processes of performance, such as special preparations for the instruments and musicians, the musicians' orientations towards the instruments and audience, their training and standing, gender, clothing, and so forth. Here, I limit myself to two main aspects: the spatial and temporal orientations of the music and their subdimensions. The spatial "where" is the Lingsar temple, the temporal "when" is during the festival—a place and time that immediately conjure images and meanings to Lombok residents. Other "wheres" include particular pavilions, courtyards, and processions; other "whens" include the timings of performances and the relationships with particular days, rites, actions, processions, and so forth. Coupled with participant responses, these two formal performance aspects reveal values given to the arts.

Several studies have examined the levels of staging of religious events, for example Kapferer (1983), Feld (1990), Davis (1987), Wong (2001), and Dibia (1985). These studies discuss the spatial and temporal orientations of the performing arts in relation to the design of the event and the efficacy of the arts. Regarding Sinhalese exorcism rituals, Kapferer (1983:178–206) states that music and dance control the stages of events, signal transitions and transformations of meaning, and order the experience of the context. Davis's work on Catholic ritual in the Dominican Republic involves two entirely different musical and religious dimensions coexisting in the same event, with men associated with one discourse (African-derived) and women another (European Catholic-derived). While gender in musical performance is not manifest this way at Lingsar, Davis's statement that each discourse is spatially anchored to its respective sacred site (1987:44) resonates with the orientation of respective performing arts. Wong (2001) explores how one ritual (*wai khruu*) and its music define so much about Thai culture. Similar to the Lingsar festival, the ritual process Wong describes addresses nobility and legend, contains multiple histories, outlines a syncretic and multifaceted cosmology, evokes powerful responses, and embodies tradition yet is a vehicle for modification.

An episteme—an understanding based on knowledge and experience—reflects the way culture members are taught to comprehend certain nonverbal aspects of reality. Music, a form of sensuous knowledge, communicates information in tandem with and about our temporal and spatial environments discerned through processes mediating music knowledge and how culture members treat, realize, or conceive of that knowledge (Laskewicz 2003:228). The Lingsar festival music is *multimedial*—something fully contextualized that the whole body experiences. Though specific to Lingsar, it reflects an active way of engaging the world.

The semiotic character of music and dance, particularly within the charged festival context, is key in identity formation. Experiencing the festival's history and symbolic packaging is a force for realizing personal and collective identities. Identities "are at once individual and social; they are the affective intersection of life experiences variably salient in any given instant" based on "what we know best about our relations to self, others, and world. . . ." (Turino 1999:221). Music and dance—affective ways to knowing—help construct these identities.

Turino's work (1999) linking semiotics and identity seems particularly pertinent to Lingsar. Crediting Peirce, Turino asserts that music meaning is simplified by defining it as the actual effect of a sign (ibid.:224). Particularly relevant is his explication of "index" as a "sign that is related to its object through co-occurrence in actual experience" (ibid.:227). For example, as Balinese grow up listening to *gong kuna* music at temple festivals, "festival" and its associated values become indexed by the music. Indices generated by music "become the mortar of personal and social identity . . . tied to the affective foundations of one's personal life . . . unreflexively apprehended as 'real' or 'true'" (ibid.:229). The index phenomenon relates to *ramé*, where activated distinct systems (performances, offerings, activities) in temporal concurrent interaction create a lively and bustling (and sometimes "unreflexivity apprehended") environment for spiritual experience and identity formation. The indices bring performance events and what they symbolize into the present and make them real and dynamic.

Experiential Dimensions

The discussions here and in Chapter Five have addressed signs and codes embodied in the structures of music and musical instruments and the contextual interactions that bring inherent meanings to life. Signs and codes are useful for identity formation, for the realization of myth, for the construction of ethnicity, for the negotiations of traditional and modern, and for meeting the needs of individual and collective spiritual experience. They have a ritual power that transforms time, space, and nature.

The discussion now concerns how participants experience the music and festival, and how participation contributes to a hermeneutical wellspring that informs future participations. The festival experience, regardless of an individual's background, can be profound. The word "experience" here basically refers to "how events are received by consciousness" (Bruner 1986:4).

Music is a prime way that members experience their culture and is an exceptional way that participants experience the Lingsar festival. Context is essential. Ritual music performed out of context has as little meaning as an offering not ritually brought to life; both present archetypal form without living force. For the music to be "meaningful" and experienced as such, the environment must be properly set. At Lingsar, this prepared environment manifests when the symbolisms of ritual objects have been activated and intermixed. The charged context sets the stage for meaningful, memorable experience. When ritual actions are performed collectively, congregants are prepared to transcend individual experience through the shared existential worlds of the performing arts. Within the performing arts exists the possibility of experiencing together the "one experience," where participants "commune" in the "same vivid and continuous present" (Kapferer 1986:190).

Although participants share the same ritual intentions, they differ in their positions within and experience of the ritual frame—the experience of shared ritual phenomena is not the same for all individuals. Balinese and Sasak, of course, interpret different experiences, and interviews reveal that experience also varies greatly within each camp and between individuals. Among the Balinese, noble descendants, urban Balinese, farmers, and those from Bali rather than Lombok all have varying interests and are affected differently. The same is true for the Sasak. Waktu Telu, the Sasak organization, sympathetic villagers and guests, reformist Muslims, government bureaucrats, curious students, and *haji* all undergo separate individual experiences and distinct takes on collective experiences despite sharing events. Caste or class, background and origin, personal disposition and ethnicity influence the experience.

Ritual protocol signals spiritual and political hierarchy (Hefner 1985:73). The Sasak *pamangku* and his aides, the *padanda*, and the Balinese *pamangku*, and the principal Krama Pura members thrive in the festival and are clearly the leaders. The Sasak *pamangku* and the Balinese *padanda* are the only individuals who can present the most significant offerings to the deities and (apart from the performing arts) invoke their presence, and thus they are credited with festival successes. Agung Biarsah and other noble descendants assume a high profile. It was perfectly appropriate when, in 1988 during Mabanten and *gadoh* prayers, Agung Biarsah assumed the front position just before the main altar and remained there alone in worship and meditation for perhaps twenty minutes throughout a torrential rainfall that caused all others to flee for cover under pavilions. Some were deeply impressed with his "power" at retaining spiritual concentration despite the downpour. His behavior, however, was not unpredictable. As the grandson of the last king of Lombok and directly linked to the history of the temple, he has a unique status and a responsibility to the festival. In fact, some Balinese may have credited him with helping to create the rainfall, a major goal of the festival.

Turner (1986:36) asserts that deep experiences of cultural performances are subject to an objectivism that allows for interpretation; this transforms normal experience into <u>an</u> experience, and into what he called a "peak experience" (Turner 1982:11). Most long-time participants demonstrated the ability to abstract and objectify their experience, to distance themselves from the events, and to contextualize their experience and give it meaning. The notion of expectancy no doubt has an impact on later interpretations of the festival, as individuals prepare mentally, physically, and spiritually for the event and rely on previous experience for their preparation.

Through multiple encounters, participants shape their subjectivity to interpret the codes and signs in arts and ritual action. The quote in Chapter One—"Our elders never told us about the meanings of offerings or of the festival. We had to discover these for ourselves"—speaks to the development of agency and interpretive modes in the festival context, and suggests that the more experienced the participant, the deeper the experience. Participants learn the spiritual dimensions of Lingsar not through storytelling traditions but via the performing arts. As Becker (1993:2, 5) suggests, an "enriched self" results from performance encounter: a "feeling of unity beyond oneself, a transcendental experience." Participants develop a spiritual sensitivity for this experience that emerges from the narrative and aesthetic properties of performance and the resultant state of *ramé*. The refinement of these perceptions can lead to the experience of a "dissolution of the boundaries between oneself and the thing perceived" (ibid.:7). At Lingsar this means achieving union with performance, offerings, and the divine, and this experience creates intra- and interethnic unity. For both Balinese and nominal Muslims, events like the Lingsar festival constitute main expressions of faith and opportunities to participate in and experience spiritual modes of being.

Many others, however, never achieve, nor perhaps want to achieve, such mystical experiences. The Sasak present who are unsympathetic to Waktu Telu beliefs clearly have different agendas. Some are curious, others (such as government officials) may want to pay their respects or show their presence to participants, many come as vendors, and a few may want to cause trouble.

APPLICATIONS TO THE PERFORMING ARTS

Music and dance are reconsidered below in light of context, formal aspects of performance, experience, and semiotics and identity. Each of these overlap in several ways to illuminate the multifaceted meanings of the festival and its performing arts.

Balinese Music and Dance

"There is an ability in Balinese culture, in many ways unique, to maintain very formal structures, while allowing for great variety, as each person, group, or situation breathes life into that form" (Herbst 1997:115). Though Herbst is referring to performance forms such as *wayang* or *topeng*, the idea also resonates with temple festival programs. Each program is its own take on the form or template for such rituals in Balinese culture. The historically constructed program at Lingsar is indeed unique to Lingsar; each art breathes its own life and character into the event.

While some Balinese relish the experience with divine forces and the resulting internal transformations, others, particularly farmers, seek not to transform their mental state but rather to achieve the practical results of ritual efficacy: rainwater, fertility, and, if they have made such vows, health and prosperity. A variety of participant experience is perfectly appropriate. Barth (1993:6–7) suggests that Balinese culture as a model encourages and generates variation, that numerous "particu-larisms" exist and are accepted. Regardless of their experiential background and individual position within the ritual frame, all resonate with and contribute to the *ramé* atmosphere that is charged with spiritual and social energy generated from the performing arts and ritual actions.

Ramé is that Indonesian notion of charged energy generally involving large groups and combining various activated symbolic orders. Mass social, political, and religious events are interpreted positively as *ramé* throughout much of the country. In Balinese culture, *ramé* incorporates collective spirituality and is the main ideal and goal of all communal events (Wallis 1973:14). This is an aesthetic state in which the possibility arises for individuals to transcend themselves, to more strongly identify with socially and religiously constructed realities, and to be part of the "same vivid and continuous moment."

Gong Kuna

The gamelan *gong kuna* opens the festival and signals the transition from mundane and linear time to sacred and cyclic time. This performance provides the power-ful "bang" that is necessary to mark the transformation of time dimension, and it initiates the energy of the festival. Ida Padanda Ketut Rai stated that a second function is to announce the festival and call human and deity worlds together to Lingsar. This music is iconic, and, however interpreted, a stable connection between these worlds.

The players perform off and on all day and the gamelan as a set is never moved. The *gong kuna* is positioned on the *balé gong* in front of the *gadoh* for the general attendants. The *balé gong* is outside the temple, not close to the main altars within the *gadoh*, but perfectly positioned to welcome participants. All participants walk by the *balé gong* and experience *gong kuna* music, as if to transform them, before entering the temple. Gedé Wija used the verb *mandikan* (to bathe) to describe the effect upon people. The resonating music floods the *gadoh* and *kemaliq* as well, so that participants hear *gong kuna* music no matter where they go within the com-plex. As the cosmologically structured music is imposed upon the environment, it affects and helps transform the inner domain of the participants. One participant stated that it "cleans the hearts" of congregants.

Large gamelan like *gong kuna* are normally positioned in a second or third courtyard of a large Balinese temple. Although it attracts deities and spiritually affects participants, the music is not considered as efficacious as, for example, the Sanskrit mantra of the *padanda*, who from his or her elevated space in front of the main altars invokes the presence of Siwa within his or her body to create holy water. The *gong kuna* music is also too loud for the more refined environment of the inner sanctum. Since the second courtyard at Lingsar is shared with Sasak, and the third a bathing area, the gamelan is instead placed outside the *gadoh* on the path into the courtyard.[1] From the *balé gong*, the *gong kuna* signals the beginning of the festival to human and divine participants, welcomes both, and in general bridges human and divine worlds.

Apart from opening the festival, the *gong kuna* music is not affixed to any particular rite but rather is performed throughout the day; it bears no temporal relationship with any specific activity. However, as Gedé Drawi and Ida Wayan Pasha first intimated and I later corroborated with *gong kuna* musicians, the repertoire uses larger forms as the day proceeds and this is deliberately fashioned to better express and enhance the spiritual experience.

The compositional forms, with structures homologous with cosmology, progressively expand. Performance begins with *gangsaran* pieces, the "bang" which initiates the day; these pieces use forms of eight, sixteen, or thirty-two beats per gong. After one or two such pieces, musicians begin *lelambatan* compositions. As more and more activities commence throughout the day and there is a livelier atmosphere, the performance proceeds from pieces in *tabuh empat* (64 beats per gong), to *tabuh enam* (96 beats) and finally to *tabuh kutus* (128 beats), the most comprehensive spiritual/musical statement. Several participants have noted that the festival and all ritual activities (including those of the *padanda*) become immersed in the power—what Becker or DeVale might call a sonic mandala—of the *gong kuna* music. This is when the atmosphere becomes alive and *ramé*; when events, actions, and performances interlock and intermingle; and when inclined participants are bathed and purified by the music. *Gong kuna* music signifies and indexes "ceremony" and conveys, through homology, notions of the sacred. But since it does not generate any particular rite and is not contextually constrained, its role is to spiritually stimulate and provide the background for ritual action.

While some teachers say that this particular music makes their thoughts peaceful or alters their mental condition from daily concerns to a religious state, few Balinese spend time listening to the *gong kuna*. The music is directed at deities as much as humans, it establishes a lively and spiritual atmosphere, and it is experienced as soundscape. In those so inclined, it produces an aural mandala on which they can focus to purify their inner selves. The *gong kuna* and its music are associated with the Hindu-Javanese-Balinese strata of cultural experience and resonate with the imagery of that time period and its conception of reality.

This music and other activities stop for Mabakti prayers, which proceed with concentration on God and the *padanda*'s mantra recitation and *genta* bell.[2] Throughout the day the *gong kuna* music has generated the expanding spiritual soundscape of the festival in approach to the festival apex—the prayers. Though mostly static, the music accompanies the gradual unfolding of festival rites and inner transformations of participants. As a kind of aural mandala, its statement is somewhat restricted to cosmology; it does not embody the emotive melodies of the other music forms, for example, that of the gamelan *baris*. *Gong kuna* music also lacks the more exciting characteristics of the gamelan *gong gilak*.

Gong Gilak

The *gong gilak* ensembles consist of the gongs and drums from the *gong kuna*, with *réong* instruments and extra processional cymbals added. These gamelans are used in the Mendak Tirta, Mailahang Kebo, and Penglemek or Melukar processions;

they are temporally affixed to the processions and spatially affixed to their routes and destinations.

The ensembles are arranged spatially at the end of particular segments of procession participants. In the Mendak Tirta procession, for example, three temple areas—Pura Ulon, Pura Lingsar Gadoh, Pura Manggis (behind the temple wall)—include a leading *pamangku*, a body of participants, and a trailing *gong gilak*. The ensembles spatially mark the three divisions, as the music shakes the earth and announces the mission. Some have suggested that these three sections unite an anthropomorphic tripartite structure, and that, with this arrangement, participants are safely sandwiched in the middle. The *baleganjur* ensemble that circles the interior of the *gadoh* during Purwédaksina, and the Sasak *baleganjur* that joins Sasak processions similarly join the back of their respective processions.

The *gong gilak* is the Balinese ensemble chosen to accompany, sanctify, and protect the Balinese or shared processions and their sacred missions. The music, associated with excitement, contracted gong-cycles, a marching pulse, and fast circulating cycles, creates an energetic festive mood in the participants as they walk to complete the procession's mission. The music is associated with *buta kala* and works, along with the proper sacrifices, as an offering to them, either transforming them into helpful agents for the procession or frightening them away (both interpretations are expressed). The music thus has an exorcism function. The processions with *gong gilak* occur in the afternoons of opening and closing days: Mendak Tirta begins at about 3:00 p.m. on the opening day, Mailahang Kebo sometime after Mendak Tirta concludes, Purwédaksina follows Mailahang Kebo, and Penglemek occurs on the late afternoon of the final day.

These ensembles create *ramé* by means of powerful sound and movement through space. Processions, parading valued objects and exhibiting stratified but unified social arrangements, greatly heighten spiritual energy, and *gong gilak* releases that energy into outside spaces in one steady stream of meaning, expression, and experience. Balinese processions form a "huge, glorious moving theatre" that uses a road "as a stage" (Dibia 1985:64), and at Lingsar they involve thousands of people moving and creating the moment together.

The Mabakti prayer held at the crossroads on the opening day is similarly participatory, and prayers are enveloped in the sound of *gong gilak* and gamelan *tambur*; these prayers welcome and receive the major deities of Bali and Lombok, linking the Balinese origin and present. The connection between Bali and Lingsar is made explicitly clear. Batara Gunung Agung and Batara Gunung Rinjani are siblings who oversee their respective islands; Batara Alit Sakti directed the Balinese to Lombok; and Batara Gedé Lingsar brought the Balinese to him, supplied the spirit army that guaranteed victory, and permitted their rule for seven generations (see Chapter Three). The gamelan *tambur* represents the forces of Lombok, while the *gong gilak* represents those of Bali. The intermixing music of these two in the Mendak Tirta procession and (usually) for the Mabakti prayers protects the congregants and unifies the martial energies of both islands. The performance expresses the dual ethnic identity of the Balinese of Lombok.

Kidung

Kidung singing is a new music element, introduced in the mid-1990s. While common in Bali at festivals, *kidung* had been very rare in Lombok. At Lingsar it has been held primarily in the *kemaliq* preceding prayers; in 2001 I also heard amplified *kidung* singing coming from the *gadoh*, spreading throughout much of the complex. The praise poetry in the Middle Javanese and High Balinese languages is very appropriate to the event; the language, text, and emotive contours affect participants. One woman commented that it assisted her in remembering God. In the *kemaliq*, it adds a clear Hindu and Balinese element.

Dances

The two historic ritual dance forms are Topeng Sidha Karya (or another *topeng* performance) and Canang Sari, both performed on the main festival day; the new dance is Rejang Déwa. *Topeng* performances are rare in Lombok, and now also rare at Lingsar, but they can be held at temple festivals and life-cycle rites. The dancer/actors adjust the performance to the context. Topeng Sidha Karya, as discussed in Chapter Five, is a masked theater of two or three male dancers who act out many different characters, each with its own mask and manner of speaking, dancing, moving, and acting. At Lingsar, the performance weaves participants and locale into the Balinese chronicles, calling this past into the present. The story specifies the founding of Lingsar and the coming of Balinese righteousness, and the performance features Sidha Karya, a mischievous but benevolent archetypal figure and potent symbol of the efficacious dance and festival.[3] The clowns narrate the story, host the journey into the past, and help articulate that past and its value for the audience.

The performance is held beside the *balé gong* (the usual positioning of *topeng* in Bali is in a second or other courtyard). The *gong kuna* on the *balé gong* assumes the *gong kebyar* form and accompanies the dances with *topeng* repertoire. The performance begins just before Rejang Déwa or Canang Sari, and it is meant to coincide with the main rites of the *padanda*, enhancing and supporting the efficacious power of those rites. There is therefore a direct temporal relationship between *topeng* and the *padanda*, a relationship found also at festivals on Bali.

Topeng Sidha Karya is a ritual with shamanistic, transformative qualities. Characters come from and create the feeling of another historical and spiritual time (Herbst 1997:88). The narrative represents a parallel world in the present; dancers and musicians traverse this world, bringing the audience with them and playing the past in the present (Gold 2004: 106). The performance provides a bridge to the ancestors and dramatizes the coming of the Balinese to Lombok, the institution of dharma and righteousness, and the legitimacy of the mission. Like *gong kuna* music, the dance dissolves time and seeks to impose its order on the environment. Since performances have been held outside the *gadoh* during the main day, only a minority of Balinese participants, along with some Sasak, have watched in any given year; most Balinese are in one of the temples at that time. However, the performance is audible almost everywhere and its message is clear.

Topeng theater, like Canang Sari, has always existed in villages outside of royal control; the target audience are common Balinese and the main discourse is in common Balinese, which functions to bring the legendary past into contemporary focus for all participants. Although farmers may identify with clowns and nobles with heroes, the notions of righteousness and order are understood by all as all share the same social experience. The performance establishes a strong and needed sense of place and legitimacy for the migrant, minority Balinese.

Many believe that the performance either helps entertain the deities as they are invoked or helps invoke them along with the *padanda*'s rituals. Others state that the deities are already present but are called forth to receive offerings as they are honored by the performance. In either case, there is a direct temporal link between *padanda*, *topeng*, and deities. The human audience also enjoys the performance as the clown characters gradually reveal the story of the mandates for authority and chronicle of the lives of heroes, especially since they occasionally step outside the story to poke fun at a character or the plot and to add contemporary reflection to the story.

Since the late 1990s Rejang Déwa, a modern-style dance with specific *gong keb-yar* accompaniment, has been performed in the *gadoh*. Though based on an older form in Karangasem, the dance is relatively new and to my surprise is considered sacred. From the various accounts I collected, it seems that many consider this dance, more than Topeng or Carang Sari, to represent the notion of sacred in Bali; it symbolizes modern Bali, Balinese roots, and everything Bali may represent. Participants responded that Rejang Déwa was "Balinese," "from Bali," and "a sacred dance from Bali." This modernized form of *rejang* (female temple dance) is an offering dance performed while the *padanda* and *pamangku* are presenting offerings, thus it is appropriately positioned before the prayers. I suggest that this is a religious "rite of modernization" within Balinese arts (Laskewicz 2003:185). While undermining traditional notions of ritual dance, the dance redefines notions of the sacred and religious identity. The dancers are proud to perform within the temple.

Canang Sari, the last dance, has a deep tradition of performance not only at Lingsar but also at many Balinese temple festivals in Lombok. The Lingsar version used to involve five male volunteers who danced and thus activated the fertile power of the *canang sari* offerings. Today, the offerings are simpler and are danced by just about anyone who wants to perform, but an element of fertility may still provide foundation for the event.

Unless another gamelan is brought into the *gadoh*—a rare occurrence due to space limitations—the *gong kuna* remains in its *gong kebyar* form (used for *topeng* and Rejang Déwa) and accompanies from the *balé gong*. The composition usually played is "Tabuh Telu," a moderate-tempo piece; others may be used depending on the group. The temporal orientation of Canang Sari interlocks with the rites of the *padanda* and the final stage of the ceremony before the prayers.

Though its meanings have changed, Canang Sari symbolizes the entrance of offerings into the temple; immediately afterward, the *padanda* and *pamangku* begin to consecrate the hundreds of offerings, and collective prayers follow. There are no narrative elements and the dancers simply improvise, but the audience watches closely as they transverse from the outer space to the inner temple space, symbolizing as it does their own physical and spiritual journey into the temple. The dancers, usually commoners, show that the participants, not the officials, are generating this rite, and that the participants are momentarily directing the energy of the festival and reveling in it. Teachers report a sense of place and well-being as a result of the dance, and a recognition of ensuing divine presence. The dance marks the first moment of organized worship within the *gadoh* and prepares congregants for prayer.

Table 6.1 below marks the generalized functions, experiences, indices, and activated behaviors for both the Balinese and the Sasak performing arts.

Interpretive Modes

In each art, energy is released into the environment, and this allows things to happen. The *gong kuna* initiates this energy by marking the transition into festival time. The *gong gilak* permits and symbolizes the missions of processions. The dances prepare participants mentally, emotionally, and spiritually for the coming prayers. *Topeng* signals the coming of deities, the righteousness of Balinese ancestors, and the stage of *padanda* ritual; Rejang Déwa, a modern offering dance, reminds participants that they are modern Balinese and part of the greater Hindu world; Canang Sari presents offerings to the deities in preparation for prayers. Music and dance allow the festival process—its spiritual experience and identity formation— to begin and move forward.

Balinese intellectuals and artists often refer to the concept of *desa/kala/patra* (place/time/context) as a way of explaining and discovering meaning from acts and arts. The concept is context-sensitive and multidimensional (see Herbst 1997) and gives a "sense of place" on social and metaphysical levels; if something does not fit into a place/time/context, then it must be out of context (ibid.:1). The idea can also reveal different meanings for the same form or item, depending on its time or place or context, or its particular reference or perspective. It thus is flexible and can accommodate multiple perspectives. Forms and items at Lingsar are subject to philosophizing. Many Balinese, particularly older nobles and priests, can speak extensively on these subjects and their interactions with objects, actions, arts, and symbolism. *Desa/kala/patra* is a way of understanding phenomena at the festival.

The performance elements and their symbolic codes coalesce to structure and give meaning to the festival. Gamelan music, for instance, is associated with the element of sound or voice (*sabda*), one of three elements, sometimes called Trikaya Parisuda (the three good acts), necessary to complete the experience of Balinese ritual. The other two elements—thought (*idep*) and action (*bayu*)—are considered fulfilled by prayer and dance respectively (Harnish 1990:204). In a conversation with me, Ida Bagus Putu Basma, a religion specialist with the Ministry of Education and Culture suggested that gamelan music is an elaboration of the *padanda*'s *genta* bell, prayer is an embellishment of the *padanda*'s mantra recitation, and dance is an extension of the *padanda*'s *mudra* hand gestures. From this point of

TABLE 6.1. Generalized Function, Experience, Index, and Activated Behaviors at the Festival

INSTRUMENT	FUNCTION	EXPERIENCE	INDEX	BEHAVIOR ACTIVATED
Gong Kuna	Signals deities/humans with activities	Participants bathed in sound, sound purification	Religious Ceremony	Festival itself
	Expands with activities			Participant energy
Gong Gilak	Follows processions	Protects; is martial	Movement	Walk to holy spots
topeng	Entertains deities; reenacts chronicles	Tells myth; is educational	Narrative; Ancestors	*padanda* rites
Rejang Déwa	Presents offerings; entertains	Modern Balinese	Sacred Balinese Dance	Offerings gathered; preparation for prayer
Canang Sari	Escorts offerings into *gadoh*; temple dance	Joy, involvement	Participant offering	Offerings gathered; preparation for prayer
Tambur	Leads processions	Protects; is martial	Ancestral power	Proceed through space safely
Baris	Performs at entrance; follows processions	Protects; stirs emotions, memories	Myth; Dances	Movement/dances
Preret	Bridge to ancestors Accompanies offerings	Suspended time Sound purification	Ancestors; Deity(ies)	Initiates or concludes offering production
Gong Sasak/*Baleganjur*	Plays off and on Follows processions	Modern gamelan; Protects	Gandrung; Procession	Dance; walk/circumambulate
Gendang Beleq	Follow processions Play off-and-on	Modernized culture	Cultural presentation	Dance/walk
Baris dance	Leads processions; intimidates	Protects; is martial	Ancestral power	Proceed through space safely
Batek/Baris	Follows processions; Entertains deity	Myth/emotive	Narrative; fertility	Movement; prayer
Gandrung	Performed occasionally	Enjoyment	Fun; fertility	Watch; participate

view (which prioritizes brahminical Hinduism), the performing arts and prayer link with the rites of the *padanda*. *Gong kuna* music is played throughout the festival and Topeng Sidha Karya (when present), Canang Sari, Rejang Déwa, and dance music are performed while the festival approaches the prayer stage, at which point all of the participants and deities are present and the symbolisms and offerings have been "brought to life."

It is the intermingling of various symbolic codes that provides the deep meaning of Balinese ritual (C. Geertz 1980:114), as these codes in their interaction recreate what they symbolize. The *penyor* poles become male and mountain symbols, and the *lamak* weavings become female and water symbols, forming a union of both gender and geography. Holy water vessels become consecrated containers of divine boons; the colorful flags in the altars become the deities they represent; the dances make the ancestors present; the music becomes the dharmic order of the cosmos; and the *padanda* transform into Siwa. These transformations trigger the *ramé* atmosphere that generates collective spirituality and unifies Balinese participants, and the whole becomes greater than the sum of the parts.

Participants are aware of connections between the performing arts and the *padanda*'s rites. These intertwine to produce the proper experience: Hindu-Buddhist-Javanese-Balinese value mixes with Sanskrit Indic value to signify the unity of various experiential worlds. The *gong kuna*, Canang Sari, Rejang Déwa, *kidung*, and especially Topeng Sidha Karya are arts that support the *padanda*'s rites. The experience of all these acts and performances simultaneously presents a temporal climax, when the meanings of all activities and arts reach an apex and the Indic world of the *padanda*, mantra, and *genta* unifies with the Balinese world of *topeng*, Canang Sari, and *gong kuna*. The different worlds of Indian theology and Balinese collective ancestral worship are reconciled and experienced together, generating a state of *ramé*.

Unlike many decades ago, the Balinese now have the opportunity to chant together "Trisandya"—the Sanskrit mantra formerly restricted to priests—that allows direct participation with the Indic world of festivals. Sanskrit is a code and the *padanda* an icon for elite, brahminical Hinduism. Collective participation expands the sense of festival co-creation and communitas and broadens the festival experience to include multiple worlds of religious practice. Of course the Balinese farmer, the urban dweller, the modern intellectual, the noble, and the priest experience different subjective dimensions of the same collective experience.

Although Balinese society is stratified, caste divisions tend to evaporate during rituals, especially during temple festivals, which assert the spiritual unity of villagers against their status inequalities (C. Geertz 1973b:452). Every Balinese ritual, in fact, establishes a sort of equality of status and purpose: the groom and bride at a wedding become Siwa and Parvati, and every corpse is a divine king for a day (Boon 1986:245). At temple festivals, everyone is a respected and honored participant.[4] Each congregant ritually bathes before departing to the temple, and they wear their finest ceremonial clothing to emphasize the special occasion and their special status.[5] All are addressed equally over the loudspeakers in High Balinese, the language normally directed at the nobility, and all contribute to the event. The sense of communitas and common purpose—instigated by the performing arts that in turn trigger *ramé*—strengthens the experience.

Because the Lingsar festival attracts Balinese who normally have no reason to come together, the communitas achieved may be even deeper. This experience of active community is incessantly instilled by the performing arts. The *gong kuna*, *gong gilak*, Topeng Sidha Karya, Canang Sari, Rejang Déwa, and *kidung* performances embrace the Balinese in distinctive ways and reenact spiritual pasts, reminding them of their common heritage, that they are all linked to the same sacred source, and that this source is essentially what they are worshipping. The event becomes successful on a spiritual level, and the operative political myth is that they have recreated the righteous continuum of Balinese-Majapahit power in contemporary Lombok.

When participants undergo this experience, the festival is successful and they expect to receive sufficient rainfall or other boons. The experience of being enveloped within the state of *ramé* is primarily collective, since the participants themselves have created it despite their different positions in the ritual frame. Everyone works for the collective experience regardless of status. Variations in individual experience are normal and accepted; in fact, these contribute to the sense of *ramé* by incorporating and activating greater diversity. The Lingsar experience also reestablishes a sense of self, because it is Lingsar that is the primary source of Balinese identity in Lombok.

Sasak Music and Dance

Sasak performing arts are not well known outside of the island, and few scholarly works have been dedicated to discovering indigenous theories of aesthetics, philosophizing, self-orientation, group identification, and so forth. This lack of data frustrates deeper explorations of context-specific meanings, semiotics, and experience at the festival. The fact that many Sasak are struggling with religious identification and behavioral codes further blurs the situation. To suggest that any experience might be deemed "religious" or "spiritual" within a non-Islamic context and performing arts is problematic in today's contested Lombok. Apart from comments by outsiders such as Martinom and the late Rahil, and some insiders such as Saparia and the late Amaq Jasira, few Sasak have offered insights regarding internal experiences of the event.

Gamelan *Tambur/Baris*

The gamelan *tambur/baris* sets up on the *balé kembar* across from the *balé gong*, on the opposite side of the entrance into the *gadoh*. The musicians begin around midday and tend to play when the *gong kuna* musicians rest, but they also often play simultaneously with the *gong kuna*. This is the ensemble that represents the official Sasak aesthetic, and their performance generally indicates that the morning activities of the *kebon odeq* and *pesaji* offerings (in the Sasak compound) are completed;

the performance marks a new stage of the given day. The equal stature of the *gong kuna* and the gamelan *tambur/baris* seems meaningful to Sasak teachers: all participants entering the temple encounter equal Sasak input and contribution to the festival.

On the opening day the gamelan *tambur* leads the Mendak Tirta procession to Pura Manggong directly following the Baris dancers (the Batek dancers do not usually participate). Just in front of the *tambur* and gong are musicians carrying the remaining instruments of the gamelan *baris*, which are only rarely played, and following the *tambur* are the *pamangku* and entourage from Pura Ulon. Teachers agree that the *tambur* and gong produce voices of the sacred past, as it is believed that this ensemble is as old as the temple. Their position at the very front symbolizes their function: to boldly announce the solemn mission to any and all creatures of the invisible and visible worlds and to challenge any competitors as if going to war. The simple music makes a simple statement. The music is not considered related to the *buta kala* or other creatures; it simply embodies the timeless messages of warfare and legendary moral authority. The processions would not go without the gamelan *tambur*. When the *redeb* and *suling* are added to the gamelan *tambur* in this context, they perform "Janggel," which is overlaid upon the "Tak Tak Pong" music of the *tambur*.[6]

This ensemble also accompanies the Muspa/Mabakti prayers of the Balinese at the crossroads at the conclusion of Mendak Tirta. Like the *gong gilak*, the *tambur* keeps playing and preserves its function of protecting the congregants while they pray. The gamelan *tambur* is the official, sanctifying agent for all processions during the festival (except Purwédaksina, which is held in the *gadoh*); it always assumes the front position, and it continues playing until the entire event has ended. The position and function indicate its prominent status.

This gamelan represents concealed spiritual power, *kesaktian*, which is directly related to the deity, the *kemaliq*, and to the ancestors in general. The parading and sounding of the two instruments are meaningful events associated with virtuous and powerful Sasak ancestors triumphantly marching through impure space to discover the water springs of Lingsar. This mythic past, and the general world of the ancestors, is recalled into the present for communion with Sasak descendants. The music has curative powers and speaks of past martial power. The fact that the gamelan *tambur* leads all processions supports the contention of Sasak leadership in the festival; i.e., that Sasak contributions guarantee prosperity and sufficient rainfall. Participants refer to gamelan *tambur* particularly as *khas* Sasak (original Sasak culture), and many feel it symbolizes their past in general.

The gamelan *baris* has a more diverse contextualization. It adds a Sasak identity to the soundscape outside the temple in the *balé kembar*, where gamelan *baris* and *gong kuna* function as flankers of the temple, symbolically bridging and protecting the space. The pieces played there are usually ones that include long melodies within single *gongan*, and these have direct emotional associations. The music is not specific to the temporal dimension of the festival (successive pieces do not gradually expand like the *gong kuna* repertoire); instead, pieces that demand more virtuoso performance technique, such as "Telek" and "Jepon," are included. *Balé kembar* performances allow musicians to play pieces unconnected with the Batek Baris dance repertoire, and they enliven and increase the volume of these pieces with vigor as they proudly demonstrate their skill. These constitute the stationary ceremonial repertoire spatially anchored to the *balé kembar*.

This gamelan is played in processions around the temple area—Mendak Tirta, Mendak Kebon Odeq, Ngilahang Kaoq, Ngilahang Kebon Odeq, Ngilahang Pesaji, Mendak Pesaji, and Ngaturang Pesaji—and normally joins the Beteteh procession. The most frequent piece in processions is "Janggel." The term refers to walking and the piece is an index for moving through space. The dancers usually walk along until they reach important parts of the spatial discourse. During Ngilahang Kaoq, for example, the dancers are given time to perform in front of the main temple gates and entrances, and, during the initial parts of the processions into the *kemaliq* (Mendak Kebon Odeq, Mendak Pesaji), they perform in the outer courtyard of the *kemaliq*. These are special points in the processional route, relating to the orientation of the festival and to the entrances (considered orifices) into the temple and *kemaliq*.

The pieces used during procession dance breaks are "Tamburan" for the Baris dancers and usually "Nyanyi" for the Batek/Telek dancers. These pieces and dances evoke the precolonial mythic period of the Sasak ancestors, and, like Balinese music, they call this period with its Panji, Datu Wali Milir, and Wali Sanga associations into the present. The processions into the *kemaliq* grandly announce and accompany the *kebon odeq* and *pesaji* offerings; the male and female *kebon odeq* are as king and queen and the *pesaji* as entourage in a royal procession. The Batek/Telek performance in front of the *kemaliq* at the conclusion of several processions is the main form of refined entertainment for the deity who enters the rocks of the altar. The rocks, vessels of the divine, are also charged with energy as they are sprinkled with holy water and dressed in ceremonial colors of yellow and white. All of these meanings merge and intermingle in a charged atmosphere honoring the ancestors.

The last of the required gamelan *baris* pieces is "Pejarakan," which is a request to the deities that they return home. It is played during the Beteteh procession that concludes when the *kebon odeq* are thrown into the Sarasuta river. The Batek/Telek dancers often perform on a small bridge above the river as a way to send off the *kebon odeq* and symbolically terminate direct contact with the deities.[7] This moment symbolizes the ancestors returning to their world. "Pejarakan" is associated with this act and features glissandi to express sadness or melancholy, or, as one teacher put it, "the sudden shadow of the mountain," over the departure of the ancestors.

The gamelan *baris* performs emotion-laden melodies and recalls the past in multiple ways. One teacher stated that the music encourages listeners to "remember," and several commented on how melodic contour represents particular emotional states. The piece "Janggel," played so often during processions, inserts the image of *wayang* theater and the travels between mythical (righteous and impure) spaces.[8] Much of the remaining repertoire continues the sensation of traveling through space, as the *tambur* and gong maintain a four-to-one ratio and *redeb* and *suling* melodies are laid above this structure. This juxtaposition harmonizes two meaningful worlds: gamelan *tambur* with its evocation of the sacred ancestor world, and gamelan *baris* with its suggestion of a world of early Sasak emotions and belief. Combined, they embody the sensation of moving between stages and spaces as within *wayang* theater. The second repertoire, with its long single *gongan* structures, provides a sense of suspended time; this role is marked by the spatial orientation of the gamelan *baris* on the *balé kembar* across from the *gong kuna*.

The constituent parts of the gamelan *baris* reference different worlds and can be divided into three parts: the *tambur* and gong, the percussion instruments related to *wayang* Sasak, and the *redeb* and *suling*, with their gender and Javanese associations. Most Sasak believe that Java is the origin of much of their culture, and they strive to follow the cultural and religious ideals of both mythic and contemporary Java, while downplaying the many cultural traits they share with Bali. The *redeb* and *suling* instruments evoke East Javanese palace life and the union of sexual energies. The instruments also speak of the literary traditions and poetry of early Lombok, thus unifying the mythic worlds of Java and Lombok. The participants can therefore experience various dimensions that sanction actions and identifications in one single performance.

Preret

The *preret* (the discussion is in the past tense here) formerly constituted its own dimension in the festival. It opened the festival for the Sasak with its loud, shrill sound, and, with "Turun Daun," set the stage for the preparation of the *kebon odeq* offerings. There were direct temporal and spatial relationships with the *kebon odeq*, the most important of all festival offerings. The musicians performed within the same courtyard before, during, and after the creation of these offerings. They also performed in close proximity in processions including *kebon odeq*, and maintained the same relationship with *pesaji* offerings in other processions, where they served generally as a vehicle intersecting the divine, the offerings, and the participants. Some teachers, including Sanusi, reported that the sound helped purify the space, time, and participants. He and a few others explained that the music transforms time, rises up to contact deities, gives the deities voice, and bridges the ancestor and human worlds. The *preret* signaled the completion of offerings and the first main Sasak ritual stage each day. This initial, daily framing rite consecrated the offerings and enhanced the sacred time and space of the event.

The instrument was also used in the Sasak processions and sometimes in the shared Beteteh procession, performing either "Pendaratan Alep," associated with walking, or "Turun Daun." The players walked immediately behind all of the offerings in procession, and their performance sanctified and presented the offerings to the deities, while enveloping the participants within its sacred sound. They continued performing during worship periods within the *kemaliq*, maintaining a link to the deities as the offerings evoked the double-gendered, tripartite divine they represented. The instrument played specific pieces to accompany prayer periods and others to accompany the removal of offerings. The *preret* was thus affixed both spatially and temporally to offerings and to some of the most crucial rites of the festival.

The instrument was the code for communication with deities. With its altered voice, it made contact with deities, invoked them, entertained them, helped transmit prayers to them, symbolized their voice, and acted as a bridge for their entrance into the festival. The *preret* was an icon of the ancestor and deity world. Most participants did not hear the *preret* when it accompanied the work on the *kebon odeq* and *pesaji* offerings in the Sasak compound, for this time when sacred creations were initiated and completed was a secret part of the festival, cordoned off from the general attendants. The instrument's aural codes, however, were publicly and readily available during the processions and in the *geria* ceremonies in the *kemaliq*. The music continually presented offerings and prayers to the deities and represented deity/ancestor value to the participants. Some teachers stated that they concentrated on the sound during prayer, much like the Balinese concentrate on the mantra recitation and *genta* bell of the *padanda* during prayer. Like the *padanda*'s chanting and the *genta*'s ringing, the *preret* was a conduit to and from the deities. The disappearance of this code, and the changing indices in the soundscape, mark a transition in both Sasak participation at the festival and in general sociocultural orientation.

Gamelan *Baleganjur/Gong* Sasak

For decades the Sasak gamelan *baleganjur* club has participated in processions, helping to complete the musical offering. Its function appears to be very similar to that of the *gong gilak*. Musician Amaq Wati confirmed that the gamelan chases malign spirits away and serves to protect participants; his friend Amaq Rena stated that the sound made everything more *ramé*.

The *baleganjur* instrumentation is assembled from the *gong* Sasak, sometimes called *gong gandrung*, from Montor village. This gamelan is performed on the *balé bundar*, the furthest *balé* from the temple in the complex. Though the music has little direct temporal or spatial orientation with other events, Amaq Wati stated that the "*suaranya penting*" (the [gamelan's] voice is important) to the festival. It adds another bronze gamelan aesthetic (with inherent values) and contributes to a *ramé* atmosphere.

Gendang Beleq

Gendang beleq makes the atmosphere much more *ramé*. Saparia said that the ensemble "*lambangkan jaman ini*" (symbolizes the current era); it's clear that, despite the former gamelan image, *gendang beleq* now signifies both Sasak "tradition" and "modernity." The musicians of two or three clubs form part of processions (notably excepting Mendak Tirta) and are placed behind the gamelan *baleganjur*. In faster-paced processions (e.g., Ngilahang Kaoq), the gamelan plays with little choreography; in slower processions (i.e., Ngilahang Kebon Odeq/Pesaji) the musicians have several opportunities to show their stuff. On these occasions, the *ceng-ceng* players perform tight and coordinated choreography, winding in and out, raising and clanging their cymbals together, forming snaking and circling lines, and shaking their hips. In 2001 I watched older participants who, I assumed, retained belief in the rites as they circumambulated the *kemaliq*. Most did not heed the dance and tried to avoid the musicians; my impression was that they were annoyed by the extra noise and distraction. To me, the ensemble represented the changing value of the festival for Sasak participants from "religious" to "public display," and from "offering" to "sanitized, presentational culture."

The ensemble produces "traditional" music that features bronze instruments, *pélog*-like tuning, and gong cycles. However, considering how it is packaged (set choreography, dressed youth) and its absence of history at the festival, my feeling is that experienced participants do not know how to place the performance. Arbainjulianda, the son of the Sasak official for Pura Ulon, said that while the multiple ensembles add more *ramé* atmosphere, they "*tak begitu perlu*" (aren't really needed). From what I gathered, the traditional signs were not interpreted as supporting the local foundations for the festival. Since this was an addition, the new sounds represented a change that undermined those same foundations (see Chapter Seven).

Despite the fact that the players did not appear to respect the inherent beliefs of the temple and festival, they accepted holy water within the *kemaliq* (while in procession) like other participants: with arms outstretched, head bowed, and water sprinkled upon them before drinking. Of course, the water on a hot day is very refreshing (I can attest to that), but some players appeared to have experience with receiving holy water. Their performance remains a rite of modernization that encourages further change and detraditionalization. The traditional music elements, out of place in the festival's history, erode the meanings that some say go back centuries. Yet the underlying signs within the ensembles, the music, and the players' actions are not entirely foreign to the Lingsar context.

Dances

The Baris dance—soldiers with rifles in Dutch outfits—presents one of the most powerful images in Lombok's history. Clearly, these outfits did not exist before the twentieth century. Sanusi reported that the earlier dancers wore black *kain* material with yellow *slendang* scarves and headpieces. He was uncertain when the outfits changed or why precisely, though he did say that Dutch soldiers were "*kuat sekali*" (very strong), and it seems that this image of power carried over into new costumes.

The dance ideally consists of eight soldiers and one commandant, together constituting the sacred number nine, which is interpreted as a periphery (eight) around a center (commandant) and also as a representation of the legendary Wali Sanga evangelists. Just as the dancers are not real soldiers, most of the rifles are not real rifles, yet the dance constitutes a moving sacred form safeguarding the processions and festival in general. Securing the festival guarantees its efficacy, and the Baris dance, with its association with the sacred gamelan *tambur* and the original history of the temple, completes this message. The fact that Balinese officials and participants have always allowed, apparently without complaint, the Baris dancers to precede every shared procession indicates a similar acknowledgement.

The Batek/Telek dance evokes East Javanese palace life and Panji, the legendary hero and lover. The dance is associated with Datu Wali Milir (or some other hero) and his coming to Lingsar, with Panji representing Milir and the other characters his entourage. Datu Wali Milir is celebrated as the great king from Java, and he embodies the Javanese imagery of heroism. Panji is from Java, Milir (according to most teachers) comes from Java, and the title *wali* indicates Islam and Milir's connection to the Wali Sanga Islamic evangelists. (Sanusi claimed Milir was sent by the Wali Sanga.) The hero introduces Islam and affirms the teaching as he transforms the landscape with his sacrifice. The water springs are an index for all he represents, regardless of his name. Gushing springs equal the hero, early Islam, and fertility. The cross-dressing of the characters promotes this message. Sanusi indicated that the mixing of sexes in the dance made everything "*lebih subur*" (more fertile); this was corroborated by other Sasak such as Saparia and by some Balinese, such as the late I Wayan Kartawirya. In this way the deified ancestor is conflated as the spring and credited with fertility regeneration.

The dance also speaks of the *telek* myth of forlorn lovers singing of their folly as they circle the grounds in penance. This narrative together with the one above unite the worlds of the Javanese (Panji, Milir, Wali Sanga) and the Sasak (*telek*, Milir) in a single performance. Though there were later times when Sanusi sought to discredit the *telek* connection, when I asked him which of these narratives was the correct one in 1987, he said without further comment, "*keduaanya*" (both of them).

When appearing at Lingsar, the Gandrung dance has no direct temporal relationship with any other event, though its timing naturally avoids the processions and prayer periods. It is performed in a Sasak space (generally the compound near the *kebon odeq* courtyard) and may occur on one or more afternoons or even in the evening (though this sometimes obligates security). While everyone considered Gandrung cathartic fun, most teachers deemed it a fertility dance. The dancer (in the 1980s, Padmawati) received incense in a courtyard from the Sasak priest and momentarily transformed into the female divine inviting local men to dance briefly with her; her dancing in close proximity with men promoted fertility.

This form is changing. Gandrung is rarely performed and not regarded as essential to the event. Its former status as a flexible but necessary fertility dance seems to have transitioned to a less sacred, marginalized display case. When I asked Parman in 2001 if the dance was needed for fertility purposes, he smiled, shook his head, and answered "*ndak*" (no). In the 1980s Parman was one of the teachers who saw a benefit for fertility in the dance.

Table 6.1 shows the generalized functions, experiences, indices, and activated behaviors of both the Sasak and the Balinese performing arts.

Interpretations

The performing arts formerly completed the processions, along with other enlivened symbolic codes (such as the *kebon odeq*, *pesaji*, *momot*), and transformed Sasak rites into meaningful streams of activated symbols associated with earlier beliefs in the ancestors and culture heroes. Today, much of this ritual system remains (such as the Batek Baris or gamelan *tambur*), though some of it seems to be transitioning into more secular dimensions that reflect the evolving Sasak orientation. Regardless, the arts articulate the beliefs and orientations of the participants, and they create powerful and *ramé* atmospheres as the varieties of music and the activities intermingle to produce heightened states of meaning. Every rite, including each procession, is filled with music, dance, and action. The diverse arts generate diverse ritual behaviors and experiences.

One way in which Sasak performing arts are distinct from their Balinese counterparts is that they are often paraded altogether. Gamelan *tambur/baris*, Baris/Telek dance, *gendang beleq*, and *baleganjur* participate in nearly every procession; the same arts may be performed during worship periods. The exceptions have been the gamelan *baris* performing without specific temporal constraints on the *balé kembar*, the gamelan *gandrung* accompanying the dance, and the *preret* framing the creation of the offerings. To contrast, the Balinese arts are separated by function; dances and some music happen only at specified times, often on one occasion only. Gamelans *gong kuna* and *gilak* do not perform simultaneously, and Canang Sari performs separately from Topeng Sidha Karya and Rejang Déwa; each of the three dances occurs but once. Ida Wayan Pasha stated that the Sasak prefer everything to happen "*sekaligus*" (together). The inherent meanings of each art are thus juxtaposed into the wide variety of rites in which they appear, once again generating diversity.

Most Sasak attend the festival with high spiritual expectations that have accumulated over years of experience. The desire for communitas and divine communion may be stronger among the Sasak since Lingsar is the last major annual context in the western plain to worship the natural/ancestral powers. This is the only public setting for worship directed toward these particular powers, and it is important for those Sasak remaining in the area who hold Waktu Telu beliefs to participate in some way. The various performing arts supply a rich mosaic of spiritual symbols that express the necessary experience to attain communitas and divine communion. Sasak participants are quite diverse. Some originate near Lingsar, others come from different districts; some are Waktu Telu who have little association with Islam, others live in Muslim communities; and still others are bureaucrats, moderate Waktu Lima, and even *haji*. Some are farmers, others are traders, some have received school education, others have not. The subjective experience of the Sasak is probably more varied than among the Balinese, because each Sasak has a different interest in and benefits from the festival in a unique way.

The quality of *ramé*, a goal shared with the Balinese, reaches its zenith when the gamelan *tambur/baris*, *preret* or *gendang beleq*, and *baleganjur* are played simultaneously in conjunction with the processions and the *geria* ceremonies. Here the worlds of the nominal Muslim Sasak come together in space and time, and gain definition and focus. The gamelan *tambur/baris* and Batek Baris dance unify the worlds of Java and Sasak in resonance with the world of deities and the water springs. Different rhythms, melodies, and musical sounds combine to create a unified whole between these worlds and their values. This, I believe, is the experience sought by most Sasak, and it occurs multiple times in suitable places for its realization.

Mendak Tirta is the first procession of the festival, Beteteh the last. Between these two processions shared with the Balinese are the shared Ngilahang Kaoq procession, the three Sasak Mendak Kebon Odeq/Pesaji processions, and the three Ngilahang Pesaji processions. There are three shared processions (Mendak Tirta, Beteteh, Ngilahang Kaoq), three Sasak Mendak processions (one Mendak Kebon Odeq, two Mendak Pesaji), and three Ngilahang processions (one Ngilahang Kebon Odeq, two Ngilahang Pesaji). Saparia noted that this makes a total of nine, the same total as the elements within *kebon odeq*, the number figurations of *pesaji* and *topat*, and the number of Baris dancers. The three Ngilahang processions in the *kemaliq* similarly circle the altar three times, thus again equaling nine.

These three-part and nine-part configurations demonstrate that processions and circumambulations relate to mandala-like forms found within Waktu Telu cosmology and numerology. Sasak processions, easily more numerous than their Balinese counterparts, occur on the three important days of the festival. Perhaps the Sasak are more obsessed with the numbers three (after all, *telu* does mean three) and nine than their Balinese neighbors; these numbers appear throughout the festival and may indicate that generating and unifying binarisms such as microcosm/macrocosm or Balinese/Sasak, and making the two into one, thereby equally three is one main goal of the festival. Three is further realized in the number of *geria* ceremonies, which follow a symbolic prescription of initiation, life, and death, while the number nine equals the number of legendary Wali Sanga evangelists. Sanusi, Saparia, and others discussed the importance of numerology in ritual actions, and how the entire festival process is structured upon divisions of three and nine, a process tacitly realized by participants with accumulated festival experience.

Temple structures are also subject to numerological philosophizing. Reflecting increasing religiosity, these efforts have concentrated on mapping Islamic numerology onto structure. For instance, Sanusi in the 1980s and Arbainjulianda in 2001 asserted that the nine outdoor bathing spots equated with the Wali Sanga, that the five showers within the *pesiraman* equaled the five pillars of Islam, and that the seventeen steps between *gadoh* and *kemaliq* reflected the *rukun* (basic principles of Islam). A variety of interpretative modes are available to those who seek a more Islamic experience.

Each ritual stage includes as many performing arts as possible, which unify the respective worlds they symbolize. "Temporal climaxes" are frequent—beginning with Ngilahang Kaoq and continuing through each Mendak Kebon Odeq/Pesaji and Ngilahang Kebon Odeq/Pesaji procession, through each *geria* ceremony, and concluding with the Beteteh procession. It is within this context that I suggest *gendang beleq* is acquiring a meaning that resonates with modernity, as its musical signs, presentational style, and functions become engrained. The ensemble and its music represent transition and may become metaphors for the lived experience of many participants. Its ingredients are appropriate: the elements are largely traditional, but the packaging—the visual presentation, the performance itself, and the viewers' experience is modern and nonritual. In the meantime the music adds a powerful voice to the construction of a *ramé* environment.

The *geria* ceremonies provide an opportunity to sit directly before the deity and to experience the incense, the holy water, the prayers, the flowers used for praying, and (formerly) the sound of the *preret*. The additional sounds of gamelan *tambur/baris* and gamelan *baleganjur* flood the *kemaliq*, and these sound worlds coincide together to realize various pasts, invoke the divine, and to balance and purify the space and time of the occasion. The congregants in the *kemaliq* are a mixed group: Sasak commoners and farmers, nominal Muslims, a few orthodox Muslims (including one or two *haji*),[9] and many Balinese commoners and farmers. Most of these are associated with the temple or with the village of Lingsar, and they come to commune with the divine and experience *ramé* and communitas.[10] They do not pray to the same notion of the divine, and they undergo different subjective experiences. Yet they share the moment of collective experience together, and they pray for the same types of results (rainwater, prosperity, health, and so forth).

The social distinctions of this group and others in the *kemaliq* disappear during the festival. The sense of equal purpose and spiritual unity in religious participatory action is the same as for the Balinese. Sanusi claimed to welcome everyone and anyone, and his successor Min says the same. The *kemaliq* rites are subject to a wide range of interpretation. The priest's formulas are silent, and this contributes to variation since the participants do not know what names are given to the divine or the language used. The *kemaliq* group, more diverse than that in the *gadoh*, achieves a deep solidarity. They are unified in collective action and share the experience of communitas and *ramé* atmosphere. This unity from such heterogeneity does not occur elsewhere; similar syncretic rites are obsolete in most of modern Lombok.[11]

Sasak participants learn how to behave and how to interpret the events and the performing arts. Sanusi mentioned that new participants would stand to the side of most rites and were shy until they learned what behavior was appropriate. They learn that the deities are made present by ritual action, that the experience of the ancestors is generated by the performing arts, and that Islamic values can be accommodated. Since this experience has become rare outside of Lingsar, active participants join in almost every procession and are present in or around the *kemaliq* during ceremonies (whether in the sanctum or not) to sense as much of this experience as possible. Their participation realizes the Sasak presence and creates the festival; they help formulate their own experience.

The conception of the local divinity (Datu Wali Milir, Datu Selaparang, Batara Lingsar, Haji Abdul Maliq, no-name) may be confusing for some participants, leading to wider interpretations. The culture hero is the deified ancestor of the *kemaliq*, sent by the Wali Sanga, who sacrificed himself to create the spring and prosperity, according to several teachers. The entire deity/ancestor world inhabits the *kemaliq* and its altar stones, according to others; Allah guided the hero, who then introduced Islam, according to still others. Active Sasak participants accept one or more of these interpretations, depending upon the circumstance and the particular context and activity, but they share an understanding that the divine is actualized at Lingsar, that there is an opportunity to ask for boons or pardon or rainwater, and that the performing arts, in conjunction with the offerings, other ritual objects, actions, and the officiates make this possible.

Participant interests reflect positions in the ritual frame. Farmers are the majority and have the greatest stake in the festival's success; for them, rainwater and fertility (land and human) are the major goals of the festival. Others—traders, small businessmen, artists, and students—may receive these same benefits or the fulfillment of personal vows. Many Sasak participants are afraid that not attending would spell disaster for them. The lure and tradition of the festival and its performing arts are hard to discontinue despite the power of reformist Islam and modern thinking.

The popular festival interpretation emphasizes the unity of mythic Javanese and Sasak worlds, implying a continuum of religious and cultural values between these two. Bali is denied a major role in the discovery of Lingsar, in festival leadership, and in the Javanese/Sasak bond. An important aspect of the experience is to create a border with the Balinese and to stamp a Sasak identification onto the festival and the arts as something uniquely their own. These efforts have been crucial in the formulation of a contemporary Sasak identity in connection to Lingsar. The denial of Balinese affiliation, as well as the increasing Islamic associations, allow for continued participation. The musical traditions are something that Sasak leaders and participants can proudly call their own. With the exception of *preret* music (which may have ceased), the arts at Lingsar have been removed from debates over what is acceptable for contemporary Sasak identity and what is non-Islamic and forbidden. The *tambur/baris* and *gendang beleq* illuminate part of the problem. The *tambur/baris* couples Waktu Telu and Waktu Lima elements; with its label as *khas* Sasak it is a protected sound. *Gendang beleq*, though traditional in sound and instrumentation, has been decontextualized and validated as authentic Sasak expression and activity. Most importantly, neither ensemble is Balinese or has Balinese associations.

To some Sasak, every important rite represents "authentic" "traditional" Sasak culture, and indicates that it all began with their ancestors. This has been important in contemporary Lombok, as forces have struggled to find living traditions and customs that express Sasak cultural identity without links to animism or Balinese culture. Through reinterpretations and redefinitions, the festival and its performing arts (without *preret* and perhaps without Gandrung) are *khas* Sasak and acceptable experiences for molding and formulating identity. The festival is now a foundation to conceptualize the past and to embrace the present, as the Sasak evolve into a more modern and Islamic entity. Despite this transition that ultimately rationalizes the festival for Sasak participation, that participation seems to be decreasing, for the core participants are older and dying. Young people may come, but they stay mostly on the sidelines, watching as spectators. Part of the rationale for adding *gendang beleq* may have been to lure younger people into the festival to maintain Sasak presence and offset the increasing numbers of Balinese.

The Festival as a Whole

The festival is an enormous and evolving multidimensional text. Each element of its realization—the temple, the histories, the spatial and temporal settings, the participants, the performing arts, the ritual objects, the numerous rites and circumambulations, the experiences, the religious officiates—contains multidimensional subtexts. The participants are drawn to Lingsar to sense its multiple realms, to experience, as Fernandez (1986:165) indicates for African religious movements, the "organizing images that are at play in ritual performance and see how microcosm and macrocosm, inner things and outer things, centers and peripheries, upper things and lower things, time-present and time-past, are related" and how they lead to a "return to the whole." This is the wholeness of communitas, when the divine is revealed and the individual and community are unified and absorbed within it. Among the Sasak, it is important to note only those with Waktu Telu sympathies (that is, those who participate actively) desire such unity. The increasing Islamic interpretations of the festival are now contesting the notion of "returning to the whole" of a pre-orthodox Islamic period.

The efficacy of the music is to enact the transformation of time and space, to reactualize the structures of microcosm and macrocosm (and male and female) and three- and nine-part forms, and to manifest the mythic pasts they reference. Music is the mechanism that generates the festival, marks its stages, and provides the spiritual soundscape for both individual concentration/prayer and martial processional action. The performing arts in general activate the lives, symbolisms, and meanings of the offerings and other static structures. The interlocking of musical sound and musical instruments with all of the ritual acts and objects creates the state of *ramé* and the spiritual balance and harmony for the successful festival. Music unlocks and sanctions energy and allows the actions and behaviors of the festival to unfold.

Any occasion in Balinese or Sasak culture derives "increased meaning and value from the presence of struck instruments" (Wallis 1979:84). The festival presents a rich array of percussion ensembles not found elsewhere together. *Gong kuna, gong gilak, tambur, baris, gendang beleq, gong* Sasak and *baleganjur* all "strike" in addressing the multiple meanings of the festival with their respective human and divine audiences. The festival messages are "epitomized in each move and magnified by the very evidence of the profusion of sounds and symbols" (Abrahams 1982:167). Music affects every participant at the festival, expresses the festival's messages to all, and reactualizes the histories of Balinese and Sasak culture.

As the participants shape their temperaments in such a context and develop their own subjectivity, music and dance regenerate that subjectivity and are the positive agents in the creation and maintenance of the sensibility developed during this learning process (C. Geertz 1973b:451). The participants learn how to interpret and experience the performing arts as referencing the necessary images and realities to create the festival.

The goal of most festivals is for all the participants to undergo the "sense of experiencing together the one experience" (Kapferer 1986:190). The experience at Lingsar is both one and two. The "two" are the respective experiences of the Balinese and the Sasak that are sometimes constructed in opposition to one another. The "one" is the resulting unification of the two, realized during Perang Topat, *kemaliq* prayers, and the Penglemek/Beteteh procession. The Perang Topat is perhaps the single most meaningful event of the festival, because it draws Balinese and Sasak farmers, high-caste participants, and even orthodox Muslims together to throw the *topat* at each other, thereby (unbeknownst to some) activating the symbolic power of the *topat* as offering. The cathartic moment of the Perang Topat binds the community as one body working together for everyone's mutual benefit. One main function of the festival is to reconcile the tension between Balinese and Sasak, and the three occasions noted above that link all participants in collective action realize this transformation.

Through referencing myths, the performing arts help erect boundaries between Balinese and Sasak as histories are constructed through the interpreted semiotics of the contents (signs, indices), embodiments, and actions. However, the cosmological structures (unifying tripartite and binary dimensions) and indices of these arts act to transcend respective ethnicities and create interethnic union. Participants of both camps frequently describe the festival in terms of creating "oneness," and imply that an identity merging both groups arises. Certainly this unity is not interpreted the same way by the great diversity of participants, but most everyone uses the same terms to define a union with the other camp. I believe that the resulting balance provides spiritual experience, social cohesion and well-being, and is necessary for the ongoing relationship of the parties and for cooperative distribution of irrigation water and other resources.

The social and religious dimensions of a given ritual receives its highest expression in musical sound (Wallis 1979:232). The rich musical expressions are made available to everyone and participants of both groups revel in the combinations of referential sounds. Musical messages communicate images and values already integral to the participants' worldviews. Balinese and Sasak music aesthetics and worldviews are similar enough for each to respond to the other's music. Many Balinese have mentioned their enjoyment of *preret* and gamelan *baris*; many Sasak have said the same of the *gong kuna*. Just as a collective significance arises when *preret* or *gendang beleq* is performed simultaneously with gamelan *baris* and *baleganjur*, a larger significance emerges when the music of the Sasak and of the Balinese are performed simultaneously. There is a greater intermingling and more comprehensive sense of *ramé*, as a still larger heterogeneous group is unified.

The positioning of two Indonesian flags at the front of all the major processions is more than empty symbolism of the Indonesian principles of mutual ethnic trust and harmony. This harmony does, in fact, occur; it is a continuing feudal-period actualization of Pancasila. Harmony is ritually brought to life in the festival through all of the ritual agents, but especially by the performing arts, Perang Topat, prayers, and the Beteteh/Penglemek procession. Differences must be reconciled for a successful festival. Without harmony, there is little *ramé*. Harmony, a primary by-product of the festival, reflects the greater realization of the spiritual balance achieved. The balance among participants and the divine creates prosperity and plentiful rainfall for irrigation water and bountiful rice yields. Balance designates the unification of disparate Balinese and Sasak ethnicities.

This unification helped the Balinese kingdoms rule for two centuries. It was necessary for the Balinese to subordinate the Sasak (as the mystical extension of Majapahit), yet achieve harmony with them at given moments of the year. In the later nineteenth century, the harmony in Lombok disintegrated into frequent ethnic battles, and the full efficacies of the Lingsar festival and other major rituals did not take hold. The Balinese soon fell. Several Balinese teachers suggested that unsuccessful festivals created disorder that led to the decline of the courts and the victory of the Dutch. The Sasak, despite Balinese colonization, have approached the binarism by positioning themselves as the elder and the Balinese as younger; they place themselves as the keepers of the tradition and the Balinese as guests. Sanusi implied that Sasak were female and charged with fertility, while Balinese were male and martial, that Sasak were cool whereas Balinese were hot, and that the two must be unified for the festival to have efficacy.

Today, as perhaps a hundred years ago, the spiritual and social role of the festival is to generate harmony, *ramé*, and the quality of communitas. Social structure and ethnic divisions dissolve as the immediate identification of "Balinese" and "Sasak" is forgotten and participants lose their respective ethnic selves. Both Balinese and Sasak have demonstrated that they need to experience this sense of community in which music and dance are primary ingredients.

CHAPTER SEVEN

Changing Dimensions, Changing Identities

THIS CHAPTER highlights changes in the festival, in the officials, in the performing arts, and in the sociocultural identities of the participants over the last twenty years. "Change" is, of course, necessary for any major public festival to remain meaningful to its participants, but the changes at Lingsar have surprised me, and the forces involved in these changes—local government, religious leaders, Sasak and Balinese leaders—have uniquely revealed their intentions (see Harnish 2005). Little is hidden in the agendas of the concerned parties. I am nevertheless astonished at the rate of change, as I had assumed that such a significant event with religious underpinnings would have to change slowly to maintain its popularity.

Many participants would disagree with me about the degree of change. Most Balinese and Sasak say that the festival has preserved its major functions and that only a few peripheral elements have evolved. One farmer I spoke with did not observe any change at all. Thus from many perspectives, nothing of significance has happened. My own perspective as an outsider who talks with most parties at Lingsar (and who analyzes the rites in ways that differ from participants) is that a number of elements have changed and that these and other elements will continue to change, perhaps more quickly. My more-than-twenty-year history of attendance at the festival and my (primarily) nonparticipant role also distinguishes my perception from participants over the same period. I submit that the reasons for change are bound up with shifting expressions of Sasak and Balinese ethnicity in Lombok. External forces—that is, globalization and alliances between nationalism and religious identity—are clearly influencing the direction of these changes.

STRUCTURAL AND LEADERSHIP CHANGES

One cause for change is connected to Indonesianization and the national arts agendas, and the related drive for music and dance on fringe islands like Lombok to be more like those in Java (see Sutton 2002), and for institutions like the Lingsar festival to represent local culture to both domestic and international outsiders. New leadership over the past twenty years has triggered a number of changes in interpretation and practice; additional changes have arisen in the way that these individuals have responded to pressure from outside forces.

The Loss of Mangku Sanusi

Many changes since 1993 can be traced to the death of Mangku Sanusi and his replacement by his younger brother, Mangku Asmin (Min). Though Min's family had been involved for generations and Min himself had always lived close by, he had apparently never even attended the festival. Yet he inherited the right to become *pamangku*, and he chose to do so. According to everyone in a position to know, Min has not absorbed the essence and meanings of the rites, nor has he learned some of the proper techniques of carrying them out; moreover, he remains unable to discuss them either with insiders or outsiders. His nephew, Parman, taught Min much about the rites (along with Min's older sister Inaq Mar, who is with him during much of the festival), but Parman says that Min remains *buta* (blind).

While some of the harshest criticism has come from Parman, Parman himself never lobbied for the position, and if Min dies, he would probably still opt not to assume the *pamangku* role. In terms of knowledge about the festival, Parman asserts that he is *tertua* (eldest); some people even call him Mangku, a term of respect for *pamangku*. The Balinese leader Kereped made it clear that he would welcome Parman as *pamangku*. I believe, however, that Parman, who has a background of government service in the Ministry of Law, will never want to serve. To become *pamangku*, with its Waktu Telu association, would compromise Parman's claim to be a modern, Islamic civil servant, and the public profile he has crafted would dissolve. He also could not criticize relationships with the Balinese or the handling of ceremonies since he would have to take responsibility for both. Parman wields more power now, with a weak *pamangku*. Not being the visible leader, he can work quietly behind the scene to further the Sasak position, to isolate the Balinese from government acknowledgment, and to undermine ritual elements he dislikes through his criticism of Min. If he survives Min, he will have a very strong hand in selecting the next *pamangku*.

Changing Leadership within the Krama Pura

The preparations for the festival and the relations between Balinese and Sasak were fairly consistent each year until the first part of the 1980s. At that time the provincial Education and Culture Department conducted a project on the festival that resulted in a video and a large section of a book. Almost immediately afterward another book, supposedly penned by Syrani, appeared. All of these products used almost only Sasak consultants and officials at the festival. The government, which had formerly allowed the festival to continue on behalf of the older beliefs, the Balinese, and farmers, had suddenly taken a stand supporting the Sasak myths and meanings of the temple and festival. The Balinese, apparently unaware of these developments until they were completed, were startled and a crisis of leadership ensued. As Wayan Kartawirya once said, *"Bagaimana Krama Pura biarlah begitu?"* (How could the Krama Pura allow this to happen?)

The Balinese community responded, and Agung Biarsah became *bendesa*, the traditional Balinese term for leadership over a temple. Agung Biarsah certainly had the right credentials. Born in Lombok, he is of noble caste, grandson of the last king, and a traditional healer respected for his abilities; he seemed like the right man. With some Sasak blood in him and a direct connection to the temple—his grandfather is credited with building the newer *pura*—even Sasak officials thought that Agung Biarsah was the appropriate leader. Agung Biarsah, however, apparently had difficulties with the government, and he frequently missed meetings at Lingsar; he also rubbed some people the wrong way, including Sanusi. While many remarked, *"Dia masih mudah"* (he's still young), as a way of rationalizing these problems, others were concerned about the direction of leadership.[1] For a number of reasons, Agung Biarsah stepped down as *bendesa*, and the position was taken up by Gusti Madé Arnaiya and later by Gedé Wija, both of whom were known as intolerant toward increasing Sasak demands. (Parman said about Wija, *"Dia keras kepada orang Sasak"* [he was stern toward the Sasak]). According to Kartawirya, neither Gusti Arnaiya, nor Wija, were open to suggestions by other Balinese; both were very suspicious about finances and the *kemaliq*'s independence from the *pura*. It was Gusti Arnaiya who approved the deals for the new temple gates and parking structure with the government; perhaps he thought that the temple gates, based on Balinese models, further Balinized the temple.

Wayan Kereped became leader of the Krama Pura in 1995, much to the relief of the Sasak organization. Born and raised in the village of Lingsar, with old family connections to the temple and a resumé of Krama Pura service and knowledge, he was the obvious choice. Some believe he did not immediately succeed Agung Biarsah because he was a commoner and leaders had always come from higher castes; however, when there was a clear need for new leadership after Gusti Arnaiya and a few interim years with Wija, he was considered for the position. Kereped and other leaders within the Krama Pura thought it more appropriate to use the title *ketua* (head) rather than *bendesa*, a term laden with history for it referred to a traditional arrangement over a temple and in Lombok related to the feudal period of Balinese colonization. *Ketua* is Indonesian, resonates with the Independence period, and presents the Krama Pura as a modernist organization; since Kereped is a commoner (not party to royal history), *ketua* is also much more suitable than *bendesa* for such a public temple.

With Kereped as *ketua*, surface relations with the Sasak improved; Kereped had known Sanusi, Min, and Parman for decades. Parman, in fact, admitted to personally liking and admiring Kereped; they are often seen together at festivals. Like Agung Biarsah, Kereped has been hesitant to increase government connections, as he does not want to further compromise the *pura*; this has allowed Parman to pursue these connections on behalf of the *kemaliq*. Kereped is not happy that tourist guides explain the origins and meanings of Lingsar only from the Sasak perspective. He finds the notion that the *kemaliq* is separate from the *pura* particularly disturbing as he feels that Balinese and Sasak will no longer be united and may start fighting like parties in the former Yugoslavia.

One other significant structural change was the appropriation of the Pura Ulon, once an independent entity, by the Krama Pura in the mid 1990s. Although they participated in the Perang Topat and the major processions, the descendents of the original founding figures in Karang Bayan had for centuries conducted most of their own rites, headed by their own priests and featuring their own gamelans in the Pura Ulon. Now the Krama Pura selects priests, oversees rites, and financially supports the festival at the temple. Although Karang Bayan participants have generally brought a processional gamelan to represent themselves, the Krama Pura hired an outside gamelan *gong kebyar* club to perform in the Pura Ulon in 2001. When I witnessed this at the festival, it seemed to symbolize the total absorption of Pura Ulon by Pura Lingsar.

Balinese and Sasak Relations

Over the last twenty years the relationship between Balinese and Sasak has deteriorated in most respects. The Sasak and *kemaliq* organization, working in tandem with the government in the early and mid-1980s, isolated the Krama Pura from public acknowledgment, and went so far in 1988 as to invite the governor without consulting or informing the Krama Pura. These actions, and the resulting rhetoric generated by the government book and video, did not foster good will. The Balinese responded in 1989 with the booklet *Pura Lingsar Selayang Pandang* which attempted to link the Balinese rites with the Vedas, legitimizing Balinese rites and actions by invoking antiquity and authority and completely ignoring the Sasak. Some acts of vandalism and violence marked the 1990s, threatening to undermine the foundation of interethnic tolerance and solidarity. Kereped, Parman, and to a lesser extent Min seemed to mediate various parties and resolve the issues. Parman continued working with government offices, particularly with Tourism, to further the Sasak position; he also galvanized villagers in Lingsar to work for, support, and secure the festival. While this has disturbed Kereped, he is happy that the Sasak have found rationales to continue participating.

Kereped and Gdé Mandia (head of the Parisadha Hindu Dharma) state that Lingsar is a *warisan* (inheritance, heirloom); for Sasak it is *budaya* (cultural), for Balinese it is *agama* (religious). This is the official line publicly articulated by the Sasak, the Balinese, and the government. Lalu Wiramaja, a modernist and educated Sasak, really wanted me to distinguish between *agama* (religion, some-times glossed as "world religion") on the one hand, and *kepercayaan* (belief) or *adat* (custom) or *budaya* on the other. Though Mandia (and many other Balinese) indi-cated to me privately that he sees the Sasak practice at Lingsar as relating to *agama*, Wiramaja, like most modernists, insists that the Waktu Telu beliefs are not *lengkap* (complete), not *sempurna* (perfected); that their *ajaran* (teachings) are not *lengkap*. Waktu Telu and Sasak participants are Muslim; if they conduct practices that appear to contradict Islam, their behavior denotes incomplete or inaccurate understandings of Islam and therefore cannot represent religion. Most Balinese would rather have Sasak participation acknowledged as "religious," but they will take "cultural" or "customary" or "traditional" if that is necessary to maintain Sasak involvement.

It is clear to me that the Balinese need to have the Sasak at Lingsar; the reverse is also true, but to a lesser extent. The Sasak camp has set its sights on represent-ing early Islamic Sasak culture in West Lombok. All of the steps they have taken— separating the *kemaliq* from the *gadoh*, receiving external support and terminating traditional support from the Balinese royal family (Agung Biarsah), and the con-stant evolution in myth—are consistent with such an effort. The recent progress towards a more visible Islamic role in the festival and its history are means of legiti-mizing Sasak claims. The motive has been, in my estimation, to establish owner-ship over the temple, the temple lands, and the festival. In contrast, the Balinese position, both in myth and in their booklet, remains consistent: the *pura* includes the *kemaliq* and was built by Balinese, who also founded Lingsar; the Sasak came later to work and share in the temple and festival. The Sasak play an important role but are subordinate to the will of the deities and the mantle of righteousness. The presence of the Sasak at this temple, however, is an absolute necessity because it symbolizes the unity of the island of Lombok (and its Sasak inhabitants) with the island of Bali. Lingsar represents that unity, and without Sasak participation the whole Balinese notion of the temple and festival is dismantled. Creating unity with the Sasak is thus a religious necessity. The temple and its myth explain why and how Balinese are in Lombok, and Sasak participation rationalizes one of the cornerstones of Balinese existence on the island.

The Sasak position is not so dependent on such a pact. Many Sasak, though they disagree with the past Balinese role as overlords, concur that unity with the Balinese is essential for the maintenance of social harmony and the coordination of rice-field irrigation. Some Sasak, however, are moving further away from the notion of unity with the Balinese and are beginning to see the festival as an occa-sion for ethnic celebration; a few have related that they have been oppressed by the Balinese and view each festival as an opportunity to express their opposition.

Kereped is a conflicted man. He said that his primary concern as leader of the Krama Pura is to keep active Sasak participation in the festival. He accepts new myths about the festival as long as the Sasak continue to participate. He acknowl-edges that Sasak participants' religion is Islam (not Islam Waktu Telu), but thinks that they should maintain *budaya* and *kewajiban kepada leluhur* (obligations to ancestors). He is having a difficult time tolerating the guides' stories to tourists that the *kemaliq* is separate from the *pura*. This one point deconstructs the Balinese position and exerts the Sasak myth. As of early 2002 he had taken no action to stop this story that separates the *kemaliq* and *pura*, although he promised that he soon would. He may also have to confront the new Sasak myth with the hero Haji Abdul Maliq and decide whether to accept it, to help maintain Sasak participation, or to challenge it, to help prevent escalating friction.

The Balinese will not stop being Balinese and Hindu, but the Sasak participants are transforming into orthodox Muslims. As I have suggested elsewhere (1988, 1998b), the modern economy, media, telecommunications, nationalism, and internationalism all favor the empowerment of reformist Islam over the Waktu Telu. Thus despite the greater openness toward the festival on the part of religious leaders, earlier Sasak beliefs involving the temple and festival are transitioning towards moderate Islam. Mangku Sanusi seemed to push for more Islamic rhetoric and elements in the 1980s, and Min has continued the trend; the idea is that the festival is a local expression of Islam and participants are enacting a traditional and cultural duty. Lalu Gedé Suparman, a culture official with the government, worries that changes at Lingsar indicate decreased value (*nilai*) of the whole event.

Meanwhile, the symbols of Islam have dominated the media in Lombok and are at work in schools and public discourse as never before. As Saparia said, young people now have more *agama* and *ilmu* (science) and are less attracted to faith in the ancestors and the powers of the land. Sasak youth—now better educated, following Islamic ritual prescriptions, and attending mosques on Fridays—have been turning away from traditional Sasak culture, customs, and beliefs. Sasak officials have been responding by creating a more Islamic component for the history and practice of the festival in order to maintain participation and the acceptance of government and religious leaders.

The village of Lingsar is a good example of increasing Islamification. Sanusi's own children, who could have become *pamangku* in succession, have instead become modern Muslims and want nothing to do with the temple. The same is true for the children of Mangku Bar, the last *pamangku* of the Pura Ulon *kemaliq*. Much of the next generation is moving away from active participation. Many younger people still involved, such as the *gendang beleq* musicians and Batek Baris dancers, clearly do not have the same understandings of the festival as their parents. None of these individuals seem to participate in prayer in the *kemaliq*, and one dancer joked that his male friend only participated in the festival "*oleh karena wanita*" (because of the girls). This transition from "traditional" to "modern" understanding is directly noticeable in the secularization of some of the performing arts (such as the *gendang beleq*) that now dominate the soundscape.

Balinese culture is in transition as well. Twenty years ago the Balinese in Bali and Lombok knew little about each other. Since then media, communications, and religious occasions have brought them closer together. Many officials at the Sekolah Tinggi Peguruan Agama Hindu Dharma (STPA, the school for educators of Hinduism) have come from Bali, modernist Hindu organizations (such as

Parisadha Hindu Dharma) are in close contact on both islands, and educational opportunities have led many local Balinese to Bali and back again. Influences and ideas from Bali have consequently flooded Lombok Balinese communities. Further, Hindu reform movements such as the Sai Baba community and Haré Krishna International have had a modest impact on local belief and practice. Local Balinese and institutions like the Krama Pura have been negotiating their own changes; the expectations are that everyone is becoming better-practicing, more informed Hindus and modern Indonesian citizens. The introduction of Rejang Déwa and *kidung* are perhaps the best examples of the festival giving up some of its local flavor and emulating Bali. Local Balinese traditions unique to Lombok, such as *preret* performance (see Harnish 1992), are waning and subject to replacement by forms originating from Bali and promoted by centralized Hindu offices.

The move toward further Hinduization or Balinization parallels the Sasak's further Islamification. Both groups identify with larger communities—national and international—and are inspired by elements of modernization such as nationalism, media, telecommunications, mobility, and education. As a consequence, local custom, community, and identity decrease in importance. Forces of modernization thus work to homogenize practice and to dismantle heterogeneity and local authority.

New Relations with the Government

Since 1983, the first time I witnessed it, the festival has become intricately connected with the government. In 1983 there was no formal relationship with any regional government office, though village and district leaders were invited to feast with Sanusi in the Sasak compound, and military police had since the 1970s routinely provided security. The Education and Culture Department conducted projects in the mid 1980s and Tourist offices were busing guests to the festival by the late 1980s (hotels often arranged their own tours). The governor was invited and attended in 1988, establishing an enduring direct relationship with the highest office in the region. The government clearly recognized that the Lingsar festival could be used to promote regionalism, nationalism, tourism, and other projects. Several offices assisted in financing the parking structure, performance pavilion, and new temple gates in the late 1980s (completed in 1993).

In the 1990s more ambitious plans were formulated. Tourist offices paid for the training and certification of five guides at the festival, and, in association with the Education and Culture Department, provided seed monies for the development of *gendang beleq* clubs throughout Lombok; these offices still supply some funds for select clubs to perform at Lingsar. Other projects, sometimes without Krama Pura approval, aimed to attract even more domestic, national, and international attention to the festival. For instance, Parman worked to secure funds from the Ministry of Tourism to hold a stick-fighting dance, Paresian, in the late 1990s on the day prior to first festival day. His logic was that, similar to ritual cockfights held the same day, some blood is spilled, thus satiating malevolent spirits; in the meantime, another staged performing act could draw more tourists and revenue. The Krama Pura was appalled and complained, and Paresian did not appear again at the festival. Saparia mentioned that the Krama Pura took this action because officials were afraid that the performing arts, and maybe the festival itself, were becoming only entertainments (*tontonan*).

Musicians and dancers from Lingsar were twice taken to the Indonesian capital, Jakarta, to perform: once at Taman Mini and another time at the well-known Hotel Mutiara. For these occasions the Batek Baris dance, in particular, was "improved" (*diperbaiki*) for staged presentation to a sophisticated Indonesian audience (see Dances below). These interventions—dance improvements, Paresian, *gendang beleq*—demonstrate that the government has directly and deliberately impacted the performing arts at Lingsar.

My Role

I learned long ago that teachers often wanted to tell me either what they wanted me to know to promote their own agendas, or what they thought I wanted to hear. I have also come to understand that what one teacher tells me in public may entirely contradict what that person tells me in private. This has made learning about the festival a sometimes confusing, drawn-out process, and it has revealed the many biases of differing perspectives. I am convinced that most teachers desired to be sincere and honest, but their own insights were often constrained by their positions, histories, and feelings about the festival, its music, and the other parties involved. Many people, particularly farmers and those who had never before spoken with a foreigner, were reluctant to share much of their experience. This has changed slightly over twenty years; younger people in particular feel more comfortable in exchange. One major change I had to negotiate was the transition from free and extensive discussions with Sanusi to short and uninformative chats with Min.

Sasak and particularly Balinese teachers felt that it was my job to clear up the problems of Lingsar. Many felt that the acknowledgement of the festival internationally would be a boon to all, adding prestige and possibly new revenue via tourism to the event. Some Sasak, such as Parman and Arbainjulianda, asked that I confirm the claims of the Sasak; several Balinese requested that I state as fact the Balinese founding of Lingsar and then give copies of my book to every government office in Lombok to prove their point. The voice of a foreign scholar was thought to provide the final judgment, to lay to rest any disagreements. I frequently told teachers, "*Saya tak bisa berpihak*" (I cannot be biased toward any side), and I am certain that this manuscript will not fulfill their expectations, though I hope they will still feel a sense of pride in the exposure.

CHANGES IN MYTHS

The Balinese story of Lingsar clearly changed between the 1930s and the present, but it seems to have been consistent for decades and perhaps since early Independence; the myth probably gradually adjusted to the dramatic sociopolitical changes under Indonesian administration. I Gusti Ketut Karangasem (sometimes called

Anak Agung Ketut Karangasem or Gusti Ngurah) and his entourage arrive in Lombok (invited by either Datu Selaparang or Datu Pejanggik), they meet with Banjar Getas, Batara Gedé Lingsar calls the party to Lingsar by creating a water spring and providing a spirit army, and the entourage goes on to defeat unjust Sasak kings. A few details have changed over decades and each teacher had their own take on the history, but the essential story and the characters remain the same.

This cannot be said for the Sasak story. Datu Wali Milir (sometimes Datuk Milir or Raden Mas Sumilir) is the main hero in most versions; Datu Selaparang is cited in some written literature, and Haji Abdul Maliq is the figure in Parman's emerging story. Many Sasak mentioned Datu Wali Milir as the name of the deity; some, however, indicated Batara Lingsar; and several said that the name of the deity is unknown or cannot be spoken. The other story characters are relatively unimportant and change in nearly every account. The land is generally described as dry and fallow, and the hero's sacrifice returns or generates fecundity. The consistent element concerns the introduction and systemization of an early form of Islam. The hero initiates a new era of belief and livelihood, and restores and preserves the fertility of the land. He magically disappears into the spring in all versions.

Clearly the accounts have been politicized to assert ownership over the land (see Chapter Three). Parman's emerging version will add yet another voice to the cacophony. He feels that the current period of openness and relaxed censorship is the appropriate time to bring forth the "real" (*yang benar*) history of Lingsar. This new story projects another strong claim over the land and temple and establishes Lingsar as an important nexus of early Islam and the ancestral deities for all of Lombok.

Myth is the rationalization for ritual around the world, and this is true also at Lingsar. I believe, however, that farmers and others attached to the land would attend the festival whether or not they knew anything about the formal myths of the temple. Indeed, I have met people who did not seem to know any of the surface features (character names, formal narratives) of any myth but came nonetheless. The springs alone—the source of irrigation—have the power to attract ritual participants, and many bring their own version of folklore. The springs demonstrate the area as the center of fertility, and the minimal story framework of righteousness, sacrifice, and unity is enough for many to rationalize participation. Many others, however, need a more comprehensive story that meets identity or existential challenges, and both parties need to explain in today's modernist world how the festival figures into socioreligious and cultural life. These more elaborate myths, in addition to indicating the importance of history and the positioning of ethnicity, have also proven to illuminate contemporary ideology, interethnic relations, and music/dance interpretations.

CHANGES IN MUSIC AND DANCE

There have been changes in both Balinese and Sasak performing arts. Most of the latter originate during Min's tenure as *pamangku*. The nature of sociocultural life in Lombok over the past few decades, however, has been so malleable that these or similar changes might have occurred even if Min had not been *pamangku*. Balinese life, for a number of similar reasons, has been changing almost as much as Sasak life.

Balinese Changes

The arrangement of the gamelan *gong kuna* on the *balé gong* has not changed: these groups are still selected by a Krama Pura member or they volunteer their services to the temple. To my knowledge, no club has played in consecutive years; the service continues to rotate. Whichever club performs on the *balé gong* must be able to transform into a gamelan *gong kebyar* and a gamelan *gong gilak*.

The loss of the second gamelan *gong kuna* through its return to Bali affects not only the members of Karang Ketéwel (the gamelan performed in the Pura Manggis behind the temple proper) but the soundscape of the whole temple. The *ramé* atmosphere, so crucial to ritual events, has decreased. Kereped regretted the return of the gamelan to Bali but felt it consistent with Balinese notions of the elder (in this case the "home" village in Bali) making decisions over owned products (gamelan), and there was a need for the gamelan in Bali. Karang Ketéwel also lost their gamelan *gong gilak* (largely assembled from the *gong kuna*) and now either borrows one or presents a gamelan *baleganjur* for rites and processions.

Decades ago a gamelan *gong kuna* performed regularly in the Pura Ulon. By the 1980s the gamelan was in ruin, so the musicians brought only the gamelan *gong gilak* instruments. Sometime in the 1990s those instruments had apparently fallen into such disrepair that the musicians started to bring a gamelan *baleganjur* (which omits the *réong* kettles); however, for reasons not explained the club did not perform in 2001, though I was told that "they would probably come next year." In the meantime the Krama Pura hired a gamelan *gong kebyar* to perform standard pieces (not the ceremonial repertoire) within the Pura Ulon. The music presentations representing the Pura Ulon have thus changed considerably.

The Canang Sari dance appears in a new form. In the 1980s five men danced the *canang sari* offerings into the temple and up to the acting priests. The offerings were intricate works of art, each with a unique and beautifully woven plait in the rice-goddess shape. Today, just about anyone (men, women, boys) can dance if their *karang* or *banjar* (ward) makes one of these offerings. There were over twenty performers in 2001 and numbers of dancers now fluctuate each year. Most of the offerings no longer have plaits and instead substitute simple bamboo strips; some for boys and women are smaller, and none are as ornate as those I saw in the 1980s. The former prescription for both dance and offerings was clearly relaxed as a new understanding of the dance and its function took hold.

Rejang Déwa is a new women's dance, instituted in 1997. Created in Bali from a combination of movements and costumes from sacred dances in East Bali by a famous choreographer associated with the college conservatory (Swasthi Widjaja Bandem) and wife of the then-director (Dr. Madé Bandem), it was introduced into

Lombok in the latter 1990s. There are differing stories of its introduction. Ni Madé Darmi, a famous dancer decades ago who maintains a small school in Cakranegara, stated that she learned the dance while in Bali and introduced it to her students in Lombok. The dance creator, Swasthi Bandem, lived and studied with Darmi years earlier while in high school, and they remain close. Another story indicates that dancers came from Bali and introduced it to dance students at the STPA Hindu Dharma school. It is likely that both stories are true. Many clubs, including the school's and Darmi's, now perform the dance for all major (and some ward) temples in Lombok. The club at the 2001 festival, Sanggar Tari Suci, was associated with the school.

I asked why such a dance would be instituted at Lingsar, a temple with its own rich history of performing arts. The answers, though often evasive because teachers were not always sure, were fascinating: "Because it is a sacred dance," "Because it is a sacred dance from Bali," and similar responses were common. Kereped gave one of these answers and then admitted that he did not really know how or why Rejang Déwa came to Lingsar. This dance is different from every other sacred dance. While traditional sacred dances are "old," improvised with simple movements, and accompanied by differing repertoires in various villages, Rejang Déwa is newly choreographed, it requires training and specific costumes and headdress, and it features set music. Rejang Déwa provides a uniform art that links Lombok Balinese directly with imagined notions of "sacred" in Bali. It may have filled a void in Lombok, and perhaps it relegitimizes the festival through constructing a modernist Balinese religiosity.

Interestingly, this dance and similar modernized *rejang* dances have also been growing in popularity in Bali. The first experiments with modernizing *rejang* appeared in the early 1980s, and in its ultimate form it was presented at a large temple rededication in 1988, when it was specifically choreographed for that event. Some scholars believe that the dance has been introduced into most festivals that did not have a prior tradition of *rejang* dance, but a few have suggested that the modern form has replaced older forms of *rejang* at several temples.[2] In a personal communication to me, Garrett Kam, one of these scholars, asserts that standardization of dances and a uniform look are means of exerting control and power. The Parisadha Hindu Dharma is, in fact, imposing its authority and giving new shape to Hindu religious practice on both islands. Left unchecked, festivals will become more uniform in coming decades.

The position of Topeng Sidha Karya (or any other *topeng* form) at the festival seems tenuous at best. Though the dance was probably never performed annually for years on end, it had an important role in the festival, and the dancers performed a specific story (abstractly told) relating the history of Lingsar. Kereped "thought" it would be performed in 2001, but it was not. He and others were concerned about the new time constraints resulting from the involvement of government officials and new elements like Rejang Déwa (which clearly have priority). The performance is now peripheral to the festival and will perhaps be held only on rare occasions when it appears that sufficient time is available.

The singing of *kidung* praise poetry had been rare in Lombok; in the 1980s I witnessed performances on perhaps only two occasions. With help from such organizations as STPA Hindu Dharma and Parisadha Hindu Dharma, clubs were organized in the 1990s and soon began to perform at temple festivals and *kidung* first appeared in 1996 at Lingsar. In 2001 I saw a club associated with STPA Hindu Dharma from Mataram, Sekar Alit, perform in the *kemaliq*. While observing the women singers, a woman next to me said, "*Dulu preret*" (It used to be *preret*). This was a keen perception and resonated with my past research (see especially 1992) where I discovered that Balinese *preret* players in Lombok performed the same function as *kidung* choruses in Bali. In this case the Sasak *preret* players had become inactive, but they were, in a way, replaced by Balinese *kidung* singers. It is clear that some Balinese still miss the *preret* players; since much of my earlier research concerned *preret*, I miss them too.

Sasak Changes

As mentioned above, one of the major traditions at Lingsar, the playing of *preret*, has nearly disappeared. From one perspective, Min appears not to have understood the importance of the instrument and its repertoire. Since 1993 the players have only come once or twice; Min often "forgets" to invite them or to pay for their transportation. In 2001 Amaq Sari came to the festival but only to play for the Balinese purification of the *kemaliq*. This seemed oddly appropriate to me: the Balinese invited a Sasak player with a rich association with Lingsar to perform in the shared space of the *kemaliq*. They could have selected a Balinese player, but they invited Sari due to his connection to the temple and because he is Sasak and could represent the *kemaliq* and perhaps the indigenous land. Min once again did not invite the players, and it is likely that the Sasak tradition will discontinue. In a very telling statement, Ida Wayan Pasha, a teacher and former culture official, said, "*Kalau membuat kebon odeq tanpa preret, itulah seperti membuat penyor sebagai dekorasi*" (Making *kebon odeq* without *preret* is like making *penyor* [the Balinese bamboo poles with male and mountain symbolism] as decoration). From Pasha's perspective, the *kebon odeq* and their creation have become empty symbolism with "*nilai spiritual hilang*" (no spiritual value).

When I began researching the festival again in 2001, I asked a number of people about the *preret* players Sari and Salih. A few said that they had died; one said that one player had died. When I was told that the players had rarely come to the festival since Sanusi's death, I asked why. The answers were again varied: "They were sick," "The festival occurred during Ramadan and they didn't have enough strength to play," etc. Parman intimated that Min had not offered transportation. These answers may have been partially true but did not satisfy my curiosity. Just before the festival began, I finally realized that Min did not appreciate the *preret*'s role and probably had never invited the players; I then realized that officials had tacitly agreed to let the tradition discontinue. Teachers like Parman and Kereped did not want to say that outright, and kept giving me bits and pieces of the answer. Interestingly, in response to my inquiry, both Parman and Kereped said that, since I was so interested in them, they themselves would invite the players to the festival. I told them that I wanted the festival to go as planned, though due to my bias, I was disappointed that the seemingly vital tradition of Sasak *preret* performance had ceased. Interestingly, two Balinese *preret* players performed "Turun Daun" in several processions and during Mabakti at the crossroads, thus keeping the sound tradition alive.

The most dramatic musical change at the festival is the addition of gamelan *gendang beleq*, and not just one ensemble but several. In 2001 four ensembles performed, and three of them entered the *kemaliq* for each procession. Some of this change is related to the 1990s promotion of *gendang beleq* as the central Sasak traditional music experience in Lombok. Government seed money helped many groups get started, buy instruments, and find teachers. Within a few years the numbers of *gendang beleq* grew rapidly. The government and regional leaders felt that membership in gamelan *gendang beleq* would be good for the young men of the island and could represent Lombok at all levels. *Gendang beleq* has become the "official" music/dance of Lombok and seems to be a vehicle to mold Sasak youth identity and ethnicity. Competitions and presentations were set up in many places, and by 2001 the numbers of clubs on the island exceeded 500. The Ministry of Tourism still pays part of the fee for the groups to come to Lingsar; the other part is paid by the *kemaliq* organization.

The earlier tradition of *gendang beleq*—performing for weddings, other life-cycle rites, in processions, and at harvest festivities—was in decline for decades as Waktu Telu culture ebbed. Government efforts—removing the ensemble from its contexts and making it presentational—essentially secularized the ensemble, thus making it compatible with efforts to nationalize the youth, have them participate in displayed culture, and involve them in village and regional life. Since the ensemble was detraditionalized, religious leaders did not complain about the activity, and thus *gendang beleq* was promoted by many forces and struck a powerful chord with communities, youth, and families. Its dominance at Lingsar (in terms of numbers of ensembles and volume) imposes a modernist Sasak element into the festival.

Saparia, the former culture director for the informal Sasak organization, was disappointed with the addition of *gendang beleq* on the grounds that it was something without an historic precedent to rationalize a presence (he seems to have been "fired" for complaining). Lalu Gedé Suparman felt that this was "decoration" that might make the festival "*seperti permainan*" (like a game). Though these sentiments come from differing perspectives (Saparia, a formerly active participant; Suparman, a government official with a stake in preserving culture), they agree on one significant issue: the legitimacy of the festival is in question. Both felt that this addition undermined what the festival represents. While only few participants hold these sentiments, I sense that those with years of festival experience do. Parman asserted that a long-obsolete ensemble, *gandut* or *dut*, performed at Lingsar "*dulu*" (long ago), and that this rationalized *gendang beleq* today; however, no other teacher ever suggested such a possibility, and, as I watched him speak, I was not sure even he believed what he was saying.

Since the 1980s most core members of the gamelan *baris* have died and been replaced by other, related musicians. Their position in the festival has not changed and, though the deceased members had many years of experience (such as *suling* player Amaq Raina, *kendang* players Amaq Sarwi and Ratima, and the lead dancer, Amaq Jasira), the club has maintained most of the same repertoire. Amaq Raidin, the *redeb* player, is about eighty years old, and he is credited with the continuity. It is, however, now difficult to hear the ensemble in processions because of the power of the *gendang beleq* ensembles. The gamelan *gong* Sasak club similarly continues its role as before, although when it is in *baleganjur* form, it is also overwhelmed by *gendang beleq*. One day during a respite in 2001, Balinese *baleganjur* musicians and Sasak *gendang beleq* squared off and briefly played against each other. The *baleganjur* was quickly drowned out.

Dances

The Baris and Batek/Telek dances still occur as in earlier years. The dancers, however, have changed and, more importantly, the choreography has changed. In the mid 1990s Lalu Gedé Suparman and a few other government officials took the Batek Baris dancers and musicians to Jakarta to perform at Taman Mini, the auditorium that represents in miniature the entire country and features performances from around the country. Suparman asked for help with the choreography from officials at the Education and Culture Department (now the Culture and Tourism Office). Abdul Hamid, a well-known Sasak choreographer, and Endah Setyorini, a Javanese dancer with a background of study in Sasak dance, worked with the performers to change parts of the choreography and to codify it.[3] The performance was a success, and the dancers have since maintained and taught the modified choreography. The main dancer, the *komanden*, Juniadi, said simply that the new movements were *lebih bagus* (more appealing).

The dances (Baris and Batek/Telek) have been gradually undergoing secularization for decades. Long ago these dances were performed only in context at the festival; as such they formed part of the special mystic power of the event. In the 1980s they were performed at some national holidays and on rare occasions for tourists. Performances can now be arranged to promote ethnicity in Lombok (in local parades), to represent Lombok (at the national level), and to entertain any high bidder (to generate revenue). The medium has gone from a sacred and somewhat secretive form to a public-display vehicle. Today the dancers still perform a portion of the "original" choreography, and the government is credited with "improving" the dance while replacing local authority.

Though it is not performed as regularly as during the 1980s, Gandrung is still occasionally held at the festival. It is apparently no longer a requirement as a fertility dance. I could not get the story straight: in 2001 some said that it was held once during the festival, some said twice, but I could not verify either statement and do not believe that it happened at all. The dance can still occur almost anywhere on the premises, but its function is not understood as it once was or is not now needed as it once was. This change is consistent with others; the fertility element, belief in agricultural spirits, and the mixing of sexes do not concur with the increasingly Islamified profile of Sasak participation.

Questions

How can a music or dance form that was once so instrumental in the festival suddenly cease to have the same importance? How can a new form suddenly appear? The answer to both questions lies in the changes in Lombok's cultures. Sasak participants are transitioning out of earlier beliefs and becoming moderate Muslims, while Balinese participants are embracing an identity more rooted in Bali and contemporary Hinduism. The identity of the festival itself has been modifying as well and can proceed without *preret* initiating the Sasak offerings; without Gandrung, *topeng*, and the second *gong kuna*; without the earlier Batek Baris choreography; and with the additions of *gendang beleq*, Rejang Déwa, and *kidung*.

Nationalizing the Arts

Indonesian government intervention in the arts expanded from 1970s through the 1990s. During these years of President Soeharto's New Order regime, the government promulgated national concepts of art (*kesenian*) that could be divorced from cultural context and colorfully, ahistorically staged to represent and domesticate "ethnicity" (Aragon 1996:425). The Taman Mini complex and auditorium exemplify this policy. That the gamelan *baris* and Batek Baris dancers—some would say the most sacred arts at Lingsar—should go to Jakarta to present decontextualized culture before a national audience demonstrates that the value for these forms has transitioned from purely ritualistic to (re)presentational.

One of the major successes of arts development projects in Lombok is the dramatic rise of *gendang beleq* clubs since the 1990s. These national projects were spearheaded by the regional Education and Culture Department's Arts Section under the direction of Haja Dra Sri Yaningsih in the 1970s. The Arts Section first undertook *menggali* ("to dig up")—creating an inventory of existing arts in Lombok. Selected styles were "improved" (*diperbaiki*) to represent Lombok and meet Indonesian aesthetic standards, then promoted and "developed" (*dikembangkan*) around the island. This process privileged certain forms, like *gendang beleq*, and served to make these forms uniform while discouraging clubs and styles with unappealing or uneven tonalities, crude costumes or masks, and dances without aesthetic or movement vocabulary.

These projects have been meant to modernize and display the arts. *Gendang beleq* was selected because it is an ensemble that can accommodate over twenty players. It also uses traditional instruments and the unique *gendang beleq* (large drums), but is not affixed to a set ritual context, and performers can be easily trained to play and execute choreography. Clubs also wear traditional and colorful costumes; these, along with the choreography and the powerful sound, combine into an appealingly impressive visual and aural experience. Youth were "naturally" attracted to the form; thus with government and community backing, clubs could form in many villages throughout Lombok. In consideration of the regional goals of modernizing and nationalizing youth via an ethnic cultural form, local clergy dropped reservations normally applied to traditional arts, and performing *gendang beleq* became a quintessential Sasak male youth activity.[4] Acciaiolo (1985) describes such national efforts as "contrived" spectacles, where regional diversity is honored but only at the level of display, not belief. Such projects engage the regional but empower the national. While *gendang beleq* is the clearest example of such a development in Lombok, the other Sasak arts at Lingsar such as Batek Baris and Telek may be slowly undergoing a parallel transformation from "ritual" to "presentational."

All of the above new or obsolete items do not register as "change" to some participants, who see the function of the festival—praying for rain, coordinating irrigation, unifying Balinese and Sasak—as fixed. Although I have perhaps sometimes overlooked the forest for the trees, the changes seem significant enough to me to alter the flavors, perspectives, and meanings of the festival. I feel that these changes are symptomatic of Lombok's struggling to come to grips with national and international religious movements, as well as with the instruments (telecommunications, education, etc.) of a modernization partially driven by increasing globalization and partially imposed by a government seeking to modernize and shape its citizenry.

Currently, one can see transitions ongoing within the performing arts via processes of detraditionalization and rites of modernization. Batek Baris and Batek/Telek dances are detraditionalizing, becoming unfixed from the Lingsar context and previous meanings, while *gendang beleq* has already gone through that process and thus can perform in the new context of Lingsar. The original musical rite of modernization was *gong kebyar*, which contributed a modern voice to festival programs after the 1930s. While *kidung* was included to both update and re-Hinduize the festival, Rejang Déwa was added as a clear rite of modernization, meant to promote new notions of the sacred, of greater Bali, of greater Hinduism, and of a modern citizenry. *Gendang beleq* performance is another such rite; its presence contests "tradition," reflects change in regulation and orientation, and invites further change and decontextualization.

Every year is a new festival and every festival is something new. From my earlier experiences to the 2001 festival, I noticed the trends listed above; in five or ten years there may be new national or regional goals, and the trends may again change.

THE 2001 FESTIVAL

The festival began on December 28, 2001, and concluded on January 1, 2002. Most of the festival events have been discussed earlier in this manuscript, but three other things happened that I had not experienced before.

It never rained. The previous three times I witnessed the ceremony it poured for at least part of the festival and particularly on the main day. Since the festival prioritizes fertility and water, rain is an auspicious and necessary sign. Reports over recent decades indicate that at least some rain fell during nearly every festival. None fell in 2001.

The *momot* bottle was opened at the Sarasuta River instead of at the Sasak compound. With the help of the *lang lang* security forces, I was escorted to within a meter of Min as he conducted the ceremony. After praying for a short while, he allowed all of the implements—offerings (including *kebon odeq*), parasols, baskets, etc.—to be taken by anyone who wanted them. And a great many people wanted them. I was nearly knocked into the river by participants clamoring over the items.

As Min opened the *momot* bottle, there was either so little water that it barely registered or there was none at all. I could not tell for sure. He looked twice and appeared disappointed for a brief moment. In my previous experience I had never seen the bottle so empty.[5] In my own mind, it was as if the deities were displeased by all the changes and had not bestowed any of the precious liquid. They had also offered no rain throughout the festival, no indication that there would be sufficient irrigation water or fertility for the next year.

Min handed the bottle to an assistant, stood up, took the bottle back, and tucked it under his arm, and quietly left for home. In the chaos that erupted over scavenging the other items, no one seemed to notice him or the empty bottle.

CHAPTER EIGHT

The Final Gong

THE LINGSAR Pujawali festival uniquely joins together two ethnic groups—migrant Hindu Balinese and Muslim Sasak—and is a cultural site of both struggle and reconciliation. A combination of activated myth narratives, participant fore-knowledge and expectation, sequenced liturgies, expanding music repertoires and structural homologies, intermingling arts, and released energies interact to create the atmosphere that allows for both intraethnic and interethnic union. Through the power of the performing arts, Balinese and traditional Sasak spiritual and political values are constructed for self and group engagement. Identity formation is a key element as participants negotiate notions of ethnicity, history and moder-nity, and locate themselves and their party within the event.

The festival has had to adapt to new times. Officials have been the major agents of change. They have responded to external forces—government interven-tion, national agendas, political and religious organizations—and made decisions on performance programs, ritual actions, and, in the case of the Sasak, rationales for participation. While "preservation" and "tradition" are exalted, some music and dance forms seemingly out of step with life or ideology were modified or mar-ginalized. This book has recounted several significant changes over the past two decades, each one negotiated through a complex agency and reflecting a shift in identification. The increasing Islamic orientation of the Sasak can still be accommodated, though further distance between the realms of traditional custom and faith will advance the festival's transformation from religious to cultural and presentational. Indeed, the music changes among the Sasak demonstrate a transition from *agama* to *budaya*.

From among the many socioreligous venues historically established for direct Hindu-Muslim interaction, only Lingsar has been maintained as an interface. After the mid-1960s slaughter, Waktu Telu culture sharply contracted and Sasak participation at Lingsar was quickly challenged by reformist forces. Through the agency of Sasak and particularly Balinese individuals (some via the Krama Pura), Sasak were able to continue their involvement, but it came at a cost that would be exacted later: participation would mostly become a cultural obligation detached from religion. I believe that this one change can explain many others arising in performing arts, myths, and agendas—even among the Balinese.

The festival is not, however, in any danger of disappearing. On the contrary, it remains vital, is central to most participants' beliefs, and has managed to survive and even thrive in contemporary Lombok. Despite government imposition, it has not become "folklorcized" to legitimize state culture (see Wong 2001:249 and Turino 1993:231); officials and participants still construct performance spaces and meanings. The compromises that have been made may have further empowered participant positions.

This chapter summarizes and reorders the data from earlier chapters, blending discourses that contextualize and explicate meanings of performing arts/rites with those that address negotiations of sociocultural change and resulting impacts on the arts.

RITUAL STRUCTURE AND ARTICULATION OF MEANING

The temple organizes a complex of beliefs and values. Lingsar is the navel temple of the Balinese, akin to the mother temple of Besakih in Bali, and considered the source of fertility and rainwater for both groups. It is one of the last major holy places of the Waktu Telu, and still attracts a number of Sasak from throughout Lombok who maintain "traditional" or "localized" beliefs. It is a main forum in which to request cures or boons and to pray for success in business or for happiness; it represents the mythic center of natural and ancestral powers of the island.

The myths illuminate how players organize events to explicate particular units of meaning, how the units are based upon cosmological notions and values of the past, and how they address contemporary sociopolitical problems. The accounts explain the Balinese/Sasak relationship, how they view and try to dominate the other by placing themselves in the superior political position—which, by extension, speaks to which group has the legitimate claim over the temple, its festival and its land. This position states that it is *their* group that discovered Lingsar, *their* group that directs the festival, and *their* deities that control prosperity. The histories of Lingsar are embedded into the elements and functions of the performing arts. Music, in particular, tells the stories of Lingsar.

Music interlocks with other activated sets of symbolism—offerings, rites of the priests, incense, dance, and ritual objects like parasols, *penyor*, and *lamak*—to create the state of heightened spiritual awareness known as *ramé*, in which mysteries of the past are revealed and experienced. Each set of symbols represents a particular aspect of the divine and has its own voice. The resulting polyphony creates a more comprehensive divine order and a deeper sense of *ramé*. An "affective alliance" of these voices is available to each participant for individual and collective spiritual experience. Music and dance help organize the spiritual experience of *ramé*, and this experience generates communitas and spiritually bonds participants together. The arts also permit or frame actions and behaviors necessary to complete the festival.

Through signs, indices, and associated actions, Balinese and Sasak music offers each group the possibility of a return to a "whole" of their respective culture—to sense their history and identity and how these reflect upon contemporary times. The varieties of music also intermingle to affect a symbolic reconciliation and unification between the Balinese and Sasak—a return to the whole of their combined culture on Lombok.

The "antistructure" element so common in festivals worldwide is this unity of Balinese and Sasak and the combined whole. Just as male and female instruments synchronize in performance, Balinese and Sasak harmonize when undertaking and experiencing the festival. It is within this balanced whole that the divine exists, that divine communion is possible, and that fertility and plentiful rain can be guaranteed. The participants all work together to create this experience, but it is the performing arts that as active agents work on the human and divine to alter reality—to transform normal experience into this eternal whole. After the festival the relationship gradually returns to tension and suspicion.

"Tradition" embodies authority and is the continuum through which one meets the divine. The notion of tradition for each group lies largely in Java, where an imagined uncorrupted moral order prevails. For the Balinese, the legendary Majapahit signifies this order; for the Sasak, the celebrated Wali Sanga primarily does. The ritual music at Lingsar articulates these places and orders, and imposes them upon the festival. The festival, in turn, comes to represent these places and their moral authority. The music, then, expresses the place of Lingsar temple, the spiritual and moral center of Lombok.

The music also encourages specific actions, attitudes, and mental states. Many participants have indicated the effect of the music, how it transforms their thoughts and emotions and prepares their minds for prayer. A common understanding among participants is that negative and disturbing thoughts contribute an impurity to the proceedings. This impurity can, in turn, disrupt the state of spiritual balance and harmony that is the larger goal of the festival. Balance and harmony create prosperity and fertility. Participants therefore negotiate negative feelings towards the other camp and embrace the transforming efficacy of the performing arts to achieve a spiritual mental state. Despite the reenactments of the myths that allow each group to experience its sociocultural identity in opposition to the other, the larger function of the ritual performances is to create a unity that transcends this opposition.

The most powerful manifestation of the divine is the merging of male and female attributes in offerings, actions, and arts. The ultimate Siwa is when he is either united with his consort, Parvati, or when he shows female attributes. The Waktu Telu deity conception couples male and female principles, and traditional Sasak rites and offerings unify these binary powers. Gender is similarly unified in music, as male and female gamelan instruments interlock and perform together. This complementary duality, unified in music performance, constitutes a balanced offering to the divine and also represents this merging of duality within the divine.

The varieties of music construct ethnicity and boundaries (partially through associations with myths), in which Balinese and Sasak claim the festival and establish intraethnic dimensions for spiritual experience. As religious minorities, both need this experience of community. On another level, however, the forms of music freely intermingle, and both camps understand the values of the performances. Many Balinese declare their enjoyment of listening to gamelan *baris* and *preret*, and some dance with the Gandrung. Sasak enjoy listening to Balinese music; Parman, in fact, offered that listening to the gamelan *gong kuna* was a noble and powerful experience. The functions and signs of Balinese and Sasak music reflect a shared worldview that recognizes tripartite and binary cosmological divisions and number constructs of threes and nines. When performed in context, the resulting experience can transcend ethnicity and envelope both groups in spiritual union. Both kinds of music, in tandem with shared action (that is, Perang Topat and processions) and prayers, construct a larger, more diverse identity that bonds Balinese and Sasak. Like ritual objects and music, this social union simultaneously represents and is an offering to the divine and becomes a force for spiritual balance, fertility, and prosperity.

The sound worlds mixing together symbolize this union. While *gendang beleq*, gamelan *baris*, and gamelan *baleganjur* are performing in the *kemaliq*, the amplified vocalizations of *padanda* and *kidung* clubs float above the soundscape. Similarly, when *gong kuna* or gamelan *gong gilak* are performed, Sasak music audibly intermingles in the atmosphere. Shared musics and actions construct a unified and powerful whole.

CHANGE AND LOCAL NEGOTIATIONS

Changes in the festival—in the music, the myths, and the politics—indicate local negotiations of national and regional pressures. Some pressures have been intended to increase the public display of *agama* (world religion) and religiosity; all have been linked to realizing notions of modern Indonesian citizens (see Aragon 1996).

Sanusi, Parman, Min, Kereped, and Krama Pura members have all been players in these negotiations. The government first imposed its presence upon the festival in the 1980s. Sanusi worked with Education and Culture officials during those years to craft a public Sasak identity for the festival, and he invited the governor to the festival, a precedent now permanently in place. Min and particularly

Parman have actively participated in the process of modern change by delimiting certain performing arts, integrating new arts, furthering the myths, and by working closely with the government and developing a tourist guide system.

It is no mere coincidence that the Sasak *preret* players have been so rarely invited since 1993 (the year of Sanusi's death). The instrument and its repertoire constitute an icon of Waktu Telu ceremony, and the changes initiated by Sanusi, the government, and Parman do not concur with such expression. The *preret*, directly linked to Waktu Telu (i.e. non-Islamic) religious ritual, plays no part in the evolving profile of the festival as a cultural or customary duty for Sasak participants. Although some Sasak remain Waktu Telu, this is clearly the wrong image for the festival in contemporary Lombok—where all Sasak are ostensibly modern Muslims.

Sasak participation is in transition. While the older Sasak congregants still pray in the *kemaliq* along with Balinese, their numbers are lower now than in the 1980s and younger Sasak do not participate. (The idea of praying with the Balinese [non-Muslims] would be strange and perhaps offensive for modern participants.) The Waktu Telu complex of beliefs has continued to decline in the Lingsar area since the late 1960s; similarly, the *preret* as an index of ritual and *kebon odeq* is no longer relevant for most Sasak participants. While it may be to blame for the demise of the *preret* tradition, the cognitive separation of culture and custom from religion has allowed Sasak participation at the festival to continue.

The most powerful representation of Sasak participation is now gamelan *gendang beleq*; this ensemble "fits" the new public Sasak image at Lingsar. The multiple clubs in performance literally drown out any competitors. This former ritual ensemble, without precedence in the festival and detraditionalized through government projects, was added to construct a modern, sanitized Sasak ethnicity reflecting the shift from "religious" to "cultural" identification. The choreographic element symbolizes a shift from ritualistic to presentational in many Sasak performing arts. The emergence of *gendang beleq* is part of the regional project to advance the ensemble as the quintessential Sasak musical expression across Lombok. At Lingsar the project combines government offices (Education and Culture, Tourism) and the Sasak organization in modernizing and "improving" the performing arts at Lingsar. The Sasak can thus be pictured as fulfilling a cultural duty while maintaining themselves as modern Muslims and Indonesian citizens. The *gendang beleq* represents a modern ethnic Indonesian project. Not integral to any rite, yet dominating in performance, its ascendance at Lingsar symbolizes a change from ritual function in the arts to presentational showmanship.

Changes in dance support the picture. Gandrung was marginalized and deritualized; it rarely is held and no longer links the feminine divine with the congregation. The Batek Baris and Baris dances feature modernized choreography, and these dances have been shifting from "ritual" to "show" over most of the last twenty years. They have been partially secularized in compromised performances for tourists, for secular holidays, and in national ethnic presentations in Jakarta. These dances, along with *gendang beleq* and many of the Sasak festival rites, have been designated *khas* Sasak by the government. As "owned" by the Sasak people (particularly in the current autonomy period), these may be subject to further government intervention and definition.

Though not a party to the above changes, the Balinese Krama Pura accepted government monies to erect new, modern-style temple gates (from Ministry of Religion) and a modern performance stage (from Ministry of Tourism); thus the very appearance of the temple now conforms to the modernized Balinese ideal of a sacred space. These changes parallel political changes within the organization. The leadership transferred from Agung Biarsah, the grandson of the last king who was credited with building Pura Lingsar, to Kereped, a common Balinese and village resident, and the Krama Pura became a modernist Balinese institution. Shortly afterward, apparently to better unify and codify the festival, the Pura Ulon lost its independence and was subsumed under the jurisdiction of the Krama Pura.

To appear more Balinese and modern, more Hindu and progressive, and less local and conservative, the Rejang Déwa dance, a new dance from Bali, was embraced as an integral and sacred rite within the liturgy. In keeping with modern Balinese-ness, *kidung* singing was added to the ceremonies in the *kemaliq*, and participants now wear uniform ceremonial colors. Other forces created other changes: one gamelan *gong kuna* was "returned" to Bali and time constraints generally prevent the performance of *topeng*. Many of the changes can be linked to the coordination of the Krama Pura with the modernist Hindu organization, Parisadha Hindu Dharma (some individuals are members of both organizations). It was the latter organization that pushed to incorporate Rejang Déwa and *kidung* and imposed the dress code. The agenda is clearly to modernize the arts and liturgies, to centralize religious practice, and to link the Lombok Balinese with Bali and the greater Hindu world.

While processes of detraditionalization have affected some Sasak arts, rites of modernization are apparent in both Sasak and Balinese arts and are clear in the liturgy. The performance of *gong kebyar*, although a part of the sound world for perhaps fifty years, is one such rite. *Kidung* is a new Balinizing and Hinduizing agent, and Rejang Déwa, a contemporary performance form, at once connects Lombok to the greater Bali and Hindu world and transforms and modernizes the profile of Balinese arts.

PAST AND FUTURE, BALINESE AND SASAK

Despite greater centralized control, the uniform religiosity expected of Balinese, and the cultural participation for Sasak, many individuals contest these changes. Some older Sasak come for religious reasons, some Balinese voice concern over the decreasing local flavor, and a few Sasak work to undermine or subvert the proceedings. The local perspective is that the festival has changed little, that the goals and ritual processes remain the same. The adage that festivals symbolically restate the arrangement of the social world seems confirmed. Balinese and Sasak renegotiate and redefine themselves in this autobiographical festival.

The past two decades have demonstrated how change and new interpretations occur within the festival. In 1983 and 1987 only two Batek/Telek dancers were present. In 1986 there were five dancers, and in 1988 there were four. When I asked Sanusi and Saparia about these discrepancies in 1988, they responded that there have always been four dancers, the number that appeared that year. Parman asserted in 2001 that there have always been three dancers (the number that year, and also in support of the emerging myth). In the slippery negotiations of "tradition," my questions to Sanusi, Saparia, and Parman may have been irrelevant. For many parties whatever is presented is what "tradition" requires, even if "tradition" changes from year to year.

Such rationalizations are not required for all dimensions of the event. The worship periods within the *gadoh* and *kemaliq* are fairly consistent; the *gong kuna*, gamelan *tambur/baris*, and *gong* Sasak/*baleganjur* groups perform the same repertoire; procession routes are unchanged; and the Perang Topat is as wild as ever. It is possible that my long experience with the festival, my surprise at new elements, and my personal attachments to some of the discarded traditions have privileged festival changes.

The Balinese have official approval from the Hindu Section of the Ministry of Religion to undertake the festival. The Sasak do not enjoy such sanction. The festival is clearly not Islamic, and it is held jointly with the non-Islamic Balinese. In the 1980s Sasak participants received government endorsement on the grounds that all Sasak participants are obviously Muslim and thus behave out of "cultural" rather than "religious" duty. This rationale increased Sasak participation, and I felt at the time that the government had underestimated the importance of Lingsar for Sasak farmers and others with Waktu Telu sympathies. Those congregants are now older, and younger Sasak are rarely participating in the same way. Recent developments—*gendang beleq*, revised myth—may be efforts to maintain festival numbers. Kereped has stated his approval of such strategies as long as they do not undermine the central Balinese foundation of *gadoh* and *kemaliq* unity. These developments, however, imply Sasak ownership of festival and separation of *kemaliq* from *gadoh*, and they clearly challenge the Balinese position.

Thus the temple and festival reveal the many tensions of interethnic relations, the minority vs. majority status of each party, the pressures placed on participants by outside forces, the negotiations with current political trends and officials, the apprehensions surrounding rice fields and irrigation waters, the locations of self and collective identities, and the annual reencounter with each other and respective and shared histories. There remains a lot at stake in the festival. Officials and participants, dealing with these tensions, construct each festival through their own agency, and sometimes this requires discarding or inserting new elements—which are then rationalized through a reinterpretation of "tradition."

The strategies of maintaining and reinventing parts of the festival were successful in increasing attendance from both parties over the past two decades. Balinese participation has perhaps doubled, and more people come from Bali. Sasak numbers, on the other hand, have stagnated and may decline. In 2001 many younger Sasak lacked what Saparia called the *niat* (devoted intention) to actively participate and to return year after year.

Though distinct in several ways, Balinese and older Sasak participants share a worldview that values the past and the experience of *ramé*. Their languages, clothing, method of prayer, and attitude toward the performing arts are similar. They undertake separate rites, but they come together for the major processions and the Perang Topat, and these are the rites that are the most meaningful for many participants.

These are moments of communitas, when ethnic tension dissolves, and when the participants forget momentarily who they are. Abrahams (1986:62) calls this a "Big Experience," when, in agreement to enter such a realm together, "we achieve a particular relief from responsibility . . . . We are able to say that we are not ourselves . . . in such a state." At Lingsar this "temporal climax" is a state of communitas driven by the *ramé* atmosphere generated by the performing arts in interaction with other ritual events. It is especially the music that first triggers this experience through signs and indices already integral to participant subjectivity. The music spiritually affects those participants who expect, desire, and need such an experience.

This experiential process is similar for participants, regardless of social status, position within the ritual frame, and personal disposition. Individuals tend to gravitate toward those symbols (representing ethnicity, social union, social order, the past, God, etc.) they find most meaningful. These symbols are realized somewhere within the diverse and complex communication networks of the performing arts. The festival in this respect encourages variation of individual experience, but this diversity has always empowered the festival. Each festival experience is unique, informs that of the next festival, and is never repeatable. Individual experience—achieved by accumulated participations, matured subjectivity, and partial distantiation—is phenomenological and constantly changing.

Balinese and Sasak contribute equally to the festival. The Sasak provide the most important of all offerings, the *kebon odeq*, and the performing art without which the festival cannot be held, the gamelan *tambur*. The Balinese contribute a myriad of offerings, many prescribed for the *kemaliq*, and the performing art that initiates the energy of the festival, the gamelan *gong kuna*. Other arts have further separated meanings and indices. The Sasak appear to maintain the traditions more related to the rain and fertility needs of the festival. Most of the Balinese performing arts and liturgical traditions at Lingsar can be found in other festivals and are not specific to Lingsar. Although the Balinese unite the two islands through a marriage of waters during Mendak Tirta, the Sasak preserve the sacred water spring in the *kemaliq* and fulfill the *momot* ritual that manifests the most sacred water for the benefit of the farmers and the land. The Sasak also contribute the Batek Baris dance (and, on occasion, Gandrung) that helps generate fertility.

Sanusi made a number of curious statements about the Balinese. He acknowledged that they were the main financiers of the festival, that they had always guarded the festival, and that they had political power over the temple. He similarly respected the efficacy of Balinese rites and performing arts at Lingsar and confirmed many parts of their myth. He always positioned himself, however, as "inner"—the internal leader of the festival—while the Balinese were "outer," forming a complementary duality. Sanusi indicated that this duality was necessary; that the Balinese were "male" (with political power), "outside," and "younger" (newer to the island), while the Sasak were "female" (encharged with fertility), "inside" (encharged with ritual), and "elder" (older to the land). He seems to have thought that this ritual unification was essential in creating harmony and activating fertility. From this perspective the Balinese and Sasak were like king and queen, like male and female *kebon odeq*, and like male dancer to Gandrung.

Khas Sasak is a defining element for many Sasak teachers. The Sasak have had a chaotic past full of painful colonizations. Their reaction has been to sweep away most traces of it and to more strongly embrace a religion from without. Orthodox Islam offered hope and liberation from the social order, *adat*, and beliefs that had failed to protect the society from cultural poverty and external forces. This response, however, left the Sasak without a coherent ethnic identity. Leaders have recognized the potential danger of further cultural disintegration as tourism and modernization have strongly impacted Lombok.

Khas Sasak designates what remains of original Sasak culture and is useful to articulate a cultural foundation. The gamelan *tambur*, Sasak festival rites, and the entire festival are considered *khas* Sasak by many individuals and institutions in Lombok. I found it interesting that a few Sasak and Javanese government officials who had never attended its festival were surprised to learn that Balinese also worshipped there. In their minds the event was *khas* Sasak and exclusively Sasak because that is how the event had been promoted. The festival—its myth and performing arts—has become *khas* Sasak for those striving to both advance Sasak culture and formulate and maintain ethnic identity and pride in the face of the many challenges striking Sasak society.

Among the Balinese, Lingsar is the mother temple, their source and origin; the festival is the legitimation of their culture and serves to reconsecrate Balinese culture to Lombok. Nowhere else in Lombok and in only a very few places in Bali do four *padanda* (two in the *gadoh*, one in the *kemaliq*, one in Pura Ulon) officiate at an annual festival. The array of performing arts and the crowds in excess of ten thousand testify to the festival's significance. Though not always given equal consideration, Sasak participation is a cornerstone of the Balinese myth and essential to festival success. The more forceful expression of Sasak myth and meaning at Lingsar since the 1980s has challenged the Balinese on several fronts.

Contestation and unity both mark the relationship between Balinese and Sasak. I was sometimes surprised to see warm interaction at the festival among particular Balinese and Sasak who had spoken privately about their basic dislike of the other. For example, Parman and Agung Biarsah are often next to each other in procession and may even hold hands as they walk together. Such actions do not merely make public or personal statements, they are representative of the festival's power in normalizing relations.

Lombok's future is unpredictable. The emerging Islamic identity among Sasak and the centralization of Hindu religious practice among Balinese will surely impose new changes on the festival. However, the festival has demonstrated some flexibility and still prospered, and, through fresh agency, will likely adapt to these forces. The festival, of course, serves its participants, and whatever shape the festival may assume will reflect their needs and the present reality of Lombok. With so many forces at work, there is no question that the processes and interpretations of the festival will continue to change.

Regardless of change, the music will still formulate cultural identity, will still reference the past, will still interlock with context to create meaning and experience for the participants, and will still intertwine with agency. If music somehow fails these tasks, the festival will discontinue. Music is the framework for the life of the festival, for the transmission of its diverse meanings and experiences. The festival starts and concludes with music, and music runs through virtually all major rites and events. Music encapsulates the sacred time, cosmology, and identity of the Lingsar festival; it explicates social, religious, and political changes within the festival and Lombok as a whole; and it drives the diverse festival experience toward its goal of *ramé*, intraethnic and interethnic unity, and communion with the divine powers of Lombok.

Notes

CHAPTER ONE: Encounters, Constructions, Reflections

1. Since the initiation of regional autonomy in 2001, the district government of West Lombok has greater authority over this water. To my knowledge some rice fields in Central Lombok still receive irrigation water originating from Lingsar, but this could change in the near future.

2. When I returned to Lingsar in 2001, several people mentioned that I should confer with a foreign man whose study of the festival was "complete" (*lengkap*). This person had talked to everyone, including Sanusi, and had even danced at one point. Names, something like "Tam" and "Fil," were offered for this person. At first I thought that someone else had come to research the festival, then it finally became clear that that mystery person was me.

3. In 1987 I invited Larry Polansky and Michelle Chin (both in Indonesia at the time) to help me document the festival. Larry and I ran video in different parts of the temple, and Michelle and I took still photos. In 1988 I invited Lisa Ho (in Indonesia at that time) to the festival and she took photos in outer courtyards while I was inside. Their assistance is very much appreciated.

CHAPTER TWO: Festivals and Cultures of Lombok

1. In general, the more heterogeneous the festival, the deeper the sense of constructed community as distinctions of particular forces dissolve into the experience.

2. The *uku* can also be viewed as six periods of the intersection of five- and seven-day weeks. In a few villages this period of 210 days is considered only half a year. The *saka* is based on twelve cycles of new moons, and a leap month is inserted approximately every

thirty months. See C. Geertz (1973a: 396–398), Ramseyer (1986:135), Goris (1960:115–116), and especially Eiseman (2000) for more information on Balinese calendars.

3. In her paper Hildred Geertz requested that this report not be cited since she felt that it was incomplete. However, I telephoned her requesting permission to quote her, and she consented.

4. There is no consensus on precisely which six temples constitute the *sad kayangan* in Bali. Goris (1960:80) lists four of six as consistently being Pura Penataran Sasih, Pura Batu Kau, Pura Yeh Jeruk, and Pura Goa Lelawah. Some intellectuals have attempted to formulate a *sad kayangan* complex in Lombok, although again no consensus exists to identify those six temples. Pura Lingsar is always one of the six, and the others are generally said to be Pura Pengsong, Pura Narmada, Pura Suranadi, Pura Batu Bolong, and Pura Méru. Duff-Cooper (1985:20) includes Pura Segara as one of the *sad kayangan*. However, Pura Segara is a sea temple related to temples of the dead and would be a curious addition.

5. Teachers report that the last king of Lombok, A. A. Ngurah Karangasem, deliberately prevented the formation of *pura dadia* (joining several villages together through a common ancestor) in Lombok, and at the same time discouraged Balinese from returning to Bali to attend festivals at the *pura dadia* there. The intention was to sever the Balinese from their relationships on Bali to make them completely loyal to the Lombok courts. This has left Lombok Balinese with a decreased familial identity.

6. Gerdin (1982:225) reports that many poor Balinese do not attend festivals at these large public temples because they feel that they do not share in the esteemed Balinese ceremonial life, lack appropriate dress, and are intimidated. This reflects how accustomed some common Balinese have become to a decreased level of public ceremony. These large temples were "owned" by the courts during colonial times, and commoners played only a small role in festivals, although they did contribute financially and through their participation. Following the Balinese defeat, festivals at some of these temples were reportedly very small, commoners' participation and financial contributions almost vanished, and the Balinese in general felt intimidated and uncertain. The high caste (*triwangsa*) shouldered as much financing as they could for festivals, and, as Gerdin (1975:190–191) reports, many continued their own lavish life-cycle feasts until they went bankrupt. Today, many more Balinese are attending festivals at public temples (especially Lingsar), yet some older commoners still feel uncomfortable and participate only marginally.

7. In general, *odalan* and *piodalan*, which are terms used to define festivals at most home, ward, village, and clan temples, follow the *uku* year for festivals, while *usaba*, *aci*, and *pujawali* apply to temples in more remote areas or to large public temples and generally follow the *saka* year. There are far more of the former than of the latter temples. In Lombok, the term *odalan* is normally used for home and ward temples and *pujawali* for major public temples.

8. The concept of Triangga consists of upper and pure (*utama*), middle (*madya*), and lower and impure (*nista*) worlds, and is related to the concepts of Triloka (three stratospheric regions) and Tri Hita Karana (three causes of goodness) (Budihardjo 1986:33), meaning that everything in the world consists of three parts. The cosmos—with divine, human, and demonic worlds—follow this concept, as do the construction patterns of temples, many villages, and home compounds. The Hindu Trinity (Brahma, Wisnu, and Iswara or Siwa) and the three village temples in Bali (*pura puseh, pura desa, pura dalam*) similarly follow these concepts, as do dance movements and the physical structure of musical instruments (see Harnish 1991b). The three-part taxonomy for the performing arts and their spatial dimensions developed by I Gusti Bagus Sugriwa in 1971 and popularized by Bandem and deBoer (1995), is based upon a similar scheme.

9. Three courtyards, normally called *jero* (inner), *jaba tengah* (middle outside), and *jaba* (outside), represent the ideal number for a temple according to some sources. However, there are an equal number of temples with two courtyards, and many with only one. The tripartite concept is often manipulated to apply to these temples.

10. In Bali, it appears that until Indonesian Independence only a single representative member of each family engaged in collective prayer, even though others worked for the success of the festival. There has consistently been more participation among Balinese in Lombok, where living in a predominantly Islamic and monotheistic island helped influence the development of the belief that all participants should participate in prayer and establish an individual relationship with God. This concept also evolved in Bali, where *brahmana* priests inserted a greater level of monotheism into Balinese Hinduism in 1950s. Ramseyer (1986:93–94) notes that after Indonesian Independence and the formation of the national ideology of Pancasila (five principles) with its first principle of belief in a single god (Ketuhanan), there developed a stronger concept of an abstract Oversoul for the deity that could encompass various manifestations and natural and ancestral deities. A concept of monotheism was necessary for Hinduism to be recognized as a "world religion" (*agama*) in modernizing, postcolonial Indonesia.

11. Many people today called "Sasak" came from Java within the last seven hundred years, often as part of a ruling noble family and entourage or for trade; many of these are thought to have "stopped momentarily" (*simpan*) in Bali, sometimes for up to a hundred years, before proceeding to Lombok. Over the centuries and today as well, Balinese can become Sasak simply by proclaiming themselves Muslim and following the tenets of Islam.

12. Van der Kraan (1980), Hägerdal (2001), and Clegg (2004) present various aspects of Balinese colonization, the Dutch conquest and colonization, and the transformation of local Balinese from empowered to minority. The Balinese were strongly oppressed during early stages of Dutch colonization and were intimidated by the Dutch and Waktu Lima, and their religion became nearly invisible. Many temples and all of the courts were destroyed in the war or afterwards by marauding Dutch and Sasak. After some years, many Balinese nobles received back their lands and became representatives and tax collectors, but minority status and reduced revenues prevented further development of Balinese culture in Lombok.

13. The *lontar* (palm-leaf manuscript) *Pegambuhan*, written in nineteenth-century Lombok, demonstrates the existence of *gambuh* theater and music. Secondary confirmation comes from a few local informants and scholars. Several individuals report that there were at least two *Semar pegulingan* orchestras, one of which was rumored to still exist in the Central Lombok home of an old Sasak noble. I was unsuccessful in my attempt to find this orchestra. I believe that both gamelans (as well as many others) were either destroyed, removed from Lombok, or had their bronze parts reforged to produce either new instruments or weapons during the Japanese occupation. The former is better documented. After the 1930s popularity of gamelan *gong kebyar* in Bali, many local groups sought to acquire or produce such gamelans to emulate the style.

14. Proyek Inventarisasi dan Dokumentasi Kebudayaan (1984), Harnish (1985), McVey (1995), and Clegg (2004) describe the Islamic expeditions to Lombok by Javanese Sufi evangelists. Later expeditions to East Lombok from Java and especially from Sumbawa and Makassar were led by orthodox Muslims. Exact dates are unknown and the efforts of these missions have been mythologized. Today, the Sasak and virtually all Indonesian Muslims recognize their faith as orthodox, meaning Sunni Islam. However, the early Sufi influence is still apparent in some performances of literature used by Sasak Muslims, such as the *Barzanji*, a collection of hymns and prayers relating the Prophet's life (see Harnish 1998b).

There are also several Islamic works in the Malay language, indicating that Muslims from coastal Sumatra and perhaps also Malaysia played an important role in providing literature, such as *The Thousand and One Nights* and other *hikayat* manuscripts. The Malay language was the early vehicle of Islam.

Islam grew as a rallying point among the Sasak as they rebelled against the Balinese colonialists in the late nineteenth century, spreading and legitimizing orthodox Islam as a viable alternative and reaction.

15. The ceremonies for the dead and ancestors mentioned by Cederroth (1981:96, 55–59, 102–120, 179–212), Krulfield (1974:93, 101–102, 183), and Polak (1978:140–178) are almost bewildering in their number and variety. The Balinese, who also have a large number of death ceremonies, cremate the dead, while the Sasak bury the dead in nearby cemeteries. Perhaps having the physical and spiritual remains of the ancestors within the village environs promoted the development of such impressive death and ancestor ceremonies.

16. Some believe that "Waktu Lima" indicates an individual in a transitional stage between the nominal and orthodox, and not an orthodox Muslim, who needs no such labels.

Waktu Telu, living up to their name, like to do things in threes and embrace three-part beliefs, though the number nine seems to be an equally important ritual construction, and the complimentary duality of two (male/female, living/dead, east/west, human/rice, mountain/sea, body/soul, etc.) is acknowledged in a wide range of rituals (see Polak 1978:126–278).

17. The meaning of Waktu Telu is vague, and different villages have different interpretations, indicating that Waktu Telu villages and practices are not uniform. Some non-Sasak have assumed that Waktu Telu pray three times a day, or that they pray or fast on three days of Ramadan, or that they pray three times a year (see Adonis 1987:88), and guidebooks to Lombok include a great many other sets of three. In many communities, only the *kiyai*—the religious (Islamic) official and counterpart of the *pamangku* who manages pre-Islamic practices—observes the prayers and fasting of Ramadan (Leemann 1989a: 26). Two Sasak teachers, Sanusi and Saparia, felt that some Waktu Telu in the western plain pray at three different periods of the year (as suggested by Adonis 1987).

The origin of the terms Waktu Telu and Waktu Lima are unknown. Some Sasak have asserted that the Dutch created them as a way to manipulate local control. Leemann (ibid.:30–32) reports that the terms were not used by officials visiting Lombok during the Balinese colonial period of the mid-to-late nineteenth century, and that during the early Dutch colonial period, officials began to separate the "*adat* party" from "orthodox Islam." The words were employed regularly in the early twentieth century, and Sasak used them to identify themselves and each other; these terms clearly led to greater polarization. As Waktu Lima religious ideology gained ground, the proverb "*agama hilang adat*" (religion [i.e. Islam] makes *adat* disappear) was used by Sasak to describe the ascension of religion (and Islamic religious officials such as *kiyai* and *penghulu*) above *adat* (and the pre-Islamic official, the *pamangku*) (Leemann 1989b:194).

18. Variations of this story all picture Islam entering Lombok via Bayan, a center of Waktu Telu culture. In the *lontar Pangeran Sangupati* in Bayan, Sangupati brought Islam to Lombok, his elder son founded the Waktu Lima, and his younger son founded the Waktu Telu (Muller 1991:55). The older son's followers were struck by accidents, disease, and famine, while the younger son's followers prospered. It was then decided that the Waktu Telu religion should be observed and the Waktu Lima teachings were thrown into the sea.

Marrison (1992) and Leemann (1989a) discuss this and other *babad* (chronicles) that present a diversity of stories on the coming of Islam to Lombok.

Many Balinese believe that Pangeran Sangupati was the same Javanese saint, called Padanda Wau Rau, who introduced Bali to the proper form of Hinduism, and, after introducing Islam into Lombok, continued to Sumbawa where he was known as Sunan Kalijaga.

19. See Krulfield (1974), Harnish (1988), Leemann (1989a, 1989b), and McVey (1995) for the evolution of a Waktu Telu village to a Waktu Lima one. Many Waktu Telu pledged allegiance to the Waktu Lima faith because Islamic ceremonies demanded far fewer resources than traditional ones. Many could no longer afford to undertake the required and expensive traditional ceremonies.

In Java, the term *adat* is maintained by most practicing Muslims, though it refers to manmade customs, unlike *agama* (religion), which involves laws prescribed by God. On the other hand, nominally Islamic Javanese, especially those practicing the Kejawan or Tengger religion, regard *adat* as including some divinely prescribed elements in addition to customs. In Lombok many modern Muslims seem to ignore the term *adat* altogether, relegating it to pre-Islamic customs that they no longer acknowledge. *Adat* in Lombok, according to these people, is something followed by nominally Islamic Sasak and Boda, while true Muslims follow only Islamic law. However, some Waktu Lima villages continue certain *adat* practices, such as reciprocal work patterns (Leemann 1989b: 62–63).

20. Before 1958 Hinduism was not considered a religion but rather a set of beliefs something akin to *adat*. Through the efforts of religious leaders in Bali, the national office of the Ministry of Religion acknowledged Hinduism as a religion in 1958.

21. Cederroth (1981:50–51) reports that Waktu Telu mosques were set aflame by Waktu Lima. There are many stories of Waktu Telu gravesites and shrines destroyed by ardent Muslims. Leemann (1989a:47) states that the army assisted the Waktu Lima in threatening and intimidating Waktu Telu after 1965. Several teachers, as well as Cederroth (1981:77), have mentioned that Waktu Telu are still often physically assaulted if they do not attend the Friday service in the orthodox mosque or do not practice the obligatory five daily prayers. Some Waktu Lima have also resorted to economic persecution of Waktu Telu by refusing to trade or make loans to them.

22. In the Waktu Telu village of Sapit, Krulfield (1974:93) states that villagers acknowledge two kinds of religious rituals: Gawé Urip, life-cycle and agricultural rites, and Gawé Bedina, all funeral and mourning ceremonies.

23. The term *wariga* also refers to a body of instructional literature in Bali and to a type of wooden calendar carried by Balinese priests and used for divination. The Sasak *wariga* calendar seems to closely parallel the *saka* (though apparently one month off), but it is rarely used today and has yet to be thoroughly researched.

24. To help substitute for traditional festivals and promote modernized ethnicity, the government has frequently sponsored a yearly processional festival (*pawé*) that engages performing arts from all over the province. This festival was developed to parade traditional and contemporary arts, clothing, and other cultural badges, and to help establish a regional identity and provide a forum for the different ethnic groups to meet. Although some music representative of the Waktu Telu is performed in this and other government events, most orthodox Muslims do not complain because of the secular format and the attitude that the music is a traditional art and is not actively engaged in accompanying Waktu Telu rites.

There also exists the unique Bau Nyalé (Catch sea worm) "event," a ritualized courting affair apparently derived from the Putri Nyalé or Denda Sukadana myth, which involves a beautiful princess who, for reasons of proper etiquette, cannot choose a suitor and so throws herself into the sea and is transformed into one or many sea worms (see further Ecklund 1977:107–110). The annual event brings tens of thousands of Sasak to the southern and eastern beaches to catch the *nyalé* sea worms, and hundreds of young people engage in a spontaneous form of ritualized singing as they display themselves and strive to impress the opposite sex. While there remains some belief in the power of the worms to increase fertility, evidenced by some farmers creating a substance from them and placing it in irrigation channels, the meaning of the event is primarily secular. The provincial Education and Culture Department now often holds a major theater performance at one of these beaches that dramatizes the legend, and this and other government-sponsored changes have inadvertently led to lower local attendance at the traditional event since the 1990s. Some predict that local attendance will continue to decline over the next few years if the government proceeds with catering the event for tourists and dignitaries.

25. Waktu Telu villages that still have them generally celebrate Ngayu-ayu annually or once every two or three years. Some Boda villages hold two such festivals annually. "Gawé" and "Alip," though sometimes referring to life-cycle ceremonies that are not generally calendrical, also refer to grave-cleaning festivals and village-wide celebrations that may occur annually, once every two or three years, or even once every eight years. Some of these festivals demand so many resources that they can only be undertaken after long intervals. Today it is financially impossible to carry out some of these festivals, such as the Alip festival of Bayan, which should be performed every eight years but has not occurred since 1957; Cederroth (1975:170) believes that it will never be held again (another major ceremony, however, the Gawé Beleq [great ceremony] was undertaken in 1997). The demand of many resources and elaborate preparations, combined with further Islamification, impoverishment, loss of land, and loss of youth to urban centers, have led most villages to discontinue festivals that promoted the fertility of the land.

26. Cederroth (1981:54) reports that villagers in Suren hold Batara Indra, the Hindu lord of the gods, as their original ancestor and the high deity of Mt. Rinjani. Van Baal (1976:11) asserts the same for Bayan, and many Boda villages concur. Marrison (1992:1) states that "Rinjani" derives from "Anjana," the mother of the monkey general Hanuman from the Hindu epic, Ramayana. This evidence demonstrates the degree of early Hindu influence and the prevalent beliefs associated with mountains. This identification with mountains and other natural sites shows the "tendency to 'ancestralize' territorial spirits and even the territory itself" (Hefner 1985:75).

27. Cederroth (1975:169–173) and van Baal (1976:10–16) describe how Bayan is constructed to become "the navel of the world," and how the buildings throughout the village represent different levels of meaning and the social divisions and castes among the villagers.

28. Officials claim that some "naughty" younger people show up and throw rotten eggs hidden in *topat* leaves. Some used to throw rocks, but the local security forces have a reputation for quickly and roughly removing anyone doing so, and now these problems are rare.

29. Perang Topat occurs in at least some of the Ngayu-ayu festivals. I have never heard of any ritual activity called "Perang Topat" in Bali, although there does exist the Perang Sampian at Pura Saluman Tiga near Gianyar and the Perang Déwa at several temples in the Karangasem area. The former involves participants throwing all the offerings up in the air as the last rite of the festival at Pura Saluman Tiga, while the latter involves ritual

fighting between supernatural beings. *Topat* are, however, important parts of Balinese ritual offerings, and, in certain contexts they are considered magical charms in Central Java.

CHAPTER THREE: Myths, Actors, and Politics

1. The water spring in the pond of Pura Ulon is merely a trickle from June through August. However, by November the spring is powerful, with far more force than that of Pura Lingsar. After December the spring again loses strength. I do not know of any explanation for this except that the rainy season begins around November, and the river that feeds the spring must swell with rainwater. Since water in the rice fields is particularly important from November through January, some people in Lombok feel the increased water flow is in response to prayers.

2. Gerdin (1982:74) includes an account of the Balinese myth that corresponds closely to the ones presented in this chapter. A more recent publication by Agung (1991) discusses the lineage of Balinese nobles leading up to the events outlined in the myth; it also presents the dilemmas the Balinese faced as they went to Lombok and omits most of the information concerning the Sasak.

3. Since Balinese, like most Indonesians, consider old charters to be most authoritative, Blambangan's version would probably be very influential if it were well known. Ngurah's account has recently spread among interested Lombok Balinese, and this may adjust a few of the minor differences I encountered during my interviews, though rival houses will maintain the distinctive features of their stories. Agung's book (1991) is very slowly spreading into Lombok and may have an impact in the near future.

4. In contrast, Hägerdal (2001), relying on *lontar* such as *Babad Lombok* (Chronicles of Lombok) and Dutch sources, presents the Balinese conquest as deliberate and brutal, and suggests that Banjar Getas is a literary motif (p. 62).

5. This altar configuration indicates the generalization of meaning from a family temple in Pura Ulon to a public Balinese temple in Pura Lingsar. One other temple in Lombok has a similar altar structure and an inner courtyard called *gadoh* (the inner courtyards of other temples are called *jeroan* or *dalam*). The Pura Pamaksan Karang Songkang in East Cakranegara includes a *gadoh* with a central altar dedicated to Batara Alit Sakti and his mother, side altars to Batara Agung and Batara Rinjani, and an additional altar for Batara Gedé Lingsar. This temple was reportedly built by a king of the Karangasem-Singosari dynasty in the early eighteenth century so that the inhabitants in the area would have their own Lingsar temple and would not have to travel so often to Lingsar. It is clear that this temple was modeled upon Pura Ulon.

6. There is a *lontar* that supports Datu Selaparang as Lingsar's founder. I was informed about this *lontar* at Agung Biarsah's palace compound in Cakranegara when a portion of it was read during a meeting. Apparently the *lontar* includes several stories about Lingsar. After consideration, Agung Biarsah and his party decided (perhaps conveniently) to disregard the portion concerning Datu Selaparang. Dutch officials took a great many *lontar* from the palaces following their victory over the Balinese, and many of these are today housed at the Leiden University Library and the National Museum. Marrison (1992) has studied some of these *lontar*. None that he reports on specifically mentions Lingsar, but it is likely that some others do.

7. Waktu Telu followers would not agree that Déwi Anjani, the deity within Danau Rinjani, came to Lombok in the sixteenth century. She is a local, ancient, powerful ancestral deity. Traditional Sasak often pray and make requests of Déwi Anjani. Dalang Budiman, a

wayang Sasak puppeteer, told me that he often asks her for mantras to protect himself. He also said that if he wanted to kill someone, he would ask her for mantras to eliminate his enemies.

8. Rice temples that help regulate the rice cycle and flow of irrigation, usually called *pura ulon siwi* (temple of head terraces), are vital in all rice-growing areas in Bali and are found in or near most villages. Technically, its name indicates that Pura Ulon should be a rice temple, and it is clear that for perhaps hundreds of years, water from Pura Ulon has served to irrigate rice fields and farmers have presented offerings there. However, Pura Ulon, with its family and expedition associations, is an exception to the norm and Pura Lingsar seems to have superseded it in this function, even though water from the Pura Ulon spring is still used to help irrigate the fields.

9. Pancasila is declining in importance in post-Soeharto Indonesia. The five principles—belief in one Supreme God, nationalism, humanitarianism, consultative government, and social justice—are upheld by the current administration, but the rhetoric is vanishing from public discourse. During the Soeharto era, these principles were often manipulated to rationalize authoritarian government, and many Muslims today prefer to look to Islam for civil guidance.

10. Sanusi and his supporters claimed that he was directly descended from the first Sasak priest at Lingsar. This type of lineage, called *turun wali* (witness descent), must be patrilineal and is almost mandatory to assume Waktu Telu religious positions. However, Parman admitted that Sanusi's claim is actually invalid because his descent is partially based on a recent matrilineal line. Sanusi's grandfather had no male descendants, and his daughter, Sanusi's mother, became priest. Sanusi, who was about seventy-two when he died in 1993, inherited the position from his brother, and now the position has gone to the youngest brother, Asmin. In the 1980s Parman said that priests had to be "chosen" by the Lingsar deity, not by mortals or descent; in 2001 he stated that the position is inherited and the individual may choose to become *pamangku*. In the 1980s the Balinese responded that the Krama Pura must affirm any successors (the Krama Pura also appoints the Balinese common priest for Lingsar); due to the loss of interest among the Sasak family, today they would accept any tolerant male who claims family relations. Both parties agreed that Min could assume the position of priest in 1993.

11. Sanusi had been receiving individual donations and support from government agencies, and the *kemaliq*, unlike the *gadoh*, remains active all year long. The priest performs a number of services and ceremonies and receives compensation, all of which promote independence. The growing separation of the *kemaliq* from the Krama Pura during the last years of Sanusi adversely impacted interethnic relationships; most Balinese assumed that it was never Sanusi himself, but other Sasak, who were interested in appropriating the festival and land. Since 1993 the relationship between Min and the Krama Pura has been cooperative, though some Balinese have complained that Min has introduced more Islamic elements into the festival, further dividing Balinese and Sasak. Both Min and Parman have promoted Islamic interpretations. I believe, however, that these were necessary for continued Sasak participation in contemporary Lombok.

12. Biarsah was a disappointment to some Balinese, who perhaps had unreasonable expectations. He stepped down from his position in 1989 and was replaced temporarily by I Gusti Madé Arnaiya, then by I Gedé Meija until 1995, when I Wayan Kereped assumed the position. Though Biarsah, like his father, is an acknowledged *dukun* (ritual specialist), he neither provided strong community leadership nor demonstrated deep knowledge of local culture and tradition. He frequently missed meetings and often suspiciously fell ill. Some Balinese, and even Sasak, criticized him simply by saying, "*Beliau masih mudah*" (He

is still young). He was suspicious of government efforts to make contributions, fearing a compromise in the Balinese position. (Later leaders have tended to accept some government assistance.) Although he resigned as *bendesa* (overseer) of the Krama Pura of Pura Lingsar, Biarsah still retains symbolic authority there and maintains this position in the Krama Pura of one other major temple, Pura Méru. By 2001 his status had risen and most Balinese felt that he had matured and become very knowledgeable about history. In many respects he is still the leader of the Balinese community on Lombok.

13. Sanusi never talked about Bar unless directly asked. His stand on the Pura Ulon *kemaliq* was that it was recently built and thus less legitimate than that in Pura Lingsar. Until the early 1980s the Pura Ulon *kemaliq* maintained the Sasak offerings for the festival that Sanusi claimed were exclusive to the Pura Lingsar *kemaliq*. It is uncertain why Bar gradually phased out these offerings and reduced his participation. Some believe that he was pressured by his son, an orthodox Muslim in government service. It is unlikely that anyone will again assume the position of priest at the Pura Ulon *kemaliq*. The Sasak attendants who become *petunggu* (waiters) do not conduct ceremonies but tend to the *kemaliq* and escort people inside for worship.

14. Circumcisions distinguish Balinese and Sasak. Lalu Wiramaya, a modernist Sasak and retired teacher and administrator, stated that when former Waktu Telu become Muslims the circumcision ceremonies are called "Islamifying" (*diIslamkan*).

Although Sasak men wore traditional headpieces (*udeng*) and sarong or *kain* cloth in past decades, they now sport headpieces (*songkok* or *peci*) and sarong associated with a pan-Indonesian, Islamic nationalism. In some areas Sasak have no "traditional" clothing at all (see Clegg 2004). Similarly, women's wear has become more conservative and Islamic since the 1970s. People wearing the most Islamic-associated clothing are often the most respected (apart from government employees at work, who sometimes wear only the headpieces). Sasak have a predilection for clothing and visual presentation; as a social and religious badge, clothing now further distinguishes Sasak from Balinese.

15. Through literature and poetry, the scholarly Balinese position is that the legendary prime minister of Majapahit, Gadjah Mada, corrected the unjust rule of the native kings in Bali in 1343, the year Majapahit conquered the Balinese kings. Just as Java freed Bali from the tyranny of native oppressors, Karangasem freed Lombok from evil native kings. This concept is perpetuated to glorify the Javanese-Balinese heritage of the Lombok Balinese noble families.

CHAPTER FOUR: Temple Units, Performing Arts, and Festival Rites

1. Min does not live at the Sasak priest's compound, but prefers to reside in his nearby home west of the compound. He sometimes moves into the compound shortly before the festival and returns home afterwards. His and other small neighborhoods west of the compound are populated with people historically linked to the temple. Sanusi preferred to live most of the year in the compound.

2. Rinjani's altar is an elevated, wooden "seat," with a pandanus-leaf roof, while Agung's *padmasana* is an elevated, uncovered "seat" made of brick and cement with depictions symbolizing the cosmos. Generally, the *padmasana* and *sanggar agung* altars are dedicated to the One God from which all else emanates, called either Ida Sang Hyang Widi Wasa, Siwa, or Surya. *Sanggar agung* may refer to altars for the Hindu Trinity of Siwa (or Iswara), Wisnu, and Brahma. For reasons that are unclear, the *padmasana* was chosen to honor Batara Gunung Agung (perhaps to indicate an omnipotent character of Batara Gunung Agung, suggesting a being such as Siwa as Mahadéwa). Interestingly, within the

inner courtyard of Pura Méru, the largest Balinese temple in Lombok, are two enormous *padmasana* altars: one for Batara Gunung Agung and the other for Batara Gunung Rinjani.

3. In the early part of this century the altar and pond in Pura Lingsar were separate, as they are in Pura Ulon, with the altar situated about five meters in front of the pond. With financial assistance from either the Dutch (according to some) or the Chinese merchant Cing (according to others), the altar was moved and placed next to the pond to facilitate *kemaliq* processions.

4. The Krama Pura booklet *Pura Lingsar Selayang Pandang* notes a (presumably) male deity in the *kemaliq*, Sang Hyang Parama Gangga, though I had never heard this particular name before.

Bali scholar Michelle Chin attended the festival with me in 1988 and noted the lack of female deities in the Pura Lingsar *gadoh*. A makeshift altar is constructed in the Pura Lingsar *kemaliq* for the river goddess Batari Gangga, though some gloss this deity as male ("Batara"). The rice goddess Déwi Sri is not directly represented at Lingsar, yet she is connected through rice cultivation. Since the festival occurs before the transplantation of seedlings and not during harvest (Sri's main domain), Gangga is the more important goddess due to her association with water and its accumulation. Déwi Sri has a second connection through her consort, Batara Wisnu, for together they unify the water and harvest cycles.

5. Parman reports that the current pavilion was preceded by another that was, in fact, circular. The newer rectangular pavilion simply inherited the name.

6. Parman mentioned that the eels' skin is "like that of a snake," and that no one is brave enough to eat those that live in the ponds. Eels are associated with fertility in Bali and Lombok, but it is normally acceptable to catch and eat them. At the conclusion of the Alip festival of Bayan, the bamboo tubes used in temporary structures that are disassembled and thrown into the river afterward are thought to transform into these eels, thus symbolizing the festival's success and general prosperity (van Baal 1976:77).

7. Some Balinese feel that the Batek Baris and particularly the gamelan *tambur*, were originally Balinese contributions to the festival and that these became Sasak over time. A few say that since gamelan *tambur* is known in Bali—I have seen two ensembles in Karangasem region—and the word *baris* refers to a martial dance in Bali, these must have been Balinese performing arts.

8. The associated festivals include two at ward temples, Karang Songkang and Karang Ketéwel in Cakranegara, and one at a large "public" temple, Pura Méru. (Pura Pengsong—at the small mountain that is part of the discovery myth—is also associated with Lingsar, but festivals are not connected.) These temples all have histories intricately linked to Lingsar, and in the past the Batek Baris group was invited to perform for their festivals.

9. The prevailing thinking was that migrants from Karang Ketéwel in Bali brought the gamelan with them to the ward Karang Ketéwel in Lombok, and that, when requested, it had to be returned to Bali. I have doubts about that contention. The instrumentation is the same as other *gong kuna* in Lombok, and these appear to have been styled upon models in north Bali; thus I do not think the gamelan originated in the Ketéwel area or was brought to Lombok by those original migrants. I did not feel it appropriate, however, to offer my own opinion on the matter.

10. The *gong kuna* group at Pagutan apparently used to perform regularly at Lingsar because villagers built the shrine in the *pesiraman* (and perhaps the *pesiraman* itself) and therefore had a direct investment in the festival. However, for many decades performance has been initiated by a group contacting the Krama Pura. If two (or no) groups request to play, then a Krama Pura member must select a club.

11. *Bebaliq* is what Balinese call the material, *kemaliq* is what Sasak call it; both refer to the sacred nature of the material. The Sasak *pamangku* conducts ceremonies for Balinese children called Nugel Bebaliq ("cut" *bebaliq*, which refers to the material worn by the child that is ritually severed). Some say that the ritual allows Balinese to enter the *kemaliq*; others that Balinese must conduct this ritual to marry Sasak women; still others that Balinese must conduct this ritual to enter Balinese temples on Lombok. Although some Lombok Balinese no longer follow this ceremony, those from Cakranegara still have this ritual held for their children by the *pamangku* in the *kemaliq*. The ritual is conducted for many Sasak children as well, and some of the material hung is from both Sasak and Balinese ancestors. The hanging of these *bebaliq* and *kemaliq* is not integral to the festival, yet the *pamangku* arranges them for every festival. When asked, neither Sanusi nor Min would say much about this activity.

Traditional Muslim children throughout Lombok undergo similar cloth-cutting ceremonies. Krulfield (1974:96–97) describes a Waktu Telu ceremony in Sapit called Lelampaq or Kekombong Umbaq, where special holy cloths are ritually woven after a child is born and will be ritually severed following a naming and hair-cutting ceremony. The cloth is kept by the *pamangku*, who uses it to create medicines to cure the child. Bolland and Polak (1971:149–170) discuss various types of Sasak sacred cloth, and Bolland (1971:171–182) compares the processes of producing sacred cloths and weavings on Lombok and Bali.

12. Bolland and Polak (1971:168) suggest that a distinction exists between cloth connecting a *pamangku* and *kemaliq* and that used for children's ceremonies and medicinal purposes. As the Waktu Telu migrated (escaping Islamic courts), they left behind their lands and original sacred places and thus the cloth associated with *kemaliq* declined in importance.

13. Only three cockfights are generally allowed at other Balinese temples in Bali and Lombok. At Lingsar, each temple structure/orifice (Pura Ulon and Pura Lingsar *gadoh* and *kemaliq*) requires an individual series of cockfights. Nine cockfights for a festival is a unique development, though nine is also a symbolically important number.

14. Leap months in the *saka* calendar, inserted about every thirty months, push back opening days to late December. The 2001 festival, for instance, began on December 28 and ended on January 1, 2002.

15. Proyek Inventarisasi (1984:113) states that *kebon odeq* are (or used to be) prepared for marriage ceremonies of the Sasak noble classes. I heard conflicting reports about *kebon odeq* at rituals in other *kemaliq* and *pedéwaq*, but never saw any others myself.

The compound within the *pamangku*'s complex was modified in the 1990s. The door was moved from opening into the compound to opening outside the compound. The new opening allows for processions to depart and return more easily.

16. Two men carrying flagpoles with Indonesian flags precede the Batek Baris in every major festival procession. They are a recent addition (1960s to 1970s according to most teachers). The flags display nationalism and proudly symbolize the unifying aspects of Pancasila, the five principles of Indonesian political philosophy, just as Balinese and Sasak are united at the festival.

17. I received conflicting reports as to whether some water from Lingsar is carried in this procession in the Batara Gedé Lingsar bottle and then mixed with water at Pura Manggong. I was also told that water from another temple further east may be used in this bottle.

18. Sanusi mentioned that these processions were performed by one unified group long ago and that their destinations were once further eastward and westward than they are today. Balinese teachers tended to agree that the procession destinations have been shortened. Sasak participation may have been more active at this earlier time.

19. Sanusi used the titles Upacara Geria and Ngaturang Pesaji interchangeably for this ritual. I later discovered that a *geria* is a ceremony within *kemaliq* or *pedéwaq* shrines. The name of this *geria* ceremony is Ngaturang Pesaji. Min does not appear to understand these ceremonies as Sanusi did, but he conducts them in a similar manner.

20. The fact that the name of the deity must be silent is consistent with the system of taboos found at *kemaliq*. According to Pepplinkhuizen (1991:36), this phenomenon, in which the name of the worshipped divinity cannot be pronounced by anyone (including the officiating priest, who may be the only who knows the name), is common in Indonesian cultures east of Bali. Sanusi never told me the name of the deity, and I personally feel that it is not likely to be Datu Selaparang or Haji Abdul Maliq (see Chapter Three).

21. The *kiyai* should be Waktu Telu, especially for the Balinese. Since there are few if any *kiyai* who admit to being Waktu Telu, those from Lingsar whose ancestors were attached to the temple are requested to perform this task. Generally, two additional buffalo are slaughtered for feasts on the last day of the festival.

The buffalo is hung in the *kemaliq* tree to demonstrate the sacrifice. The remains of the Balinese buffalo may later be added. These remains do not generate a bad smell, which participants claim is because of the power of the offering. The right front hoof is hung in the tree because buffalo begin walking with that hoof; the right leg is therefore the most important limb and symbolizes the animal's journey into the spirit world. As I watched proceedings in the *kemaliq* in 2001, I did not at first realize that I was sitting directly beneath the buffalo head. The huge head was a meter above me. It did not smell, but I soon found another sitting area.

22. Unlike the Sasak, the Balinese rarely invite outsiders. Officials feel that asking outsiders—presumably Sasak or Javanese Muslims—would turn their rituals and activities into entertainment for their guests, which would be awkward and inappropriate. Fortunately, the officials had no such problems inviting me.

23. Since Pura Ulon is "older" than Pura Lingsar, some say that Balinese must pray there first. However, many Balinese are unaware of this rule and fail to visit Pura Ulon.

24. According to Sasak legend, the Perang Topat should occur when the *waru* flower wilts in the late afternoon (*raraq kembang waru*). This is supposedly the time of day when Datu Wali Milir achieved *moksa* in the water spring. The Perang Topat symbolizes the items that his followers then threw into the spring. A Balinese *pamangku*, the late Mangku Saka, mentioned that he felt Perang Topat symbolized the Adiparwa story (from the Mahabharata epic) of the war between the deities and a demon giant in trying to gain *amerta* (the elixir of life) after it had been produced by the demon pulling the *naga* serpent that holds Mt. Mandara in place. The *topat* are carried back to the rice fields after the Perang Topat and symbolize the fertility aspects of *amerta*.

Perang Topat still occurs at a few of the remaining Waktu Telu and Boda festivals. The symbolism of the rite appears similar at these other festivals, though the celebrated myths differ.

25. The regional government now regulates the agriculture cycle and offers a number of options to farmers and *subak*. Farmers are allowed to plant seedlings in the fields after November 1, a date that precedes the festival and reduces some of its agrarian significance. However, most farmers still wait until after the festival to plant their seedlings and the temple supports this traditional system by releasing more irrigation water at that time.

Lansing (1987:326–341) describes how a rice terrace is an entire ecosystem, and not just part of an irrigation chain, that is dependent upon coordination with neighboring terraces to prosper. This coordination includes assuring the proper mineral elements in the terrace to maintain fertile soil and allows for a mutual fallow period that prevents pestilence. His description of the role of Pura Ulon Danu Batur as the supreme water temple in Bali (serving 204 *subak*), and its festival as part of a scheduling system for irrigation and coordination of the rice cycle, could probably be used for Pura Lingsar and its festival, particularly during the period of Balinese colonization. The festivals are timed in accordance with the water and sunlight needs of the rice, and they allow for the main harvest during the dry season. In Bali and West Lombok, farmers achieve two harvests; following the main harvest, they plant a faster-maturing variety of rice, harvest again, and then allow a short fallow period that minimizes pest populations. The regional government on Lombok has given farmers flexibility in following this schedule and has introduced faster-maturing rice. Many farmers, however, continue the past practice.

Pura Lingsar is often associated with Pura Ulon Danu Batur among Lombok Balinese, because Pura Lingsar is connected to the lake, Segara Anak, within the crater of Gunung Rinjani, just as Pura Ulon Danu Batur is located on Gunung Batur in proximity to the lake, Danu Batur. Both temples are sources of fertility, and the lakes are the homes of Déwi Danu (Batur) and Déwi Anjani (Rinjani), goddesses considered givers of water for irrigation. Although Déwi Anjani is not directly represented in the altars at Pura Lingsar, she completes the male Batara Gunung Rinjani and is associated with Batari Gangga (goddess of rivers) and Batara Wisnu (god of fertile water). A major ancestral deity, she also forms a part of the emerging Sasak myth.

26. Proyek Inventarisasi (1984:120) reports that other forms, such as the shadow play, the Sasak *kayaq* theater, and the Balinese *légong* classical dance have been performed at the festival. *Légong* was presented as recently as 1993.

27. The late Mangku Saka explained that there should be two processions within Balinese temples: the first on the first day to bring down the deities by circling counterclockwise, representing descent from the Himalayas, then the second on the last day to symbolically send the deities back by circling clockwise. (He also said that the processions could be interpreted as participants ascending to the Himalayas, then descending.) Although he participated at Lingsar for over sixty years, he did not know why the two (especially the first) processions go clockwise. Apparently, it has always been so at Lingsar.

At the 1988 festival the events on the opening day were delayed, causing confusion and apparently preventing the first procession from taking place.

28. Ida Wayan Pasha, a highly respected former official of the Education and Culture Department official who had a Balinese father and a Sasak mother, explained that the Sasak attend the festival (and other pre-Islamic rituals) to remember an event in the mythic past, while the Balinese come to worship the active power of nature of Batara Wisnu in the embodiment of Batara Gedé Lingsar. Within the traditional Sasak worldview, natural deities are incarnations of ancestors; Batara Rinjani, for example, is considered the first, original ancestor. Datu Wali Milir (or other name for the founding hero) is also an ancestor, and, for some, Batara Gedé Lingsar is the residing ancestor deity. Perhaps Haji Abdul Maliq will become an ancestor for those who know his story.

29. A Sasak group east of Kumbung in the hills overlooking the Lingsar area mentioned in 1988 that local religious leaders would not allow them to attend the festival. So instead they prepare the appropriate offerings and face them towards Lingsar from their homes for the duration of the event. This type of intimidation, as well as more direct measures such as physical violence and public ostracism, has declined as the attitude toward cultural

participation has evolved. Parman, the nephew of the Sasak *pamangku*, stated that government and religious leaders should understand that "Muslims at Lingsar are like those everywhere, but we have a different culture."

30. When I showed films from the festival with this *haji* in them to Muslim government officials, they were dismayed that someone who had gone to Mecca could actively participate at the non-Islamic shrine of Lingsar.

CHAPTER FIVE: Music: History, Cosmology, and Content

1. The analyses in this chapter are restricted to defining the varieties of music and instruments at Lingsar to support this study's themes of meaning, homology, hermeneutical encounter, and behavior generation. For further information, see Harnish 1991a.

2. Becker and Becker (1981) allude to Hindu-Buddhist constructs underlying particularly Javanese gamelan. It is important to acknowledge, however, that Islam has become the prominent idiom in Java and Lombok and that Hindu-Buddhist cultural notions do not now resonate among Javanese as they did decades ago.

3. *Pélog* refers to a hemitonic heptatonic scale, while *slendro* refers to an anhemitonic pentatonic scale in Java. These terms are not truly indigenous to Bali but have become well known. They are also known among the Balinese and Sasak on Lombok, but are more restricted to the areas of strong Balinese influence in West Lombok. The further one goes from West Lombok, the further the musical tonality diverts from *pélog/slendro* matrices.

4. In his essay on the *Aji Gurnita*, Vickers (1985:146) states that music can cause "emotions relating to sexual desire and passion." The emphasis on Semara, the god of sensual love, in discussions concerning the development of gamelan in both *lontar* indicates the sensual and affective qualities of music (see Harnish 1998a).

5. McPhee (1966:38) positions these relationships differently. *Ding* is related to Siwa, *dong* to Iswara, *deng* to Mahadéwa, *dung* to Brahma, and *dang* to Wisnu. Unlike the *Prakempa*, McPhee sequences the tones *ding-dong-deng-dung-dang*, as they occur in the gamelan *gong* in Bali. In Lombok, however, the sequence of tones begins with *dong* and progresses *deng, dung, dang*, and *ding*. No one I have asked knows why the ordering of tone names among the Lombok Balinese differs from that in Bali; the pitches themselves are equivalent.

The *Prakempa* also associates goddesses with the five tones of the *slendro* scale: *ndang* with Mahadéwi, *nding* with Saraswati, *ndeng* with Gayatri, *ndung* with Sri Déwi, and *ndong* with Huma Déwi (Bandem 1986:72–73). When placed within the mandala configuration of ten tones, however, the goddesses transform into the gods Mahesora, Sangkara, Ludra, Sambhu, and Buddha. These gods and their tones are placed within the subdivisions of the four cardinal directions, with Buddha placed in the center along with Siwa. Buddha and Siwa are at other times different names for the same center.

Wallis (1979:102) asserts that the *Aji Gurnita* includes magic syllables, five-day cycles, and body parts for each of the five tones, although the deities indicated differ from those of the *Prakempa*. *Ding* is related to Bamadéwa, south, the day Paing, blood, and red; *deng* is related to Tatpurusa, west, Pon, sinews, and yellow; *dung* is related to Agora, north, Wagé, bones, and black; *dong* is related to Isana, center, Kliwon, marrow, and grey; and *dang* is related to Sakiojata, east, Manis, skin, and white. He adds that five *mudra* hand gestures of the priest during rites are also related to the five tones, and he discusses how tones and other cultural phenomena are positioned together to create cosmological design.

6. Over the last few decades several villages and the conservatories have ordered new sets of gamelan *gong gedé*, thus somewhat reviving the style.

7. Some Dutch and Sasak may have destroyed or looted gamelan following the Balinese defeat in 1894. Several teachers state that the Japanese melted down some gamelan to forge bullets during their occupation (1942–1945).

8. The *bendé* is a small hanging gong with a sunken boss. It is usually played with a small wooden hammer on the boss or shoulder and can be damped or open to produce a variety of percussive sounds. It follows the fastest density pulse and is more aligned with the cymbals than the punctuation. *Bendé*, also called *babendé*, are frequently found in the *gong kuna* but only played in particular pieces.

Another instrument, a single kettle-gong called *petuk*, is sometimes included. Normally called *kempli* or *kajar* in Bali, the *petuk* is played on the main pulse and is more common in gamelan *gong gilak* and *baleganjur*. *Petuk* refers to this timekeeping instrument in virtually all Balinese ensembles in Lombok and in many Sasak gamelans.

9. Former culture official Ida Wayan Pasha said that this piece is sometimes called "Remrem" (Dark). Another teacher, I Wayan Kartawirya, added that during the Balinese colonization, the piece used to accompany and signify the coming of the king to a ritual event.

10. Most teachers believe that it is the *kempli* strokes that govern the form of *tabuh*. Rembang (1985:9–10) asserts that the *tabuh* number indicates both *kempul* and *kempli* strokes.

11. For purposes that appear to be purely musical (i.e., increasing tension or cadential), an extra *kempul* stroke is added on the beat before the gong stroke at the end of the cycle.

12. The higher register can be realized only by the two-octave *trompong*, not by the single-octave metallophones.

13. The flow of a *lelambatan* piece is virtually always the same in Lombok, though occasionally the terms for transitional sections and technique differ from club to club. Apart from the main sections, terminology and practice varies further in Bali, where the elaborate transitions and rhythmic breaks (*angsel*) that mark the Lombok style are absent. How Lombok's form and style began is a mystery, although there is some evidence that these may have originated in Buleleng and not in areas more commonly associated with the gamelan *gong* (see Harnish 1992).

14. In several areas of East Bali, there are some gamelan *baleganjur* that are complete (i.e., not derived from other ensembles) and do not include kettle-gongs, just like the Lombok version. Today in Bali more *baleganjur* (with kettle-gongs) are manufactured as complete ensembles due to the *kreasi beleganjur* (*beleganjur* creations) movement that has attracted young people for competitions. Bakan (1999) reports that the *kreasi beleganjur* craze inspired clubs to order gamelans for that purpose only; thus these are also complete unto themselves and not assembled from larger gamelans.

15. The *padanda* is an aloof character. Deriving from the highest-status caste (*brahmana*), *padanda*, especially after achieving priesthood, do not often associate with commoners. At most festivals the *padanda* enters the temple, conducts the ceremony, creates holy water, and then returns home or leaves to officiate at another festival or life-cycle rite. They rarely have any deep attachment to one temple and seldom stop to socialize.

16. Some state that long ago the offerings were held with both hands to emphasize their importance in the dance. Today, however, the offerings are held in either hand (though it is considered much more appropriate to hold them in the right, "pure" hand) as they enter the temple dancing. In the 1980s some Balinese said that these dances had changed and were now sometimes humorous; in 2001 the few I spoke with acknowledged the changes and were disappointed with the quality of the offerings.

17. According to Rio Helmi (personal communication) and other scholars and specialists on the Balinese Studies Internet list, Rejang Déwa (and the unique *kompol* headdress)

derives from East Bali. I Wayan Dibia suggests that an early Swasthi Bandem attempt at new Rejang Déwa was performed at an event in 1983 (Schaareman, personal communication), and Garrett Kam (personal communication) reports that the current dance was first performed publicly in 1988 at Pura Dalem Sekarmukti in Singapadu. Kam (1993:78) enjoyed it until he noticed that the dance was soon spreading to other temples. Rucina Ballinger (personal communication) stated in 2003 that the dance is performed "at almost every temple festival" she has attended in recent years, usually at temples that have no earlier tradition of *rejang*. On occasion, Kam asserts, Rejang Déwa may have replaced previous temple dances, and he views the spread of the dance as a political "means of control and exerting power," since the new form originated at the government academy and was promoted by Hindu and government offices (the costume color, yellow, is also associated with the ruling Golkar political party). Since the dance is also performed outside of temple festivals (in concerts abroad, at state cultural spectacles), Rejang Déwa is not a sacred performance from a "traditional" point of view; at Lingsar, it is sacred.

18. Since Sumbawa and Makassar (in South Sulawesi) extended influence into East Lombok, some Sasak in that district feel a stronger affinity with those locations than with Java. See Clegg (2004) for more historical information.

19. Some government officials and cultural leaders have sought to divide Balinese and Sasak arts, and to discourage any style that shares Balinese elements. For example, Drs. Arzaki, the head of a cultural organization, claimed that arm movements in dance that rise to or above the head indicate Balinese influence, and he argued that officials should stop these movements in Sasak dance. Several officials, however, have countered that the movements are not necessarily Balinese. A few have articulated that since some of these influences originated in Java, discerning what is Balinese and what is Sasak is problematic.

20. I hoped to interview Rahil again in 1995 to record more of his ideas, but was saddened to learn that he had died. His outspokenness and directness in proclaiming himself a Waktu Telu distinguished him. He was also an intellectual and founder of both an arts community and a social welfare community organization in his village of Lenek.

21. In areas of Balinese influence such as West Lombok, Sasak ensembles seem to be more similar to *slendro* and particularly to *pélog*. Beyond these areas Sasak music largely diverges from *pélog* and *slendro* tonality, and there are a number of tetratonic forms—in compositions for gamelan *beleq* and *kamput*, for example. The gamelan *beleq* features a gong chime of four kettle-gongs, along with a gong, drums, usually a small set of cymbals, and other bronze percussion instruments. Many other ensembles, such as the gamelan *oncer* and *barong tengkok*, include similar tetratonic gong chimes. The nearly obsolete *kamput* ensemble consists of *preret*, gong, drums, cymbals, and bronze percussion instruments. Although the *preret* (and all wind instruments in the above ensembles) has a comfortable heptatonic capability, most of the *kamput* repertoire is tetratonic and players stay with the tonal material. "Traditional" ensembles do not acknowledge more than five tones. Newer Islamic-inspired ensembles, however, often include violins and plucked lutes that accompany vocal songs with sometimes heptatonic and nearly tempered tonality (Harnish 1998b).

22. Occasionally the drum is left uncovered. The few gamelan *tambur* in Bali are also wrapped in *kain poleng*. This material often appears on people and objects subject to strong negative energy. Many strong warrior figures in *wayang* theater, for example, wear *kain poleng*.

23. Ida Wayan Pasha said that the story line of two Sasak theater forms, Baris Arog and Amaq Darmi, follow similar themes. Both include two *telek* figures who wear the same *gulungan* (arched) headpieces as at Lingsar, although the dancers are often men and one of

them dresses as a woman. My research on Baris Arog in the village of Longseran indicates that they once had such a tradition and that there is probably a strong link between Baris Arog and Batek Baris. Pasha reports that this story is related to another, older one concerning the legendary Banjar Getas and the queen of the East Lombok kingdom, Selaparang. When their love was discovered, they had to circle the kingdom singing. However, no other teacher has offered this version. Telek dancers are included in performance of the gamelan *barong tengkok* and hobbyhorse riders for marriage ceremonies held in several Central Lombok villages. The term *telek* is also known around Lombok as a common, nonnarrative Sasak dance.

24. This association is restricted to the ceremonial repertoire; in ensembles the *preret* has no specific pre-Islamic links.

25. "Pang Pang Pau," like "Turun Daun," uses a *pélog*-like pentatonic tonality. "Jodak Digol" uses a *pélog*-like tetratonic tonality, and both pieces are based on two-line *lelakaq* poetry. "Jodak Digol" has been transcribed and analyzed (Harnish 1985:233–299); it is a core piece in several villages and is sometimes used among Balinese communities to accompany female offering dances. There is clearly a connection between this piece and offerings. Salih stated that it was appropriate to play the piece whenever offerings are picked up and removed.

CHAPTER SIX: Explorations of Meaning

1. Bandem and deBoer (1995) explicate a theory that categorizes performing arts at temple festivals in terms of the courtyard in which they take place. This theory, with sacred (*wali*), semi-sacred (*bebali*), and secular (*bali-balihan*) categories, was first postulated by I Gusti Bagus Sugriwa, a noted Balinese intellectual on the performing arts and theological matters. The three-ness is related to other tripartite structures (heaven, sky, earth; mountain, earth, sea; head, body, leg, and so forth). Though limited because it is based exclusively upon spatial orientation, the theory was crafted by Balinese intellectuals and has been useful for categorizing the arts.

2. The prayers are silent. Some concentrate on the individual gods addressed through each *sembah* (hands clasped with fingers holding a flower, which is thrown forward to the god) of the prayers. This is often called Panca Sembah due to the five times of *sembah*, though usually one *sembah* is "empty," that is, not addressed to a specific god or manifestation of God. Others go through the motions but think of God, with thoughts in Balinese language.

3. Members of the Krama Pura stated that Topeng Sidha Karya had been presented at the temple for at least as long as they could remember. I received a report that Topeng Pajegan was held rather than Sidha Karya during the 1990 festival. Topeng Pajegan functions similarly in recontextualizing the past into the present and reactualizing legendary figures into the temple's history and into the lives of the participants. Although the performance does not include the figure Sidha Karya, the single Topeng Pajegan dancer/actor/singer reinvents history in a ritualistic fashion considered very appropriate for temple festivals.

4. This is generally true throughout Balinese society. Participants should be "respected equals in a single religious community" (Wallis 1979:56). Sometimes, as with Lingsar, one noble or those generally of noble caste (*kesatria*) may be treated with extra respect and sit in front of the altars during prayer. At Lingsar there is no hard rule for this, but Agung Biarsah and his family usually sit right in front of the altar for Batara Alit Sakti and Batara Gedé Lingsar in the north-center position of the *gadoh*. Ritual protocol therefore preserves

parts of the social order, despite the assertion that festivals benefit all participants equally and should therefore treat them all equally.

5. As Gerdin (1982:225) suggests, some poor Balinese farmers do not feel that they have the proper clothing to attend important festivals like Lingsar, and apparently many others who contribute *topat* never enter the *gadoh*. They may not enter the *kemaliq* either, but they probably feel a closer spiritual affinity with the *kemaliq* since its altar is associated with irrigation water. *Kemaliq* ceremonies also are less formal, participants are not as well dressed, and the atmosphere may be more comfortable for poor or uneducated commoners. Kartawirya and others recounted that during Balinese colonization, Balinese commoners were not allowed in the *gadoh* and instead participated in the *kemaliq*. This story was difficult to confirm.

6. The *redeb* player, Amaq Raidin, has not participated in Mendak Tirta processions for many years; he feels he is "too old" and "not needed." The *suling* player normally participates. It is easier to walk with a *suling* than with a *redeb*.

7. In this and other chapters, active Sasak participation is linked with "deity" or "deities." This creates obvious problems with Islamic interpretation and with the contention that Sasak participation is "cultural" rather than "religious." Most participants have used terms like *roh* (spirit, deity) to describe the presence at Lingsar.

8. The spaces/settings of *wayang* Sasak are palace, nature/forest, and war scenes, and mosques or holy places. "Janggel" and its variations are played for the transitions to and from all of these settings (see Harnish 2003). These spaces can be interpreted to have representations in the *kemaliq*, the temple in general, and in spaces outside of the temple complex.

9. I played some video footage to officials (mostly Javanese, a few Sasak) at the Culture and Education Department that showed a *haji* seated and praying next to nominal Muslims in the *kemaliq*, and they were appalled. *Haji* are supposed to be orthodox Muslims who pray only to Allah and follow Islamic regulations, requirements which clearly do not allow for prayer in a "heathen" shrine. I think this indicates, however, just how important the *kemaliq* and Lingsar are to traditional Sasak villagers. In addition to being the source of fertility, prosperity, rainwater, irrigation water, divine cures, and so forth, the festival can be considered a local expression of Islam.

10. Many of these congregants probably want to ask pardon, seek divine cures, or request specific boons, since the *kemaliq* is available for such requests.

11. To my knowledge, fewer Islamic elements appear in rites in more strongly Waktu Telu communities like Bayan. Many of such elements at Lingsar have emerged since the late 1960s, and my thesis is that these elements have helped protect the festival from religious pressures that seem to have eliminated other such rituals in nearby areas.

Several other Balinese temples in West Lombok, such as those at Suranadi and Narmada, include *kemaliq* spaces and at one time Waktu Telu participated at festivals in these temples. Teachers were unsure when this participation stopped. Sanusi disagreed that these were true *kemaliq* courtyards, since in his rhetoric only the *kemaliq* at Pura Lingsar was the true courtyard. He contended that Sasak had participated at other temples only because they could not come to Lingsar. It seems likely that the 1960s slaughter probably terminated subsequent Sasak participation at these other Balinese temples. Due to strategies by both Balinese and nominal Muslims, Lingsar was protected and Sasak participation could continue.

CHAPTER SEVEN: Changing Dimensions, Changing Identities

1. Over the years Agung Biarsah's status and reputation have been restored and enhanced. He is now considered a good leader and very knowledgeable about the temples, the histories, and all of the traditions. He also has a home in Denpasar, the capital of Bali, and spends much of his time there; his children are being educated in Bali. He told me in 2001 that attending the festival is a top priority for him, but he was unable to attend that year due to commitments on Bali.

2. I thank Garrett Kam, Rucina Ballinger, Rio Helmi, and Danker Schaareman for their ideas on the spread of Rejang Déwa.

3. The new movement vocabulary was not radically new, but it introduced notions of gender and character; the vocabulary between characters, however, remains very similar.

These officials also helped organize the choreography of many of the *gendang beleq* ensembles, including two of the clubs at Lingsar; choreography was included in the cultural packages the government offered. On one occasion I attended a practice of a club in Narmada. Throughout the practice officials, particularly Endah Setyorini, were adamant about the teenaged boys maintaining vertical male movements and not shaking their hips, which Setyorini insisted was a female movement. I noticed that the four groups at Lingsar generally performed the hip-shaking movements and that most others do as well. I did not inform Setyorini, a Javanese with clear notions of gender-specific movement vocabulary, about the performances because I thought she would be gravely disappointed to learn that performers were deviating from her instruction. Her efforts to upgrade Sasak performing arts to a Javanese standard are somewhat typical of Indonesian government policies in outer regions.

4. One reason that clergy relaxed their reservations is that the government, unlike decades ago, now consists largely of Sasak *haji* or former *tuan gurus*. *Gendang beleq*'s rise as a decontextualized male youth project was to some extent patterned after Bali's *kreasi beleganjur*, the display gamelan *beleganjur* style originated in 1986 (see Bakan 1999). Both were processional gamelan models, both were state-developed for the same reasons, and both targeted male youth.

5. Teachers in early 2002 told me that the bottle has been empty before, but I had neither seen nor heard of it being empty over twenty years. A few teachers also indicated that festivals have been held without rainfall, but again I had neither experienced nor heard about that happening over the period. The harvest that year, while not bountiful, was sufficient.

Glossary

adat custom, customary law.

adharma opposite of dharma and order; chaos.

agama religion, world religion.

Aji Gurnita a *lontar* manuscript on the courtly arts, probably written about a hundred years ago.

akasa/pertiwi/apah sky/earth/water, the three worlds of the macrocosm.

alip Sasak term for festival and feast; see also *gawé*.

arja Balinese romantic, sung dance theater based on the Panji or Malat stories of East Java.

badede indigenous form of Sasak poetry of various types, frequently using a couplet form.

balé an open pavilion.

balé banten open pavilions for offerings.

balé bundar the open pavilion for the gamelan *gong* Sasak and its performers.

balé gong the open pavilions in front of the *gadoh* and in the Karang Kétewel shrine area (Pura Manggis) for gamelan performance.

balé kembar the "paired" open pavilion across from the *balé gong* in front of the *gadoh*. The gamelan *baris* is often positioned on this *balé*.

balé pewédaan the open pavilion in front of the altars in the *gadoh* of Pura Lingsar and Pura Ulon for the *padanda* and Vedic recitation. Also called *balé peliangan*.

baleganjur a Balinese-style processional gamelan; adopted by a Sasak club at Lingsar. Often spelled *beleganjur* in Bali.

banten offerings. *Banten suci* (also called *banten luhur*) refers to offerings for deities, *banten sor* for lower-world *buta kala* spirits.

barangan refers to a gong chime of twelve kettle-gongs played in continuous interlocking parts in the *gong kuna*. Also called *trompong barangan* or *réong*.

baris "line"; refers to the Baris dance of eight soldiers and a commandant held during the Lingsar festival. Also called Batek Baris, and refers to the gamelan that accompanies the performance.

batek refers directly to two of the four dancers of the Batek or Telek dance who wear arched headpieces. The term often refers to the entire dance, and hence indirectly to all of the dancers, including these two, the general and the king.

bebaliq a ceremonial cloth of the Sasak; also called *kemaliq*.

bendé a small or medium-sized hanging gong with a sunken boss whose function is more aligned with the drums and cymbals than with the punctuating instruments.

bendesa overseer of a temple and temple organization.

Beteteh "discard"; the Sasak term referring to the final day and sometimes also to the final procession of the festival.

budaya culture, also *kebudayaan*; often contrasted in Lombok with *agama*.

buta kala mischievous underworld spirits that can cause sickness and suffering.

canang sari "essence of betel nut"; required temple offerings of betel nut, flowers, and other ingredients with woven plaits. Also refers to the offering dance (Canang Sari or Ngolahang Canang Sari) in which dancers carry the offerings into the *gadoh*.

ceng-ceng a large set of cymbals used in ensembles, a single set of paired and hand-held cymbals, and a single set of paired cymbals with halves on a base struck by counterpart halves.

cili rice goddess figure.

daksina "south"; a required temple offering. Also an offering reportedly made for the gamelan *baris*.

daya/lauq Sasak terms for north or toward the mountain and south or toward the sea.

desa/kala/patra "place, time, and circumstance," used for placing activities and philosophizing.

gadoh the exclusively Balinese courtyard in Pura Lingsar and Pura Ulon. Also refers to the main courtyard of Pura Bukit in Bali, and of Pura Pamaksan Karang Songkang in Cakranegara Timur.

gambuh the refined court dance of Bali based on the Panji tales, considered the source of almost all Balinese music and dance forms.

gamelan an ensemble; originally a Javanese term.

***gamelan* baleganjur** the processional ensemble consisting of a gong, a timekeeping kettle-gong, cymbals, and drums. Often spelled *beleganjur* in Bali.

***gamelan* baris** the Sasak ensemble that features *redeb*, *suling*, *kenat*, *kajar*, *kendang lanang* and *wadon*, gong, and *tambur*, and is performed in procession and on the *balé kembar*.

***gamelan* bebonangan** a processional ensemble on Bali similar to the gamelan *bale-ganjur*.

***gamelan* gambuh** the gamelan that accompanies the Gambuh dance drama on Bali and formerly on Lombok.

***gamelan* gandrung** sometimes used to label the gamelan *gong* Sasak club that plays at Lingsar.

***gamelan* gong** the standard pentatonic Balinese ensemble consisting of gongs, metallophones, gong chimes, drums, and cymbals.

***gamelan* gong gedé** the large ceremonial gamelan of Bali, counterpart to gamelan *gong kuna*.

***gamelan* gong gilak** a Lombok Balinese ensemble derived from the instrumentation of gongs, drums, and cymbals in the gamelan *gong kuna*, with additional bronze percussion instruments.

***gamelan* gong kebyar** the modern, virtuoso Balinese gamelan *gong* ensemble.

***gamelan* gong kuna** the standard ceremonial gamelan of the Lombok Balinese.

***gamelan* gong Sasak** the Sasak version of the gamelan *gong kebyar*, incorporating elements of other Sasak gamelans *oncer* and *tawa-tawa*.

***gamelan* oncer** another name for the *gendang beleq* ensemble.

***gamelan* Semar pegulingan** a court gamelan of Bali formerly found also in Lombok.

***gamelan* tambur** the sacred ensemble "owned" by the *kemaliq* of Pura Lingsar that consists of a *tambur* drum and gong; it is associated with warfare and magical power.

***gamelan* tawa-tawa** a Sasak processional ensemble.

***gamelan* wayang Sasak** the Sasak gamelan that accompanies the shadow play, *wayang* Sasak.

Gandrung "love"; the social dance involving a single woman dancer who invites dance partners from the audience.

gangsa jongkok resting-bar metallophones that sound the core melody in the *gong kuna*.

gangsaran the faster ceremonial repertoire of the gamelan *gong gedé* and gamelan *gong kuna*.

gawé Sasak term for festival or feast; see also *alip*.

gendang beleq Sasak "big drum" ensemble, sometimes called gamelan *gendang beleq*, consisting of two large drums, *réong* kettles, many cymbals and usually a *suling*.

gending "composition"; referring generally to both instrumental music and vocal music.

genta the bell of the Hindu *padanda* priest.

geria a ceremony including collective prayer held in front of the *kemaliq* altar, occurring once on the opening, main, and final days. Also called Ngaturang Pesaji, or, for the first day, Ngaturang Kebon Odeq.

gilakan the repertoire of the *gong gilak*.

gong refers to an ensemble, the gamelan *gong*, and its variants.

gong gedé the large, ceremonial gamelan of Bali.

gong gilak a processional gamelan of the Lombok Balinese.

gong kebyar the modern, virtuoso Balinese gamelan.

gong kuna the ceremonial gamelan of the Lombok Balinese.

gongan the length between gong strokes, a gong cycle.

haji a male Muslim who has undertaken the pilgrimage to Mecca.

ikan tuna the fresh-water eels that live in the *kemaliq* ponds and are frequently found in irrigation channels and irrigated rice terraces in Lombok and Bali. Called *julit* or *bejulit* in Balinese.

isteri "wife," referring to one of the *kebon odeq* offerings.

jegogan the two large suspended-bar metallophones in the *gong kuna*, *gong kebyar*, and *gong* Sasak supplying punctuation to the core melody.

kaja/kelod Balinese terms for north or toward the mountain and south or toward the sea.

kajar a single kettle-gong with a sunken boss played in figuration with the *kenat* kettle-gong in the gamelan *baris*.

karang a ward or sub-village unit. Also called *banjar*.

kayangan tiga the three-temple grouping typical of many villages in Bali, consisting of a temple of origins (*pura puseh*), a central village temple (*pura balé agung* or *pura desa*), and a temple of the dead (*pura dalam*). This grouping does not exist in Lombok.

kebon odeq the main Sasak offerings at Lingsar and found in a few other villages in Lombok, consisting of a male (*lanang*) and female or wife (*isteri*). Represents microcosm and macrocosm.

kemaliq "place of supernatural sanctions"; refers to the second courtyard at Lingsar and to its altar.

kempli a single, horizontally mounted kettle-gong providing secondary punctuation in the *gong kuna*.

kempul a medium-sized hanging gong used for secondary punctuation in the *gong kuna*, and the only gong normally used for the *baleganjur*.

kenat a single kettle-gong played in figuration with the *kajar* kettle-gong in the gamelan *baris*.

kendang cylindrical double-headed drums, consisting of male (*lanang*) and female (*wadon*), included in the *gong kuna*, *gong gilak*, gamelan *baris*, *gong* Sasak, and *baleganjur* ensembles at Lingsar.

kepercayaan "beliefs"; often used to define religious-like practices that do not fall under *agama*.

ketua head, director.

khas *Sasak* original Sasak culture.

kidung Balinese Hindu praise poetry, originally from Java, often sung by female choirs.

krama pura Balinese organization responsible for a temple and its festivals. The organization at Lingsar is Yayasan Krama Pura Lingsar.

lelakaq Sasak poems of love, nature, and parting.

lamak woven plaits with symbols; also considered the abode of the gods.

lanang "male," referring to one of the *kebon odeq* offerings, and also to male drums and gongs.

lang lang Sasak community security forces; also *pecalang*.

lelambatan the slow, stately, ceremonial repertoire of the gamelan *gong gedé* and gamelan *gong kuna*.

lontar manuscripts made of palm leaf.

Mabakti "to do devotional worship"; refers to Balinese prayer periods in the *gadoh* and at the crossroads on the opening day. Also called Muspa and Panca Sembah. Requires five occasions of raising a flower between the middle fingers of clasped hands while in collective prayer.

Mailahang Kebo the Balinese term for the procession that circles the entire Pura Lingsar structure three times clockwise with a water buffalo.

mandala a pictorial depiction of the structure of the cosmos.

Mawéda "to recite Wéda": refers to the general rite of Vedic recitation during the *padanda*'s rituals.

Mendak Kebon Odeq the procession that takes the *kebon odeq* from the Sasak priest's home compound to the *kemaliq*, where they are positioned for most of the festival.

Mendak Tirta "meet holy water"; the procession on the opening day that proceeds to Pura Sarasuta and Pura Manggong to collect water representing four high deities of Bali and Lombok: Batara Alit Sakti, Batara Gunung Agung, Batara Gedé Lingsar, and Batara Gunung Rinjani.

moksa divine unification with representative spiritual energy remaining at the place of transcendence.

momot the bottle ritually sealed on the morning of the opening day and opened after the conclusion of the main events on the final day.

Nawa Sanga the Balinese nine-part system of deities and their attributes mapped onto the universe that dictates traditional architectural form, rice planting, deity invocation, and so forth.

Ngaturang Pesaji the name of a ceremony with a collective prayer rite (also called *geria*) held in front of the *kemaliq* altar.

Ngilahang Kaoq the Sasak term for the procession that circles the entire Pura Lingsar structure three times clockwise with a water buffalo.

Ngilahang Pesaji the name of the procession that circles the *kemaliq* altar three times clockwise. Ngilahang Kebon Odeq sometimes refers to the first one of the three processions (one for each of the main days), held on the opening day.

padanda the high Balinese priests. Must be from the *brahmana* caste.

padanda istri the "wife" of the *padanda*. May accompany their husbands or provide services as *padanda* after their husbands' deaths.

padmasana the altar for Batara Gunung Agung in both the Pura Lingsar and Pura Ulon *gadoh* courtyards, though normally the altar for Batara Surya, Siwa, or Ida Sang Hyang Widi Wasa, the Supreme Being. Sometimes refers to the *kemaliq* altar. Also called *sanggar agung*.

palinggih the altar or "seat" for the deities, often considered those directly honored by temple festivals. Also called *palinggihan* or *pasimpangan*, although this latter term often refers to altars for "visiting" deities.

pamangku the common Balinese priests in charge of rites and upkeep of temples; also the title of Sasak priests of the Waktu Telu.

Panca Sembah the ritual act of praying five times during Balinese ritual.

Pancasila the five national principles of Indonesia, formulated by the first president of Indonesia, Soekarno.

Panji the legendary crown prince of the mythic East Javanese kingdom of Kahuripan. The stories based on this character are often called Serat Malat, and they provide the basis for Balinese *arja* and *gambuh* theater, as well as for the Batek/Telek dance.

pantun a rhyming-couplet poetic form found throughout the archipelago, used for several gamelan *baris* songs.

Parisadha Hindu Dharma the Hindu organization that oversees the religion in Indonesia; Bali and Lombok have their own branches.

pedéwaq stone altars of the traditional Muslims.

pélog a seven-tone scale system developed in Java that spread throughout much of Indonesia, primarily throughout Java and in Bali and Lombok.

Pemendak "meet" or "welcome"; one of the Balinese terms for the opening day; it refers to meeting and escorting the deities and their representational water during the Mendak Tirta procession.

Penaek Gawé "beginning of festive work"; the Sasak term for the opening day.

pendede a subgenre of Sasak *badede* poetry directed at ancestral and natural deities.

Pengadagang "birth" or "creation"; a Balinese term referring to the opening day.

pengawak the "body" of a Balinese composition.

pengawit the introduction ("what comes first") in a Balinese composition.

pengecet an allegretto or final section to a Balinese composition.

Penglemek "fertile soil"; a Balinese term referring to the last day of the festival.

penyor large Balinese ceremonial poles with mountain and male symbolism, sometimes coupled with female symbolism to create a unified whole; other times meant to balance the *lamak* weavings with their female symbolism. Constructed for ceremonies.

Perang Topat "war of the rice squares"; the mock war held in the shared outer courtyard where participants hurl the *topat* at each other. This activates the fecund power of the *topat*.

peras gong an offering for the gong and its spirit, which represents the entire gamelan. Placed by the gong of the *gong kuna* and *tambur* ensembles.

pesaji the secondary Sasak food offerings, made in increments of nine.

pesiraman the courtyard for bathing at Pura Lingsar, divided into sections for men and women.

petuk a single kettle-gong used as a timekeeper in the gamelan *baleganjur, gong kebyar*, and *gong* Sasak ensembles.

pokok the core melody in Balinese music.

polos/sangsih the terms for the two Balinese interlocking musical parts.

Prakempa a *lontar* manuscript on music and theology, probably written in the mid-to-late nineteenth century.

preret a double-reed, wooden wind instrument sometimes used for solo performance by the Sasak at Lingsar and in ensembles throughout the island. The Balinese also have a tradition of solo *preret* performance at temple festivals.

Pujawali "worship return"; the name of the festival at Lingsar and of some Balinese festivals following the *saka* calendar. Also a term for a few Sasak festivals and interpreted as "worship to Wali," the Sasak culture hero credited with discovering the water springs at Lingsar.

pura a Balinese temple.

pura bukit hill temples; Pura Bukit is also a specific temple, located in East Bali, in the Lombok Balinese myth in coming to Lingsar.

pura desa central village Balinese temple, also called *pura balé agung*.

pura dalam Balinese temple of the dead.

pura jagat "world" Balinese temple, also called *pusering jagat*.

pura pamaksan Balinese ward temples.

pura puseh a Balinese temple of origin; these do not exist in Lombok.

Pura Ulon the "head" temple of Lingsar, located a little over a hundred meters east of Pura Lingsar.

pura ulon siwi name of a Balinese temple located at the head channel of a terrace irrigation system. Pura Ulon and the Pura Lingsar *kemaliq* both function as rice-irrigation temples.

pura umum a "public" and generally large Balinese temple.

Purwédaksina "east-south"; refers to the circumambulating processions within the *gadoh* on the opening and final days.

Rainan Karya "day of (creative or festive) work"; the Balinese term for the main day of the festival.

ramé the state of bustling liveliness that is the goal of communal events.

redeb a two-string spiked lute played with a bow of horsehair in the gamelan *baris*. Also called *rebab*.

rejang a generic term for a Balinese offering dance.

Rejang Déwa a modern offering dance that has spread to temples in Bali and Lombok.

réong two kettle-gongs in a single frame in the *gong gilak*. Term refers to smaller kettle-gongs played in interlocking parts, and to a gong chime of twelve kettle-gongs in the *gong kebyar* and *gong* Sasak ensembles. Sometimes spelled *réyong*.

rincik a smaller set of paired *ceng-ceng* cymbals used in the gamelan *baris*.

sad kayangan the six temples supposed to link Bali together as a whole, sometimes also applied to Lombok. However, it is difficult to establish just what temples constitute these six on either island.

saka the solar-lunar calendar used to determine the Lingsar festival.

sampiran used in couplet poetry; refers to the first two lines, organized not for their direct meaning to the poem but to create rhyme and assonance.

sembah the act of clasping the hands in prayer.

slendro an anhemitonic five-tone scale system, developed in Java and spread throughout much of Indonesia but primarily throughout Java and in Bali and Lombok.

subak the irrigation organizations of Bali and Lombok.

suling bamboo flutes, such as those used in the gamelan *baris*.

tabuh "strike"; refers to instrumental compositions and their forms such as in the *lelambatan* repertoire. *Tabuh empat* (four strikings), *tabuh enam* (six strikings), and *tabuh kutus* (eight strikings) are examples.

tambur a large barrel-shaped drum, played as part of the gamelan *tambur* and the gamelan *baris*.

telek refers to the two *batek* dancers with arched headpieces whose roles are based on a story of the Lingsar area of a princess and commoner. Also called *batek*.

tirta "holy water" refers to the water from the *kemaliq*, the water following prayers in the *gadoh*, and the water in the *momot* bottle.

topat hardened rice squares fastened with palm leaves that are used in offerings of various kinds and in Perang Topat.

topeng "mask"; also refers to masked dancing.

Topeng Sidha Karya the masked dances featuring the Sidha Karya character at the end of the performance.

Triangga a concept that maps three spheres onto the manifest world.

Triloka a concept that maps three spheres onto the cosmos.

trompong a gong chime of ten kettle-gongs providing melodic leadership in the *gong kuna*.

tuan guru an Islamic religious leader, usually a commoner, in Lombok.

uku a Javanese-Balinese calendar of 210 days, also called *pawukon*.

upiti/setiti/pralina "birth/life/death," from the ritual formulae of Balinese *padanda* priests.

utama/madya/nista "upper/middle/lower"; the tripartite structure of the manifest world as formulated by the Triangga concept.

wadon "female," referring to female drums and gongs.

Waktu Lima Sasak orthodox Muslims, though sometimes considered an intermediary stage towards becoming "pure" Muslims.

Waktu Telu Sasak traditional or nominal Muslims.

Wali Sanga The legendary "nine friends" or "witnesses" of Islam, credited with spreading Islam throughout Indonesia and incorporating Islamic elements into several forms of performing arts.

wariga a Sasak calendar used for determining rituals; also a Balinese calendrical system used for divination.

wayang kulit the shadow play of Bali (and Java and other areas) normally featuring stories from the Mahabharata.

wayang *Sasak* the Sasak shadow play featuring the Serat Menak stories of world Islamification.

windu a Javanese and Sasak eight-year calendar used, among other things, to determine Islamic holy days.

Bibliography

Abrahams, Roger D. 1982. The Language of Festivals: Celebrating the Economy.
In *Celebration: Studies in Festivity and Ritual*, edited by Victor Turner, 161–177.
Washington, D.C.: Smithsonian Institution Press.
———. 1987. An American Vocabulary of Celebrations. In *Time Out of Time: Essays
on the Festival*, edited by Alessandro Falassi, 173–183. Albuquerque: University of
New Mexico Press.
Acciaioli, Gregory. 1985. Culture as Art: From Practice to Spectacle in Indonesia.
Canberra Anthropology 8 (1–2):148–172.
Adonis, Tito, ed. 1987. *Suku Terasing Sasak di Bayan, Daerah Propinsi Nusa Tenggara
Barat.* Jakarta: Departemen Pendidikan dan Kebudayaan.
Agung, Anak Agung Ktut. 1991. *Kupu Kupu Kuning yang Terbang di Selat Lombok.*
Denpasar (Bali): Upada Sastra.
Anderson, Benedict. 1972. The Idea of Power in Javanese Culture. In *Culture and Politics
in Indonesia*, edited by Claire Holt et al., 1–69. Ithaca: Cornell University Press.
Appadurai, Arjun. 1981. The Past as a Scarce Resource. *Man* (n.s.) 16:201–219.
Aragon, Lorraine V. 1996. Suppressed and Revised Performances: *Raego'* Songs of
Central Sulawesi. *Ethnomusicology* 40 (3):413–439.
Baal, J. van. 1976. *Pesta Alip di Bayan.* Translated from the Dutch by Nalom Siahaan.
Jakarta: Bhratara.
Bakan, Michael B. 1999. *Music of Death and New Creation: Experiences in the World of
Balinese Gamelan Beleganjur.* Chicago: University of Chicago Press.
Bandem, I Madé. 1986. *Prakempa: Sebuah Lontar Gambelan Bali.* Denpasar: Akademi
Seni Tari Indonesia Denpasar.

Bandem, I Madé, and Fredrik Eugene deBoer. 1995. *Kaja and Kelod: Balinese Dance in Transition.* Kuala Lumpur, New York: Oxford University Press.

Barth, Fredrik. 1993. *Balinese Worlds.* Chicago: University of Chicago Press.

Becker, Judith. 1979. Time and Tune in Java. In *The Imagination of Reality: Essays in Southeast Asian Coherence Systems,* edited by A. Yengoyan and A. L. Becker, 197–210. Norwood, NJ: Albex Publishing Corp.

———. 1981. Hindu-Buddhist Time in Javanese Gamelan Music. In *The Study of Time, Papers from the Fourth Conference of the International Society for the Study of Time, Alpbach-Austria,* edited by J. T. Fraser, N. Lawrence, and D. Park, 162–172. New York, Heidelberg, Berlin: Springer-Verlag.

———. 1993. *Gamelan Stories: Tantrism, Islam, and Aesthetics in Central Java.* Arizona: Arizona State University.

Becker, J., and A. L. Becker. 1981. A Musical Icon: Power and Meaning in Javanese Gamelan Music. In *The Sign in Music and Literature,* edited by Wendy Steiner, 203–215. Austin: University of Texas.

Belo, Jane. 1953. *Bali: Temple Festival.* Locust Valley, NY: J. J. Augustin.

Blacking, John. 1995 (orig. published 1969). Expressing Human Experience through Music. In *Music, Culture, and Experience: Selected Papers of John Blacking,* edited by Reginald Byron, 31–53. Chicago: University of Chicago Press.

Blambangan, I Goesti Bagoes Djlantik. n.d. Riwajatnja Poera-poera dan Pedewa'-pedewa' di West-Lombok. Unpublished manuscript.

Bohlman, Philip V. 1996. Pilgrimage, Politics, and the Musical Remapping of the New Europe. *Ethnomusicology* 40 (3):375–412.

Bolland, Rita. 1971. A Comparison between the Looms Used in Bali and Lombok for Weaving Sacred Cloths. *Tropical Man* 4:171–182.

Bolland, Rita, and A. Polak. 1971. Manufacture and Use of Some Sacred Woven Fabrics in a North-Lombok Community. *Tropical Man* 4:149–170.

Boon, James A. 1986. Symbols, Sylphs, and Siwa: Allegorical Machineries in the Text of Balinese Culture. In *The Anthropology of Experience,* edited by Victor W. Turner and Edward M. Bruner, 239–260. Urbana: University of Illinois Press.

Brinner, Benjamin. 1995. *Knowing Music, Making Music: Javanese Gamelan and the Theory of Musical Competence and Interaction.* Chicago: University of Chicago Press.

Bruner, Edward M. 1986. Experience and Its Expressions. In *The Anthropology of Experience,* edited by Victor W. Turner and Edward M. Bruner, 3–32. Urbana: University of Illinois Press.

Budihardjo, Eko. 1986. *Architectural Conservation in Bali.* Yogyakarta: Gadjah Mada University Press.

Campbell, Joseph. 1988. *The Power of Myth,* with Bill Moyers, edited by Betty Sue Flowers. New York: Doubleday.

Cederroth, Sven. 1975. Symbols of a Sasak Community in Northern Lombok. Unpublished manuscript.

———. 1981. *The Spell of the Ancestors and the Power of Mekkah: A Sasak Community on Lombok.* Goteborg: ACTA Universitatis Gothoburgensis.

Clegg, Kendra. 2004. Ampenan: Constructions of Nationality, Ethnicity and Identity in Urban Lombok. PhD dissertation, Deakin University, Australia.

Cornell, Stephen. 2000. That's the Story of Our Life. In *We Are a People: Narrative and Multiplicity in Constructing Ethnic Identity,* edited by Paul Spickard and W. Jeffrey Burroughs, 41–53. Philadelphia: Temple University Press.

Cosentino, Donald J. 1986. Real Vodoun is Always Changing: Pentecostal Aspects of Vodoun Celebration. Presentation at the conference *Festivals: Issues and Interpretations—Local to International Perspectives*, University of California, Los Angeles.

Davis, Martha Ellen. 1986. "Native Bi-Musicality": Case Studies from the Caribbean. *Pacific Review of Ethnomusicology* 4:39–55.

DeVale, Sue Carole. 1977. A Sundanese Gamelan: A Gestalt Approach to Organology. PhD dissertation, Northwestern University.

———. 1991. Musical Instruments and the Micro-Macrocosmic Juncture. *Tradition and Its Future in Music, Report of the SIMS 1990 Osaka*, edited by Yoshihiko Tokumaru et al., 255–262. Osaka: Mita Press.

DeVale, Sue Carole, and I Wayan Dibia. 1991. *Sekar Anjar*: An Exploration of Meaning in Balinese Gamelan. *The World of Music* 33 (1):5–51.

Dibia, I Wayan. 1985. *Odalan* of Hindu Bali: A Religious Festival, a Social Occasion, and a Theatrical Event. *Asian Theatre Journal* 2, 1 (Spring): 61–65.

Drewel, Margaret Thompson. 1986. The Reinvention of Festival: The Imewuro Annual Rally of Southwestern Nigeria. Presentation at the conference *Festivals: Issues and Interpretations—Local to International Perspectives*, University of California Los Angeles.

———. 1992. *Yoruba Ritual: Performers, Play, Agency*. Bloomington: Indiana University Press.

Duff-Cooper, Andrew. 1985. Duality in Aspects of a Balinese Form of Life in Western Lombok. *Cosmos* 1:15–36.

Ecklund, Judith Louise. 1977. Marriage, Seaworms, and Song: Ritualized Responses to Cultural Change in Sasak Life. PhD dissertation, Cornell University.

———. 1979. Tradition or Non-tradition: Adat, Islam, and Local Control on Lombok. In *What is Modern Indonesian Culture?*, edited by Gloria Davis, 249–267. Athens, OH: Center for International Studies, Ohio University.

Eiseman, Fred B. Jr. 2000. *Balinese Calendars*. Bali: Fred Eiseman.

Eliade, Mircea. 1959. *The Sacred and the Profane: The Nature of Religion*. New York: Harcourt, Brace and World, Inc.

———. 1963. *Myth and Reality*. New York and Evanston: Harper & Row.

Falassi, Alessandro. 1987. Festival: Definition and Morphology. In *Time Out of Time: Essays on the Festival*, edited by Alessandro Falassi, 1–10. Albuquerque: University of New Mexico Press.

Faruqi, Lois Ibsen al. 1983. What Makes "Religious Music" Religious? In *Sacred Sound: Music in Religious Thought and Practice. Journal of the American Academy of Religion Studies* 50, 1, edited by Joyce Irwin, 21–34. Chico, CA: Scholars Press.

Feld, Steven. 1990. *Sound and Sentiment: Birds, Weeping, Poetics, and Song in Kaluli Expression*. Philadelphia: University of Pennsylvania Press.

———. 1994. Communication, Music, and Speech about Music. In *Music Grooves*, edited by Charles Keil and Steven Feld, 77–95. Chicago: University of Chicago Press.

Fernandez, James W. 1986. The Argument of Images and the Experience of Returning to the Whole. In *The Anthropology of Experience*, edited by Victor W. Turner and Edward M. Bruner, 159–187. Urbana: University of Illinois Press.

Foley, Kathy. 1992. The Medium and the Message: *Sintren*, Trance Performance of Cirebon. In *Essays on Southeast Asian Performing Arts: Local Manifestations and Cross-Cultural Implications*, edited by Kathy Foley, 23–53. Center for Southeast Asia Studies, Occasional Paper no.18. Berkeley: Regents of the University of California.

Geertz, Clifford. 1960. *The Religion of Java*. New York: Free Press.

————. 1973a. Person, Time, and Conduct in Bali. In *The Interpretation of Cultures: Selected Essays by Clifford Geertz*, 360–411. New York: Basic Books, Inc.

————. 1973b. Deep Play: Notes on the Balinese Cockfight. In *The Interpretation of Cultures: Selected Essays by Clifford Geertz*, 412–454. New York: Basic Books, Inc.

————. 1980. *Negara: The Balinese Theater State in the Nineteenth Century*. Princeton, NJ: Princeton University Press.

Geertz, Hildred. 1988. The Life of a Balinese Temple: A Social Biography of Pura Desa Batuan. Presentation at the Society for Balinese Studies annual conference, Denpasar, Bali, Indonesia.

————. 1992. Preface. In *Masks of Bali: Spirits of an Ancient Drama*, edited by Judy Slattum, 8–9. San Francisco: Chronicle Books.

Gerdin, Ingela. 1975. Ruinous Feasting: Changed Effects of the "Big Feast" among Balinese in Lombok. *Ethnos* 40, 1–4:185–193.

————. 1982. *The Unknown Balinese: Land, Labour and Inequality in Lombok*. Goteborg: ACTA Universitatis Gothoburgensis.

Gold, Lisa. 2004. *Music in Bali: Experiencing Music, Expressing Culture*. New York: Oxford University Press.

Goris, Roelof. 1960. Holidays and Holy Days. In *Bali: Studies in Life, Thought, and Ritual*, 113–130. The Hague: W. van Hoeve, Ltd.

Hägerdal, Hans. 2001. *Hindu Rulers, Muslim Subjects: Lombok and Bali in the Seventeenth and Eighteenth Centuries*. Thailand: Hans Hägerdal.

Harnish, David D. 1985. Musical Traditions of the Lombok Balinese: Antecedents from Bali and Lombok. MA thesis, University of Hawai`i at Manoa.

————. 1988. Religion and Music: Syncretism, Orthodox Islam, and Musical Change in Lombok. *Selected Reports in Ethnomusicology* 7:123–138.

————. 1989. Music at Balinese Temple Festivals: Five Criteria for Investigating the Meaning of Music in Ritual Contexts. Presentation at the Society for Ethnomusicology national conference, MIT, Boston.

————. 1990. The Preret of the Lombok Balinese: Transformation and Continuity within a Sacred Tradition. *Selected Reports in Ethnomusicology* 8:201–220.

————. 1991a. Music at the Lingsar Temple Festival: The Encapsulation of Meaning in the Balinese/Sasak Interface in Lombok, Indonesia. PhD dissertation, University of California at Los Angeles.

————. 1991b. Balinese Performance as Artistic Offering. *Asian Art* 4 (2):8–27.

————. 1992. The Performance, Context, and Meaning of Balinese Music in Lombok. In *Balinese Music in Context: A Sixty-fifth Birthday Tribute to Hans Oesch*, edited by Danker Schaareman, 29–58. Forum Ethnomusicologium 4. Winterthur: Amadeus.

————. 1994. The Future Meets the Past in the Present: Music and Buddhism in Lombok. *Asian Music* 25 (1–2):29–50.

————. 1997. Music, Myth, and Liturgy at the Lingsar Temple Festival in Lombok, Indonesia. *Yearbook for Traditional Music* 29: 80–106.

————. 1998a. Bali. In *Garland Encyclopedia of World Music*, vol. 4, *Southeast Asia*, edited by Sean Williams and Terry Miller, 729–761. New York: Garland Publishing, Inc.

————. 1998b. Nusa Tenggara Barat. In *Garland Encyclopedia of World Music*, vol. 4, *Southeast Asia*, edited by Sean Williams and Terry Miller, 762–786. New York: Garland Publishing, Inc.

————. 2001. Like King and Queen, Like Balinese and Sasak: Musical Narratives at the Lingsar Temple Festival in Lombok, Indonesia. *Ethnologies* 23 (1):63–88.

————. 2002. Teletubbies in Paradise: A Social History of Music in Bali. Presentation at the Society for Ethnomusicology national conference, Estes Park, CO.

————. 2003. Worlds of Wayang Sasak: Music, Performance, and Negotiations of Religion and Modernity. *Asian Music* 34 (2):91–120.

————. 2005. New Lines, Shifting Identities: Interpreting Change at the Lingsar Festival in Lombok, Indonesia. *Ethnomusicology* 49 (1):1–24.

Hauser-Schaublin, Brigitta. 1991. Poleng, the Dualism of Black and White. In *Balinese Textiles*, edited by Brigitta Hauser-Schaublin, Marie-Louise Nabholz-Kartaschoff, and Urs Ramseyer, 80–93. Singapore: Periplus Editions (HK) Ltd.

Heelas, Paul. 1996. Detraditionalization and Its Rivals. In *De-traditionalization: Critical Reflections on Authority and Identity at a Time of Uncertainty*, edited by Paul Heelas, Scott Lash, and Paul Morris, 1–22. Cambridge, MA: Blackwell Publishers.

Hefner, Robert W. 1985. *Hindu Javanese: Tengger Tradition and Islam*. Princeton: Princeton University Press.

Herbst, Edward. 1997. *Voices in Bali: Energies and Perceptions in Vocal Music and Dance Theater*. Hanover: Wesleyan University Press (University Press of New England).

Herzfeld, Michael. 1982. *Ours Once More: Folklore, Ideology and the Making of Modern Greece*. Austin: University of Texas Press.

————. 1985. Levi-Strauss in the Nation-State. *Journal of American Folklore* 98 (388):191–208.

Hooykaas, Christiaan. 1973. *Religion in Bali*. Leiden: Brill.

Kahin, George McT. 2003. *Southeast Asia: A Testament*. London: Routledge Curzon.

Kam, Garrett. 1993. *Perceptions of Paradise: Images of Bali in the Arts*. Bali: Yayasan Dharma Seni Museum Neka.

Kapferer, Bruce. 1983. *A Celebration of Demons: Exorcism and the Aesthetics of Healing in Sri Lanka*. Bloomington: Indiana University Press.

————. 1986. Performance and the Structuring of Meaning and Experience. In *The Anthropology of Experience*, edited by Victor W. Turner and Edward M. Bruner, 188–206. Urbana: University of Illinois Press.

Keeler, Ward. 1975. Musical Encounter in Java and Bali. *Indonesia* 19:85–126.

Kraan, Alfons van der. 1980. *Lombok: Conquest, Colonization and Underdevelopment, 1870–1940*. Singapore: Heinemann Educational Books (Asia) Ltd.

Krulfield, Ruth. 1974. The Village Economies of the Sasak of Lombok: A Comparison of Three Indonesian Peasant Economies. PhD dissertation, Yale University.

Kunst, J., and W. Kunst-V. 1925. De Toonkunst van Bali. *Tijdschrift voor Indische Taal-, Lande en Volkenkunde* 73 (1933): 220–256.

Lansing, J. Stephen. 1987. Balinese "Water Temples" and the Management of Irrigation. *American Anthropologist* 89:326–341.

Laskewicz, Zachar. 2003. *Music as Episteme Text Sign and Tool: Comparative Approaches to Musicality as Performance*. Brussels: Saru Press.

Leach, E. R. 1972. The Structure of Symbolism. In *The Interpretation of Ritual*, edited by J. S. LaFontaine, 239–275. London: Tavistock Publications.

Leeman, Albert. 1989a. *Internal and External Factors of Socio-cultural and Socio-economic Dynamics in Lombok (Nusa Tenggara Barat)*. Zurich: Geographisches Institut Abt. Anthropogeographie Universitat Zurich.

————. 1989b. Verdrangt der Islam das Adat? Eine Fallstudie aus Lombok (Indonesien). *Regio Basiliensis* 30 (2–3):191–204.

Levi-Strauss, Claude. 1963. *Structural Anthropology.* Vol. 1. New York: Basic Books.

————. 1966. *The Savage Mind.* Chicago: University of Chicago Books.

Marin, Louis. 1987. Notes on a Semiotic Approach to Parade, Cortege, and Procession. In *Time Out of Time: Essays on the Festival*, edited by Alessandro Falassi, 220–228. Albuquerque: University of New Mexico Press.

Marrison, Geoffrey E. 1992. *The Literature of the Sasak of Lombok: A Survey of Javanese and Sasak Texts.* Special issue of the Centre for South-East Asian Studies, University of Hull, England, edited by Geoffrey E. Marrison.

McPhee, Colin. 1966. *Music in Bali: A Study in Form and Instrumental Organization in Balinese Orchestral Music.* New Haven: Yale University Press.

McVey, Ruth. 1995. Shaping the Sasak: Religion and Hierarchy on an Indonesian Island. In *Kulturen und Raum: Theoretische Ansatze und Empirische Kulturforschung in Indonesien.* Festschrift fur Professor Albert Leemann, edited by Samuel Walty and Benno Werlen, 311–331. Chur/Zurich: Verlag Ruegger AG.

Mendoza, Zoila S. 2000. *Shaping Society through Dance: Mestizo Ritual Performance in the Peruvian Andes.* Chicago: University of Chicago Press.

Muller, Kal. 1991. Wetu Telu: Mix of Islam and Traditional Adat Practices. In *East of Bali: From Lombok to Timor*, edited by Kal Muller, 54–55. Berkeley-Singapore: Periplus Editions, Inc.

Nketia, J. H. Kwabena. 1990. Contextual Strategies of Inquiry and Systematization. *Ethnomusicology* 34 (1):75–98.

Pepplinkhuizen, Coen. 1991. Religion: Visions of Duality and Balance. In *East of Bali: From Lombok to Timor*, edited by Kal Muller, 36–42. Berkeley-Singapore: Periplus Editions, Inc.

Polak, Albert. 1978. *Traditie en tweespalt in een Sasakse boerengemeenschap (Lombok, Indonesie).* Amsterdam: Koninklijk Instituut voor de Tropen.

Proyek Inventarisasi dan Dokumentasi Kebudayaan. 1984. *Upacara Tradisional dalam Kaitannya dengan Peristiwa Alam dan Kepercayaan di Nusa Tenggara Barat.* Mataram: Departemen Pendidikan dan Kebudayaan.

Proyek Penelitian dan Pencatatan Kebudyaan Daerah. 1988. *Sejarah Daerah Nusa Tenggara Barat.* Mataram: Departemen Pendidikan dan Kebudayaan.

Qureshi, Regula Burchkhardt. 1986. *Sufi Music of India and Pakistan: Context and Meaning in Qawwali.* Cambridge: Cambridge University Press.

————. 1987. Music Sound and Contextual Input: A Performance Model for Musical Analysis. *Ethnomusicology* 31(1):56–86.

Ramseyer, Urs. 1986. *The Art and Culture of Bali.* Singapore: Oxford University Press.

————. 1991. Bebali: Borderlines between the Sacred and the Profane. In *Balinese Textiles*, edited by Brigitta Hauser-Schaublin, Marie-Louise Nabholz-Kartaschoff, and Urs Ramseyer, 59–72. Singapore: Periplus Editions (HK) Ltd.

Ramstedt, Martin. 1993. Traditional Balinese Performing Arts as Yajnya. In *Performance in Java and Bali: Studies of Narrative, Theatre, Music, and Dance*, edited by Bernard Arps, 77–87. London: School of Oriental and African Studies.

Rembang, I Nyoman. 1985. *Hasil Pendokumentasian Notasi Gending-Gending Lelambatan Klasik Pegongan Daerah Bali.* Bali: Departemen Pendidikan dan Kebudayaan Direktorat Jendral Kebudayaan Proyek Pengembangan Kesenian Bali.

Rice, Timothy. 1994. *May It Fill Your Soul: Experiencing Bulgarian Music*. Chicago: University of Chicago Press.

Seebass, Tilman, I Gusti Bagus Nyoman Panji, I Nyoman Rembang, and I Poedijono. 1976. *The Music of Lombok: A First Survey*. Bern: A. Franke AG Verlag.

Simms, Robert. 1993. Aspects of Cosmological Symbolism in Hindusthani Musical Forms. *Asian Music* 24 (1):67–90.

Slattum, Judy. 1992. *Masks of Bali: Spirits of an Ancient Drama*. San Francisco: Chronicle Books.

Spickard, Paul, and W. Jeffrey Burroughs. 2000. We Are a People. In *We Are a People: Narrative and Multiplicity in Constructing Ethnic Identity*, edited by Paul Spickard and W. Jeffrey Burroughs, 1–19. Philadelphia: Temple University Press.

Stokes, Martin. 1994. Introduction: Ethnicity, Identity and Music. In *Ethnicity, Identity and Music: The Musical Construction of Place*, edited by Martin Stokes, 1–27. Oxford: Berg.

Stuart-Fox, David J. 1991. Pura Besakih: Temple-State Relations from Precolonial to Modern Times. In *State and Society in Bali*, edited by Hildred Geertz, 11–42. Leiden: KITLV Press.

Sugarman, Jane C. 1997. *Engendering Song: Singing and Subjectivity at Prespa Albanian Weddings*. Chicago: University of Chicago Press.

Sumarsam. 1995. *Gamelan: Cultural Interaction and Musical Development in Central Java*. Chicago: University of Chicago Press.

Sutton, R. Anderson. 1993. *Semang* and *Seblang*: Thoughts on Music, Dance, and the Sacred in Central and East Java. In *Performance in Java and Bali: Studies of Narrative, Theatre, Music, and Dance*, edited by Bernard Arps, 121–143. London: School of Oriental and African Studies.

———. 2002. *Calling Back the Spirit: Music, Dance and Cultural Politics in Lowland South Sulawesi*. New York: Oxford University Press.

Syarani, H. Achmad. 1986. *Sejarah Timbulnya Bangunan Kemaliq Lingsar*. Lombok: H. Achmad Syarani.

Tenzer, Michael. 1990. Temporality in Context: Some Paradigms Drawn from Recent Balinese Music. Presentation at the American Musicological Society, Society for Ethnomusicology, and Society for Music Theory conference, Oakland, CA.

———. 1998. *Balinese Music*. Berkeley and Singapore: Periplus Editions, Inc.

———. 2000. *Gamelan Gong Kebyar: The Art of Twentieth-Century Balinese Music*. Chicago: University of Chicago Press.

Turino, Thomas. 1993. *Moving Away from Silence: Music of the Peruvian Altiplano and the Experience of Urban Migration*. Chicago: University of Chicago Press.

———. 1999. Signs of Imagination, Identity, and Experience: A Peircian Semiotic Theory for Music. *Ethnomusicology* 43 (2): 221–255.

Turner, Victor. 1969. *The Ritual Process: Structure and Anti-structure*. Chicago: Aldine Publishing Company.

———. 1982. Introduction. In *Celebration: Studies in Festivity and Ritual*, edited by Victor Turner, 11–29. Washington, D.C: Smithsonian Institution Press.

———. 1986. Dewey, Dilthey, and Drama: An Essay in the Anthropology of Experience. In *The Anthropology of Experience*, edited by Victor W. Turner and Edward M. Bruner, 33–44. Urbana: University of Illinois Press.

———. 1987. Carnival, Ritual, and Play in Rio de Janeiro. In *Time Out of Time: Essays on the Festival*, edited by Alessandro Falassi, 74–90. Albuquerque: University of New Mexico Press.

Turner, Victor, and Edith Turner. 1982. Religious Celebrations. In *Celebration: Studies in Festivity and Ritual*, edited by Victor Turner, 201–219. Washington, D.C.: Smithsonian Institution Press.

Vickers, Adrian. 1985. The Realm of the Senses: Images of the Court Music of Pre-Colonial Bali. *Imago Musicae* 2:143–177.

Wallis, Richard Herman. 1973. Poetry as Music in Java and Bali. MA thesis, University of Michigan.

———. 1979. The Voice as a Mode of Cultural Expression in Bali. PhD dissertation, University of Michigan.

Woodward, Mark R. 1989. *Islam in Java: Normative Piety and Mysticism in the Sultanate of Yogyakarta*. Tucson: University of Arizona Press.

Wong, Deborah. 2001. *Sounding the Center: History and Aesthetics in Thai Buddhist Performance*. Chicago: University of Chicago Press.

Zakaria, Fath. 2001. *Geger, Gerakan 30 September 1965: Rakyat NTB Melawan Bahaya Merah*. Lombok: Penerbit Sumurmas Mataram.

Index

About the Author

DAVID HARNISH is associate professor of ethnomusicology and director of the Balinese gamelan Kusuma Sari at Bowling Green State University in Ohio. Although he specializes in the music of Indonesia, he has also studied in Japan and India and has explored Latino music culture in northwest Ohio. He has served as a consultant for the National Geographic Society, the Smithsonian Institution, and the British Broadcasting Corporation. As a guitarist he has recorded Hindustani Indian rock and jazz, and he currently performs with old time, Afro-Caribbean, blues, rock, *conjunto,* and country bands.

PRODUCTION NOTES FOR HARNISH, *BRIDGES TO THE ANCESTORS*

Book and cover design and composition by Diane Gleba Hall
Text set in Baskerville and Gill Sans Condensed
Printing and binding by the Maple-Vail Book Manufacturing Group
Printed on 60 lb. Text White Opaque, 426 ppi